STUDIES IN MEDIEVAL AND EARLY MODERN CIVILIZATION
Marvin B. Becker, General Editor

Charity and Children in Renaissance Florence: The Ospedale degli Innocenti, 1410–1536 *Philip Gavitt*

Humanism in Crisis: The Decline of the French Renaissançe *Philippe Desan, editor*

Upon My Husband's Death: Widows in the Literatures and Histories of Medieval Europe *Louise Mirrer, editor*

Wife and Widow in Medieval England *Sue Sheridan Walker, editor*

The Rhetorics of Life-Writing in Early Modern Europe: Forms of Biography from Cassandra Fedele to Louis XIV *Thomas F. Mayer and D. R. Woolf, editors*

Defining Dominion: The Discourses of Magic and Witchcraft in Early Modern France and Germany *Gerhild Scholz Williams*

Women, Jews, and Muslims in the Texts of Reconquest Castile *Louise Mirrer*

The Culture of Merit: Nobility, Royal Service, and the Making of Absolute Monarchy in France, 1600–1789 *Jay M. Smith*

Clean Hands and Rough Justice: An Investigating Magistrate in Renaissance Italy *David S. Chambers and Trevor Dean*

"Songes of Rechelesnesse": Langland and the Franciscans *Lawrence M. Clopper*

Godliness and Governance in Tudor Colchester *Laquita M. Higgs*

The Social Politics of Medieval Diplomacy: Anglo-German Relations (1066–1307) *Joseph P. Huffman*

The Strozzi of Florence: Widowhood and Family Solidarity in the Renaissance *Ann Crabb*

The Philosophers' Game: Rithmomachia in Medieval and Renaissance Europe with an Edition of Ralph Lever and William Fulke, *The Most Noble, Auncient, and Learned Playe* (1563) *Ann E. Moyer*

Illegitimacy in Renaissance Florence *Thomas Kuehn*

Illegitimacy in Renaissance Florence

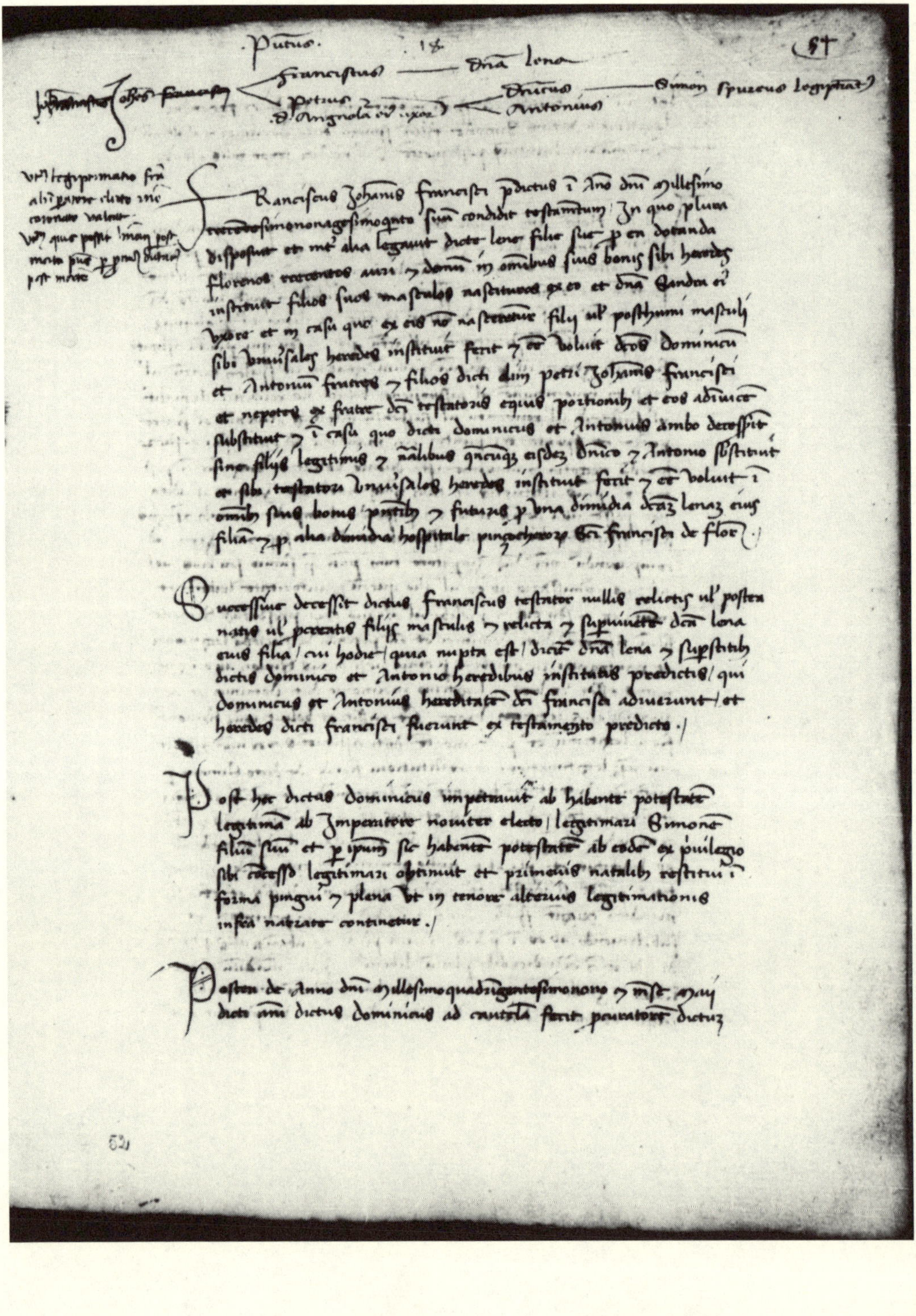

·Putius· ·18· (54)

Johannes [illegible] Francisci — Franciscus — Dna Lona
— Petrus — Dnicus — Simon spurius legiptimatus
— Angnola [illegible] — Antonius

Franciscus Johannis Francisci pictor [illegible] Anno dni Millesimo trecentesimononagesimoquarto suum condidit testamentum. In quo plura disposuit et inter alia legavit dicte Lone filie sue pro eius dotanda florenos trecentos auri et domum. In omnibus suis bonis sibi heredes instituit filios suos masculos nascituros ex eo et dna [illegible] eius uxore et in casu quo ex eis non nascerentur filii vel posthumi masculi sibi universales heredes instituit fecit et esse voluit dictos Dominicum et Antonium fratres et filios dicti dni Petri Johannis Francisci et nepotes ex fratre dicti testatoris equis portionibus et eos ad invicem substituit et in casu quo dicti Dominicus et Antonius ambo decessissent sine filiis legitimis et naturalibus [illegible] eisdem Dnico et Antonio substituit et sibi testatori universales heredes instituit fecit et esse voluit in omnibus suis bonis presentibus et futuris pro una dimidia dictam Lonam eius filiam et pro alia dimidia hospitale [illegible] Sci Francisci de Flor.

Successive decessit dictus Franciscus testator nullis relictis vel postea natis vel procreatis filiis masculis et relicta et superviventi dicta Lona eius filia, cui hodie, quia nupta est, dicitur dna Lona et superstitibus dictis Dominico et Antonio heredibus institutis predictis, qui Dominicus et Antonius hereditatem dicti Francisci adiverunt et heredes dicti Francisci fuerunt ex testamento predicto.

Post hec dictus Dominicus impetravit ab habente potestatem legitimandi ab Imperatore noviter electo legitimari Simonem filium suum et per ipsum sic habente potestatem ab eodem ex privilegio sibi concesso legitimari obtinuit et primevis natalibus restitui in forma pingui et plena ut in tenore alterius legitimationis infra [illegible] continetur.

Postea de Anno dni Millesimoquadringentesimonono et mense Maii dicti anni dictus Dominicus ad cautelam fecit procuratorem dictum

62

Illegitimacy in Renaissance Florence

Thomas Kuehn

Ann Arbor
THE UNIVERSITY OF MICHIGAN PRESS

Published in the United States of America by
The University of Michigan Press
Manufactured in the United States of America
♾ Printed on acid-free paper

2005 2004 2003 2002 4 3 2 1

A CIP catalog record for this book is available from the British Library.

Library of Congress Cataloging-in-Publication Data

Kuehn, Thomas, 1950–
Illegitimacy in Renaissance Florence / Thomas Kuehn.
p. cm. — (Studies in medieval and early modern civilization)
Includes bibliographical references and index.
ISBN 0-472-11244-9 (acid-free paper)
1. Illegitimacy—Italy—Florence—History. 2. Paternity—Italy—Florence—History. I. Title. II. Series.
KKH9851.13.K84 2001
346.45'51017—dc21 2001005530

Frontispiece used by concession of the Ministero per i Beni e le Attività Culturali della Repubblica Italiana

For my parents

Preface

This book began years ago, as I completed study of emancipation, by which a child was removed from the legal power and the family of the father. The logical and natural counterpart to that study was an examination of a process by which persons were subjected to paternal power. Only adoption and legitimation in civil law had the capacity to manufacture *patria potestas* where there had been none. As a subject for investigation, however, adoption had a distinct disadvantage. It hardly ever happened—not in the full formal, legal sense (as opposed to fostering a youngster in one's household). Adoption continued to be discussed as a legal institution in the law schools. It even happened once in a great while. But it simply was not possible to study adoption as a viable social and legal institution for Renaissance Florence or anywhere else.[1]

Compared to adoption, the rare act of legitimation seems almost common.[2] Legitimation necessarily deals, as does emancipation, with children and their natural father. Legitimation thus points to a pool of possible candidates—illegitimate children, the irregular circumstances of whose birth and paternity were a matter of public record. Recognition of paternity and its responsibilities did not inevitably entail legitimation, but legitimation could not occur without it. So to study legitimation at all seemed to require first locating and studying this pool of candidates, to find out who they were socially and to figure out why they found their way to legitimation. Thereafter one could begin to take stock of effects, legal and otherwise, of legitimation. The very process of legitimation—or indeed the very existence of an illegitimate within society and family—

1. Cf. my "L'Adoption à Florence à la fin du Moyen Âge," *Médiévales* 35 (1998): 69–81.

2. As my "Reading between the Patrilines: Leon Battista Alberti's *Della Famiglia* in Light of His Illegitimacy," *I Tatti Studies: Essays in the Renaissance* 1 (1985): 161–87, now in my *Law, Family, and Women: Toward a Legal Anthropology of Renaissance Italy* (Chicago, 1991), chap. 6.

entailed much more than emancipating a child (something paternal death would accomplish in the normal course of events). An outcast was given a social identity and personhood more in line with that of others. It was the acquisition and the dimensions of that personhood that forms the story in this book.

Study of illegitimacy allowed investigation of a second matter, no less important, that also arose from my study of emancipation—the roles of law and jurists in a Renaissance city-state. The legal situation was undoubtedly complex. On the one hand there were the texts and terms of a learned law expounded in schools, which aspiring jurists had to attend. These were texts of Roman law as compiled at the command of the emperor Justinian in the sixth century, to which were added other bits (like feudal law); and there was the equally important and still-developing body of canon law. On the other hand were the local acts of legislation and custom, unlearned and partial in comparison to what became known as *ius commune* (common law), but undeniably a type of positive law bound to functioning courts and administrative bodies that were the actual sites in which jurists could hope to exercise influence.

Illegitimacy was necessarily a difficult area of law, setting off a vital concept (legitimacy) and touching on an extremely vital area of social and legal life (inheritance). In an era of weak (though slowly strengthening) government, jurists were called on to use their expertise to make sense of legal confusions and apply the law in comprehensible fashion to the problems that arose in practice. They operated with their sense of the law while facing competing social, economic, and political interests they could also understand and share. This book is also the story of the "lawmakers" (jurists, legislators) who facilitated, or not, the interests of social actors, while validating certain results or avoiding others. It became the story of the ways in which illegitimacy was partially overcome and never really forgotten, how a social and legal paradox was carefully managed and maintained.

In her philosophical study of illegitimacy, Jenny Teichman remarks that "the legitimacy/illegitimacy distinction is situated at a multidimensional interface of human institutions and natural facts about human beings."[3] Sexual reproduction, kinship, inheritance and property, as well as morality are all involved in illegitimacy. Illegitimacy thus impinges on vast areas of social life, many of which are of current interest to histori-

3. Jenny Teichman, *Illegitimacy: An Examination of Bastardy* (Ithaca, N.Y., 1982), 10.

ans. What began for me as an interest in a legal institution with parallels to emancipation has broadened into an investigation of dimensions of law and legal practice, social and cultural life, theory and practice.

Illegitimacy and legitimation (so also emancipation) were a means for people to craft an ambiguity—the child who was, but also was not, part of a family—that could be used to advantage. Creative manufacture, maintenance, and management of such ambiguities was one of the hallmarks of life in a Renaissance city-state, if not of all societies. It was related to the more celebrated creativity of a city like Florence in the arts and humanism, and not simply because some of the best-known artists and humanists (Boccaccio, Alberti, da Vinci) were themselves born illegitimate. At the core of illegitimacy lay the seeming inconsistency that a penalizing and shameful status fell on the child as a result of parental acts that themselves were illicit but not unnatural. Strictly speaking it was not the guilty—or the guilty alone—who were punished. The parents' experience resulted in a child come into the world in an "irregular" manner, tangible evidence of parental transgressions. The child of sin, or love, was itself seen as sinful. On the other hand, the child had come into the world and was not necessarily or totally a social outcast. Parents might be intent on treating the child as an object of value, as a social person. The apex of value was to be treated as legitimate, but making an illegitimate into a legitimate carried conceptual costs, at the least.

As a life without honor was considered a living death,[4] the dishonor of illegitimacy had to be denied or circumvented. If shame could not be removed either by getting the seducer to marry his victim or simply by denying the illicitness of the procreative sexual act, there was little choice but to abandon the child. But some chose another way that resulted neither in the removal of the child nor the denial of illegitimacy. It becomes intriguing to see some men both acknowledging illegitimate paternity (thus also fixing the mother inalterably as a bastard-bearer) and yet keeping that child, with that status. Why bring an object of shame near, recognize that shame, and yet in some respects treat him or, less often, her as any other child? How could the contradictions between shameful status, in and beyond the law, and association with the father, his family and property, be reconciled? Were they? These are intriguing questions.

One is constrained to take what the sources give, and that is not much. Even in periods like the present when illegitimacy is relatively common

4. Cf. Francis William Kent, *Household and Lineage in Renaissance Florence: The Family Life of the Capponi, Ginori, and Rucellai* (Princeton, N.J., 1976), 201.

and carries little social stigma, it has never been something people admitted easily. It has always been tainted with sin and/or dishonor in varying forms and intensities. The subsequent reticence of the sources makes it a difficult challenge actually to locate and study illegitimates.

The general sense of what illegitimacy means to a society has shifted broadly over time. Projected back to the Renaissance, the bastard child was socially dangerous and disruptive. He was Edmund in *King Lear,* capable and ambitious, but caught "in the plague of custom," while perhaps of "more composition and fierce quality" than the less passionately generated legitimate son, and whose desire to usurp the legitimate heirs' place brings tragedy, loss, and dishonor. By the Enlightenment the bastard had become Diderot's quietly desperate characters of *Entretiens sur le bâtard* and *La religieuse,* whose subjection to exclusionary and discriminatory treatment becomes an indictment of hypocrisy and the demands of family stifling individual talent and initiative. In the nineteenth century and on into the late twentieth, illegitimacy is a social pathology. Not only was there sexual transgression behind illegitimacy—as there always was before—but there is no provision for careful familial nurturing. The illegitimate child becomes the dangerous adult now not because of the circumstances of procreation but because of the disadvantaged circumstances of socialization. Modern illegitimacy is about "unwed mothers" ostensibly, but it is really about absentee fathers, a larger matter to which divorce and desertion contribute.[5] It is about household poverty and social maladjustment. Failure to follow the legal niceties of formal marriage makes little social difference where the couples cohabit and raise their children.

Illegitimacy in a late medieval Italian city-state was about something else. It was about the honor of father and mother; it was about lines of kinship and inheritance; it was about abandonment or raising by a father. It too was about possible household poverty and social maladjustment, about social paternity, but it could be resolved by abandonment to foundling homes. Illegitimacy most mattered, however, when the illegitimate mingled with legitimates or was found where they were expected—in the paternal household.

5. For one interesting perspective on twentieth-century concerns, see Janet Fink, "Natural Mothers, Putative Fathers, and Innocent Children: The Definition and Regulation of Parental Relationships outside Marriage, in England, 1945–1959," *Journal of Family History* 25 (2000): 178–95.

Acknowledgments

The longer it takes to research and write a book, the more debts one accumulates. This book has taken a long time. I offer my appreciation to the staffs of the Archivio di Stato, Florence, and the Biblioteca Nazionale Centrale for their kindness, generosity, and professionalism. I am grateful also for the help and hospitality I received at the Library of Congress, the Vatican Microfilm Collection at St. Louis University, the Robbins Collection at the University of California Law School Library (especially from its director, Laurent Mayali), the University of Chicago Libraries, and the Center for Research Libraries in Chicago. Professor Paolo Grossi of the University of Florence generously allowed me use of the incomparable collection of legal historical materials housed there. Clemson University Library's dedicated staff in the Interlibrary Loan Office processed my innumerable requests for materials. Research support and two sabbaticals from Clemson University have given my work a boost at various stages. A summer stipend from the National Endowment for the Humanities allowed me to investigate the 1458 catasto and other sources.

Without the contributions of Elaine Rosenthal, Osvaldo Cavallar, the late David Herlihy, and Anthony Molho, this would be a much thinner book in more ways than one. To former students Mike Sutton, Jonathan Fowler, William Allsbrook, Theron Davis, and Jean Burke I owe thanks for helping me computerize data. The enthusiastic support of Roger Grant, as chair of the Clemson Department of History, sustained the enterprise in its final stages. My friend and colleague, David Nicholas, gave an insightful reading of the entire first draft. Julius Kirshner, friend and mentor, has been a constant source of encouragement, information, and ideas over the years, as well as a penetrating and critical reader of an earlier draft. He has kept the bar high; I hope I have not fallen too far short. Tom Green gave me invaluable editorial advice.

I cannot leave unmentioned those who shared my moments of enthusiasm or frustration—especially Teresa Suggs for her unflagging support as this book rounded into shape. My daughter, Allison, kept me aware of the joys of paternity. Finally, although the irony of dedicating a book about illegitimate children to one's parents is not lost on me, it is wholly fitting, because in the process I have gained enormous insight into what I have inherited from them.

Contents

Figures and Tables

Introduction

> It is clear that the society [of Renaissance Florence] . . . inculcated precious few individualistic qualities in its members; nor, to turn the formulation around, did its members aspire to such individualistic and modern behavior. An immersion in the Florentine culture of the fifteenth century leads one . . . to an uncompromisingly nonmodern world.
>
> —Anthony Molho, *Marriage Alliance in Late Medieval Florence*

In 1408 a Florentine named Domenico di Pietro di Giovanni took his young bastard son, Simone, before a count palatine, who held privileges delegated by the Holy Roman emperor, in order to have him legitimated. Unmarried and otherwise childless, Domenico thus positioned this boy as his heir. His kin, however, did not accept his arrangement. Following his death the next year Lena, daughter of his paternal uncle, Francesco, brought suit to prevent Domenico's estate, including property come to him from Lena's father, from falling into the hands of the now legitimate son. The clash between Domenico's inheritance strategy and Lena's material interests traversed dense and difficult legal terrain. The case, therefore, was passed by the Florentine court to three learned, university-trained jurists (none of whom was Florentine) for their professional opinion and decision *(consilium)*. They had to consider arguments made on behalf of Lena that the legitimation was invalid on any of a number of technical points and arguments that, if the legitimation were technically correct, the *legitimatus* Simone was still not truly legitimate in order to inherit property, according to the terms of the uncle's testamentary substitution and the Florentine statute governing intestate inheritance.

The lengthy *consilium*, authored primarily by a Milanese, Signorino degli Omodei (d. 1419?), ended up awarding the estate to Simone. In reaching that conclusion, the jurist studded the opinion with references to the canonical texts of civil law (that is, the Justinianic *Corpus iuris civilis*) and canon law, feudal law, the authoritative writings of academic jurists, other case opinions, and relevant passages from Florence's statutes, as well as the language of notarial texts (the uncle's testament, the acts of legitimation). In affirming the validity of Simone's legitimation and confirming his inheritance, these jurists were validating one man's strategy to perpetuate his family line through his son. They also characterized legitimacy as an inherent natural state, metaphorically likening legitimation to a parting of the clouds to reveal the blue sky or a threshing away of the husk to disclose the grain within. Still, these jurists also conceded something to "common usage" (and Lena's point of view) and allowed that Simone was *legitimatus,* not in fact *legitimus* by birth (so a portion of the patrimony went to the paternal grandmother).[1]

At the heart of this case lay an admitted illegality, embodied in the person of Simone, fathered in adultery with an unnamed woman. But through the efforts of his father he was being brought ever more closely within legal bounds. Social patterns of interaction and legal rules stood on his side, as they also stood on the side of those, like Lena, whose interests in the inheritance opposed his. This book is the story of fifteenth-century Florentines like these—the illegitimates and their legitimate kin and those notaries, legislators, and jurists who were called upon to grapple with the normative difficulties raised by patterns of social interaction.

The world into which Florentine bastards were born differs enormously from that which greets the many illegitimate children born today. Foundling homes do not dot our landscapes; infant abandonment is not a regular feature of social life, although child abuse disturbs us. Some bastards are raised by both parents (in relationships that approximate what was meant by concubinage in late medieval *ius commune*); many more have only a mother, perhaps supported by welfare agencies; some are adopted; few, it seems, are raised by their fathers. The effective force of any distinction between legitimacy and illegitimacy seems dramatically lessened in a world where, due to divorce primarily, so many legitimate children are found in truncated or reorganized households, and their fatherlessness has become a matter of public concern. Legal disabilities on illegitimates have been erased in many nations. What remains of ille-

1. Cf. my "'As If Conceived within a Legitimate Marriage': A Dispute concerning Legitimation in Quattrocento Florence," *American Journal of Legal History* 29 (1985): 275–300, reprinted with some emendations in my *Law, Family, and Women,* chap. 7.

gitimacy is largely the (weakening) sense of sexual transgression—"proof of acts best left unrecorded."[2]

Yet not so long ago the situation was different. Foundling homes functioned in Italy and elsewhere in the nineteenth century, largely as dumping grounds for illegitimate children.[3] Illegitimacy linked to senses of blood and nationality continued to demarcate a lower status and a diminished citizenship. True, French revolutionary legislation had abolished distinctions between bastards and legitimate children (provided parentage was substantiated), which itself was based on a rejection of illegitimacy as irrational, unnatural, aristocratic, and priestly. However, the revolutionary law was never really enforced and was widely objected to, not least for its consequences for marriage as a civil institution.[4] The disabilities of illegitimate birth, especially where the identity of the father was in doubt, were reinstituted after 1804.[5] Subsequently the nineteenth century produced a real explosion of illegitimate births, as it also enshrined individualism in law and culture. Moralistic stigmas remained; as did economic disadvantages for those raised and supported by a single parent, the mother.[6]

The destigmatizing of illegitimacy in twentieth-century societies coincided with a culturally embedded notion of individualism. The bastard became—legally and socially—a subjective agent capable of controlling his or her actions, exercising his or her rights, and contributing to the world and/or self. Kinship relations for any individual were extrinsic, rather than necessary, so the lack of relationships on the part of bastards

2. So goes a line from Patricia Stone's poem "Illegitimacy," *New York Review of Books*, 26 April 1984, 21.

3. David I. Kertzer, *Sacrificed for Honor: Italian Infant Abandonment and the Politics of Reproductive Control* (Boston, 1993). In a recent article he discusses how foster families in the nineteenth century continued to care for foundlings placed with them even after they ceased to receive payments: cf. Wendy Sigle, David I. Kertzer, and Michael J. White, "Abandoned Children and Their Transition to Adulthood in Nineteenth-Century Italy," *Journal of Family History* 25 (2000): 326–40.

4. Crane Brinton, *French Revolutionary Laws on Illegitimacy* (Cambridge, Mass., 1936).

5. See Anne Lefebvre-Teillard, "Ius sanguinis: L'émergence d'un principe (Eléments d'histoire de la nationalité française)," *Revue critique de droit international privé* 82 (1993): 223–50.

6. *Time* for 25 February 1935 ran a story under the heading of "medicine" concerning "the scarlet thread of bastardy" in New York City, which reported about the women (mainly young domestics) who had these children.

was no longer a priori legally or socially disabling.[7] Women could even contemplate deliberate single parenthood.

Anthropologists, who have wrestled with the social meaning of personhood since a celebrated essay of Marcel Mauss,[8] have taught us that individualism is a distinctly Western version of social personhood:

> The Western conception of the person as a bounded, unique, more or less integrated motivational and cognitive universe, a dynamic center of awareness, emotion, judgment, and action organized into a distinctive whole and set contrastively both against other such wholes and against its social and natural background, is, however incorrigible it may seem to us, a rather peculiar idea within the context of the world's cultures.[9]

Or, again:

> We take persons to be, first, cultural elements, topics of knowledge and discourse. Persons are constructs deemed capable of experience, will, action, identity, and the like. Actual beings may be treated as persons in a culture, but we do not take them to be persons by definition. Indeed, not all humans need be persons in a culture, nor are all persons likely to be human.[10]

Personhood is not necessarily tied to a physical body. The necessary condition for personhood is completion by some sort of psychological identity, which is essentially social, although modern law takes it as having developed outside its purview.

For our purposes it is worth noting that in some societies "the bound-

7. Marilyn Strathern, *After Nature: English Kinship in the Late Twentieth Century* (Cambridge, 1992), 78.

8. J. S. LaFontaine, "Person and Individual: Some Anthropological Reflections," in *The Category of the Person: Anthropology, Philosophy, History,* ed. Michael Carrithers, Steven Collins, and Steven Lukes (Cambridge, 1985), esp. 133.

9. Clifford Geertz, "'From the Native's Point of View': On the Nature of Anthropological Understanding," in his *Local Knowledge: Further Essays in Interpretive Anthropology* (New York, 1983), 59. More broadly see Richard A. Schweder, *Thinking through Cultures: Expeditions in Cultural Psychology* (Cambridge, Mass., 1991), esp. 113–55, 156–85; Robin Fox, *Reproduction and Succession: Studies in Anthropology, Law, and Society* (New Brunswick, N.J., 1993), 96–98.

10. Geoffrey M. White and John Kirkpatrick, "Exploring Ethnopsychologies," in *Person, Self, and Experience: Exploring Pacific Ethnopsychologies,* ed. Geoffrey M. White and John Kirkpatrick (Berkeley and Los Angeles, 1985), 9.

aries of a person may be conceptualized as extending far beyond the physical body. For example, all members of a nuclear family might be assumed to share an essence distinct from those outside the family, which in turn binds them, as a unit in relation to those others."[11] Notions of blood and honor that permeated Florentine families played such a role, extending the boundaries of personhood, especially for fathers of families managing patrimonies. Insofar as notions of blood and honor touched bastards, their personhood could meld with that of their kin and they could lose their distinctive (and divisive) individuality. This, though, was the individuality of an asocial or presocial being who is not a person: "where personhood is a status reserved for defined categories of people, parents or men, by implication those who are not persons are individuals."[12] The same negative sense of individuality has also been applied to women.[13] We can begin to conceptualize the legitimation of Simone di Domenico as a process transforming him from an individual into a social person, except that we first have to account for the degree of social personhood already vested in him by paternal recognition and upbringing. Personhood resulted from an additive process across one's life as useful and socially defining relationships developed.[14]

The person is also a social agent. When Simone di Domenico and other bastards were legitimated, their greatly expanded agency (in regard to officeholding, inheritance, and the like) was noted in notarial charters. In the modern Western notion of the individual, agency is linked to subjectivity and becomes authorship, conceived as individual, singular, and possessive.[15] Such is not the case in societies anthropologists study, where agency is affected by the requirements of a relationship; persons are multiply constituted with no innate unity.[16] The persons we will study were part of a western European society and culture. They came from the tradition in which the modern notion of the individual as a sub-

11. Jane Fajans, "The Person in Social Context: The Social Character of Baining 'Psychology,'" in White and Kirkpatrick, *Person, Self, and Experience,* 370.

12. LaFontaine, "Person and Individual," 133.

13. Marilyn Strathern, "Self-Interest and the Social Good: Some Implications of Hagen Gender Imagery," in *Sexual Meanings: The Cultural Construction of Gender and Sexuality,* ed. Sherry B. Ortner and Harriet Whitehead (Cambridge, 1981), 187.

14. LaFontaine, "Person and Individual," 137.

15. Marilyn Strathern, conclusion to *Dealing with Inequality: Analyzing Gender Relations in Melanesia and Beyond,* ed. Marilyn Strathern (Cambridge, 1987), 284, and her introduction.

16. Marilyn Strathern, *The Gender of the Gift: Problems with Women and Problems with Society in Melanesia* (Berkeley and Los Angeles, 1988), 269–74.

jective agent arose. The historian of such a society cannot ignore this tradition and its effects in the actions of social persons variously affected by Christian moral teachings and legal theories that incorporated forms of conscious voluntarism and rights.

Historians have placed the origins of individualism at a number of locations across the centuries. Brian Tierney looks to the twelfth century, yet he has to concede that theories of natural rights only reached a complete form in the seventeenth century.[17] The early canonists did not expect a language of subjective rights, he says, "to justify a moral universe in which each individual would ruthlessly pursue his own advantage," derived from greed or egotism. Rather the canonists viewed humans as free, rational, moral, and acting within "the ties of justice and charity that bound individuals to one another."[18] As we will see, in law the bastard recognized by his father was conceded a minimal right to material support; he did not gain a form of anticipatory ownership of paternal property that went to a legitimate son. Property, it can be said with some truth, is always about relations between people, no matter how much it is posed as a matter of persons and things.[19] Kinship was both a definer of persons and a means of access to resources.

In Western countries individualism has been enshrined in the linking of subjectivity to the notion of a legal person, the protagonist of acts, operating with motives and interests. The "myth" of personality, as Paolo Zatti terms it, thus underwrites a sense of juristic humanism.[20] The bastard, like any other legally free human, is such a *persona.* Only those not yet come of age or those whose mental capacities are proved defective ordinarily lack full *persona*—are deemed incapable of being active, even as passively they possess rights and in that sense are persons.

Illegitimacy was a deeply ambiguous area of law and social practice. It was the sort of legal matter that easily generated "trouble cases," which touched conceptual boundaries and gray areas. As such it could both expose to our view underlying assumptions and prejudices, legal and cultural, and also reveal a functional retreat back into opacity, as too much

17. Brian Tierney, *The Idea of Natural Rights: Studies on Natural Rights, Natural Law, and Church Law, 1150–1625* (Atlanta, 1997), 30–34, 51–52.

18. Ibid., 77.

19. Cf. Ann Whitehead, "Women and Men; Kinship and Property: Some General Issues," in *Women and Property—Women as Property,* ed. Renée Hirschon (London, 1984), 176–92.

20. Paolo Zatti, *Persona giuridica e soggettività: Per una definizione del concetto di "persona" nel rapporto con la titolarità delle situazioni soggettive* (Padua, 1975), 176–79.

clarity, too firm resolution could be deeply disturbing, throwing up to view contradictions patched over or best ignored. Desire to limit legal rights of bastards nonetheless also confirmed the existence of some sort of rights. Legitimation, whether by imperial, ecclesiastical, or civic auspices, further strengthened the assimilation of the bastard, but if it went too far, it could denude legitimacy of its core meaning. Here was an area of law well served by the lack of a doctrine of judicial precedent, so no single, well-meaning, forcefully written opinion could forever redefine matters.

Jurists held a preeminent role as interpreters of law and social practices. Perhaps at no other time did jurists enjoy the sort of civic prestige and prominence that they had in fifteenth and early sixteenth centuries, before more overt political control of courts and their staffing by a professional judiciary.[21] The fifteenth century saw the expansion of legal treatises summarizing particular institutions and issues, including crucial treatments by Florentine jurists of illegitimacy and legitimation and commentaries on local statutes. *Consilia* were collected and copied—more authoritative ones later to be printed. From these writings it was possible to develop juristic "common opinions" on matters of dispute within law. In the end we will find Florentine jurists, by a variety of paths, coming only to a general agreement to respect and abide by legal processes like legitimation without totally eradicating illegitimacy. The birth status of Simone di Domenico and so many others like him was not to be forgotten, no matter how favored by paternal treatment and the law.

The problem with bastards was that they were part of a family, but not totally. They were an anomaly. Like many an anomaly, they were best dealt with by being disposed of or forgotten. Such was indeed the fate of many bastards—a fate made easier in fifteenth-century Florence by the establishment of the foundling hospital of the Innocenti. Like Simone's father, however, a number of Florentine men (illegitimacy was

21. Cf. Luigi Lombardi, *Saggio sul diritto giurisprudenziale* (Milan, 1967); Mario Ascheri, *Tribunali, giuristi e istituzioni dal medioevo all'età moderna* (Bologna, 1989); Mario Sbriccoli, *L'Interpretazione dello statuto: Contributo allo studio della funzione dei giuristi nell'età comunale* (Milan, 1969); Adriano Cavanna, "Il ruolo del giurista nell'età del diritto comune," *Studia et documenta historiae et iuris* 44 (1978): 95–138; and three essays: Julius Kirshner, "*Consilia* as Authority in Late Medieval Italy: The Case of Florence"; Vincenzo Colli, "*Consilia* dei giuristi medievali e produzione libraria"; and Thomas Kuehn, "*Consilia* as Juristic Literature in Private Law," all in *Legal Consulting in the Civil Law Tradition,* ed. Mario Ascheri, Ingrid Baumgärtner, and Julius Kirshner (Berkeley and Los Angeles, 1999), 107–40, 173–225, 229–53.

a matter of paternity, not maternity) chose to recognize paternity and see to the bastard's upbringing. Even anomalies have something going for them. The bastards may have been the result of relationships that were legally unrecognized or even illegal, but they were related to people. Nature and blood mattered, in law and in culture. Bastards may not have had the full status of legitimate persons, but they were also fully capable legal actors in many regards, including their own ability to own property, marry, and propagate a legitimate line of descent. Thus they might also prove to be suitable heirs, at least when a man had no legitimate progeny. On the moral level bastards were the product of sin, and so unworthy of approaching the altar or donning a religious habit by canon law. But they too were God's creatures, possessed of an immortal soul and the right to life (including alimentary support and baptism).

The essential ambivalence of illegitimacy was felt most closely by those who were related to a bastard, who were asked to share a home or even an inheritance. But it was also felt broadly in fifteenth-century Florence, buffeted by demographic factors at the outset, finally growing in population before facing the confusion and crises of the wars at the end of the century. The establishment of the Innocenti was only one note in a legislative symphony that took cognizance of illegitimacy in its different movements. Citizenship legislation, the *monte delle doti,* the fiscal device of the catasto excluded, limited, and admitted bastards (in that order). The fifteenth century, then, is also a pivotal century in which to examine illegitimacy from the point of view of Florentine history. This was the century in which the most eloquent and forcefully written evocation of the ideals of Florentine patrician family life was penned by Leon Battista Alberti, ironically a bastard scion of this formerly powerful and wealthy clan, itself besmirched by lengthy exile in the first decades of the century.[22]

Bastardy in Renaissance History

The irony of Alberti's birth was lost on Jacob Burckhardt when, in his classic *Civilization of the Renaissance in Italy,* he enshrined bastardy in the historiography of the Renaissance. He drew a simple equation between the illegitimacy of despotism as a political form and illegitimacy in the line of descent of a despot's family: "Closely connected with the

22. Cf. Kuehn, "Reading between the Patrilines."

political illegitimacy of the dynasties of the fifteenth century was the public indifference to legitimate birth." Burckhardt also saw illegitimacy underlying the stunning and individualistic achievements of some of the great figures of the era: Petrarch, Boccaccio, Alberti, da Vinci. Freed of constraints posed by family, guild, church, and more, these men of genius were free to explore ancient texts and art forms and develop new modes of expression. This "golden age" for bastards ended, said Burckhardt, with the straitlaced moralism of the Counter Reformation.[23]

Burckhardt's observations have served as the basis of a hardy stereotype of the Renaissance as a "golden age" for bastards. No less a figure than Sigmund Freud attributed not just psychological but artistic aspects of Leonardo da Vinci's life to his bastardy. Freud obviously had no historically accurate sense of family life in the Renaissance.[24] Historians who do have remarked on the seemingly comfortable presence of bastards in households. As one historian has it, "the Tuscan *famiglia* of the *trecento* was a far larger and more elastic organization than the modern family; not only wives, but concubines, had their place there; not only sons, but bastards."[25]

The notion of an age of bastards, like the concept of the Renaissance that spawned it, has also enjoyed geographical expansion. The French and English nobility have been cited as prolific bastard-generators in the fifteenth century.[26] David Nicholas examines illegitimacy in his analysis of families in Ghent, and he finds that "widespread concubinage and high

23. Jakob Burckhardt, *The Civilization of the Renaissance in Italy,* trans. S. G. C. Middlemore, rev. ed. Irene Gordon (New York, 1960), 51, 283, 310–14.

24. Sigmund Freud, *Leonardo da Vinci: A Study in Psychosexuality,* trans. A. A. Brill (New York, 1955). Among other things, Freud presumed that Leonardo was not part of his father's household before the 1458 catasto, where he showed up as a five-year-old (47), which is crucial to Freud's sense of Leonardo as fatherless. However, later Freud saw Leonardo in a more "normal" oedipal rivalry with his father and posed that as father to his artworks "he created them and then troubled himself no longer about them, just as his father did not trouble himself about him" (94).

25. Iris Origo, *The Merchant of Prato: Francesco di Marco Datini,* rev. ed. (Harmondsworth, 1963), 170. See also Kate Simon, *A Renaissance Tapestry: The Gonzaga of Mantua* (New York, 1988), 145.

26. For now, see J. P. Cooper, "Patterns of Inheritance and Settlement by Great Landowners from the Fifteenth to the Eighteenth Centuries," in *Family and Inheritance: Rural Society in Western Europe, 1200–1800,* ed. Jack Goody, Joan Thirsk, and E. P. Thompson (Cambridge, 1976), 302; Françoise Autrand, "Naissance illégitime et service de l'État: Les enfants naturels dans le milieu de robe parisien xive–xve siècle," *Revue historique* 267 (1982): 289–303; Mikhail Harsgor, "L'essor des bâtards nobles au xve siècle," *Revue historique* 253 (1975): 319–54.

incidence of bastardy" demonstrates "unblushing acceptance of behavior totally at variance" with Christian morality.[27] Myriam Carlier has similarly argued that acknowledgment of illegitimate paternity carried no stigma, as opposed to "denying paternity against all rationality and leaving the child to fend for himself."[28]

From Robert Davidsohn, who attempted the first modern comprehensive history of Florence, to Lauro Martines, who has authored one of the most recent surveys of Renaissance Italy, this image has been maintained.[29] Its essential factual basis, in each case, remains an awareness of the presence of bastards in princely, noble, and patrician families and their visible role at times in affairs of state. Only Martines, who has studied law, has sounded a cautionary note: "Bastardy—whatever Burckhardt and others may have said about its political place in the Italian Renaissance—generally carried a stain of some sort, especially in urban society, although men could be made to overlook it by the force of power and place or by means of money and a dispensation."[30] Flaunting the rules of conventional behavior that applied to social inferiors redounded to nobles' honor and reputation. Where, as Martines insightfully has it, power and image were sides of the same coin, bastardy communicated important messages for the powerful.[31]

Stephen Greenblatt argues that the term *individualism* was a nineteenth-century invention and that, *pace* Burckhardt, "individual identity

27. David Nicholas, *The Domestic Life of a Medieval City: Women, Children, and the Family in Fourteenth-Century Ghent* (Lincoln, Neb., 1985), 59, 168.

28. Myriam Carlier, "Paternity in Late Medieval Flanders," in *Secretum scriptorum: Liber alumnorum Walter Prevenier,* ed. Wim Blockmans, Marc Boone, and Thérèse de Hemptinne (Leuven, 1999), 245.

29. Robert Davidsohn, *Storia di Firenze,* vol. 4: *I primordi della civiltà fiorentina,* part 3: *Il mondo della chiesa, spiritualità e arte, vita pubblica e privata,* trans. from German by Eugenio Dupré-Theseider (Florence, 1973), 697; Robert S. Lopez, "Hard Times and Investment in Culture," in *The Renaissance: Six Essays* (New York, 1953), 47–48; Nino Tamassia, *La famiglia italiana nei secoli decimoquinto e decimosesto* (Milan, 1911), 221–22, though he contests Comines (225–26); Anna T. Sheedy, *Bartolus on Social Conditions in the Fourteenth Century* (New York, 1942), 73. Among legal historians, cf. Hermann Winterer, *Die rechtliche Stellung der Bastarden in Italien von 800 bis 1500* (Munich, 1978), 59–60. Also George R. Marek, *The Bed and the Throne: The Life of Isabella d'Este* (New York, 1984); Pierre Hurtubise, *Une famille-témoin: Les Salviati* (Vatican City, 1985), 317–19; Maurice Baudin, *Les bâtards au théâtre en France de la Renaissance à la fin de xviie siècle* (Baltimore, 1932), 20–22.

30. Lauro Martines, *Lawyers and Statecraft in Renaissance Florence* (Princeton, N.J., 1968), 28.

31. Lauro Martines, *Power and Imagination: City-States in Renaissance Italy* (New York, 1979), 239.

in the early modern period served less as a final goal than as a way station on the road to a firm and decisive identity with normative structures."[32] Natalie Zemon Davis contributes the insight that the boundaries around the conceptual self and the bodily self were not only not isomorphic but were not firm and closed. "The example of the sixteenth century," she concludes, "suggests the importance of seeing the person as part of a field of relations and of being open to paths and modes for the constitution of the self different from those in nineteenth century thought."[33] Peter Burke has likewise argued that the "self" in the Renaissance was not single but multiple.[34] The fluidity between public and private, the sharing of risks and honor by family members, kept people in close but not necessarily intimate relations.[35] Families, in turn, required relations with others for their survival, and though these relations varied enormously between the elites and the humble folk, there was always an openness to the scrutiny of others.[36]

Certainly the tendency in the historiography of family and kinship in Florence has been to stress the imperatives of patrilineage in shaping the lives of men and women.[37] The tendency is to see kin solidarities as becoming over time less horizontal and more vertical, less spatial and

32. Stephen Greenblatt, "Fiction and Friction," in *Reconstructing Individualism: Autonomy, Individuality, and the Self in Western Thought,* ed. Thomas Heller, Morton Sosma, and David E. Wellbery (Stanford, Calif., 1986), 35.

33. Natalie Zemon Davis, "Boundaries of the Self in Sixteenth-Century France," in Heller, Sosma, and Wellbery, *Reconstructing Individualism,* 54 and 63.

34. Peter Burke, "Representations of the Self from Petrarch to Descartes," in *Rewriting the Self: Histories from the Renaissance to the Present,* ed. Roy Porter (London, 1997), 28. Aaron Gurevich finds that in the Middle Ages and Renaissance people had a sense of individuality that was rooted not in "accidental traits of character" but in prototypes related to office, social place, and group: *The Origins of European Individualism,* trans. Katharine Judelson (Oxford, 1995), 14, 50–53, 197–98, 249.

35. Philippe Braunstein, "The Emergence of the Individual: Toward Intimacy, the Fourteenth and Fifteenth Centuries," in *A History of Private Life,* ed. Philippe Ariès and Georges Duby, vol. 2: *Revelations of the Medieval World,* ed. Georges Duby, trans. Arthur Goldhammer (Cambridge, Mass., 1988), 535–630.

36. These themes are especially evident in the third volume of *A History of Private Life,* entitled *Passions of the Renaissance,* ed. Roger Chartier (Cambridge, Mass., 1989), especially in essays by Nicole Castan (21–67, 403–45), Jacques Gélis (309–25), Maurice Aymard (447–91), and Arlette Farge (571–607).

37. Cf. Kent, *Household and Lineage;* Christiane Klapisch-Zuber, *Women, Family, and Ritual in Renaissance Italy,* trans. Lydia G. Cochrane (Chicago, 1985), and *La famiglia e le donne del Rinascimento a Firenze* (Bari, 1988). A notable exception to this tendency is Richard Goldthwaite, *Private Wealth in Renaissance Florence* (Princeton, N.J., 1968).

more temporal.[38] There continue to be those who invoke a conventional Burckhardtian image of individualism and locate it in the Renaissance or even earlier.[39] Such continued attachment to a sense of increasing individualism in the Renaissance makes sense in view of the voluntarism found in humanistic ethics or of the undoubted individual achievements of figures varying from Lorenzo Valla to Michelangelo. But in the realm of law, politics, and family, the self was implicated in a rich pattern of social personhood. Study of the personhood of Renaissance bastards can contribute a great deal to this debate. We have the difficult dual task of trying to determine what a person was generally thought to be or could be in Florentine society and what actual, single human actors did.[40] Florentine jurists faced much the same task in the illegitimacy cases that came to them.

In fifteenth-century Florence one key to the rehabilitation of a bastard was the legal process of legitimation. By this means men otherwise childless could designate illegitimate children as their heirs and alleviate the disabilities of illegitimate status. Forms of legitimation existed in civil law, were revived and expanded by canon law, and were permitted and enlarged in civic statutes. The anthropologist Jack Goody claimed that the church sought "to exercise a large measure of control in the domestic domain" and prevent consolidation of estates by forbidding remedies for childlessness like adoption and legitimation.[41] He notably failed to engage the conceptual vocabulary that explained ecclesiastical biases—notions of nature, blood, and sin—and ignored the fact that the church also made legitimation more widely available by extending legitimation

38. See the historiographical synthesis by Francis W. Kent, "La famiglia patrizia fiorentina nel Quattrocento: Nuovi orientamenti nella storiografia recente," in *Palazzo Strozzi: Metà Millennio, 1489–1989,* Atti del Convegno di Studi, Florence, 3–6 July 1989 (Rome, 1991), 70–91. Also Marzio Barbagli, *Sotto lo stesso tetto: Mutamenti della famiglia in Italia dal xv al xx secolo* (Bologna, 1984).

39. In "Inventing Sincerity, Refashioning Prudence: The Discovery of the Individual in Renaissance Europe," *American Historical Review* 102 (1997): 1309–42, John Martin has pressed against Greenblatt and others ("new historicists") that they leave no room for historical development of a Western notion of the individual. Martin finds that there was "a new emphasis on inwardness or the idea of an interior self as the core of personal identity" and an individual responsible for his or her own words and deeds.

40. Cf. Ronald F. E. Weissman, "Reconstructing Renaissance Sociology: The 'Chicago School' and the Study of Renaissance Society," in *Persons in Groups: Social Behavior as Identity Formation in Medieval and Renaissance Europe* (Binghamton, N.Y., 1985), 39–45.

41. Jack Goody, *Development of Family and Marriage in Europe* (Cambridge, 1983), 44–59, 72–74, 76, 101.

by rescript to all forms of illegitimates. Goody also ignored the sort of arguments raised by Georges Duby that "the practice of concubinage lasted because it served family interests" and that "illegitimate sons shared the lives of their legitimate half-brothers."[42]

Duby, Goody, and others tie legitimacy to inheritance strategies, especially among the nobility, for whom inheritance meant not only wealth but power, position, honor, name. They see marriage and inheritance rules from a social rather than a legal perspective. They assume behavior is rule-bound. Illegitimate, but recognized and socially placed, bastards in fact posed difficult challenges to social and legal order and to the expenditure of resources. A bastard like Simone had a personhood of uncertain dimensions; and he, his kin, and the jurists were all involved in ascertaining those dimensions. In this regard one should also note the splendid work of Ann Twinam on processes of legitimation in Spain's American colonies, where she notes that "race and illegitimate birth were not necessarily ascriptive characteristics assigned permanently at birth but could be changed, or even achieved" by conscious manipulation of disparities between public and private worlds.[43]

A crucial concept for understanding illegitimacy in Florence was honor. In the first place, honor is not a constant and clear concept but a conceptual field with paradoxes and fruitful ambiguities. What constitutes honorable or dishonorable behavior is thus open to negotiation. Honor is a matter of both conscience and sentiment and of repute and precedence (related to birth, power, wealth, sanctity, prestige, guile, and more).[44] Honor inheres both in the person as agent and in relations with others; it requires management and communication; it is a rhetorical situation, where meanings are evanescent and to be determined.[45] Honor is also an expression of family:

> the group acquires a prestige transmitted from forbears which gives it control over its history. It follows that it is more highly esteemed to inherit certain types of past rather than others. This explains the

42. Georges Duby, *The Knight, the Lady, and the Priest: The Making of Modern Marriage in Medieval France,* trans. Barbara Bray (New York, 1983), 43, 262–63.

43. Ann Twinam, *Public Lives, Private Secrets: Gender, Honor, Sexuality, and Illegitimacy in Colonial Spanish America* (Stanford, Calif., 1999), 25.

44. J. G. Peristiany and Julian Pitt-Rivers, introduction to *Honor and Grace in Anthropology,* ed. J. G. Peristiany and Julian Pitt-Rivers (Cambridge, 1992), 1–17.

45. Michael Herzfeld, *The Poetics of Manhood: Contest and Identity in a Cretan Mountain Village* (Princeton, N.J., 1985).

> manipulation of genealogies and the disappearance from the collective memory of elders who have bequeathed neither glory nor honor and, above all, those who have done the contrary.[46]

Bastards or their begetters may precisely have been the sort to be ignored, but at least for the powerful, bastardy could be redeemed by working for the family, even while being eminently more expendable.[47] To concede bastards any place in family relations was to concede them some sort of personhood, however partial.

Illegitimate children were a family resource but also a source of tension and animosity. Charles de La Roncière, in a study of Tuscan families in the fourteenth century, argued that the importance of the male line in the household's constitution meant that persons of the female line or illegitimate relations were kept there only reluctantly. On the other hand, delay of marriage for men into their late twenties and the easy availability of female slaves and domestic servants providing ready sexual outlets, ensured that family records "are filled with the names of bastard offspring." Still, "in the case of bastards and widows, the interest of the lineage won out," and they were able to stay with paternal relations despite tensions that might arise from their presence.[48]

This book, among other things, is the first study of a population of bastards and the moral, social, and legal tensions they gave rise to. It demonstrates that it is difficult to credit the notion that the fifteenth century, especially in Florence, constituted a "golden age" of bastardy. Illegitimacy was a stigma—a *macula.* Those who bore it were disadvantaged by it—not uniformly, not consistently—but disadvantaged. Those recognized and raised in the paternal home were better off than those abandoned, but they were not as well off as legitimate children. Even if legitimated, their prior status was never entirely obliterated—neither at the hands of jurists, nor legislators, nor their own kin. Bastards' membership and participation in a family was more easily conceded in some matters (as in armed vendetta); but regarding the future inheritance of property or office (matters linked to agnation, itself springing from *patria potestas*) any such concessions were more restricted. As problems

46. Maria Pia di Bella, "Name, Blood, and Miracles: The Claims of Renown in Traditional Sicily," in Peristiany and Pitt-Rivers, *Honor and Grace,* 155.

47. Pia di Bella, "Name, Blood, and Miracles," 164.

48. Charles de La Roncière, "Portraits: Tuscan Notables on the Eve of the Renaissance," in Ariès and Duby, *History of Private Life,* 2:157–309.

of family inheritance came to occupy Florentines more thoroughly in the fifteenth century, as they came to use mechanisms like the *fideicommissum* more and in a more refined manner, as they less frequently emancipated their children and bound emancipations more closely to inheritance strategies, they also needed to control illegitimates.[49] Their claims on family resources had to be removed, postponed, or limited. Abandonment to a foundling home or just consistent labeling as illegitimate effectively marginalized the bastard in society.

John Boswell arguably overemphasized this marginalization when he termed the growth of foundling homes proof that foundlings were no longer met with the "kindness of strangers" and were always nonpersons.[50] In fact the foundlings of Florence have been well studied by a number of scholars, who have found reason to contest Boswell's harsh judgments. Our attention, in contrast, will be directed to those bastards who, like Simone, were not abandoned but were recognized and raised by their fathers. The presence of bastards openly labeled as such, especially in elite families, has been taken as sufficient evidence of full and successful assimilation. The evidence is, in fact, patchy and impressionistic, limited to a few notable figures. But that seems sufficient as long as the meaning of illegitimacy is seen as an unequivocal indication of a loosening of behavior before institutions like the church and family. But the existence of legal cases and so much else shows us that bastardy was anything but unequivocal. The bastard raised in a family home, even more so the bastard legitimated, straddled the boundary between secure order (legitimacy) and dangerous disorder (illegitimacy). In the same manner that Robert Darnton used house pets, possessed of an ambiguity as mediators of binary opposites, bastards are "good to think" for gaining insight into meanings of legitimacy, agnation, and family in Renaissance Florence.[51]

49. Cf. Thomas Kuehn, *Emancipation in Late Medieval Florence* (New Brunswick, N.J., 1982), 159–61; also Samuel K. Cohn Jr., *The Cult of Remembrance and the Black Death: Six Renaissance Cities in Central Italy* (Baltimore, 1992), 171–81.

50. John Boswell, *The Kindness of Strangers: The Abandonment of Children in Western Europe from Late Antiquity to the Renaissance* (New York, 1988), 160–79, 264, 322–35, 341–44, 401–34. Contrary to his belief, children of annulled marriages were not rendered illegitimate by the annulment, if the marriage had been entered into in ignorance and good faith.

51. Cf. Robert Darnton, "The Symbolic Element in History," *Journal of Modern History* 58 (1986): 218–34.

Legal and Demographic History

Legal historians and, more recently, historical demographers are the only ones to study illegitimacy. They have sought to determine what rules of marriage, sexual activity, family membership, and inheritance were and if they were followed or enforced. Their work is vital. Yet the works of legal historians only begin to flesh out the dilemmas faced by jurists like Omodei and his colleagues; and the historical demographers have not been concerned with the experience (as opposed to the origins) of bastardy for children like Simone di Domenico.

So much legal history, especially that of civil law, comes off as a skeleton without flesh. Its focus is mainly on the sort of legal doctrines, terminology, and pedantic issues that filled academic jurisprudence.[52] Social historians have complained with dismay about the divorce of legal from social realities; about the fact that legal historians do not directly investigate the use of law by laymen, as seen, for example, in notarial documents or even in records of litigation or its alternatives. One of the presumptions and objectives of this book is to take a broader view of the law and its operation.

Specific legal historical interest in illegitimacy and legitimation has followed developments in family law. In the early twentieth century, as nations revised their law codes, socialist parties were active, and sociology began to look to the effects of industrialization on family life, there was a brief spate of legal historical studies of illegitimacy. More recently, in the aftermath of Vatican II but more importantly against the backdrop of increasing concern with matters like divorce and abortion, scholars like Hermann Winterer and Anke Leineweber have gone over the legal ground again.[53] Many of these histories betray an ideological attachment

52. Cf. Luigi Berlinguer, "Considerazioni su storiografia e diritto," *Studi storici* 15 (1974): 3–56; Julius Kirshner, "Some Problems in the Interpretation of Legal Texts *re* the Italian City-States," *Archiv für Begriffsgeschichte* 19 (1975): 16–27; the contributions of a conference, Paolo Grossi ed., *Storia sociale e dimensione giuridica: Strumenti d'indagine e ipotesi di lavoro* (Milan, 1986); Peter Goodrich, *Reading the Law: A Critical Introduction to Legal Method and Techniques* (Oxford, 1986), esp. 91–100.

53. Winterer, *Die rechtliche Stellung*, and Anke Leineweber, *Die rechtliche Beziehung des nichtehelichen Kindes zu seinem Erzeuger in der Geschichte des Privatrechts* (Königstein, 1978), but see also Corrado Pecorella, "Filiazione (storia)," *Enciclopedia del diritto*, vol. 17 (Milan, 1968), 449–56; H. Regnault, *La condition juridique du bâtard au Moyen Age* (Pont-Audemer, 1922); H. Herrmann, *Die Stellung der unehelichen Kinder nach kanonischem Recht* (Amsterdam, 1971); R. Génestal, *Histoire de la légitimation des enfants naturels en droit canonique* (Paris, 1905); Albert Weitnauer, *Die Legitimation des aussere-*

to modern notions of childhood—its innocence and need of nurturing. They are intent on explaining current laws and institutional protections for illegitimate children. From the perspective of a present "enlightened" to the peculiar nature of childhood, work on bastardy law is permeated with a concern to designate the villains who worsened the legal condition of innocent children and, on the other hand, the heroes who distinguished that innocence from parental sin.[54] So it is that Roman law has been characterized as harsher than Germanic customs regarding illegitimate offspring, yet both seem laxer than canon law, for the church's adoption of clerical celibacy and sacramentalization of marriage seem to have resulted in a worsening of the legal situation of bastards.[55] Sexual unions that did not fit the definitions of marriage were categorized as illicit and their progeny as illegitimate, with legal disabilities heaped upon them if only to discourage potential parents.[56] Procreation became the only moral basis of sexual behavior, and the "later medieval fascination with order and uniformity" posited, for Aquinas, that the chief good of marriage was not even procreation per se but the legitimacy of the children.[57] There was also the fear of miscegenation by means of a wife's

helichen Kindes im römischen Recht und in den Germanenrechten des Mittelalters (Basel, 1940), who relies in great part on Génestal; H. J. Wolff, "The Background of the Post-classical Legislation on Illegitimacy," *Seminar* 3 (1945): 21–45; Benvenuto Pitzorno, *La legittimazione nella storia delle istituzioni familiari del medioevo* (Sassari, 1904).

A small flurry of studies of illegitimacy by German scholars in the 1970s coincided with extensive discussion of legal changes in Germany. A reform of Italian family law went into effect in 1975 in the midst of heated discussions of divorce and abortion. Note the presentist tones in the sociological paper by Hans-Joachim Hoffmann-Nowotny, "Soziologische Marginalien zur Marginalisierung durch 'illegitime' Geburt," in *Illegitimität im Spätmittelalter,* ed. Ludwig Schmugge (Munich, 1994), 11–20.

54. Peter Laslett, *Family Life and Illicit Love in Earlier Generations: Essays in Historical Sociology* (Cambridge, 1977), 160.

55. For a brief synopsis, see Gilbert Joseph McDevitt, *Legitimacy and Legitimation: An Historical Synopsis and Commentary* (Washington, D.C., 1941), 1–10; Maxime Lemosse, "L'enfant sans famille en droit romain," *Recueils de la société Jean Bodin pour l'histoire comparative des institutions,* vol. 35: *L'enfant,* part 1: *Antiquité-Afrique-Asie* (1975), 257–70; Bernhard Schimmelpfennig, "Ex Fornicatione Nati: Studies on the Position of Priests' Sons from the Twelfth to the Fourteenth Century," *Studies in Medieval and Renaissance History,* n.s. 2 (1979): 23–25; Winterer, *Die rechtliche Stellung,* 58–59; Pier Silverio Leicht, *Storia del diritto italiano: Il diritto privato,* vol. 1: *Diritto delle persone e di famiglia* (Milan, 1943), 231–32; Weitnauer, *Die Legitimation,* 87–90; Génestal, *Histoire de la légitimation,* i–iii, 1–23; Regnault, *La condition juridique,* 25–30, who also maintains, therefore, that before that point "le bâtard n'est pas un objet de droits, que la droit de bâtardise n'existe pas."

56. Boswell, *The Kindness of Strangers,* 341–44.

57. John Boswell, *Christianity, Social Tolerance, and Homosexuality: Gay People in*

adultery that would result in a man raising children who were not in fact naturally his. Yet canon law doctrines, as those of civil law, were not uniformly negative. The church improved bastards' alimentary rights,[58] revived the civil law institution of legitimation by subsequent marriage and by rescript, and extended legitimation by rescript beyond the bounds set for it by civil law, as well as providing dispensations from disabilities imposed by canon law on illegitimates.[59] James Brundage concludes that the canonists "seem to have been more solicitous to improve the lot of bastard children than were civic authorities."[60]

In Italy, when there is benign treatment of illegitimates in customs and statutes (e.g., granting some succession rights and allowing legitimation), it is generally credited to Lombard influence.[61] Feudal law, on the other hand, has been accused of worsening the lot of bastards. Succession rights in a vassal's lineage and the prerogatives of lords over their fiefs served to remove bastards from the nobility and reduce them to a sort of serfdom.[62] Feudal law, notably in England, was also hostile to the idea that mere formalities of legitimation or adoption could generate legal ties to third parties.[63] But then, as Richard Helmholz has pointed out, England also had canon law courts where, in contrast to common law, alimentary rights for bastards were established and enforced.[64]

Western Europe from the Beginning of the Christian Era to the Fourteenth Century (Chicago, 1980), 165 and 270.

58. Gian Savino Pene Vidari, *Ricerche sul diritto agli alimenti: L'obbligo "ex lege" dei familiari nel periodo della Glossa e del commento* (Turin, 1970), 153–72; Leineweber, *Die rechtliche Beziehung,* 62–63; Regnault, *La condition juridique,* 57.

59. Regnault, *La condition juridique,* 17–18; Génestal, *Histoire de la légitimation,* 151–59; Adhémar Esmein, *Le mariage en droit canonique,* 2 vols. (Paris, 1891; rpt. New York, 1968), 2:40–41.

60. James A. Brundage, *Law, Sex, and Christian Society in Medieval Europe* (Chicago, 1987), 543.

61. Antonio Pertile, *Storia del diritto italiano dalla caduta dell'impero romano alla codificazione,* 2d ed., 6 vols. (Turin, 1894), 3:388–89; Leineweber, *Die rechtliche Beziehung,* 73–74; Winterer, *Die rechtliche Stellung,* 83–84, 111; *Encyclopedia of the Social Sciences,* s.v. "Illegitimacy: Legal Aspects," by A. C. Jacobs (1932), 7:582–83; J. H. Baker, *An Introduction to English Legal History* (London, 1971), 263.

62. Regnault, *La condition juridique,* 58–119; Leicht, *Storia del diritto italiano,* 1:231.

63. Cf. T. E. James, "The Illegitimate and Deprived Child: Legitimation and Adoption," in *A Century of Family Law, 1857–1957,* ed. R. H. Graveson and F. R. Crane (London, 1957), 39–55. An interesting comparison of civil and common law traditions can be found in Joseph McKnight, "Legitimation and Adoption on the Anglo-Hispanic Frontier of the United States," *Tijdschrift voor Rechtsgeschiedenis* 53 (1985): 135–50.

64. Richard Helmholz, "Support Orders, Church Courts, and the Rule of *Filius Nullius:* A Reassessment of the Canon Law," *Virginia Law Review* 63 (1977): 431–48.

The coexistence of multiple sources of law argues strongly against any reductionistic analysis of the legal status and conditions of bastards. These sources, moreover, were not thoroughly independent of each other. By the fifteenth century, civil, canon, and other legal traditions had fused in the hands of university-trained jurists into a complex legal amalgam, usually dubbed the *ius commune*. The notion of a *ius commune* was a way of asserting a semblance of order in these multiple sources, an order valid in all or most jurisdictions (hence common).[65] The bringing of these legal traditions into proximity raised problems and questions. There were also problems of jurisdiction—whether ecclesiastical or secular courts would oversee matters of bastardy, and which matters.[66] It becomes very difficult to see how one can maintain that things were better or worse for bastards in the fifteenth century in comparison to some earlier period, or in canon law as compared with civil, or in *ius commune* as opposed to local statutes, simply by looking at legal rules.

The one recent attempt to study illegitimacy in some systematic fashion within the confines of *ius commune* comes from the German historian Ludwig Schmugge. The core of his work is a computerized data bank assembled from the records of papal dispensations regarding illegitimacy between 1449 and 1533; but he has also produced an important anthology, *Illegitimität im Spätmittelalter,* with preliminary results for Spain, Ireland, and portions of Germany, as well as theoretical and legal historical papers.[67] While his work is undoubtedly valuable, it studies only one sort of source and, in consequence, deals mainly with bastards entering the clergy. We will be concerned with bastards who entered the clergy, even less so with those born of clergy, only insofar as they can tell us something about families and social personhood.

Beyond the *ius commune,* though in conjunction with it, the *ius proprium* of each commune (mainly embodied in written statutes) also governed illegitimacy. This legal level has been little studied by legal histori-

65. Cf. Danilo Segoloni, ed., *Il diritto comune e la tradizione giuridica europea* (Perugia, 1980); Paul Koschaker, *Europa und das römische Recht,* 4th ed. (Munich, 1966); and my "A Medieval Conflict of Laws: Illegitimacy and Legitimation in *Ius Commune* and *Ius Proprium,*" *Law and History Review* 15 (1997): 243–73.

66. Cf. R. H. Helmholz, "Bastardy Litigation in Medieval England," *American Journal of Legal History* 13 (1969): 360–83.

67. This volume is in the series Schriften des Historischen Kollegs, Kolloquien 29 (Munich, 1994). See Schmugge's introduction to *Illegitimität im Spätmittelalter,* 1–9. His monograph is *Kirche, Kinder, Karrieren: Päpstliche Dispense von der unehelichen Geburt in Spätmittelalter* (Zurich, 1995).

ans whose gaze is otherwise fixed on the more coherent and sophisticated *ius commune.* As we will see, statutes varied in their treatment of illegitimates, but all treated them as less than legitimate and accepted the terms, if not all the rules, of *ius commune.* By Florence's statutes, political capacity was crippled by illegitimacy (for two generations), and some markets or careers were forbidden. Lack or limitation of inheritance also meant that even as an adult the illegitimate would not stand for much. Although there was a blood connection to the father (where paternity was known or admitted), it was not one of honor created by marriage with its carefully negotiated property settlements. The illegitimate child embodied no useful or valuable relationships or property transfers in the way the legitimate child did. Abandonment of bastards in part expressed the lack (or confusion) of relationships they embodied.

The evidence regarding illegitimates in Florence further shows us the continued vitality and importance (in law and practice) of paternal power, *patria potestas.*[68] Illegitimate children did not fall under this authority, but legitimation (and adoption) could establish it, and thus agnation. This paternal *potestas* limited the autonomy of children, absorbing their persons, their agency, into the *familia.* But *familia* was also *substantia,* and children and wives had their claims on the patrimony, limiting the discretion of the *pater* as owner *(dominus)* in regard to those portions of it variously designated as dowry, *peculia, parapherna, donationes,* and more.[69] As an expression of family unity *potestas* was destined for a degree of extension in legal treatises in later centuries, as it licensed monarchic power. Not withstanding critical voices arising from influential natural law thinkers or the effects of revolutionary legislation to undercut paternal power (lessening bastardy and encouraging adoption), the nineteenth-century civil codes in Europe, including the Italian *Codice civile* of 1865, incorporated a rigorous form of *potestas.*[70]

Yet the *pater* was not free to act with regard to *dos* and *patrimonium.* The former was circumscribed in law; his controls were more usufructu-

68. Richard P. Saller, "*Patria Potestas* and the Stereotype of the Roman Family," *Continuity and Change* 1 (1986): 7–22, has argued that among the Romans *patria potestas* was not a harsh patriarchal regime. My point is that it remained an important and potentially incapacitating legal factor, beyond the fact that fathers did live into at least a portion of their children's lives and thus exercised that power.

69. Gigliola di Renzo Villata, "Persone e famiglia nel diritto medioevale e moderno," *Digesto,* 4th ed., vol. 13 (Civile), 499–501.

70. Ibid., 505–26. In Italy this power was limited to children under twenty-one.

ary than proprietary in some ways. He was bound by social expectations, intestacy rules, rights of legitim, and fideicommissary stipulations handed down from preceding generations. Only with the greatest difficulty could he disinherit a child, if he so chose.[71] These materialistic/substantive foundations and constraints were not present with regard to women one was not married to (especially poor servants and slaves) and not even to concubines or illegitimate children. In that regard, because conventional social restraints were not present, there was no legitimacy.

As the magisterial works of Paolo Grossi have reminded us, more than other legal institutions, property (as ownership) is bound to a particular anthropology.[72] Definitions of property generate questions about personhood, including that of illegitimates or women.[73] In the modern West property rights in objects to be used and disposed of inhere in individuals as subjects able to use and dispose, although the notion of absolute dominion in property, suggesting individual autonomy, is itself fallacious in that all property is in some way relational, as rights against others.[74] The early Middle Ages saw a move away from the absolute *dominium* of Roman law to a system of real situations based not on *dominium* or even multiple *dominia* but on a multiplicity of economically effective positions with regard to an object. Learned jurisprudence later recast the notion of *dominium utile,* separable from but coincident with a full *dominium*

71. On this theme in the law, see Julius Kirshner, "Baldus de Ubaldis on Disinheritance: Contexts, Controversies, *Consilia,*" *Ius Commune: Zeitschrift für Europäische Rechtsgeschichte* 27 (2000): 119–214 (a special issue on the sixth centenary of Baldus's death). Jane Fishburne Collier, in an anthropological reexamination of a Spanish village, notes that parents of legitimate children could not disinherit them and thus projected, as a mark of respect, the duty that they had taken on (in contrast to childless adults): cf. *From Duty to Desire: Remaking Families in a Spanish Village* (Princeton, N.J., 1997), 148, 246 n. 41.

72. His "La proprietà e le proprietà nell'officina dello storico," in *La proprietà e le proprietà,* ed. Ennio Cortese (Milan, 1988), 205–72; but see also his important earlier works *"Locatio ad longum tempus": Locazione e rapporti reali di godimento nella problematica del diritto comune* (Naples, 1963); *Le situazioni reali nell'esperienza giuridica medievale* (Padua, 1968); and his collected papers in *Il dominio e le cose: Percezioni medievali e moderne dei diritti reali* (Milan, 1992). Also on these themes, see Dietmar Willoweit, "Dominium und Proprietas: Zur Entwicklung des Eigentumsbegriffs in der mittelalterlichen und neuzeitlichen Rechtswissenschaft," *Historisches Jahrbuch der Goerres-Gesellschaft zur Pflege der Wissenschaft im Katholischen Deutschland* 94 (1974): 131–56; Manlio Bellomo, *Problemi di diritto familiare nell'età dei comuni: Beni paterni e "pars filii"* (Milan, 1968).

73. Also Carol Blum, "Of Women and the Land: Legitimizing Husbandry," in *Early Modern Conceptions of Property,* ed. John Brewer and Susan Staves (London, 1995), 161–69.

74. Brewer and Staves, *Early Modern Conceptions of Property,* 3; also Robert W. Gordon, "Paradoxical Property," in ibid., 95–110.

vested in others over the same objects. Such a reification of coincident ownerships is not the dominant and autonomous property of the modern capitalist world. These various *dominia* were not attributes of an owner; they were inscribed in things.

Even where the paterfamilias, the full legal person, could seem to have absolute ownership of houses, lands, and moneys, what we frequently find is the paradox that freedom in ownership implies freedom to craft restraints on that same property, to bind one's own hands or those to whom it will transfer. The outstanding example is the use of intergenerational restraints.[75] These were most notable on the types of property that for Florentines answered Annette Weiner's description as "inalienable possessions." Such items, "imbued with the intrinsic and ineffable identities of their owners," are kept across the generations, as their loss diminishes persons and the groups to which they belong. Holding onto such possessions, when otherwise involved in social relations of reciprocal exchange, requires the enormous effort of keeping-while-giving.[76] Such possessions clearly are not the exchangeable commodities of capitalist markets, ownable by anyone.[77] For Florentines these were the *casa,* the *villa,* and much else, but there was also blood and honor. Seen in this context, the Florentine illegitimate again had a unique ambiguity. Was he a stranger to whom such possessions were not to be alienable? Or was he a kinsman and thus someone who authenticated the status quo? Was he someone to whom little or no reciprocity need be shown? Was he himself a "possession" of sorts not to be alienated? Or was he to be given to others?

For demographic historians it is not the legally normative but the statistically normative that matters. The assumption of sociological research is that "why people keep the rules needs no explanation or even can have no (interesting) explanation."[78] The rule of interest to historical demographers is the so-called principle of legitimacy attributed to the anthro-

75. Gordon, "Paradoxical Property," 102.

76. Annette B. Weiner, *Inalienable Possessions: The Paradox of Keeping-While-Giving* (Berkeley and Los Angeles, 1992). Weiner's views have been powerfully seconded by Maurice Godelier, *The Enigma of the Gift,* trans. Nora Scott (Chicago, 1999). An excellent study of gift practices in sixteenth-century France is Natalie Zemon Davis, *The Gift in Sixteenth-Century France* (Madison, 2000).

77. Cf. James G. Carrier, *Gifts and Commodities: Exchange and Western Capitalism since 1700* (London, 1995), 19–28.

78. Teichman, *Illegitimacy,* 11–12.

pologist Bronislaw Malinowski, according to which no child should be born without a social, as opposed to a biological, father.[79] As Peter Laslett rephrased it, "the appearance of children for whom no mature male, permanently allied to the mother, can be held responsible, had to be prevented in order to safeguard the future of the society and of each of its constituent members."[80] The image thus invoked—the prevalent image of illegitimacy today—is that of the unmarried mother, often young, poor, ill-educated, whose offspring seem condemned to follow her fate. Illegitimacies of other sorts, from adultery to incest, do not figure in this vision. Paternally recognized and raised, then legitimated, Simone di Domenico also does not fit.

The Malinowskian perspective is patently functionalist. It is reductionistic of levels of meaning and contexts other than the equilibrium function seen as important by the social scientist. A rise in illegitimacy, therefore, has to be taken as indicative of social breakdown unleashing dysfunctional behavior. Max Weber's less biologistic thesis was that the distinction between legitimate and illegitimate arose when political and economic groups ceased to consider women merely as chattel and began to protect them "against the original discretion of the buyer" (i.e., husband). Here is where the dowry came in to protect the woman, limiting the husband's discretion by tying her to something of value.[81] Concubinage, in contrast to marriage, was, propertyless.[82] It is worth noting, moreover, that a civil law requirement for turning concubinage into marriage, and thus legitimating any children, was provision of a dowry.

Laslett has argued that "a rise in illegitimacy is not always a reliable indicator of social breakdown, of anomie, of disturbance in familial control, the ability or willingness of the local elite to supervise the doings of the local people."[83] It was the social myopia of people that led them to

79. Malinowski, "Kinship," *Encyclopedia Britannica,* 14th ed. (1929), 13:403; cf. William J. Goode, *The Family,* 2d ed. (Englewood Cliffs, N.J., 1982), 35; Shirley Foster Hartley, *Illegitimacy* (Berkeley and Los Angeles, 1975), 3.

80. "Introduction: Comparing Illegitimacy over Time and between Cultures," in *Bastardy and Its Comparative History: Studies in the History of Illegitimacy and Marital Nonconformism in Britain, France, Germany, Sweden, North America, Jamaica, and Japan,* ed. Peter Laslett, Karla Oosterveen, and Richard M. Smith (Cambridge, Mass., 1980), 5.

81. Max Weber, *Economy and Society,* ed. Guenther Roth and Claus Wittich, 2 vols. (Berkeley and Los Angeles, 1968), 1:358, 372–74.

82. On this see chap. 1; Goody, *Production and Reproduction: A Comparative Study of the Domestic Domain* (Cambridge, 1976), 50.

83. Laslett, introduction to Laslett, Oosterveen, and Smith, *Bastardy,* 60.

see illegitimacy as merely a problem of personal morality.[84] Laslett argued that illegitimacy was, in fact, disproportionately the result of a "bastardy-prone subsociety" that did not observe the broader rules of marriage and sexual behavior.[85] Illegitimacy ratios were generally low (by modern standards) in early modern Europe, on the order of 1 percent to 3 percent.[86] The problem was not sexual behavior per se; fear focused rather on the possible social and economic consequences.[87]

Demographic historians are not concerned with inheritance strategies or social assimilation of bastards but with charting levels and types of illicit sexual behavior. Only in the early modern era do they begin to find sufficient sources to track sexuality. They then run reconstitutions, checking birth and baptismal registries against marriage records to determine illegitimacy ratios and rates over time. As one such historian has remarked, however, "the study of illegitimacy through birth registration has nothing to contribute with regard to the assimilation of the child in society."[88] To put it another way, why people performed sexual acts is separable (at least in part) from how they decided to deal with the consequences nine months later.

Parallel is the problem of the social location of illegitimacy. One assumption would be that social ties were looser and more fluid in urban society, such that prenuptial pregnancies were more apt to happen and more liable to fail to result in marriage. They were also more likely to happen for lower-class women (servants, textile workers, casual laborers) often recruited from the countryside and thus away from familial

84. Ibid., 61.

85. Laslett, *Family Life,* 147; Michael Mitterauer and Reinhold Sieder, *The European Family: Patriarchy to Partnership from the Middle Ages to the Present,* trans. Karla Oosterveen and Manfred Horzinger (Chicago, 1982), 124–29. Philippe Ariès suggested that Laslett's subsocieties may simply have been the result of the insistence of conservatives on not registering births as legitimate that the parents did not agree were illegitimate. Cf. Philippe Ariès, "The Indissoluble Marriage," in *Western Sexuality: Practice and Precept in Past and Present Times,* ed. Philippe Ariès and André Béjin, trans. Anthony Forster (Oxford, 1985), 155.

86. M. Demonet, J. Dupaquier, and H. LeBras, "A Repertory of Stable Populations," in *Population Patterns in the Past,* ed. Ronald Demos Lee (New York, 1977), 298; Laslett, introduction to *Bastardy and Its Comparative History,* and his *Family Life,* 109.

87. Cf. G. R. Quaife, *Wanton Wenches and Wayward Wives: Peasants and Illicit Sex in Early Seventeenth Century England* (New Brunswick, N.J., 1979), 63 and 180. Quaife notes (57–58) that by Laslett's numbers premarital pregnancies varied between 18 percent and 39 percent of baptisms.

88. Etienne van de Walle, "Illegitimacy in France during the Nineteenth Century," in Laslett, Oosterveen, and Smith, *Bastardy and Its Comparative History,* 277.

supervision and protection.[89] Rural women caught in an illegitimate pregnancy also at times went to cities to give birth, thus swelling the illegitimacy ratio there.[90] Beyond premarital sexuality, sexual exploitation by masters of their female servants accounted for many illegitimacies from wealthy fathers.[91] The poor, it is said, had more bastards, or certainly a bastard's mother was more likely to be poor and so vulnerable.[92]

Perhaps for Florence, where concepts of honor could reinforce religiously based sexual morality, but where there were also readily available lower-class female sexual outlets (slaves, servants, or prostitutes), there was less likelihood of open bastardy for respectable women. In effect, for women of some social standing in Florence, there was a trade-off—restrictions on their actions and movements in return for legal and economic security in the form of a dowry. Their sexual fidelity was the crux of the matrimonial relation and the safeguard of the blood-transmitted honor of the group.[93] Within the home they could come to have considerable influence in shaping domestic life, including the sheltering, or not, of illegitimates.[94] Their security also traded on male promiscuity with lower-class women, where parenthood (i.e., paternity) remained dubious and/or illegitimate and so no real threat to them or their legitimate progeny. For these lower-class women there may have been sexual activity (it would not be correct to speak of sexual freedom), but while possibly facing all the dangers of gestation and delivery, they had no security that their progeny could contribute to a lasting social familial order. In the meantime, the fathers who acknowledged paternity and took on the obligation of support for illegitimates thereby asserted—all the more strongly than in the less obviously optional case of legitimate progeny—a male prerogative over reproduction and kin relationships.[95]

89. Olwen H. Hufton, *The Poor of Eighteenth-Century France, 1750–1789* (Oxford, 1974), 320. She puts the rural ratio of illegitimacies at 1 to 2 percent, for towns under ten thousand population 4 percent, for cities 12 to 17 percent.

90. Rudolph M. Bell, *Fate and Honor, Family and Village: Demographic and Cultural Change in Rural Italy since 1800* (Chicago, 1979), 37–39.

91. Quaife, *Wanton Wenches,* 181–82.

92. Keith Wrightson, "The Nadir of English Illegitimacy in the Seventeenth Century," in Laslett, Oosterveen, and Smith, *Bastardy and Its Comparative History,* 176–91.

93. Maria Serena Mazzi, *Prostitute e lenoni nella Firenze del Quattrocento* (Milan, 1991), 46.

94. Ibid., 54–57.

95. Cf. Sandra Cavallo and Simona Cerrutti, "Female Honor and the Social Control of Reproduction in Piedmont between 1600 and 1800," in *Sex and Gender in Historical Perspective,* ed. Edward Muir and Guido Ruggiero, trans. Margaret A. Gallucci with Mary M. Gallucci and Carole C. Gallucci (Baltimore, 1990), 81.

To be supported from family wealth was to be acknowledged not as an autonomous individual with rights but as part of a web of relationship. Wealth spent on a bastard, as on any family member, retained reference to those who gave it. This was most obvious in inheritance. The married woman too carried with her reference to whence she came (where she could return when the marriage ended), in the form of the dowry that would pass to the children she would have by her husband in his home. The illegitimate mother had no such. Even concubines (legally, both parties unmarried but living together) who gave birth to several bastards over years brought no dowries or family ties. The concubine lucky enough later to be married had to have evidence of a dowry to legitimate the children she had already borne, according to civil law. Conversely, the adulterous wife, whose adultery might become evident precisely by way of a pregnancy, or even the nonchaste widow could lose her dowry by law. The dowry was to help establish/procreate relations through her husband, not another.[96]

Treatment of a bastard related to this lack of ties through the mother. The bastard in and of him- or herself could be a useful resource; disadvantageous treatment (with abandonment at one extreme) was culturally driven and not the result of some crude maximization. Just as for a woman marriage (and accompanying property) gave her a social role within a domestic group, so for a child inheritance marked a social role as continuator of a domestic group. Like the woman denied marriage and a dowry, the bastard denied inheritance had no social position.

Sources and Plan of the Book

One of the problems with studying illegitimacy is the almost total silence of the bastards themselves and the general reticence of most sources to speak of them. Yet a variety of sources exist to give some purchase on them, and to quite a degree each chapter is built around a particular type of source. As law necessarily discussed them, we dispose of legal sources—the canonical texts, authoritative glosses and commentaries, treatises, and local statutes and other regulations. These will constitute the basis, above all, for two chapters laying out legal rules applicable in

96. Guido Ruggiero, *The Boundaries of Eros: Sex Crime and Sexuality in Renaissance Venice* (Oxford, 1985), 55, treats the matter of maternal adultery as an economic one—the costs of an illegitimate child. What I am adding to the equation is the symbolic and semantic dimension of property.

Florence, as we try to confront the range of ambiguities clustering about illegitimacy that faced jurists who theorized about illegitimacy or, more commonly, confronted cases like that of Simone di Domenico. Some attention will be paid to changes or doctrinal innovations arising in the course of the fifteenth century, but by and large the *ius commune* will figure as a structure within which there were numerous uncertain and contested problems. Then we will examine Florentine legislation touching on illegitimacy, a further complicating matter in law. The presumptions, experiences, and interests of Florentines, both bastards and those around them (genealogically, if not geographically), are what made for the cases that came to the courts. To get at these requires recourse to other sources. The main goal of the third chapter is a presentation of Florentine attitudes toward bastardy. Florentines' views were, in fact, unexceptionable on the matter. No doubt a similar presentation of the material, with perhaps even more expressive and revealing sources, could be crafted for other Renaissance Italian city-states. However, Florentines left an astonishing range of sources that furnish entrée to their values and attitudes, especially the literature of account books, diaries, and *ricordi*. Their senses of family, property, and honor, and their confusions in the persons of bastard children, there become apparent.

The truly unique Florentine source for the social history of that city, however, is the catasto (actually a succession of catasti at intervals between 1427 and 1480). It forms the basis for examining bastards and their families, along with another important Florentine source, the notarial texts (charters of legitimation and testaments). The fourth, fifth, and sixth chapters rest on the information I have been able to glean from archival and other sources about Florentine bastards. There we will learn about them and their families. We will learn who their mothers were, and what stages of life their fathers were in when they illicitly conceived. We will see how some of them were raised in the paternal home while others were not, what they inherited, and how some were legitimated. This will be the most comprehensive study of bastardy for a Renaissance Italian community, for all that it cannot pretend ultimately to be complete or systematic. We will see how, if anything, the fifteenth century was a golden age for contradiction, ambiguity, and liminality for bastards.

Without family reconstitutions or any consistent source listing bastards, one is left to accept the designations by contemporaries in the sources. Only when someone called a child illegitimate can we be sure we have one. The reluctance of people to apply this shameful label leaves the researcher with frustratingly few clues to follow, as well as making him or her totally dependent on the source's sense of illegitimacy—though that is where investigation properly should start and end. Those raised by their fathers and/or paternal kin had some standing in society and family; but that standing was also continuously open to question and challenge. Those challenges were nowhere more pressing and frequent than when bastards stood in line to inherit. The final chapter studies disputes, concentrating especially on the ideological accommodations worked out by jurists in their *consilia* submitted when these disputes reached the point of litigation. We will examine a half dozen cases, ranging in time across the fifteenth century and into the sixteenth. Here the jurists had to validate or avoid certain results as their professional predilections encountered litigants' interests on the uncertain terrain of the law. Thus the chapters progressively narrow their focus from generally to locally applicable law, to attitudes toward bastards and those who harbored them, to specific disputes and disputants.

These cases arose in real situations (or in hypotheticals that closely approximated real situations). They presented fairly typical problems—most typically the attempt of legitimate kin to prevent or limit inheritance by illegitimates. Microhistorical analysis of Florentine cases shows that there was a constant interplay of legal norms (classifications of illegitimacy, rules of inheritance, consequences of legitimation) and social norms and expectations (of honor, kinship, coresidence, sexual activity). These latter were disciplined by the law, for, whatever a Florentine bastard may have anticipated from paternal treatment, there were rules that came into play. Jurists' *consilia* met the needs of people and institutions for answers; they inserted law into the everyday, while confronting the law with practical needs of the concrete realities of life. "The task of the researcher is therefore to reveal again the past conversion of social relations into juristic terminology, to trace original meanings and to set the underlying events into the historical context."[97] In a detailed manner we can thus examine the broad theme of the implication of law in daily life in the society of fifteenth-century Florence.

The main problem this book confronts is that the law, which most definitely defined what and who was legitimate or not, marginalized but could not remove the illegitimate from society. Only the foundling home

97. Ingrid Baumgärtner, ed., *Consilia im späten Mittelalter: Zum historischen Aussagewert einer Quellengattung* (Sigmaringen, 1995), 9.

did that, to a great extent, and it was not an option for everyone. Interactions with the illegitimate fostered a sense of social belonging and might accord some inheritance rights or other modes of familial identification. But no Florentines, perhaps least of all the illegitimates themselves, were able or willing to remove all trace and memory of illegitimate origins. Their upbringing would be at reduced cost, their inheritance of a reduced amount, their legitimation of reduced value.

What will emerge are meanings and functions of illegitimacy that went well beyond anything envisioned in a Malinowskian functionalism or a simple notion of social control. This range of functions was possible because of the pervasive ambiguities that attached themselves, in shifting and manipulable configurations, to illegitimacy. Florentines, both laymen and jurists, actuated and tried to resist these ambiguities, but they were there, in ways they could not always anticipate until the cases arose. Bastards were both dangerous and helpful, both expensive and profitable, depending on circumstances. Certainly Simone's utility as heir to Domenico was threatening to Lena. We cannot assume that bastardy's meaning was unproblematic or that the work of jurists, therefore, was merely pedantic.

PART ONE

Norms

1
Illegitimacy and Legitimation in *Ius Commune*

Illegitimacy

There was not simply one category of illegitimate; there were several. The ambiguities in law began there. Only once the matter of exact status was disposed of could one turn to issues such as its effects on inheritance. By the beginning of the fifteenth century the work of the great fourteenth-century commentators of civil and canon law was complete. It fell to fifteenth-century legists to fill in gaps and synthesize legal precepts around relevant topics. What they found surrounding illegitimacy were varying, confusing, and even contradictory legal opinions and teachings. Two fifteenth-century lawyers, active in Florence, systematized and summarized the law on illegitimates and legitimation—Antonio Roselli (1381–1466), who wrote a *Tractatus legitimationum* in 1407, soon after receiving his doctorate in Bologna, and Benedetto Barzi da Perugia (ca. 1379–1459), author of *Tractatus de filiis non legitime natis,* written in 1456.[1] Roselli's motive for writing was to counteract the "diverse judgments and great many disputations and doubts" [diversas sententias et plurimas disputationes et dubia] entertained by law professors.[2] But for Roselli and Barzi, as for other Florentine jurists, illegitimacy would

1. *Tractatus universi iuris,* vol. 8: *De ultimis voluntatibus,* part 2 (Venice, 1584), fols. 24ra–29vb (Barzi, *Tractatus de filiis non legitime natis*) and 75ra–90va (Roselli, *Tractatus legitimationum*). The manuscript Vat. Lat. 2641, fol. 235ra, gives the date 1407, "in civitate Bononie, etiam secundo anno doctoratus mei ibidem iure legente extraordinarie infortiati et in xxvi anno etatis mee." Whereas Roselli spent most of his career in Florence, Barzi taught in Perugia, Siena, and Ferrara, as well as Florence (1435–43). For profiles of Roselli and Barzi, see Martines, *Lawyers and Statecraft,* 500 and 503 respectively.

2. Roselli, *Tractatus legitimationum,* fol. 75ra.

become more than a topic of legal theory. It would become part of their family life.[3]

Giovanni da Imola (1367/72–1436), a civilian, included illegitimacy among judicial rulings of *status personae*.[4] But the closest jurists regularly came to defining illegitimacy was in stipulating what it was not—namely, legitimacy. Defining legitimacy, of course, seemed easy. For Bartolo da Sassoferrato (1314–1357), in a technically precise manner, a legitimate child was "born to a husband and wife capable of contracting matrimony and generating children while cohabiting together during the marriage."[5] The bastard was defined by the lack of such legitimacy, hence a diminished personhood, in the same way that a slave was defined by his lack of freedom.[6] As Baldo degli Ubaldi (1327–1400) captured it, because a "child [*filius*] is an immediate person descending from a husband and wife," then "likewise bastards are not properly termed children of their fathers. . . . so wherever there is reference [in laws] to children with respect to pursuing any dignity or inflicting any penalty, it is understood to refer to a legitimate and natural child."[7] The circumstances of procreation and birth biased the law against illegitimates.

By the terms of civil law all illegitimate children were *sui iuris*—that is, not subject to *patria potestas,* which could issue only from marriage, or from judicial acts such as adoption and legitimation.[8] Canon law had an

3. In 1457 Roselli, then teaching in Padua, reported to Florentine catasto officials the existence of an illegitimate grandson named Rosello. Cf. Archivio di Stato, Florence (hereafter ASF), Catasto 809, fols. 35r–36r.

4. Giovanni da Imola to l. Saepe, De re iudicata (D. 42.1.63), *In primam digesti novi* (Bologna, 1580), 331a.

5. Bartolo to l. Filium, De iis qui sunt sui (D. 1.6.6), *In primam ff. veteris* (Venice, 1585), fol. 24rb–va: "Ille dicitur filius legitimus qui ex viro et uxore ad matrimonium contrahendum et generandum habilibus simul cohabitantibus constante matrimonio nascitur, hoc dicit." See also Paolo di Castro, *cons.* 467, *Consilia* (Frankfurt am Main, 1582), vol. 3, fol. 226ra: "Legitimi vero dicuntur propter solennitatem mutui matrimonialis consensus coniunctam huic naturali coniunctioni, quae solennitas a iure civi. est inventa."

6. It is as "ein Manko der Persönlichkeit" that Dietmar Willoweit discusses the legal situation of bastards, in his "Von der natürlichen Kindschaft zur Illegitimität: Die nichtehelichen Kinder in den mittelalterlichen Rechtsordnungen," in Schmugge, *Illegitimität im Spätmittelalter,* 62.

7. Baldo to l. Filium diffinimus (D. 1.6.6), *In primam digesti veteris partem commentaria,* in *Opera omnia* (Venice, 1577), vol. 1, fol. 35vb: "filius est immediata persona a viro et uxore descendens. . . . Item bastardi non dicuntur proprie filii patruum. . . . quia ubicunque fit mentio filii respectu alicuius dignitatis consequendae, vel poenae infligendae, intelligitur de legitimo et naturali."

8. Leineweber, *Die rechtliche Beziehung,* 50. Bartolo da Sassoferrato to l. Item in potestate De iis qui sunt sui vel alieni iuris (D. 1.6.1), *In primam ff. veteris commentaria*

additional, ethical concern with the illicit circumstances of an illegitimate's conception. All illegitimates, whether born of concubinage or incest or any form of illicit sexual liaison, were products of an immoral act. They all bore a stain *(macula)*. They all suffered from a *defectus natalium* that barred illegitimates from clerical ordination.[9] In this way sons, who were assumed to be imitators of paternal immorality, would both suffer appropriately for the *crimina paterna* and not besmirch the dignity and honor of the church by dispensing its sacraments.[10] There was, in fact, a general moral fear of the possession of family property by *illegitimi,* because of the potential they represented by virtue of being *sui iuris* for fraudulent practices.[11] Cino da Pistoia (d. 1336/37), for example, frankly stated that "when a father buys something and has the instrument of sale drawn up in the person of his *spurius,* that is presumed to be fictitious."[12] But law did not render bastards total nonpersons. They had some rights and abilities, as any others who were *sui iuris,* and they could have some family identity and claims. For example, papal decretals clearly affirmed—in contrast to civil law—that all illegitimates were entitled to maintenance and support *(alimenta)* from their mother and from their father, if his identity was known or could be proved. Civilian jurists ultimately followed the canonists' lead in this regard.[13]

(Venice, 1585), fol. 24rb: "Unde naturalis tantum non est in potestate patris, multominus spurius." Antonio da Butrio, *Repertorium iuris,* s.v. "Potestas," Vat. Lat. 11606, fol. 104ra–rb. For a discussion of *patria potestas* see Kuehn, *Emancipation,* esp. chaps. 1 and 5.

9. Leineweber, *Die rechtliche Beziehung,* 55–59, 68; Génestal, *Histoire de la légitimation,* 1–19; Richard Trexler, *Synodal Law in Florence and Fiesole, 1306–1518* (Vatican City, 1971), 37–38, 234, 235–36; and Peter Landau, "Das Weihehindernis der Illegitimität in der Geschichte des kanonischen Rechts," in Schmugge, *Illegitimität im Spätmittelalter,* 41–53.

10. Klaus Schreiner, "'Defectus natalium': Geburt aus einem unrechtmäßigen Schoß als Problem klösterlicher Gemeinschaftsbildung," in Schmugge, *Illegitimität im Spätmittelalter,* 93–99.

11. Barzi, *Tractatus,* fol. 27va: "cum inter patrem et filium propter naturale vinculum quod subsistit, de levi est praesumenda fraus cui obviandum est." Antonio da Butrio, *Repertorium iuris,* s.v. "Spureus," fol. 247rb.

12. Cino to l. Senatores, C. De naturalibus liberis (C. 5.27.1), *In codicem et aliquot titulos primi pandectorum* (Frankfurt am Main, 1585; rpt. Turin, 1964), vol. 1, fol. 321ra: "quod quando pater emit, et facit quod instrumentum sit in persona filii spurii, quod presumitur fictum."

13. Leineweber, *Die rechtliche Beziehung,* 62–63, 76–79; Pecorella, "Filiazione (storia)," 452–53; Vidari, *Ricerche sul diritto agli alimenti,* 153–72; Pertile, *Storia del diritto italiano,* 3:390; Jean Louis Flandrin, *Families in Former Times: Kinship, Household, and Sexuality,* trans. Richard Southern (Cambridge, 1977), 174–78. An important doctrinal text is Hostiensis, to Qui filii sint legitimi (X. 4.17), *Summa aurea* (Venice, 1605), cols. 1383–84.

They also conceded to canonists' sense of consanguinity measured bilaterally for the purpose of determining incest prohibitions, which also included illegitimate kin.[14]

Late medieval jurists did not settle on a general illegitimate personhood; they fashioned a hierarchy of illegitimacies parallel to the hierarchy of sexual sins. One juristic scheme distinguished children into four types: the *legitimi et naturales* (born of a legitimate marriage), *legitimi tantum* (i.e., adopted), *naturales tantum* (born of a concubine kept in one's home "maritali affectu"), and the *nec legitimi nec naturales* (fig. 1).[15] Illegitimate children fell into the last two categories. The last—the general category of *spurii*—was further subdivided between children of casual unions whose fathers were often unknown or uncertain, the so-called *vulgo quaesiti,* and children of thoroughly illicit unions (*nati ex damnato coitu,* for the knowledge of which, ironically, the identity of the father had to be known): the *incestuosi, nefarii, adulterini*—including those born of clerical concubinage.[16] According to Dino del Mugello (d. 1303?), *spurii* were those (1) whose father was uncertain, (2) whose father was not proper (e.g., a priest), and (3) children of a slave.[17] Quite simply, not all *illegitimi* were born equal. They had differing *status personae,* and determination of the effects of those differences presented jurists with the sorts of rhetorical and logical exercises for which they were well trained.

The personhood of an illegitimate was marked indelibly with the relationship at play in conception. Personhood in law was about having and being in relationships. *Naturales* were born of an ongoing, not casual, relationship; the *nati ex damnato coitu* were born in violation of a preexisting relationship; the *vulgo quaesiti* were the result of an encounter, not a relationship. It was the father's identity (and within it, his relationship with the mother) that affected the personhood of the illegitimate.

14. Cf. Gianna Pomata, "Legami di sangue, legami di seme: Consanguinità e agnazione nel diritto romano," *Quaderni storici* 86 (1994): 299–334.

15. Leineweber, *Die rechtliche Beziehung,* 46–47, 71; Pecorella, "Filiazione (storia)," 453; Leicht, *Storia del diritto italiano,* 1:230.

16. Dino del Mugello, *Tractatus de successionibus ab intestato,* Vat. Lat. 2638, fol. 1ra (also in *Tractatus universi iuris,* part 1, fols. 318ra–319vb).

17. Ibid., fol. 1vb. Lodovico a Sardi, *Tractatus de naturalibus liberis,* in *Tractatus universi iuris,* part 2, fols. 31vb, claimed the child of a *serva* and a freeman was "naturalis tantum." Benedetto Barzi's handling of the matter is also highly symptomatic (Barzi, *Tractatus,* fols. 24vb–25ra), as is Roselli, *Tractatus legitimationum,* fols. 76rb–va; Angelo degli Ubaldi to § Natura, Quibus modis naturales efficiantur sui (A. 7.1, 1 in c.), *Opus ac lectura autenticorum* (Venice, 1485), fol. 24ra.

- Legitimate (*sub patria potestate*)
  - *legitimi et naturales*
    - derived by marriage
  - *legitimi tantum*
    - derived by adoption
- Illegitimate (no *potestas*)
  - *naturales tantum*
    - derived by concubinage
  - *nec legitimi nec naturales* (*spurii*)
    - *vulgo quaesiti*
    - *nati ex damnato coitu*
      - *incestuosi*
      - *adulterini*
    - derived by fornication or illicit or damned coition

Fig. 1. Legal types of children

But paternity was not susceptible to proof so much as admission and presumption.

Legitimacy had to be publicly established. It could not result, as the canonist Antonio da Butrio (1338–1408) argued, from the declaration of a parent that a child was legitimate.[18] On the other hand, the mere assertion of a father that a child was not his also had no legal effect by itself, at least according to Bartolo.[19] There was a strong presumption of legitimacy for a child born of a married woman (termed *favor filiationis*).[20] If a wife notoriously carried on with other men, the presumption was still that her child was legitimate.[21] The Sienese jurist Mariano Sozzini (d.

18. Antonio da Butrio to c. Per tuas (X. 4.17.12), *In librum quartum decretalium* (Venice, 1578), fol. 48rb: "No. secundo quod super legitimitate hic non videtur stari dicto parentis, etiam si eum instituendo filium legitimum appellavit, quod videtur esse contra theoricam Doc. in l. i § iulianus ff de lib. agno. [D. 28.5.1, 12]. Sed veritas est, quod ex hoc probatur filius praesumptive."

19. Bartolo to l. Filium, De receptis arbitris (D. 4.8.6), *In primam ff. veteris,* fol. 24va.

20. Anne Lefebvre-Teillard, "'Pater is est quem nuptiae demonstrant': Jalons pour une histoire de la présomption de paternité," *Revue historique de droit française et étranger* 69 (1991): 331–40, and her *Introduction historique au droit des personnes et de la famille* (Paris, 1996), 281–86.

21. James, "Illegitimate and Deprived Child," 42–43; da Butrio, *Repertorium iuris,* s.v. "Legittimatio," fol. 11vb, and s.v. "Legittimus," fol. 13vb: "Natus in domo viri ex uxore que notorie se inmiscebat cum aliis presumitur legittimus."

1467) disclosed the power of that presumption when he said that, not only was a contrary assertion "minime creditur," but even if it could be shown that during the marriage the wife had been adulterous or found "outside her husband's house and in a suspicious place," her word that the child was legitimate was dispositive.[22] Sozzini consistently followed that line in a Venetian case where he upheld the eligibility for office of a patrician whose birth and parents' marriage had not been registered with the Concilio Maggiore as required by Venetian law. Legitimacy of birth, he maintained, was set by *ius commune* and not local statute.[23] Further, two marriageable people living together had to be presumed married, not in a relation of concubinage.[24] Where there was an impediment to marriage (e.g., the couple was related within prohibited degrees of consanguinity) but both man and woman in good faith believed themselves validly married (putative marriage), the children were to be treated as legitimate.[25]

Another Sozzini—Bartolomeo (1436–1507)—participated in a Florentine case that turned on proof of illegitimacy. Paradiso Macinghi refused to return property that he rented to a widow, Margherita, who claimed it as *tutrix* for her children, on the grounds that they were illegitimate and so she could not be their *tutrix*. Her husband had died in 1454, but the case only arose in 1488. Paradiso therefore disputed the testimony of the three witnesses who said Margherita and Jacopo had "treated each other as husband and wife" in part on the grounds that the witnesses would have been too young to remember and had at best partial knowledge.[26] Paradiso's arguments had been sufficiently powerful to win a summary judgment of concubinage against her. Margherita took the case to court and retained Sozzini, along with Antonio Cocco-Donati (1451–1491) and Bulgarino de' Bulgarini (d. ca. 1490).

---

22. Mariano Sozzini to c. Officii, De penitentiis et remissionibus (X. 5.38.9), *Nova et utilissima commentaria super secunda parte libri quinti decretalium* (Venice, 1593), fols. 213ra–va.

23. Victor Crescenzi, *"Esse de Maiori Consilio": Legittimità civile e legittimazione politica nella repubblica di Venezia (secc. xiii–xvi)* (Rome, 1996), 426–29.

24. Da Butrio, *Repertorium iuris*, s.v. "Concubina" (Vat. Lat. 2351), fol. 42rb. See generally Génestal, *Histoire de la légitimation*, 160–65.

25. Génestal, *Histoire de la légitimation*, 151; da Butrio, *Repertorium iuris*, s.v. "Legittimus," fol. 13vb; Dino del Mugello, *Tractatus*, fol. 2vb; Bartolo to Auth. De incestis nuptiis (A. 2.6), *Opera omnia*, 10 vols. (Venice, 1615), vol. 9, fol. 15rb. On this basis the imposter's child was judicially declared legitimate: cf. Natalie Zemon Davis, *The Return of Martin Guerre* (Cambridge, Mass., 1983), 89–91.

26. These are gathered in ASF, Carte strozziane, 3d ser., 41/10, fol. 211r–v.

Sozzini lost no time in revealing his sentiments about Paradiso's case: "I marvel that anyone who has tasted broth [that is, anyone who has been weaned] would raise such a legal difficulty."[27] The children had to be presumed to be "in quasi possessione legiptimitatis." Macinghi faced the burden of proof regarding illegitimacy, which he had met easily enough by pointing to an instrument of legitimation that disclosed the children's illegitimacy. Margherita had moved, as mother and guardian, to secure her children's inheritance by obtaining the legitimation in addition to the paternal testament and whatever could be testified about her relationship with the father. Sozzini countered that the proof of concubinage in another court had been a summary judgment and now there were more reliable witnesses who testified to the marital conduct of the couple.

Sozzini had no sympathy for Macinghi, who after all was not an heir but was trying to take advantage of illegitimacy to claim ownership. Antonio Cocco-Donati had no sympathy either. He pointed to the legal presumption of legitimacy for children of a cohabiting woman. Two other jurists, Filippo Decio (1454–1535) and Giovan Vettorio Soderini (1460–1528), signed the *consilium.* Their corroboration made the case stronger. The one serious weak point was the attempt here both to assert legitimacy by birth and also by rescript post mortem. If the first was valid, the second was unnecessary.

Legal proof of paternity raises yet another ambiguity: not only did illegitimacy violate relationships, it made them (parent and child), although they were not factually certain and were not as strong in law as legitimate parental relationships. An illegitimate child may not have been *filius,* and, as Barzi said, equally nonlegitimate fathers were not parents;[28] still, there was a relationship, and this sort of fact had a way of insinuating itself into law. It was productive of alimentary rights for bastards, and it carried numerous other implications, notably regarding inheritance. Personhood was spelled out in terms of property and symbolic qualities (such as honor) that were of the essence of legal persons, who could have, own, act, and so forth.[29]

---

27. ASF, Carte strozziane, 3d ser., 41/2, fol. 202r: "Sed certo miror quod ab aliquo qui aliquod gustavit de brodio iuris fiat talis difficultas."

28. Barzi, *Tractatus,* fol. 25ra: "quod appellatione parentum patres non legitimi non compraehenduntur."

29. See Sergio Mochi Onory, "*Personam habere:* Studio sulle origini e sulla struttura della 'persona' nell'età del Rinascimento," in *Studi di storia e diritto in onore di Enrico Besta,* vol. 3 (Milan, 1939), 417–39; Villata, "Persone e famiglia."

To pose an example at this point, from the latter part of the fourteenth century survives a *consilium* of three Florentine jurists: Francesco d'Albergotti d'Arezzo (1304–1376), Lapo da Castiglionchio (fl. 1370s), and Giovanni de' Ricci (1342–1402).[30] The case involved the children of a man named Pietro, who had both legitimate sons and *naturales.* The latter had no resources or skills by which to support themselves, but one legitimate son had enough from the patrimony to afford to feed his family and these half brothers. The jurists unequivocally said that this legitimate son had to support his brothers. Civil law set an obligation on a paternal estate to feed *naturales;* canon law expanded it to all forms of illegitimates, even those born *ex damnato coitu;* and brothers had an obligation to each other.[31] This decision seems fully in line with the doctrinal positions affirming alimentary rights of bastards.[32] This case shows us that the legal obligation of *alimenta* was seriously enforced and that distinctions between *naturales* and *spurii* mattered in practice.

By implication *filii naturales* shared something substantially important with the *legitimi et naturales;* also by implication *spurii* were somehow "unnatural" or outside the "puritatem naturae." Civil and canon law recognized a certain natural, if not legal, legitimacy in concubinage—as opposed to the rampant libido that produced *spurii.* On one level, differences between illegitimates corresponded to the degree of social and moral threat carried by sexual acts. Fornication between unmarried persons was regarded more lightly than other offenses. Ecclesiastical courts did not aggressively pursue cases in this area; they acted only when neighbors brought in accusations and complaints. A trip by a husband to the local brothel or to his servant's or slave's bed was not liable to meet with extreme penalties.[33] Adultery was a matter of concern mainly when a married person kept up a long-standing liaison outside the house or, worse, abandoned family for mistress. Here church courts contemplated use of excommunication.[34] On the

30. On whom see Julius Kirshner, "Messer Francesco di Bici degli Albergotti d'Arezzo, Citizen of Florence (1350–1376)," *Bulletin of Medieval Canon Law,* n.s. 2 (1972): 84–90.

31. Vat. Lat. 8069, fol. 350r–v.

32. For a Perugian case concerning *alimenta,* see Ottob. Lat. 1726, fols. 205r–207r.

33. Maria Serena Mazzi, "Il mondo della prostituzione nella Firenze tarda medievale," in *Forestieri e stranieri nelle città basso medievali* (Florence, 1988), 127–47 (also in *Ricerche storiche* 14 [1984]: 337–63); Jacques Rossiaud, *La prostituzione nel Medioevo* (Bari, 1986), esp. 100, 150, 187.

34. Jean-Marie Carbasse, "Currant nudi: Le répression de l'adultère dans le Midi médiéval," in *Droit, histoire et sexualité,* ed. Jacques Poumarède and Jean-Pierre Royer (Toulouse, 1987), 83–104.

other hand, forms of sodomy, as "unnatural" acts, were perceived as very threatening.[35]

Concubinage was envisioned in law as a marriagelike but informal relationship, capable even of becoming a marriage.[36] The concubine lived in the man's house, for, as Bartolo determined, a woman kept outside one's home, though loosely termed a concubine, was not such in law. Only cohabitation indicated marital "affectus."[37] However, the concubine had no dowry. The problem was to distinguish her from the servant girls also resident and regularly used sexually by their masters.[38] Drawing such a distinction was not always easy: to Angelo degli Ubaldi (1323–1400) both "concubines and prostitutes are vile persons, for their lives are prodigal and given to pleasure."[39] And in canon law concubinage as continual and seemingly unrepentant fornication was looked upon as more reprehensible (i.e., "living in sin") than transient sexual relations.[40]

Establishing the relationship between the parents, and thus the exact status of the child, was important because the different classes of illegitimates had available to them greater or lesser rights, depending where they stood on a vertical scale running from *naturales* at the top to the *nati ex damnato coitu* at the bottom. *Naturales* generally enjoyed greater rights and stronger family attachment than did the *spurii*. Jurists said that the *naturalis* had a "certain" father and so might be termed a *filius,* though not a *filiusfamilias,* because *patria potestas* was lacking. The *spurius,* on the other hand, did not have a "certain" father (even if his identity was known) and thus could only be termed a *liber* (child).[41] Along the same lines, while *naturales* and *spurii* alike could be said to belong to the "offspring" *(de generatione)* and to the people *(de gente)* of their fathers, only *naturales* could be said to retain relationship *(coniunctio)* and closeness

35. Michael Rocke, "Il controllo dell'omosessualità a Firenze nel xv secolo: Gli Ufficiali di Notte," *Quaderni storici* 66 (1987): 701–23.

36. Brundage, *Law, Sex,* 40–43, 103, 118; and broadly on Roman marriage law, see Susan Treggiari, *Roman Marriage: "Iusti Coniuges" from the Time of Cicero to the Time of Ulpian* (Oxford, 1991).

37. Bartolo to l. Concubinam, De concubinis (D. 25.7.4), *In primam infortiati partem commentaria* (Lyons, 1544), fol. 41vb.

38. Brundage, *Law, Sex,* 298.

39. Angelo, *cons.* 171, *Consilia* (Frankfurt am Main, 1575), fol. 111ra: "concubinam et meretrices [esse] turpes personas. Sunt enim earum vitae prodigae et luxurie deditae."

40. Brundage, *Law, Sex,* 369–70, 444–47, 514–16.

41. Leineweber, *Die rechtliche Beziehung,* 47; Bartolo to l. Item in potestate, *In primam ff. veteris,* fol. 24rb; Barzi, *Tractatus,* fol. 25ra; Antonio da Butrio, to c. Per venerabilem, Qui filii sint legitimi (X. 4.17.13), *In librum quartum decretalium,* fol. 53va; and his *Repertorium iuris,* s.v. "Spureus," fol. 247rb.

(propinquitas) to their fathers. Only *naturales* were capable of holding whatever honors and dignities were associated with being their fathers' children.[42] These were not just scholastic logical distinctions, however, for as we will see, these determinations affected whether civil law rules or statutes applied to bastards.[43]

Naturales, not *spurii,* were considered *agnati.* Ordinarily agnation was linked to *patria potestas,* as was membership in the *domus, casa,* or *familia,* so illegitimates would seem to have been excluded from all these categories. Even legitimate but emancipated children, because of the removal of *patria potestas* through emancipation, were considered to be "extra domum et familiam patris" and disagnated (although they retained *iura agnationis* since they could still inherit from their fathers).[44] Nevertheless, some very authoritative jurists, like Bartolo da Sassoferrato, allowed that *naturales* could be considered to be part of the paternal *domus,* if not *familia,* and permitted to bear its arms and insignia, if local customs (as in Tuscany) so allowed.[45] Still, only legitimate children (sons really) were *filiifamilias* and thus so automatically their fathers' heirs that they could be termed owners (along with their fathers) of the family patrimony and disinherited only with extreme difficulty.[46] Only with the *filiifamilias* could it be said "the person of the father and of the son are considered to be the same."[47] To medieval jurists land, temporal duration, and blood were normative factors minimizing individuality in favor of nature and group membership.[48] These factors necessarily struck illegitimates differently.

Bartolo da Sassoferrato's was the most sweeping position on the claims of bastards to be *de familia, de domo, de parentela,* and *de gente,* depending on the language employed in civic statutes. If *domus* meant agnation, the bastard did not count; if it meant "blood," he did. Likewise it did if one only referred to cohabitation, for then bastard status was not

42. Barzi, *Tractatus,* fol. 28ra: "nunquid dicti filii possint promoveri ad honores et dignitates. et in hoc concludas quod spurii regulariter sint incapaces nisi in subsidium et defectum legitimorum. . . . In filio autem naturali tamen credo quod sit capax dignitatum."

43. Barzi, *Tractatus,* fol. 25rb–va; Paolo di Castro, *cons.* 19, *Consilia* (1582), vol. 3, fol. 14vb, offers five circumstances in which the term *filius* in a civic statute should be taken to apply to illegitimates.

44. Kuehn, *Emancipation,* 18, 26–27, 32, 139, 146.

45. Sheedy, *Bartolus on Social Conditions,* 73–74; cf. Osvaldo Cavallar, Susanne Degenring, and Julius Kirshner, *A Grammar of Signs: Bartolo da Sassoferrato's "Tract on Insignia and Coats of Arms"* (Berkeley and Los Angeles, 1995), 64–65.

46. Kirshner, "Baldus de Ubaldis on Disinheritance."

47. Bellomo, *Problemi di diritto familiare,* 28–51.

48. Cf. Paolo Grossi, *L'ordine giuridico medievale* (Bari, 1995), 74–75.

at issue. The bastard counted also if *domus* referred to all those bearing the same insignia.[49] Other authoritative jurists, like Baldo degli Ubaldi, maintained that *naturales* were not *de domo,* because that term was civil and not natural.[50] In his canon law commentaries Baldo went so far as to argue that at least with regard to nobility (for which dignity there was a higher standard), natural sons were not noble nor *de domo* but "of a putrified blood."[51]

Paolo di Castro (ca. 1360–1441) agreed with Baldo that *spurii* and *bastardi* were not noble or *de domo nobilium,* and thus not subject to statutes touching those of noble houses.[52] Here then was one example of the sort of doctrinal ambiguity that could raise legal opportunities for those intent on using law to their advantage and those who had to craft arguments to defend or attack that use. *Naturales,* kept and raised in the house from the start, could claim to have been treated as sons (or daughters), not just called sons.[53] Those who accorded such membership and privileges to *naturales* were downplaying the distinction between them and legitimate offspring, so there were those such as Baldo who sought to reaffirm a distance between natural and legitimate sons with regard to *familia, agnatio, arma, domus, insignia,* and so forth. It was left to statutory law and custom to save the notion of legitimacy from overencroachment by naturalness.

Embedded in civil law and in local statutes was the goal of enforcing public obligations and protecting family units. As Guglielmus Durantis (d. 1295) succinctly captured it in his *Speculum iudiciale,* the *publica utilitas* required the preservation of paternal and grandpaternal property in the hands of the male line, the *proles masculina.*[54] Denial or limitation of

49. Bartolo to l. Tutelas, De capitis diminutione (D. 4.5.7), *Opera omnia,* 1615 ed., vol. 1, fol. 139vb; and to l. Pronuntiatio [§] familie, De verborum significatione (D. 50.16.195, 2), *In secundam digesti novi partem commentaria* (Lyons, 1544), fol. 257rb–va.

50. Baldo to l. Filium diffinimus (D. 1.6.6), *In primam digesti veteris,* fol. 35vb.

51. Baldo to c. Innotuit, C. De electione (X. 1.6.20), *In decretalium volumen commentaria* (Venice, 1595; rpt. Turin, 1971), fol. 71rb: "Per hoc patet quod bastardi non sunt nobiles, nec de domo nobilium: quia non decidunt ab aliquo fonte, que sit nobilis, sed a sanguine putrefacto."

52. Paolo di Castro to l. Ex libera, C. De suis et legitimis (C. 6.55.6), *In secundum codicis partem commentaria* (Lyons, 1553), fols. 123vb–124ra.

53. *Glossa ordinaria* to c. 10, De probatione, 2.19: "Bene dicit, nominatus et habitus, nam sola nominatio non facit filium" (cited in Esmein, *La mariage en droit canonique,* 2:39 n. 1).

54. *Speculum iudiciale* (1479), De successionibus ab intestato, fol. 202va. On the related problem of family memory, see my "*Memoria* and Family in Law," in *Art, Memory, and Family in Renaissance Florence,* ed. Giovanni Ciappelli and Patricia Lee Rubin (Cambridge, 2000), 262–74.

inheritance rights of illegitimates was the most consistent and salient element of their status in law, and this diminished capacity of inheritance rested on a lack of standing within a recognized *familia.* Agnation above all was a concept to describe classes of heirs; and bastards' lack of agnation meant loss of inheritance rights.[55] The essence of the difference between the *naturalis* and the *spurius* lay in the greater rights and possibilities of the former to inherit at least a fraction of a father's estate; *spurii* could inherit only from the mother (provided she was not of high social rank and they were not *ex damnato coitu*).[56] The parents of *naturales* could succeed to them; only the mother could succeed to a *spurius;* no parent could succeed to an *incestuosus, nefarius, adulterinus,* or other child *ex damnato coitu.*[57]

Naturales could receive only one-twelfth *(uncia)* of the father's property by testament (if there were also legitimate heirs) or on intestacy (if there were no legitimate heirs).[58] *Naturales,* however, also precluded testamentary conditions in a *fideicommissum* that spelled out contingent lines of inheritance if the heir died "without sons." For that purpose *naturales* were sons. Bartolo da Sassoferrato, however, noted that that did not apply to *naturales* "ex dignitate" (i.e., nobles) because "such offspring 'are abhorred' by persons of high standing."[59] *Spurii* were not allowed inheritance from their fathers, intestate or otherwise, legitimate heirs or no—nor even allowed to receive inter vivos gifts.[60] The canonist Pietro d'Ancarano (ca. 1330–1416) noted that *naturales* could succeed their fathers but *spurii* could not "because they are excluded from all benefit of the law."[61] Statutes giving inheritance rights to *spurii* were seen as nothing more than

55. If legitimate heirs wanted to give to a *spurius* from paternal goods, they could not; the goods would be forfeit to the fisc (Baldo to l. Certum, C. Unde legitimi [C. 6.15.5], *Opera omnia,* vol. 7, fol. 43vb).

56. By extension, two *spurii* with the same mother could succeed each other, but if they had different mothers, though the same father, they could not (da Butrio, *Repertorium iuris,* s.v. "Spureus," fol. 247rb).

57. Dino del Mugello, *Tractatus,* fol. 2ra.

58. A succinct but complete presentation is in Dino del Mugello's *Tractatus,* fol. 1rb–va.

59. Cavallar, Degenring, and Kirshner, *A Grammar of Signs,* 21.

60. Pecorella, "Filiazione (storia)," 450; Leineweber, *Die rechtliche Beziehung,* 83–85. Angelo degli Ubaldi to § Generaliter, Quibus modis naturales efficiantur sui (A. 7.1.11), *Opus ac lectura autenticorum,* fols. 24vb–25ra; Hostiensis to X. 4.17, *Summa aurea,* cols. 1381–82.

61. Pietro d'Ancarano to c. Quia ingredientibus, De testamentis (X. 3.26.2), *Super tertio decretalium commentaria* (Bologna, 1581), 221a: "quia omni iuris beneficio sunt exclusi."

an open invitation to sin.[62] Baldo degli Ubaldi came out clearly against any statute granting inheritance rights not granted in *ius commune* to *spurii.*[63] Baldo's thorough denial of inheritance rights is also a forceful response to a powerful current that admitted some form of "natural" attachment and some degree of *persona,* even to a *spurius.* Thus that powerful current, even when sped along by legitimation, could be met with stiff resistance by those whose claims might otherwise be swept away.

In general, inheritance followed legitimacy and *patria potestas.*[64] Yet the law did allow that natural attachments, as distinct from social and legal legitimacy, exerted some influence on inheritance, as in the rights of emancipated children to the paternal estate. Cino da Pistoia struck out farther in this direction than others, as he seemed willing to concede to the *naturalis* the capacity of a *filius iustus.*[65] Others, however, shied away from that extreme while still conceding something to the force of nature.[66] The natural attachment even of *spurii* (as evidenced in their right to *alimenta*) proved productive of certain doctrinal openings to inheritance from their fathers, in addition to their mothers.[67] This position rested on the argument of Bartolo that fathers could leave a quantity of *substantia* for *alimenta* or dowries.[68] Jurists discussed the possibilities for inheritance by *spurii* through mechanisms like the legacy embodied in a will. By that means a father could circumvent the prohibition of direct inheritance to a bastard son by leaving property to a third party, with the obligation to transfer it in turn to the bastard.[69] Pietro d'Ancarano contemplated a scenario whereby a *spurius* was made heir by his legitimate brother or someone else, which was not forbidden by law.[70] By the end

62. Paolo di Castro, *cons.* 34, *Consilia* (1582), vol. 2, fols. 18rb–va; Leineweber, *Die rechtliche Beziehung,* 85–86, cites the similar objections of Baldo.

63. Baldo to c. Canonum, De constitutionibus (X. 1.2.1), *In decretalium volumen commentaria,* fols. 10rb–11va.

64. Hostiensis to X. 4.17, *Summa aurea,* col. 1386; Antonio da Butrio to c. Quod nobis, Qui filii sint legitimi (X. 4.17.9), *In librum quartum decretalium,* fol. 47va: "Ultimo vides quod haec est bona consequentia, si filius est: ergo haeres, quando est legitimus: alias non."

65. Cino to l. Si competenti, De alendis liberis (C. 5.25.3), *In codicem* vol. 1, fol. 320vb, and to l. Si arrogator, De adoptionibus (D. 1.7.22), *In codicem* vol. 2, fol. 11ra.

66. Crescenzi, *Esse de Maiori Consilio,* 410–15.

67. Pecorella, "Filiazione (storia)," 454; Leineweber, *Die rechtliche Beziehung,* 88–89.

68. Bartolo to Auth. Ex complexu, C. De incestis nuptiis (C. 5.5.6 in c.), *Opera omnia,* 1615 ed., vol. 7, fol. 160vb.

69. Pietro d'Ancarano to c. Multorum, De Iudaeis (X. 5.6.2), *Super quinto decretalium commentaria* (Bologna, 1581), 51b.

70. Ancarano to c. Quia ingredientibus (X. 3.26.2), *Super tertio decretalium commentaria,* 221a.

of the century Giasone da Maino (1435–1519) could claim that it was possible for *spurii* to inherit as long as the *coheres* could be trusted.[71] Fear of fraud, however, surfaced at the thought of *spurii* holding paternal property, so cautionary limitations were broached by various jurists.[72]

Legitimation and Dispensation

The laws that created illegitimate status and disabilities could also remove them. Simone di Domenico's birth status as an adulterine *spurius* would have gained him no inheritance from his father had he not been legitimated, but as his case and others also show, even then legitimation and its effects were not beyond challenge. Legitimation worked some sort of effective rehabilitation of the legal *persona* of a bastard, but the effects of legitimation varied by the prior illegitimate status of the bastard and by the sort of legitimation that was used. For both historical and logical reasons, there were four different forms of legitimation in *ius commune,* as well as dispensation in canon law. Legitimation, in whatever form, could only complicate the essential ambiguity of the illegitimate. All those persons in the law marked by significant changes of status—*adoptivus, emancipatus, libertus, legitimatus*—generated peculiar problems.

Ecclesiastical dispensation was a fairly limited legal device, in that its focus was very specific. Under canon law bastards could not receive holy orders or obtain a benefice, and sons of priests could not receive their fathers' benefices.[73] A dispensation could release one from any of these disabilities. Illegitimates were also dispensed to enter monasteries, which was a way to do penance for parental sins.[74] A dispensation, unlike legitimation, did not free one from the *defectus natalium* but only from one effect of it.[75] There was some resistance to illegitimates finding their way into cloisters or higher clerical orders. In 1465, for example, the Domini-

71. Giasone da Maino to l. Si pater tuus, C. De haeredibus instituendis (C. 6.24.4), *In secundam codicis partem commentaria* (1573), fol. 98ra.

72. Pecorella, "Filiazione (storia)," 454. And Guglielmus Durantis, *Speculum iudiciale* (Lyons, 1556), part 4, De successione ab intestato § ii, ver. sed quid si pater, fol. 149vb.

73. Génestal, *Histoire de la légitimation,* 47; Schimmelpfennig, "Ex Fornicatione Nati," 20–24; Landau, "Das Weihehindernis der Illegitimität," 48–53.

74. Cf. Génestal, *Histoire de la légitimation,* 80–82; Roselli, *Tractatus legitimationum,* fol. 75rb and 90va; Schreiner, "Defectus natalium," 89–93.

75. VI. 1.11.2, *Corpus iuris canonici,* ed. Emil Friedberg, 2 vols. (Leipzig, 1879). Cf. Schimmelpfennig, "Ex Fornicatione Nati," 29.

cans forbade illegitimates to enter their order, and the Franciscans and others at that time were getting tougher.[76] Even where illegitimates were permitted, cloister rules frequently prohibited them from holding any important posts with control over others or over the institution's resources.[77] Those who could not afford a dispensation, who did not have fathers or relatives in a position to help them, were, of course, effectively shut off from this canon law remedy.[78] Several famous Florentine bastards, Leon Battista Alberti and Carlo di Cosimo de' Medici among them, enjoyed the benefits of purchased dispensations.

Legitimation was much more thorough than dispensation. It removed not one or two effects of illegitimacy; it supposedly removed all, or most, by addressing the underlying *status personae.* As Paolo di Castro put it, "legitimation is not done only for the sake of succession, but also for other effects."[79] It was, claimed the canonist Antonio da Butrio, "a form of respect and honor to the legitimate person, because its opposite is a form of shame."[80] Still, while legitimation indeed made the *persona* of the bastard into much more than an heir to the *pater,* the provision of a successor was clearly one of the major motives behind legitimation. Certainly back in the thirteenth century the canonist Hostiensis (Enrico da Susa, 1200–1271) had driven home the connection between legitimacy and *haereditas,* even as he made clear that it was possession of legitimacy that gave rise to possession of *haereditas,* not the other way around.[81]

Legitimation was not the only legal device by which to secure oneself an heir. Adoption also had that function. Glossators and commentators continued to expound on civil law texts dealing with adoption, and not just because adoption law furnished a locus classicus for analyzing legal fictions. They went into all the conditions for adoption or adrogation and

76. Schimmelpfennig, "Ex Fornicatione Nati," 36; Génestal, *Histoire de la légitimation,* 85.

77. Schreiner, "Defectus natalium," 101–4.

78. Ibid., 111. On "clerical careers," see Christian Hesse, "Vorgezeichnete Karriere? Die Bemühungen von Eltern, ihre unehelichen Söhne mit Pfründen zu versorgen, dorgelegt an Beispielen aus den Diözesen Basel und Konstanz," in Schmugge, *Illegitimität im Spätmittelalter,* 275–92.

79. Paolo di Castro, *cons.* 22, *Consilia* (1582), vol. 2, fol. 12ra–rb: "Nam legitimatio non fit solum propter successionem, sed etiam propter plures alios effectus."

80. Antonio da Butrio to c. Per venerabilem, Qui filii sint legitimi (X. 4.17.13), *In librum quartum decretalium,* fol. 49vb: "quidam decor et honor erga personam legitimam: quia eius oppositum est dedecus quoddam."

81. Hostiensis to c. Causam que, Qui filii sint legitimi (X. 4.17.7), *Summa aurea,* col. 1386: "non enim haereditas trahit ad se legitimationem, sed legitimatio haereditatem."

their effects, including the still restricted rights of inheritance by an adopted son.[82] Perhaps because these inheritance rights were restricted, adoption was not an institution much in favor in social practice.[83] Those in need of an heir turned not to adoption but to legitimation, which gave them an heir of their blood, however tainted. Jurists, in fact, nicely captured this prejudice toward blood. Angelo degli Ubaldi drove home the point that the *adoptivus* became *filius per creationem,* not *per generationem*—a solely efficient cause with no accompanying material cause.[84] Bartolomeo Sozzini offered a most thorough rendering of the effective prejudice against adoption:

> although an adoptive son and a legitimated son are equated . . . still in fact an argument from the one to the other is not valid. . . . For someone can easily be made an adoptive son, by a testator adopting anyone as his son, but legitimation cannot be made to happen so easily.[85]

Here again, even for the *spurius,* much less the *naturalis,* there was some sort of natural connection that, a priori at least, no adopted or adrogated heir could claim (if not otherwise adopted from among one's agnates). Paolo di Castro gave expression to the power of natural, blood connections in a *consilium:*

> And for this reason I say that adoptive sons do not come to inherit, although they are legitimate, because, as in them does not subsist any natural tie or connection of blood, there does not rest on them such an affection that a father would seem to think of them, or even the emperor . . . it is otherwise with a legitimated son, because there is an underlying natural and paternal connection by reason of which a

82. On inheritance by adopted children, see Dino del Mugello, *Tractatus,* fols. 1va and 2va.

83. Cf. my "Reading between the Patrilines"; and my "L'Adoption à Florence."

84. Angelo to l. Filiosfamilias, De adoptionibus (D. 1.7.1), *In primam digesti veteris* (1580), fol. 18va.

85. Bartolomeo Sozzini, *Consilia,* 5 vols. (Venice, 1579), vol. 2, *cons.* 226, fol. 83vb: "et licet filius adoptivus et legitimatus aequiparentur . . . tamen in proposito, de uno ad aliud non valet argumentum. . . . Nam in adoptivo de facili fieri posset filius, testatore adoptando aliquem in filium, sed legitimatio non impetratur ita de facili, unde non habet locum ratio illarum legum."

father seems to have affection for him and display it, because nature is the same for legitimates and illegitimates.[86]

Types of Legitimation

Just as there were different sorts of illegitimate children, there were different forms of legitimation, each with its own requirements, forms, and effects: (1) *legitimatio per subsequens matrimonium,* (2) *legitimatio per rescriptum principis,* (3) *legitimatio per oblationem curiae,* (4) *legitimatio ex testamento,* where *naturales* were designated as *heredes,* (5) *legitimatio ex testamento,* where they were called *filii* with no mention of their illegitimacy and three witnesses had subscribed the testament.[87]

Legitimation by subsequent marriage was designed only for *naturales.* Basic here was the legal ability of the parents to marry—something lacking for spurious, adulterine, and incestuous bastards. Civil law had made legitimation by subsequent marriage available to encourage solemnizing concubinage relationships. In the decretal *Tanta* Alexander III (1159–81), however, also expanded its scope and changed its nature. Alexander considered legitimation to arise by natural force of the sacrament of marriage, not by the mere fiction of law.[88] As a result, the basic requirement became not a preexisting state of concubinage but that the couple were marriageable at the time of conception.[89] While the civil law's treatment of concubinage arose from its ambivalence toward it as neither approved nor disapproved, the canonical emphasis on the force of marriage thus made legitimation by marriage available to less stable relationships, as long as they were not marked by concupiscence,[90] whereas civil law operated

86. Paolo di Castro, *Consilia,* 2 vols. (1522), *cons.* 461, vol. 2, fols. 236ra: "Nec per hoc dico quod veniant filii adoptivi licet legitimi sint: quia cum non subsistat in illis aliqua naturalis vel vinculum sanguinis non cadit in eis tanta affectio: ut pater de ipsis cogitare videatur vel etiam imperator ar. ff. de le. ii l. si ista quis § fi. de condi. et demon. l. fideicom. secus in filio legitimato: quia si ibi subest naturalis et vinculum paternum ratione cuius pater ad ipsum videtur affectionem habuisse et sibi prospexisse: quia natura est eadem legitimi et illegitimi ff de accu. l. hos accusare § omnibus facit l. qui concubinam in prin. de leg. iii de capi. dimi. l. tutelas."

87. Dino del Mugello, *Tractatus,* fol. 1rb; Pecorella, "Filiazione (storia)," 452–54; Winterer, *Die rechtliche Stellung,* 60–68.

88. Génestal, *Histoire de la légitimation,* 175–77; Weitnauer, *Die Legitimation,* 94–95; Esmein, *La mariage en droit canonique,* 2:40–41.

89. Génestal, *Histoire de la légitimation,* 153–59.

90. Bartolo to l. In concubinatu, De concubinis (D. 25.7.3), *In primam infortiati commentaria* (Venice, 1581), fol. 38va. See also Filippo Decio, *cons.* 154, *Consilia,* 2 vols. (Venice, 1575), vol. 1, fol. 164va; Roselli, *Tractatus legitimationum,* fol. 76va–vb.

with a very narrow definition of concubinage as a stable relationship involving the woman "retenta in domo."

As a legal institution deemed *favorabilis* for those experiencing it, legitimation through subsequent marriage was made available at any time. If, for example, the father, having procreated children on a concubine, later married another woman, after the wife's death he could return and marry his concubine and thus legitimate his children by her.[91] In addition, several canonists argued that in a case where marriage was impossible at the time of conception but was possible at birth (as by the married mother's husband's death), the child could be legitimated by marriage.[92] This bordered on letting adulterers marry, however, and canon law especially was loath to do so and thus seem to condone sin. As the purpose of marriage was procreation, Cino da Pistoia found it worth discussing whether a dying man could marry his concubine in order to legitimate their children, as the procreative purpose of marriage was thwarted in that instance. He allowed it by the trick that the hope of having children took the form of legitimating existing children—"a new quality of child is procreated."[93]

Sometimes, in imitation of an old Germanic rite, parents getting married would stand with their children under a blanket or cloak, symbolizing their generation and inclusion in the family.[94] This, however, was not a formal legal requirement for legitimation. A formal dotal instrument was, at least in civil law. Medieval canon law, however, rested marriage on the consent of the partners. On this point there was not necessarily ever agreement, even though Panormitano (Niccolò de' Tedeschi [1386–1445]) claimed that civilians had conceded this point to the canonists.[95]

The fate of the patrimony of Biagio di Jacopo da Vispignano in the last decade of the fourteenth century turned on this issue. Biagio had named

91. Pecorella, "Filiazione (storia)," 454; also Roselli, *Tractatus legitimationum,* fol. 78va.

92. Roselli, *Tractatus legitimationum,* fol. 77ra.

93. Cino to l. Nuper, C. De naturalibus liberis (C. 5.27.11), *In codicem,* vol. 1, fol. 321rb. See also Laurent Mayali, "Note on the Legitimization by Subsequent Marriage from Alexander III to Innocent III," in *The Two Laws: Studies in Medieval Legal History Dedicated to Stephan Kuttner,* ed. Laurent Mayali and Stephanie A. J. Tibbetts (Washington, D.C., 1990), esp. 56–57.

94. Pertile, *Storia del diritto italiano,* 3:391; Weitnauer, *Die Legitimation,* 97; Génestal, *Histoire de la légitimation,* 101, 146–47.

95. Génestal, *Histoire de la légitimation,* 165–67. Roselli, *Tractatus legitimationum,* fol. 77rb: "Nam sola confectio dotalium instrumentorum eos facit legitimos."

five sons as his heirs, substituting them for each other in case one died "sine filiis legitimis et naturalibus." Two sons (Jacopo and Pepo) died without issue. One, Pietro, had legitimate children. Another, Martino, had had a son (Antonio) and a daughter by a concubine (Caterina, daughter of a Gherardo from the Bolognese contado) whom he later married, but without a notarized dowry. Pietro's heirs challenged the claims of Martino's children to their share by substitution to the dead brothers, contesting their legitimacy, seeing as there was not the required *confessio dotis*. A judge, it seems, put these matters to a distinguished panel: Angelo degli Ubaldi and Antonio da Butrio, who seems to have been the chief author, and, flanking them, four prominent Florentines: Filippo Corsini (1334–1421), Giovanni Ricci (1342–1402), Rosello Roselli (fl. 1380–1400), and Torello Torelli (fl. 1400).[96]

In a contemporary case arising in Siena, a jurist had arrived at the opinion that children were legitimate despite the absence of a true dotal instrument.[97] But one of the panel, Angelo degli Ubaldi, had claimed, in a different case, that where there was no dowry such children could not be considered legitimate.[98] And in the case at hand civil law, which required dowry, governed inheritance. However, Antonio da Butrio countered with the sweeping assertion that canon law governed marriage questions. So here the dowry requirement was waived in accordance with canon law by a noted canonist. He deemed the children legitimate and thus substitute heirs to half the property of their childless uncles.

Civil and canon law also remained in disagreement, it seems, on the need for consent to the legitimation, as opposed to the marriage. Because the sacramentality of marriage bulked large in canon law, canonists considered that consent to marriage implied consent to all that it entailed. Roselli, however, argued that a father could, at the moment of marrying his concubine, reject the legitimation of their children.[99] More obvious was the disagreement about the need for consent on the part of the children who would be legitimated by the marriage; although this was more an interesting logical legal conundrum than the sort of thing that arose in practice. What bastard was likely not to want to consent to his parents' marriage? Canonists maintained the children's consent was unnecessary;

96. Vat. Lat. 8069, fols. 367r–369v.
97. Vat. Lat. 11605, fols. 202ra–203rb.
98. Angelo, *cons.* 29, *Consilia,* fols. 17va–18vb.
99. Roselli, *Tractatus legitimationum,* fol. 77rb.

legitimation was an inevitable natural effect of the sacrament.[100] Civilians, on the other hand, faced the legal consequence that legitimated children were subjected to the *patria potestas.* Just as consent was required for adoption or adrogation, which also put one under *potestas,* or for emancipation, which removed one from it, consent was required for legitimation.[101] It was not consent to the parents' marriage; it was consent to their legitimation. And it had to be an active, express form of consent *(ratihabitio)* and not just a lack of contradiction, a tacit consent. A child absent from the proceedings was not legitimated until he formally consented.[102]

Legitimation by rescript was a form more often used by Florentines, as in the case of Simone di Domenico, because the parents were so often unmarriageable. *Legitimatio per rescriptum principis* was first established by Justinian to provide for *naturales* whose mother had died or who otherwise could not be legitimated by a subsequent marriage. The institution took shape in the Middle Ages largely as a result of the famous and controversial decretal of Innocent III, *Per venerabilem,* by which the pope claimed the power to legitimate by rescript in temporal matters. Just as dispensation could be operative for any category of illegitimate, legitimation through rescript could be used for *spurii,* contrary to the Justinianic form of the institution.[103] The later practical prominence of this institution was owed in part to this extension of its use, for it was the main, if not only, form of legitimation available to *spurii.*[104]

Properly speaking, legitimation was an act of voluntary jurisdiction reserved ordinarily to the emperor alone, at least in territories and among

100. Génestal, *Histoire de la légitimation,* 167–68.

101. Roselli, *Tractatus legitimationum,* fol. 79va; Bartolo to § Generaliter, Quibus modis naturales efficiantur sui (A. 7.1.11), *Opera omnia,* 1615 ed., vol. 9, fol. 37va.

102. Roselli, *Tractatus legitimationum,* fol. 87ra.

103. Leineweber, *Die rechtliche Beziehung,* 64–66; Pecorella, "Filiazione (storia)," 453; Weitnauer, *Die Legitimation,* 34–47, 98–101; Génestal, *Histoire de la légitimation,* 181–87. For an interesting discussion of the legal qualities of *Per venerabilem,* see Kenneth Pennington, "Pope Innocent III's Views on Church and State: A Gloss to *Per venerabilem,*" in *Law, Church, and Society: Essays in Honor of Stephan Kuttner,* ed. Kenneth Pennington and Robert Somerville (Philadelphia, 1977), 49–68.

104. Pecorella, "Filiazione (storia)," 454; Winterer, *Die rechtliche Stellung,* 68–73; Leineweber, *Die rechtliche Beziehung,* 64–66; Ferdinand Kogler, *Die legitimatio per rescriptum von Justinian bis zum Tode Karls IV* (Weimar, 1904), a diplomatic study. Because, strictly speaking, there was no form of legitimation available to *spurii* in civil law, medieval jurists like Baldo could persist in referring to *spurii* as *illegitimabiles* (Baldo to l. Senatores, C. De naturalibus liberis [C. 5.27.1], *Opera omnia,* vol. 6, fol. 201va).

persons subject to him.[105] The emperor's power to legitimate by imperial rescript could also be delegated to counts palatine (generally locally prominent figures who purchased the noble title and its legal powers or received it as an honor) who could act in his name.[106] Emperor Charles IV (1346–1378) was especially important in this regard for, although he was not the first to do so, he granted palatine privileges extensively and regularized the process.[107] Important for Florence was his grant in 1364 of palatine privileges ex officio to the archbishops of the city. Prominent citizens or even doctors of law, like Antonio Roselli and Benedetto Barzi, also obtained these nonhereditary privileges from time to time.[108]

The ritual of legitimation itself imparted to participants and observers a sense of the nature of the status transformation it accomplished. In legitimation by rescript the child knelt before the count palatine while his father's petition to have him legitimated was orally presented. The child also swore an oath of loyalty to the empire before he was pronounced legitimate.[109] In this ceremony, then, the child was passive, except for expressing consent to legitimation (and thus submission to his father) and allegiance to the empire. Following this ceremony a charter was drawn up by a notary.

For those like Lena di Francesco intent on wresting an estate from the hands of a legitimated heir, one important tactic was to attack the validity of the legitimation. For this reason the requirements for validity were carefully spelled out in doctrinal writings and argued over both there and in judicial cases. The first requirement was that the father reveal the exact status of the child being legitimated *(naturalis, spurius, adulterinus,*

---

105. Roselli, *Tractatus legitimationum,* fol. 85ra.

106. As Baldo degli Ubaldi, *additio* to l. Emancipari (D. 1.7.36), De adoptionibus, *In primam digesti veteris commentaria,* fol. 44ra; Roselli, *Tractatus legitimationum,* fols. 86va–vb.

107. Bartolo, for one, was given such a privilege to legitimate with regard to his students. Bartolo to l. Gallus § forsitan (D. 28.2.29, 8), *In primam infortiati,* fol. 96va; Cavallar, Degenring, and Kirshner, *A Grammar of Signs,* 8–22. On the counts palatine and legitimation, see Winterer, *Die rechtliche Stellung,* 74, 111; Kogler, *Die legitimatio per rescriptum,* 76–83; Pecorella, "Filiazione (storia)," 454.

108. Kogler, *Die legitimatio per rescriptum,* 76–83; Roselli, *Tractatus legitimationum,* fol. 86vb; Gabriella Airaldi, ". . . bastardos, spurios, manzeres, naturales, incestuosos. . . ," in her *Studi e documenti su Genova e l'Oltremare* (Genoa, 1974), 322–23, 334. Paolo di Castro to l. ii, De verborum obligatione (D. 45.1.2), *In secundam digesti novi partem* (Lyons, 1553), fol. 4va–vb, follows the case of legitimation by a papal legate with powers "in temporalibus" in Bologna.

109. Airaldi, "Bastardos," 333. If the son were absent, the father swore the oath for him, but without kneeling.

incestuosus).[110] The second requirement was that the father declare whether or not he had other, legitimate children, for the imperial rescript could not be used to prejudice the rights of legitimate children.[111] Since the time of Charles IV a clause to that effect had been inserted in rescripts and palatine privileges. Such clauses, however, merely followed the thrust of legal thought in the universities. Whereas legitimation by subsequent marriage operated by virtue of a *favor matrimonii* (such that the children of a concubine could be legitimated by marriage even if there were legitimate children), legitimation by rescript was designed to provide a legitimate heir where one otherwise was lacking.[112] The problem became acute if the legitimating father, as happened in Florence and doubtlessly elsewhere, subsequently sired legitimate offspring. Guglielmus Durantis had argued that the force of the rescript evaporated when there were later legitimates by marriage. The rescript had been granted on condition that there were no heirs, and the condition had been removed.[113] Bartolo da Sassoferrato, however, decided that inheritance rights were not lost, not even for those legitimated by rescript.[114] Later doctrine and legal practice, however, were not always as kind to legitimated persons. The argument that legitimation remained, though inheritance might be lost, became the *communis opinio.*[115]

110. Roselli, *Tractatus legitimationum,* fol. 87vb: "Nam difficilius concedit privilegium incestuoso quam naturali." Filippo Decio, *Consilia, cons.* 306, vol. 1, fols. 339rb–va, *cons.* 579, vol. 2, fol. 228ra; Paolo di Castro, *cons.* 30, *Consilia* (1582), vol. 1, fol. 21vb; Antonio da Butrio, to c. Per venerabilem, *In librum quartum decretalium,* fol. 52rb.

111. Roselli, *Tractatus legitimationum,* fol. 87vb. Kogler, *Die legitimatio per rescriptum,* 105; Leineweber, *Die rechtliche Beziehung,* 75.

112. *Glossa ordinaria* to § Generaliter, ver. in quibus, Quibus modis naturales efficiantur sui (A. 7.1.11), *Codex,* vol. 2 (Lyons, 1612), cols. 407–8; Antonio da Butrio to c. Per venerabilem (X. 4.17.13), *In librum quartum decretalium,* fol. 52vb; Filippo Decio, *cons.* 306, *Consilia,* vol. 1, fol. 339rb; Giovanni d'Andrea, *additio* to *Speculum iudiciale,* 1556 ed., fol. 149vb; Bartolo to § Tribus, Quibus modis naturales efficiantur sui (A. 7.1.7), *Super authenticis et institutionibus commentaria* (Venice, 1580), fol. 37ra; Angelo degli Ubaldi to § Si quis igitur, Quibus modis naturales efficiantur legitimi (A. 6.1.1), *Opus ac lectura auctenticorum,* fol. 20ra.

113. *Speculum iudiciale,* part 4, De successione ab intestato, ver. sed ex facto, fol. 149vb, including the *additio* of Giovanni d'Andrea.

114. Bartolo to l. Ex facto, De vulgari et pupillari substitutione (D. 28.6.43), *In primam infortiati* (Venice, 1581), fol. 132rb.

115. Baldo to D. 28.6.43, *Opera omnia,* vol. 3, fol. 99ra; Paolo di Castro, *cons.* 22, *Consilia* (1582), vol. 2, fols. 12ra–rb; Decio, *cons.* 576, *Consilia,* vol. 2, fol. 224vb; and *cons.* 257, vol. 1, fol. 279va: "licet tollatur effectus successionis, remanet tamen legitimatio integra, et perfecta. . . . licet per supervenientiam filiorum legitimorum legitimatio prius facta non revocetur secundum communem opinionem effectus tamen legitimationis limitatur, et restringitur, quia cum ipso legitimato concurrunt filii, et ex legitimo matrimonio postea nati."

Nello da San Gimignano (b. 1373) handled a typical case, though in a somewhat untypical manner.[116] Of four brothers, only Lapuccio had issue, a legitimate daughter Piera and a bastard son Filippo, whom he had legitimated by rescript without reference being made to the daughter. It was in her interests (or that of her husband) to contest the validity of that legitimation, for then she would be sole heir to her father and his three brothers. Nello's partisan *consilium* (commissioned to bolster her case and not neutrally to resolve the dispute) attempted to dismiss the legitimation on the grounds that the father's silence invalidated the legitimation from the start. Even if legitimate children were only born after the legitimation, it was still invalid in his opinion. Nello dismissed Bartolo's arguments about the validity of completed legal acts with the claim that legitimation was really for the purpose of inheritance and so not completed until the *de cuius* died, and that when the reason for a rescript ended (here, the lack of legitimate children), its effect ceased.[117] Also, Filippo, it seems, had not been present at his legitimation and had never formally ratified it later, as he had to. Finally, even if the legitimation were valid, Filippo could succeed with this legitimate daughter; he could not exclude her as statutes allowed. Nor did it matter that Filippo could claim to be born "ex soluto et soluta," because that did not make him *naturalis*. Here obviously Nello stuck to the narrower sense, tied to a specific form of concubinage, in civil law.

In a parallel, though not similar, Pisan case involving Angelo degli Ubaldi, a legitimation was upheld against the objection that the father had declared in the rescript that the boy's mother had not been married when in fact she had (meaning the *spurius* was in fact *adulterinus*).[118] That charge was not, perhaps, as serious as that of disguising the existence of other children. That the birth of legitimate children after legitimation would invalidate the act was a greater problem. Nello's solution was not followed by others, and perhaps not by the court here.

Because the legitimated child would acquire inheritance rights, there arose a third, though lively debated, requirement: Should those who otherwise stood to inherit, had the child not been legitimated (called *venientes ab intestato*), be cited to appear at the legitimation and be given

116. Biblioteca Nazionale Centrale, Florence (hereafter BNF), Landau Finaly 98, fols. 201r–202v.

117. Fol. 201v: "Et tenendo hanc partem respondetur ad rationem Bar. quod legitimatio, ut patet ex forma eius, fit ad finem et effectum succedendi qui adhuc pendet et sic non est sortita effectum suum nisi morte secuta."

118. Angelo, *cons.* 204 and 205, *Consilia,* fols. 134va–135rb.

the opportunity to stop it by refusing to grant their approval or consent? Again, by virtue of the *favor matrimonii,* no such possibility was raised regarding legitimation by subsequent marriage. This was not just an arid issue for the exercise of doctrinal muscles; it was raised in Lena's arguments against Simone di Domenico. In that case there was denial of a need for consent from the nearest agnate (an uncle).[119] The fact that the legitimation deprived such people of inheritance did not matter, because the father whose property was at issue could always have deprived these relatives by spending his wealth or squandering it—throwing it in the sea was the image conjured up by Filippo Decio (1454–1535).[120] In short, as Bartolo said, the property belonged to the father and he could do what he wanted with it, because legitimation mainly concerned his interests and not those of the agnates.[121] However, if the father himself was heir by virtue of a substitution in favor of others, should he have no legitimate or legitimated heirs, then those others had to be summoned to the legitimation. The only other time at which the prospective heirs had to be consulted about a legitimation was when it was affected after the father's death, in which case the interests of the heirs were immediate.[122]

The father had to consent to legitimation because he acquired *patria potestas.*[123] The child had to submit voluntarily to this *potestas.*[124] The need for consent raised problems, however, in instances where it could not be readily given—as when the son was absent from the proceedings or was an infant, legally incapable of consent. These issues were treated by jurists on analogy to the emancipation of *infantes* and *absentes,* which also required the imperial rescript. There was some disagreement as to whether an *infans* could be legitimated. By and large, however, jurists

119. Kuehn, *Law, Family, and Women,* 184–85.

120. Decio, *cons.* 557, *Consilia,* vol. 2, fol. 212rb: "quia tali casu non agitur de praeiudicio agnatorum, cum pater possit bona sua proicere in mari si velit." Roselli, *Tractatus legitimationum,* fol. 87vb: "Ratio, quia pater posset privare illos bona dilapidando, ut not. l. 2 C. de inof. don. [C. 3.29.2] ergo fortius per actum civilem a iure, vel Principis privilegium concessum."

121. Bartolo to l. Gallus § et quid si tantum, De liberis et posthumis (D. 28.2.29, 5), *In primam infortiati* (Venice, 1581), fols. 95ra–va. See also Baldo to l. Nam ita divus, De adoptione (D. 1.7.39), *In primam digesti veteris,* fol. 44va.

122. Roselli, *Tractatus legitimationum,* fols. 87vb–88ra.

123. Da Butrio to c. Per venerabilem (X. 4.17.13), *In librum quartum decretalium,* fol. 52vb; Roselli, *Tractatus legitimationum,* fol. 87ra.

124. Bartolo to l. Inviti, De iis qui sunt sui vel alieni iuris (D. 1.6.11), *Opera omnia,* 1615 ed., vol. 1, fol. 25rb.

followed the affirmative opinion of Bartolo da Sassoferrato, that infants could be legitimated without their consent just as they could be emancipated, provided, of course, that both acts occurred by means of an imperial rescript.[125] Antonio Roselli and Baldo degli Ubaldi, in indicating their adherence to Bartolo's position, relied not only on the general analogy to emancipation but also on the general principle that legitimation was a favor to the infant and so could humanely proceed without his consent or knowledge.[126] Signorino degli Omodei cited Bartolo in defending Simone di Domenico on this point.[127]

Another issue that arose for Omodei in Simone's case was the use of an agent *(procurator)* to obtain the rescript. It was not clearly established whether a legitimation could be performed through agents. Bartolo allowed the practice as consistent with the law, and Baldo agreed owing to the dangers and difficulties of travel.[128] Bartolo opened the way to the use of a *procurator* by distinguishing between those legal acts that involved management of a patrimony and those that did not. Nonpatrimonial acts—adoption, emancipation, manumission—required the presence of the father in person, because he performed the act; the judge or other official only authorized it. In legitimation, however, the father was only consenting to what was really the act of the imperial official (i.e., it was the official who "legitimated" the son, not the father). So Bartolo, and Baldo following him, concluded that a *procurator* could be used in legitimation.[129] Omodei, in turn, relied on them.

The remaining forms of legitimation need detain us only briefly. *Legitimatio per curie oblationem,* available in civil law only to *naturales,* was invented by Theodosius II in 442 to benefit the civic *curiae* in the weaken-

125. Bartolo to l. Iubemus, De emancipatione liberorum (C. 8.48[49].5), *In secundam codicis partem commentaria* (Venice, 1580), fol. 113va.

126. Roselli, *Tractatus legitimationum,* fol. 87ra: "Praeterea legitimatio filii est favor, ut l. nuper, in fi. de nat. li. [C. 5.27.11] ergo in istis sine consensu fiet ipsorum. et ista pars videtur mihi humanior pro qua facit, quia talis legitimatio demum fit a Principe." Baldo to l. Iubemus, C. De emancipationibus (C. 8.48[49].5), *Opera omnia,* vol. 8, fol. 178rb.

127. Kuehn, *Law, Family, and Women,* 185.

128. Bartolo to l. Post mortem § neque adoptari (D. 1.7.25,1), *In primam digesti veteris,* fol. 29rb; Baldo to D. 1.7.25,1, *In primam digesti veteris,* fol. 43rb.

129. Bartolo to l. Gallus § forsitan (D. 28.2.29, 8), *In primam infortiati* (Venice, 1581), fol. 96vb: "quia in legitimatione pater nihil disponit, sed principi vel habenti authoritatem ab eo disponendi consentit, non enim ipse pater legitimat, sed principis authoritas." Baldo to D. 28.2.29, 8, *In primam et secundam infortiati,* fols. 69ra–rb, and to l. Neque absens, De adoptionibus (D. 1.7.24), *Opera omnia,* vol. 1, fol. 43ra.

ing imperial administration. A father could take his natural son to the *curia,* whether or not he had other legitimate sons, to be legitimated as his heir and placed under his *potestas.* A natural daughter was legitimated in a more indirect manner, by being married to a member of the *curia.* Father and child had to consent; however, a *naturalis* could also seek legitimation from the *curia* after his father's death, in which case he could not be allowed to succeed on intestacy or to break a will.[130] *Legitimatio per oblationem,* it should be noted, did not result in the full benefits of other forms of legitimation. It enabled one to inherit only, including the rights and obligations of membership in the *curia* (which were burdensome during the late Roman empire). According to Roselli this form of legitimation was no longer in use.[131] However, on occasion the government of a city like Florence undertook a similar sort of legitimation.

The powers of municipal bodies to legitimate or at least enable to inherit posed a difficult and much discussed issue on which there was no clear consensus. Baldo degli Ubaldi fought any extension of legitimation by this means to *spurii.*[132] Roselli, while conceding the legitimacy of statutes and customs as sources of law, concluded that legitimating *spurii* was not a power that fell to cities, as it could lead to irrational or sinful results: "[B]y such a statute the penalty for crime is removed and an occasion for fornicating is provided, for men not having wives or having sterile ones may take concubines, so that by them they may have sons and heirs. If therefore it gives rise to sinning, it is not possible or honest."[133] Still, despite his agreement on this score with Baldo and Bartolo, Roselli found that his own teacher, Antonio da Butrio, thought that exercise of this power time out of mind ("de cuius initio non extat memoria") was valid.[134] His was a concession to municipal practice.

Justinian allowed a father who had not otherwise legitimated his natural children during his lifetime, and who had no legitimate children, to name the natural children as full heirs *(haeredes universales)* in his testament, and that nomination was considered to affect full legitimation.

130. Roselli, *Tractatus legitimationum,* fol. 90rb–va; McDevitt, *Legitimacy and Legitimation,* 8–9.

131. Roselli, *Tractatus legitimationum,* fol. 90rb: "et quoniam haec forma hodie communiter non tenetur, ideo succincte pertranseam tantum de ea ponens."

132. Baldo to X. 1.2.1, *In decretalium,* fols. 10rb–11va.

133. Roselli, *Tractatus legitimationum,* fol. 86rb: "sed per tale statutum remittitur pena delinquenti et datur occasio fornicandi: Nam viri non habentes uxores vel habentes steriles accipient concubinas, ut ex eis habeant filios et haeredes. si ergo dat materiam peccandi, ergo non est possibile vel honestum."

134. Roselli, *Tractatus legitimationum,* fols. 86rb–va.

However, it was first necessary, as Roselli explained, for the children to petition the emperor and produce the will. In this way the legitimation became formal and public, just as the other forms were, or, as Dino del Mugello put it, they became legitimated "partly by the testator, partly by law, partly by the emperor."[135]

Effects of Legitimation

The emperor could reshape law, but only the father could shape nature, as in recognizing a child as his.[136] Legitimation and emancipation were the main avenues by which law was reshaped regarding children. Both institutions were considered to be honors, "a favor for the child," said Roselli, echoing the language of others about emancipation.[137] Both had nothing to do with the mother (except for legitimation by marriage). The operative legal matter was the abolition or creation of *patria potestas,* something impossible for a woman. Aside from some consideration of inheritance rights and alimentation, there was little discussion of legal ties between child and mother, even of cognation to her family. Likewise the doctrinal presumption was always that legitimation was contemplated for sons as heirs, not for daughters (who indeed were rarely legitimated).

Illegitimacy ended through legitimation, and the status of the person was transformed. But, whether by subsequent marriage, testament, municipal decree, or rescript, legitimation's effects were open to question. Was legitimation the same as legitimacy by birth? Was it retroactive to birth? What did it mean for inheritance? In answering these questions, jurists at times only reached a broad agreement to disagree. Invariably legitimation by subsequent marriage had slightly more favorable effects than legitimation by rescript; and *naturales,* who had less legal distance to travel to legitimacy, usually advanced farther than *spurii.*[138] But such

135. Roselli, *Tractatus legitimationum,* fol. 79va; Dino del Mugello, fol. 1rb.

136. Roselli, *Tractatus legitimationum,* fol. 87ra: "dicit quod consensus Principis habet iura legum, id est legitimationis, et per patrem iura naturae, id est quia efficitur suus patri, et sic ius naturae non habet sine consensu patris."

137. Ibid.; Baldo to l. Nam ita divus, De adoptionibus (D. 1.7.39), *Opera omnia,* vol. 1, fol. 44va. Cf. also McDevitt, *Legitimacy and Legitimation,* 45–46; Kuehn, *Emancipation,* 30–34.

138. On these matters, see Anne Lefebvre-Teillard, "'Tanta est vis matrimonii': L'écho français d'une vieille controverse," in *Hommage à Romuald Szramkiewcz* (Paris, 1998), 95–108, and "Beati possidentes," in *À cheval entre histoire et droit: Hommage à Jean-François Poudret,* ed. Eva Maier, Antoine Rochat, and Denis Tappy (Lausanne, 1999), 247–59.

are the only firm conclusions that can be derived from the evidence. In contrast to assertions that legitimated children "were in no way differentiated from those legitimately born," were capable of all rights and honors and admitted to full family membership, we find in fact that medieval jurists preserved a number of distinctions and reservations.[139]

At first sight, it would seem that legitimation should have equated *legitimati* with *legitimi* in all regards. Legitimation was said to remove the stain *(macula)* of illegitimate birth. In this regard medieval jurists made legitimation more transformative than anything envisioned in Roman law. Just as all were supposedly born free, but society enslaved some, so all were said to be born legitimate, but society branded some as illegitimate. Manumission, then, was not the gift of freedom but the revelation and releasing of primordial and natural freedom. It was metaphorically related by the *Glossa ordinaria* to the process of threshing grain, which did not create a new species of grain but merely revealed what had been hidden beneath the husk.[140] So too legitimation revealed "natural" legitimacy.[141] Thus Angelo degli Ubaldi defined legitimation:

> Strictly and properly speaking, he is called legitimated, who is brought back to said pristine state and right of descent and for whom all stain of birth is removed. So if the emperor or one having authority from him simply makes someone legitimate, he therefore takes away all stain of simplicity, naturalness, and spuriousness, which are induced by means of written laws. For by nature all men are born free and legitimate; but wars introduced slavery; lust was the occasion of inordinate passion, of the system of naturalness, and of spuriousness; and

139. The phrasing is Weitnauer's, *Die Legitimation,* 95, 102. Cf. also Génestal, *Histoire de la légitimation,* 167; Leineweber, *Die rechtliche Beziehung,* 74–76; Winterer, *Die rechtliche Stellung,* 68–71.

140. *Glossa ordinaria* to l. Manumissiones, De iustitia et iure (D. 1.1.4), *Digestum vetus,* vol. 1 (Lyons, 1612), col. 57: "cum omnes liberi nascuntur iure naturae ergo non dat ei libertatem, cum ille liber sit. His duabus rationibus, vel oppositionibus, inductus expono, datio, id est, detectio. nam cum manumitto servum, detegitur libertas servi. nam ipse semper liber est inspecto iure naturae sic qui excutit grana de spicis, non novam speciem facit: sed eam quae est: detegit." Paolo di Castro, *cons.* 180, *Consilia* (1582), vol. 1, fol. 90rb: "quia legitimare est abstergere maculam illegitimitatis, que expulsa detegitur legitimitas, quae iure naturali inerat, cum omnes a principio legitimi nascerentur."

141. Hostiensis, to Qui filii sint legitimi (X. 4.17), *Summa aurea,* cols. 1379–80. See also Winterer, *Die rechtliche Stellung,* 71; Pecorella, "Filiazione (storia)," 453.

so just as the laws introduced this so also laws, both legislated and unlegislated, can abolish the basis of this system.[142]

The restoration of natural right in the legitimated child thus generally restored his *fama.* He could legally do then whatever was in the power of the legitimating agency to give him. He could act and give testimony in any court and he was capable of all civil honors, including inheritance.[143]

As the *Glossa ordinaria* maintained, the legitimated son was legitimate as to family and agnation, civil status, dignities and honors.[144] In short, the *legitimatus* had become a full legal person in the *ius commune.* There was little question, therefore, that legitimated children were agnate to their fathers and to all other agnates.[145] *Legitimati* even held full succession rights with regard to, or in the face of, these agnates.[146] There was a certain amount of complication as to whether the *legitimatus* followed the *origo* of his father or his mother. This was not a topic of lively debate, but as a number of bastards were fathered by men away from their homes for business or other reasons, it was also not a moot point.[147]

---

142. Angelo degli Ubaldi, *cons.* 17, *Consilia,* fol. 12ra: "stricte et proprie loquendo, ille legitimatus dicitur, qui ad dictum pristinum statum, et ius geniturae reductus est, et cui omnis nativitatis macula est abolita. Unde si princeps, aut habens autoritatem ab eo, simpliciter aliquem facit legitimum eo ipso tollit omnem maculam simplicitatis naturalitatis, et spureitatis; quae post leges conditas sunt inducta. A natura enim omnes homines liberi, et legitimi nascebantur: bella autem servitutem introduxerunt: libido autem et concupiscentiae inordinatae schematis naturalitatis, et spureitatis, fuit occasio: unde sicuti leges hoc introduxerunt (ut dictis iur.) ita et leges tam animatae, quam inanimatae, huius schematis radicem abolere possunt."

143. Innocent IV to c. Per venerabilem (X. 4.17.13), *Commentaria in V libros decretalium* (Frankfurt am Main, 1570; rpt. Frankfurt am Main, 1968), fol. 481ra: "Et not. quod legitimatus restitutus famae, etc. cum quo dispensatum est in quocunque foro, sive ecclesiastico, sive civili, et omnia ea facere poterit, super quibus habuit potestatem qui legitimavit vel famae restituit vel dispensavit, poterit enim in omni iudicio testimonium reddere, ad civiles honores vocari, nisi sint talia, quae sint in alterius praeiudicium." Roselli, *Tractatus legitimationum,* fol. 80ra.

144. *Glossa ordinaria* to l. Cum legitime, De statu hominum (D. 1.5.19), vol. 1, col. 92; Winterer, *Die rechtliche Stellung,* 71.

145. Roselli, *Tractatus legitimationum,* fol. 89rb; Durantis, *Speculum iudiciale,* 1556 ed., fol. 150rb.

146. Bartolo to § Generaliter, Quibus modis naturales efficiantur sui (A. 7.1.11), *Opera omnia,* 1615 ed., vol. 9, fol. 37va; Antonio da Butrio, to c. Per venerabilem (X. 4.17.13), *In librum quartum decretalium,* fol. 53ra; Sozzini, *cons.* 226, *Consilia,* vol. 2, fols. 82va–vb; Paolo di Castro, *cons.* 34, *Consilia* (1582), vol. 2, fol. 18va; Angelo degli Ubaldi, *cons.* 17, *Consilia,* fol. 12va.

147. There were political and fiscal effects to determining *origo.* Cf. Julius Kirshner, "Mulier alibi nupta," in Baumgärtner, *Consilia im späten Mittelalter,* 147–75.

But by the beginning of the fourteenth century doctrinal developments also began to make room for contrasting arguments attempting to limit the effects and nature of legitimation. Jacopo Bottrigari (ca. 1274–1347) forged a distinction, saying that legitimation by rescript did not make someone legitimate but merely conferred on him "the rights of legitimacy."[148] He still perceived a difference between those born legitimate and those whose legitimation came only from a later formal act. The freed slave, after all, was called not free *(liber)* but a freedman *(libertus)*, and the legitimated child was similarly called not legitimate *(legitimus)* but legitimated *(legitimatus)*. There was a difference in personal history that retained linguistic resonance.

Against the "fact" of birth, legitimation operated as a legal "fiction." By juristic doctrine a fiction worked only something possible—something in imitation of nature—which was treated as a truth even though it was contrary to truth.[149] Bartolo da Sassoferrato said legitimation did not operate by fiction, that is, contrary to truth, because it truly made one legitimate who was, in "pure truth," legitimate.[150] Baldo degli Ubaldi, however, disagreed with Bartolo. Legitimated children were not "naturally legitimated but by a privilege and a fiction."[151] Elsewhere he declared that "legitimation is a form of alchemy, which makes something appear to be what it is not but that cannot transmute one species into another, for just as a *legitimatus* bears the form [*figura*] of a legitimate, still he does not have the same substance, which must derive from the nature of things, which is divine and immutable."[152] Legitimation, then,

---

148. Bottrigari to Prohemio codicis, *Lectura super codice* (rpt. Bologna, 1973), fol. 1rb: "Cave tamen quod quis legitimando non facit quod legitimum sed iura legitimationis ei confert unde removet impedimentum et reddit eum iuri nature in qua non erat discretio in coitu."

149. Bartolo to l. Si is qui, De usurpationibus et usucapionibus (D. 41.3.15), *In primam digesti novi partem commentaria* (Venice, 1580), fol. 94vb: "Fictio est in re certa eius quod est possibile contra veritatem, pro veritate a iure facta assumptio."

150. Bartolo to D. 41.3.15, ibid., fol. 95rb: "Pone ergo, lex ex certa causa vult filium in potestate facere sui iuris, filium non legitimum vult facere legitimum, et servum liberum, potest ne hoc facere? Certe sic, tamen non secundum fictionem sed secundum ipsam puram veritatem, quia vere erit sui iuris, vel legitimus, vel liber."

151. Baldo to l. Si quis aliquid, C. De his qui veniam aetatis impetrant (C. 2.44[45].4), *In primos libros codicis commentaria* (Lyons, 1546), fol. 140ra: "quia non sunt naturaliter legitimati sed ex privilegio et ex fictione."

152. Baldo to X. 1.2.1, *In decretalium,* fol. 10rb: "Legitimatio similis est alchimie, quae facit apparere illud, quod non est, transmutare tamen unam spetiem in alteram non potest, sicut legitimatus figuram legitimi gerit, sed non habet eandem substantiam, qua debet profiscisci a rerum natura, que divina et immutabilis est."

restored the child to the natural state by conferring upon him the habit of acting like a legitimate child. It did not merely remove an obstacle that covered up an ingrained, innate behavior. It was one thing, said Baldo, to be legitimate; it was something else to be legitimated, bccause a child legitimated by rescript was legitimate only to his father, not to other relatives.[153]

In medieval law the play of fiction was limited.[154] Not surprisingly, therefore, it was Baldo's less generous opinion that seems to have found the most adherents. Also unsurprisingly, if legitimation of *naturales* by marriage came off as fictive, legitimation of *spurii* by rescript was no less so. Antonio Roselli declared that a person legitimated by rescript was legitimate fictively from that moment to the past, though truly legitimate to the future.[155] Bartolo had been more insistent on the legal truth of legitimation by rescript, of its essential similarity to legitimation by marriage, but even he left room for "truer judgment."[156] Other forms of legitimation—by *oblatio* or by testament—were merely dispensative, maintained Roselli, and as such aimed only at the future and were thoroughly fictive, resulting in no agnation to the father or others.[157]

The distinction drawn by jurists like Baldo degli Ubaldi and Antonio Roselli did not arise solely from within the law. It related, to "common usage." Bartolo had conceded much to common usage, but he also maintained that the *communis usus loquendi* was a figurative understanding that could not alter the proper meaning of things.[158] Fifteenth-century jurists, actively involved in litigation as well as teaching, wrestled with "common sense" meanings. One such was Paolo di Castro:

153. Baldo, *additio* to l. Emancipari, De adoptionibus (D. 1.7.36), *In primam digesti veteris,* fol. 44ra.

154. Yan Thomas, "'Auctoritas legum non potest veritatem naturalem tollere': Rechtsfiktion und Natur bei den Kommentatoren des Mittelalters," in *Recht zwischen Natur und Geschichte,* ed. François Kervégan and Heinz Mohnhaupt (Frankfurt am Main, 1997), 1–32.

155. Roselli, *Tractatus legitimationum,* fol. 89ra.

156. Bartolo to § Tribus, Quibus modis naturales efficiantur sui (A. 7.1.7), *Super authenticis,* fol. 37ra: "legitimatio vero per rescriptum principis est idem quod legitimatio per matrimonium ut videtur probari infra eo § adoptionis [A. 7.1.11, 2]. . . . Sed salva semper sententia veriori, videtur posse dici contra. ratio, quia legitimatio retrotrahitur, et perinde habetur legitimatus ac si esset legitime natus."

157. Roselli, *Tractatus legitimationum,* fol. 89ra–rb; Angelo degli Ubaldi, to § Si quis igitur, Quibus modis naturales efficiantur legitimi (A. 6.1.1), *Opus ac lectura auctenticorum,* fol. 20ra.

158. Bartolo to l. Liberorum, De verborum significatione (D. 50.16.220), *Opera omnia,* 1615 ed. vol. 6, fol. 235va.

> It appears that, although properly speaking a legitimated person is truly legitimate and natural, by nature and the cooperating dispensation of the law . . . yet the common usage does not so consider him. Rather they are called natural, since there are two species of legitimates, because some are original and some are not, and between them there is much difference in common usage, so that each is distinguished by its own terms. . . . [Common usage] calls legitimate and natural only those originally so, not the others, whom it terms legitimated, and so the words are to be understood simply in their stronger sense.[159]

The issue was far from settled, because important practical effects were involved. Giasone da Maino made the practicalities apparent when he tackled the problem of the retroactive quality of legitimation. If retroaction meant the legitimation had favorable results for the *legitimatus* and did not prejudice others' rights, then it went into effect. If, however, rights of others were adversely affected, the legitimation was not to be treated as retroactively valid.[160] Where, for example, inheritance went by primogeniture, it was important to know if a first, illegitimately born, legitimated son recovered precedence over a later, legitimately born brother.[161]

Where the legitimated person had no legitimate siblings, there was some question of the inheritance rights lost by the agnates *venientes ab intestato*. By and large, these potential heirs lost out to the *legitimatus*, some provision having been made, as we have seen, that they be summoned to appear at the legitimation by rescript. However, in actual terms, this class of now-postponed heirs formed the pool of potential litigants, with clear interests in contesting inheritance by bastards, howsoever legitimated. Their opportunities arose mainly in two contexts. One

159. Paolo di Castro, *cons.* 252, *Consilia* (1582), vol. 2, fol. 123vb: "Constat autem quod licet legitimatus de proprio significatu dicatur vere legitimus et naturalis natura et iuris dispensatione cooperante . . . tamen communis usus loquendi non sic se habet, sed appellantur naturales, cum enim legitimorum duae sint species, quia quidam originarii, quidam non, et inter eos in multis est differentia communis usus loquendi, ut singuli eorum singulis appellationibus distinguantur . . . originarios tantum legitimos et naturales appellat, alios non, sed factos legitimos, et sic verba intelligantur in potiori significatu, et simpliciter, non secundum quid l. i § si in perpetuum si ager vect. [D. 6.3.1,1] et l. hoc legatum ff. de leg. 3 [D. 32(1).45]."

160. Giasone da Maino to l. Gallus § et quid si tantum, De liberis et posthumis (D. 28.2.29, 5), *In secundam codicis partem commentari,* fol. 191ra.

161. Roselli, *Tractatus legitimationum,* fol. 80rb–va.

involved the use of fideicommissary substitutions in wills, which defined an order of succession, and the other was civic statutes, which similarly defined orders of succession—in these instances varying somewhat from intestate succession in civil law.

There are those, like Andrea Romano, who have argued that inheritance was changing in law and legal practice in the course of the fourteenth and fifteenth centuries. A horizontally extended sense of patrimony tying together multiple complex households was giving way to a more vertical sense of the perpetual unity of a house and patrimony linked to a line of male descent. Progressive use of testaments and the ability in them to lay out substitutions marked this trend.[162] A testator could specify a line of descent through his sons and spell out what would happen to the property—that is, who would be substituted as the next heir if the sons, in turn, died without legitimate heirs.[163] Such clauses became increasingly common in the course of the fifteenth and sixteenth centuries throughout Italy. They appear not only in testaments but in various *donationes, lauda,* and other legal instruments. How legitimated bastards fit into these substitutions, if at all, became a pressing legal issue. Did legitimated sons count as legitimate for the purposes of the substitution? Did they prevent the passage of property to the specified substitute?

Baldo maintained that legitimation as fiction did not fulfill the conditions of a *fideicommissum* in favor of legitimate descendants.[164] Because as a rule wills had to be interpreted by the inferred intent of the testator *(mens testatoris),* Antonio da Butrio argued that the common conditional clause used in substitutions ("si decesserit sine filiis legitimis et naturalibus") referred to circumstances of birth (in terms of which legitimation was a fiction), and thus legitimated sons—whether by marriage or rescript—did not stop a testamentary substitution.[165] Antonio Roselli kept this distinction.[166] Others, however, had argued that a testator's

162. Andrea Romano, *Famiglia, successioni e patrimonio familiare nell'Italia medievale e moderna* (Turin, 1994), 18–19, 33–34, 43, 59, 60–61; in general on testaments see the exhaustive study of Giovanni Chiodi, *L'Interpretazione del testamento nel pensiero dei glossatori* (Milan, 1997).

163. On the *fideicommissum* and substitution, see Cooper, "Patterns of Inheritance"; and M. Caravale, "Fedecommesso (storia)," *Enciclopedia del diritto,* 17:109–14.

164. Baldo to l. Si ita quis § is cui in tempus, De legatis ii (D. 31.[1].51,1), *Opera omnia,* vol. 3, fol. 151rb.

165. Da Butrio to c. Per venerabilem (X. 4.17.13), *In librum quartum decretalium,* fol. 53rb.

166. Roselli, *Tractatus legitimationum,* fol. 80ra.

words applied only to the time of his death and not to the time of the descendant's birth. Thus Bartolomeo Sozzini declared that what mattered to a testator was keeping property within the family, that is, in male hands, and that legitimation expressed a preference for a bastard son over legitimate daughters.[167]

In the case of the heirs of Biagio di Jacopo da Vispignano mentioned above, the requirement of legitimate birth in the language of the substitution was set aside. While it was conceded that "the difference between legitimate and illegitimate is induced by positive law," it was aided by nature in that all were born legitimate primevally. Those legitimated were truly legitimate "so that they can fit into the testator's words."[168] The *consilium* thus concluded that Martino's children had rights of inheritance to their uncles by substitution and precluded any substitution to Martino's share.

The *consilium*'s interpretation of the substitution ran counter to much academic teaching on the subject "that legitimation that arises from marriage after birth is not true legitimation but such a person is taken as legitimate." So these legitimated children, while enabled in civil law, were totally excluded from any statutory clauses, because statutes could not know the fictions of *ius commune*.[169] Presumably neither could the substitutions of testators. Antonio da Butrio also recognized that the usual language of testamentary substitutions, the same language employed by Biagio da Vispignano, referred to time of birth.[170] On the basis of that distinction his student Antonio Roselli (whose father was among the six signatories) would decide that *legitimati per subsequens matrimonium* did or did not satisfy substitutions.[171] In this *consilium*, however, da Butrio avoided the usual terms associated with this line of interpretation. He did not discuss whether the legitimation was fictive or retroactive; he did not go into the problem of whether the substitution referred to time of birth.

167. Sozzini, *cons.* 63, *Consilia,* vol. 3, fol. 70rb.

168. Vat. Lat., fol. 369r: "Non ergo abusive sed cohadiuvante natura filii legitim<at>i sunt et vere legitimi ita quod cadere possunt in verbis testatoris sicut et in verbis legis canonice comprenduntur quod est plus appellatione legitime natorum."

169. Da Butrio to c. Tanta, Qui filii sint legitimi (X. 4.17.6), *In librum quartum decretalium,* fol. 45rb: "Et nota, quod legitimatio quae surgit ex contractu matrimonii post nativitatem prolis, non est vera legitimatio sed habetur talis pro legitimo."

170. Ibid., fol. 53rb.

171. Roselli, *Tractatus legitimationum,* fol. 80ra.

Conclusions

Despite the presence of synthetic treatises, by the fifteenth century the *ius commune* had not yet devised any general definition of legal personhood.[172] *Persona* was a function of legal freedom, age, sex, legitimacy, mental capacity, and so forth. Distinctions were drawn at times between an objective legal *persona,* whose rights and interests could be given theoretical expression, and the human being as subject of rights, but only in the sixteenth century, under the influence of humanistic perspectives of *humanitas,* would the distinction between living entity and legal person be drawn to the extent of postulating that, while a slave was *homo,* he was not a *persona.*[173] It would not be until the eighteenth century that Western thinkers would devise a fully subjective sense of legal personhood coincident with the reshaping of notions of childhood, including those regarding illegitimacy.

In simple terms, a *persona* in law in the fifteenth century was someone who, from involvement in relationships, had full capacity to have and to act.[174] An illegitimate was not such a person. Some actions were precluded him or her, and inheritance was limited, remote, or impossible. On the other hand, in comparison to a slave, the illegitimate at least had some sort of partial personhood. An *illegitimus* could own property, pursue legal actions regarding it, formally marry and sire a legitimate progeny (as a new line of descent, not agnate to existing lines). But the illegitimate did not possess the usual assets, attributes, and relationships that could propel a legitimate child into the life of the legal person.

Succession followed *patria potestas* in Roman law. Male filiation through *potestas* was the social and legal bond of authority; hence succession in the male line was instantaneous where it was not for inheritance descended of women, as they were incapable of authoritative power over those who were to follow them (the class of *legitimi heredes*

172. For what follows, see the intelligent discussion of Paolo Zatti, *Persona giuridica e soggettività,* esp. 51–83; also Paolo Cappellini, "'Status' accipitur tripliciter: Postilla breve per un'anamnesi di 'capacità giuridica' e 'sistema del diritto romano attuale,'" *Annali dell'-Università di Ferrara, scienze giuridiche,* n.s. 1 (1987): 29–97.

173. Zatti, *Persona giuridica e soggettività,* 69.

174. Grossi, *L'ordine giuridico medievale,* 84; Laurent Mayali, "Le droit des autres dans la France médiévale: Système de différenciation et mode d'harmonisation," in *Identité et droit de l'autre,* ed. Laurent Mayali (Berkeley and Los Angeles, 1994), 187.

in Roman law).[175] Illegitimate children were, by Roman law, associated only with the mother, but the bond of maternity was not a bond of legal authority. "Illegitimacy was a term that could properly be applied only to the act of engendering, which was an act of the man alone."[176]

In the centuries of the Christian Roman empire and the medieval world, the artificial distinctions in Roman law between kinship and authoritative agnatic descent and inheritance revolving around *patria potestas* gave ground. Women could become *tutrices* to their own children at least, and rights to alimentation were extended on the basis of filiation. In these regards, bastards all gained some greater sense of connection to mother, but even more to father (if he was known). But, at the same time, the terms of the Roman law did not go away. *Patria potestas* still defined legitimate filiation. Not only was legal personhood thus partial for illegitimates or even for different types of bastards, but it had a processual dimension. It could be changed by legitimation (just as manumission, adoption, emancipation, marriage, or just the growth process could change the personal status of people).

While the lawyers absolutely affirmed the "stained" and inferior status of illegitimates in civil law and the removal of this stain by legitimation, they introduced or kept distinctions that tended to reduce the status of those who went through legitimation. Not that all the jurists' efforts went only toward equivocation and confusion of the basic issues. A number of rules were established so as to seem virtually unquestionable. The procedures and requirements for legitimation were more or less set. Legitimation, however, was also a fiction of civil law, and so its operation was in doubt where civil law was overridden or activated by other sources of law or rights—statutes or a testator's intent, for example.[177]

---

175. Yan Thomas, "The Division of the Sexes in Roman Law," in *A History of Women in the West,* ed. Georges Duby and Michelle Perot, vol. 1: *From Ancient Goddesses to Christian Saints,* ed. Pauline Schmitt Pantel, trans. Arthur Goldhammer (Cambridge, Mass., 1992), 88. See my "Person and Gender in the Laws," in *Gender and Society in Renaissance Italy,* ed. Judith A. Brown and Robert C. Davis (London, 1998), 87–106.

176. Thomas, "Division of the Sexes," 116.

177. As both juristic fiction and reality, legitimation had its parallels to the law of acquired citizenship. Cf. Diego Quaglioni, "The Legal Definition of Citizenship in the Late Middle Ages," in *City-States in Classical Antiquity and Medieval Italy: Athens and Rome, Florence and Venice,* ed. Anthony Molho, Kurt Raaflaub, and Julia Emlen (Stuttgart, 1991), 155–67; Julius Kirshner, "*Civitas sibi faciat civem:* Bartolus of Sassoferrato's Doctrine on the Making of a Citizen," *Speculum* 48 (1973): 194–213, "*Ars imitatur naturam:* A Consilium of Baldus on Naturalization in Florence," *Viator* 5 (1974): 289–331, and "Between Nature and Culture: An Opinion of Baldus of Perugia on Venetian Citizenship as

Juristic treatment of legitimation (as of other legal institutions and constructs) tended to isolate areas of indeterminacy in the law, while also perpetuating and at times heightening those indeterminacies. The pro and contra style of argument and professional pride or jealousy also led to the elaboration and perpetuation of contrary views.[178] Even the establishment by consensus of authoritative commentaries and *communes opiniones* to be applied in practice did not remove indeterminacy. Authoritative or common views could be rejected for good reason—that too was an accepted doctrine of forensic practice.[179]

What illegitimacy more or less vigorously denied (depending on the type of illegitimate), and what legitimation more or less fully affirmed, was the existence of a web of relationships around the *illegitimus/legitimatus.* Legal relationships took their substance in terms of real and symbolic attributes. Hence the concern one finds to spell out, for bastards and *legitimati,* issues of inheritance, honors (arms, insignia), *fama,* and name. Perhaps above all a *patria potestas* was created and agnation conceded, where before there had been only blood.

Burckhardt saw bastards as individuals in an anthropological sense, in that they had fewer or more tenuous relationships. In that sense they were perhaps freer to forge relationships, to gain their own (including intellectual or artistic) capital in the world. But they were deficient in legal personhood, if not social. They were disadvantaged in relation to legitimate kin. Their very individuality marked them as peculiar, antisocial, less than persons. They stood outside, rather than inside, kin relationships—at least legally. The educations, dispensations, or other benefits and expenditures lavished on Petrarch or Boccaccio, Alberti or da Vinci, Carlo or Giovanni de' Medici were not something to which they had some legal claim and could not be predicted from the legal and moral circumstances of their birth alone.

Second Nature," *Journal of Medieval and Renaissance Studies* 9 (1979): 179–208; Joseph P. Canning, "A Fourteenth-Century Contribution to the Theory of Citizenship: Political Man and the Problem of Created Citizenship in the Thought of Baldus de Ubaldis," in *Authority and Power: Studies on Medieval Law and Government Presented to Walter Ullmann on His Seventieth Birthday,* ed. Brian Tierney and Peter Linehan (Cambridge, 1980), 197–212 and his *The Political Thought of Baldus de Ubaldis* (Cambridge, 1987), 159–84.

178. See Lombardi, *Saggio sul diritto giurisprudenziale,* 79–199.

179. See Mario Ascheri, "'Consilium sapientis,' perizia medica e 'res iudicata': Diritto dei 'dottori' e istituzioni comunali," *Proceedings of the Fifth International Congress of Medieval Canon Law* (Vatican City, 1980), 533–79.

2

Illegitimacy in Florentine Laws and Institutions

Ius commune provided the framework, procedures, and conceptual underpinning to local norms, especially with regard to family, marriage, inheritance, and similar matters.[1] Alongside *ius commune,* Florentine statutes and other legislation *(ius proprium)* erected an ever-changing array of modifications, restrictions, and exemptions. Such legislation tailored the general rules to fit local meanings and practices as well as political contingencies, and an already complicated and ambiguous area of law like illegitimacy became more complicated by the combination of *ius proprium* and *ius commune.*

With regard to illegitimacy, at least as much as any other area of law, technical meanings did not always carry over to daily life or the more informal legislation of Italian cities. In statutes and in common speech, bastards—as a general term, without distinctions as to the circumstances of conception—were linked to families and involved as a result in a network of reciprocal rights (such as inheritance) and duties (such as vendetta). Jurists were painfully aware of the disjunction between lay meanings and their own, but they were also constrained to accede weight to those common meanings in the law, especially as they informed civic or guild statutes. Statutes and customs that recognized the rights of bastards to participate in vendettas seemed to go a long way to conceding family membership indiscriminately to *naturales* and *spurii* well beyond the carefully propagated limits of civil and canon law. Accordingly, Angelo degli Ubaldi, in one of his *consilia,* said that the linkage of bastards to families

> is corroborated by common speech in Italy, which has it that by the term *filii* are included even bastards and *spurii.* . . . And it is corrobo-

1. Martines, *Lawyers and Statecraft,* 92.

> rated by custom, which in fact we see daily in Italy, because vendettas are carried out by even bastard kin. . . . For to him who is descended of the male blood of the offended person pertains vendetta and revenge (that is, the injury) of the offended, or making peace or compensation.[2]

A jurist such as Angelo did not quietly accept the vocabulary of the streets. While conceding something to the "vulgar" outlook, he insisted that bastard children were not to be identified legally with a particular father such that they could insist on paternal prerogatives or even become involved in vendettas:

> But when we speak of a legitimate for some purpose we simply call him *filius* of someone. Nor does it matter that by our customs *spurii* burn for revenge and sometimes yearn for it more than *legitimi*, because rarely is it that they are present, although sometimes it happens. So it does not follow *de iure* that to them belongs every vendetta, because it does not belong to them, who are unworthy by nature of that paternal benefit, in the absence of law.[3]

While the right to die in a vendetta can be a dubious privilege, Angelo clearly maintained that the exclusion of *spurii* on this score was punitive. No matter what "nature" gave them by common usage, they lacked sufficient natural substance for vendetta. The rules by which participants in vendetta lived, however, were those of the "communis usus loquendi." Bartolo had already recognized this disjunction between legal and "common" meanings as a general matter throughout Tuscany, and his concession of family standing to bastards lay at the heart of jurisprudential discussions, which, however, also continued to be carried out with precise distinctions between *naturales* and *spurii* that did not always creep into

2. Angelo degli Ubaldi, *cons.* 401, *Consilia,* fol. 291rb: "Ergo hoc corroboratur ex communi usu loquendi, qui habet hoc in Italia, quod appellatione filiorum comprehendentur etiam bastardi et spurii. . . . Item corroboratur ex consuetudine, quam de facto vidimus vigere in Italia, quod fiant vindictae per consortes etiam bastardos. . . . Namque ad illum, qui descendit ex sanguine masculino offensi, pertinet facere vindictam, et levare faidam id est iniuriam offensi, vel facere pacem, seu compositionem."

3. Ibid.: "Sed cum de legitimo loquimur ad aliquem finem, filium alicuius simpliciter appellamus. Nec ob. quod filii spurii secundum mores nostros ad vindictam facti ardentes, et propitius anhelant quandoque, quam legitimi: quia de raro contingentibus est, licet quandoque contingat. Non sequitur ergo de iure: Ad eos spectat omnis vindicta: quia imo non spectat: ex quo paterno beneficio sunt indigni: ut in fallentia iuris, secundum naturam."

statutes.[4] To save the legal meaning, Bartolo conceded legal effect to the common usage only where its result would benefit the illegitimate. Where a Perugian law encouraged capture of members of a magnate clan, Bartolo excluded bastards.[5] Florence's statutes gave normative expression to this familial linkage and common usage.

Perhaps the most celebrated example of this inclusion of bastards for purposes of vendetta was a rubric in Florence's famous antimagnate legislation of 1293, the Ordinances of Justice. By this statute *naturales* or any *bastardi* over fifteen were required, as much as legitimate members of magnate houses, to offer monetary guarantees to the commune for good behavior.[6] The ordinance thus recognized the role bastards might play in vendettas or other family strategies. Male relatives, including *spurii et bastardi* of a condemned magnate, could be sued for recovery of debts.[7] The concern to associate all family members in peaceful behavior did not end with magnates, however. Florence, as many other Italian cities, adopted a statute ordering *consortes* to submit common disputes to binding arbitration (to head off more acrimonious litigation or more explosive situations).[8] Expressly included among the *consortes* were even *spurii*.[9] A statute allowing parents to request of communal officials that they detain in jail a child who led a shameful and dissolute life also included bastards.[10] All these pieces of Florentine legislation thus employed more precise terms of *ius commune* so as to preclude doubts

4. Bartolo to C. 6.38.5, *Opera omnia,* 10 vols. (Venice, 1602), vol. 8, fol. 39va and to D. 4.5.7, vol. 1, fol. 139vb. See above, chapter 1.

5. Bartolo to l. Item in potestate, De iis qui sunt sui vel alieni iuris (D. 1.6.3), *In primam ff. veteris commentaria* (Venice, 1585), fol. 24rb.

6. *Ordinamenta iustitiae communis et populi Florentiae, anni mcclxxxxiii,* ed. Francesco Bonaini [extract from *Archivio storico italiano,* new ser., 1] (Florence, n.d.), 65–66, concerning "omnes et singuli legittimi et naturales, sive naturales tantum, sive qui vulgo bastardi appellantur." See also Anna Maria Enriques, "La vendetta nella vita e nella legislazione fiorentina," *Archivio storico italiano* 91 (1933): 85–146, 181–223.

7. *Statuta populi et communis Florentiae, anno salutis mccccxv,* 3 vols. (Freiburg, 1778–83), vol. 1 (hereafter Statuta 1415), book 3, rubric 61: De pena facientis congregationem vel invitatam pro violatione status pacifici civitatis Florentie vel invitando aliquam civitatem vel locum, 1:278–81 (ASF, Statuti di Firenze 29, fol. 110r).

8. Luciano Martone, *Arbiter-Arbitrator: Forme di giustizia privata nell età del diritto comune* (Naples, 1984).

9. ASF, Statuti del comune di Firenze, 16: Statuti del podestà dell'anno 1355 [hereafter Podestà 1355], Liber II, rubric 30: Quod consanguinei et consortes habentes questionem vel controversiam teneantur ipsam commictere, fols. 81r–82r; Statuta 1415, book 2, rubric 66: De compromissis fiendis inter consortes, 1:162–64.

10. Statuta 1415, book 2, rubric 96: Qualiter coniuncti possint facere capi coniunctos male conditionis, vel vitae, 1:191–92.

and disagreements, but by virtue of being phrased in distinction to *ius commune* these statutes were also more evidently positioned to be interpreted restrictively by jurists wedded to *ius commune* as the standard of justice.

Undeniably bastards seem to have been accorded generous treatment, insofar as family membership and rights in vendetta were given them, but the peculiar context and function of this legislation argues against taking it as a general cultural statement regarding illegitimates.[11] The Ordinances of Justice dealt with "magnates," whose behavior and lifestyle were seen as socially disruptive. The ordinances' avowed purpose was to avoid fraud, for which it was necessary to treat bastards as part of the problem.[12] Indeed, they might be especially useful and "expendable" in family fights in comparison to legitimate members, or more eager to demonstrate their familial loyalty by participating, as Angelo degli Ubaldi intimated. Moreover, in the context of antimagnate legislation, the rights accorded bastards can only be seen as contributing to the political disabilities heaped upon that class. If the law did not lump bastards with their families, magnate lineages might only be encouraged to pursue access to political offices and favors through illegitimate cadet lines, which did not share political disabilities but with which kinship ties—"natural" if not legal—still existed. The statute that included *spurii* in mandatory arbitration too was crafted in the most inclusive manner possible; its precautions reveal to us how kinship was a language used to various effects in feuds and vendettas.[13]

There was a certain consistency to legislated images of Florentine bastards. Even though Florence's statutes were revised and reorganized by jurists, treatment of bastards was little changed across the differing

11. In contrast to Robert Davidsohn, *Storia di Firenze*, vol. 4: *I primordi della civiltà fiorentina*, part 3: *Il mondo della chiesa, spiritualità e arte, vita pubblica e privata*, trans. from German by Eugenio Dupré-Theseider (Florence, 1973), 697–99; Leineweber, *Die rechtliche Beziehung*, 73; and in a more careful formulation Martines, *Power and Imagination*, 239.

12. Gaetano Salvemini, *Magnati e popolani in Firenze dal 1280 al 1295* (rpt. Milan, 1966), 138–59; and the equally classic Nicola Ottokar, *Il comune di Firenze alla fine del Dugento* (rpt. Turin, 1962), 90–128; Gene A. Brucker, *Florentine Politics and Society, 1343–1378* (Princeton, N.J., 1962), 29, 35, 70; Carol Lansing, *The Florentine Magnates: Lineage and Faction in a Medieval Commune* (Princeton, N.J., 1991), 189–90. Edward Muir, *Mad Blood Stirring: Vendetta and Factions in Friuli during the Renaissance* (Baltimore, 1993) has before him an illegitimate active in a series of events.

13. Cf. Osvaldo Raggio, "La politica nella parentela: Conflitti locali e commissari in Liguria orientale (secoli xvi–xvii)," *Quaderni storici* 63 (December, 1986): 721–57.

redactions.[14] The most important index of these attitudes is inheritance, for it was the most evident disability and distinction between legitimate and illegitimate in *ius commune* and beyond. Two different rubrics consistently bore on the possibilities of inheritance by illegitimates. One, first enacted in the aftermath of the great 1348 epidemic, dealt directly with intestate inheritance by bastards. It accorded those born of concubinage or at least from two unmarried people (a generous construction of *naturales*) rights to inheritance on intestacy to one or both of their parents, but only in the absence of other possible heirs. They stood in preference, that is, only to the commune of Florence as fisc. The same statute conceded a similar preference for a wife in succession to her husband. As a wife was born to another agnatic line, the equation of her claims to the deceased with those of a natural child is indicative of how weak the claims of both were. The other categories of bastards procreated in illicit coitus were given no rights to inherit from their parents or siblings. On the other hand, those related to them by paternal or maternal line could inherit *from* them "as if these bastards had been legitimately born." Thus they had no inheritance rights to speak of themselves, but they were a source of inheritance rights for others, which they were not in civil law.[15] By this set of rules the many confused and vacant inheritances left by the plague might be settled on survivors. The Florentine lawyer Alessandro Bencivenni (1385–1423), in commenting on this statute, pointed out that allowing succession to those on the paternal side modified the intestacy rules of *ius commune.*[16]

This Florentine statute was unique in comparison to legislation from elsewhere in northern and central Italy. A number of communities were content to leave inheritance by bastards to the rules of *ius commune.* Others went farther than Florence and accorded inheritance rights to

14. On statutory law see Giorgio Chittolini and Dietmar Willoweit, eds., *Statuti città territori in Italia e Germania tra Medioevo ed età moderna,* Annali dell'Istituto Storico Italo-Germanico, Quaderno 30 (Bologna, 1991), which includes Elena Fasano Guarini, "Gli statuti delle città soggette a Firenze tra '400 e'500: riforme locali e interventi centrali," 69–124.

15. Statuta 1415, Book 2, rubric 126: De successione communis Florentiae ab intestato, et de haeredibus naturalium, et bastardorum, 1:217–18; Podestà 1355, book 2, rubric 75: Quod commune Florentiae ab intestato succedat. Quod generaliter succedant naturales et bastardi, fols. 98v–99r. The more generous definition of *naturales* as those "nati ex soluto, et soluta vel descendentes ex eis licet non intervenerit legitimus concubinatus" appeared only in the 1415 statute.

16. BNF, Principale, II, iv, 435, fol. 65r–v.

bastards, usually if there were no legitimate children.[17] Venice since 1242 gave explicit recognition to legitimation by subsequent marriage and, in that event, accorded inheritance rights.[18] Ferrara (1456) denied even *legitimati* inheritance if there were other agnates, unless the legitimation could be proven to have been at the father's initiative.[19] In contrast, Arezzo in 1327–32 allowed inheritance by illegitimates in the absence of legitimate children, limiting them to two *unciae* if there were legitimates and empowering the local Podestà to legitimate.[20] Perugia in its statutes of 1342 enacted similar rules.[21] Pistoia, subject to Florence permanently from 1351, had since 1285 allowed property to be left to illegitimates as long as there were no legitimate children. Lucca's statutes of 1539 permitted testamentary and intestate inheritance to *naturales* and alimentary rights even to incestuous and adulterine bastards. Genoa did not give bastards inheritance rights, but in the other direction it not only gave the paternal line succession to *naturales* but privileged it, "these *naturales* being endowed rather by paternal power and nourishment," while the mother's line "is often presumed to be vile and abject persons."[22] The Ligurian community of Savona, by a statute of 1345, allowed anyone without legitimate progeny to leave property to an illegitimate of either sex and whatever status.[23] Florence alone drew the line laterally out to eight degrees before allowing *naturales* to inherit.

The other Florentine rubric concerning bastards was actually about the inheritance rights of women. Florence, like so many other Italian cities, had a statute excluding dowered women from inheritance in favor of male relatives. The statute explicitly stated that the exclusion was effective in the favor of males "born of a legitimate marriage."[24] Illegiti-

17. Notably Treviso, Bologna, Verona, and Cremona, printed editions of whose statutes I have consulted, made no special inheritance provisions for illegitimates.

18. *Gli statuti veneziani di Jacopo Tiepolo del 1242 e le loro glosse,* ed. Roberto Cessi (Venice, 1938), Liber IV, rubrica xxviii, Quod filius natus ante legitimum matrimonium reputetur ut haeres sit in bonis paternis, si pater eius eam legitime acceperit in uxorem, 208.

19. *Statuta urbis Ferrariae nuper reformata anno domini mccccclvi* (Ferrara, 1476), rubrica cxlii, Quod legitimati non succedant.

20. *Statuto di Arezzo (1327),* ed. Giulia Marri Camerani (Florence, 1946), Liber III, rubric lviii, De successione naturalium et spureorum, 170.

21. *Statuti di Perugia dell'anno mccxlii,* vol. 1, ed. Giustiniano degli Azzi (Rome, 1913), Liber II, rubrica 37: Che'l pate possa lassare al figliuolo spurio de gli bien suoie, 336–38.

22. For Pistoia, Lucca, Genoa, see Franco Niccolai, *La formazione del diritto successorio negli statuti comunali del territorio lombardo-tosco* (Milan, 1940), 153–56.

23. *Statuta antiquissima Saone (1345),* vol. 2, ed. Laura Balletto (Genoa, 1971), 184.

24. Statuta 1415, book 2, rubric 130: Qualiter mulier ab intestato succedat, 1:223–25; Podestà 1355, fols. 97v–98v.

mate sons thus did not have the power to "exclude" (legitimate) sisters. Given the active role of jurists in formulating and arranging the statutes of 1355 and of 1415, this statutory language can hardly be seen as accidental. Here too Florentine law embodied a prejudice against those of illegitimate birth. It was a prejudice widely found elsewhere.[25] The Florentine statute that established such an inheritance norm, in fact, served as the starting point for legal doctrinal discussions of them—at least it did for Baldo degli Ubaldi and Bartolo da Sassoferrato as a result of their practical experience.[26] Such statutes, designed to preserve family property among male agnates, often specified that these agnates, of whatever degree of relationship, must be legitimate. The statutes did not keep legitimated sons from inheriting. The problem was whether they inherited to the exclusion of women or they inherited equally with them. These statutes raised the specter of excluding legitimately born daughters, for example, in favor of illegitimately born but later legitimated sons. It would be possible in practice to argue, as Paolo di Castro did in one case, that for the sake of legitimacy women should not be deprived.[27] Antonio Roselli used the distinction between "common" and statutory law to enunciate the maxim that "the words in a statute must be taken in a true and not a fictive sense." Roselli, however, allowed that there was more than one "true" sense to be found in statutes. Either they simply referred to legitimate children, or they more precisely referred to those legitimately born. With regard to those legitimated by later marriage, then, Roselli concluded that the statutes covered them when they spoke simply of legitimates (because they were truly legitimate) but not when the statutes spoke explicitly of time or circumstances of birth (because they were only fictively legitimate by birth).[28]

By the time Giasone da Maino approached the problem, perhaps early in the sixteenth century, he could rehearse an extensive literature.

25. Cf. Niccolai, *Formazione del diritto successorio,* 65–108; Manlio Bellomo, *Ricerche sui rapporti patrimoniali tra coniugi* (Milan, 1961), 163–85; Laurent Chevailler, "Observations sur le droit de bâtardise dans la France coutumière du xiie au xve siècles," *Revue historique de droit français et étranger,* 4th ser., 35 (1957): 376–411.

26. The discussion of Baldo to l. Gallus § et quid si tantum (D. 28.2.29,5), *Opera omnia,* vol. 3, fols. 65vb–67ra, begins with a consideration of the Florentine statute. Also Bartolo to l. ii § in videndum, Ad tertullianum (D. 38.17.2,47), *In secundam infortiati partem commentaria* (Venice, 1581), fols. 176va–vb.

27. Paolo di Castro, *cons.* 252, *Consilia* (1582), vol. 2, fols. 123vb–124ra.

28. Roselli, *Tractatus legitimationum,* fol. 80ra.

Whereas Baldo had declared that a *filius legitimatus* fit the terms of such a statute and prevented inheritance by a legitimate daughter, Giasone found that Paolo di Castro had disagreed in favor of a "more powerful reading" of the statute. He even turned Baldo against himself, noting other points in his commentaries that conceded that a *legitimatus* was only "tanquam legitimus" or only had the "imago legitimorum," or "like a man medicated for an illness" still had some scars. Giasone brought forth Baldo's likening of legitimation to alchemy, giving the *legitimatus* the *figura* but not the *substantia* of legitimacy. Still Giasone agreed that legitimated sons excluded legitimate daughters from inheritance, offering no real argumentation to that effect but only the assertion "thus twice I so advised and it was so decided."[29]

The statutory language linking legitimacy to birth was also used to interpret Florentine testators' intent (presuming that they would not want to differ from their city's laws). Antonio Strozzi (1455–1523) found that Giovanni da Imola had declared that the *communis opinio* was that the *legitimatus* excluded the *substitutus.* So he declared that Bernardo di Baldassare Brunetti, a *legitimatus,* excluded his uncle Guasparre because a "legitimated son in no way differs from a legitimate and natural son." Also, in this case Bernardo's grandfather as testator had not made the substitution explicitly conditional on lack of legitimate sons but only on the lack of sons, period. But Strozzi had been hired by Guasparre, so he argued, on the support of Bartolo, Angelo degli Ubaldi, and Alessandro Tartagni (1424–77) that where one was dealing with a testator "of honest and good life or established in worthiness" there could be no presumption "that he would want to admit to his estate bastard sons," even legitimated ones.[30] There was no reason to take the testator's failure to specify legitimacy in the substitution's condition as implying his willingness to accept less than that. He had, after all, referred to his two sons as "legitimate and natural." Since he had not instituted bastards of his own, why would he want bastards of his son? The presumption regarding the testator's intent was bolstered by reference to the statute's explicit mention of legitimate birth. The desires of a testator had to be presumed to

29. Giasone da Maino to l. Cum acutissime, C. De fideicommissis (C. 6.42.30), *In secundam codicis partem commentaria,* fols. 175vb–176ra.

30. ASF, Carte strozziane, 3d ser., 41/4, fol. 508r: "Hoc dicunt doc. quod quando testator esset honeste et bone vite vel in dignitate constitutus, non est presumptio quod voluerit admictere ad suam hereditatem filios bastardos."

conform to the statute of his city; even Bartolo had said as much (though in a different context).[31] The opposing view, then, that the *legitimatus* in no way differed in law from a *legitimus* did not hold in Florence. "And also the practicing jurists maintain this about this statute, saying that the common conclusion that a *legitimatus* excludes a *substitutus* does not take place with our statute."[32] As Strozzi hastened to point out, he was far from the only one to take a narrow view on *legitimati* and their descendants in relation to substitutions and inheritance in general. We do not know if he won the case. Still, these were clearly not issues for the classroom alone, and doctrinal positions took on immediate relevance as jurists applied them in conjunction with statutes and testaments. The general rule that substitutions applied only to those born legitimate would increasingly disadvantage bastards as such fideicommissary clauses became more widespread.

Inheritance statutes aimed to protect families as patrimony. Exclusions of dowered women and bastards from inheritance were part of this. Laurent Mayali has noted that there was not a clear definition of family at work in these exclusions. Concessions had to be made to the domestic experience of the daughter or bastard, as well as to their membership within the kin. Above all, by the end of the Middle Ages, when jurists had made clear how far they were willing to go to safeguard the property rights of daughters and bastards, their exclusion became less a matter of statutorily governed intestacy and increasingly a matter of contractual arrangement in dowries, donations, arbitrations, and testaments.[33] In that regard it is interesting that, whereas Pistoia and Arezzo had statutes allowing parents to compose testaments in favor of their bastards, Florence did not. Regarding testaments and legitimation, matters in Florence remained in the realm of *ius commune*. Florence, unlike Bergamo, did not expressly encourage legitimation when there were no legitimate heirs.[34]

---

31. Ibid., fol. 509r–v.

32. Ibid., fol. 509v: "Et hoc etiam tenent pratici super dicto statuto ad finem dicentes quod illa communis conclusio quod legiptimatus excludat substitutum non habet locum stante nostro statuto de quo supra."

33. Cf. Laurent Mayali, *Droit savant et coutumes: L'exclusion des filles dotées, xiième-xvème siècles,* Ius Commune, Sonderhefte: Studien zur Europäischen Rechtsgeschichte 33 (Frankfurt am Main: Klostermann, 1987), esp. 66–74, 85–86.

34. Niccolai, *Formazione del diritto successorio,* 153. No such law, however, graced the preplague statutes. Cf. *Lo statuto di Bergamo del 1331,* ed. Claudia Storti Storchi (Milan, 1986).

A final piece of legislation of some interest in this context demonstrates concern with parental responsibility. Any free man who impregnated another's slave had to pay the costs of birth and alimentation. He also had to compensate the owner for the "deterior conditio" of the slave following parturition, that being one-third of her value (full value if she died). The child was to have the legal status of the *father,* not the slave.[35] Presumably the father was also supposed to see to the upbringing and expenses of the child. At least twice in the fifteenth century there were statutory additions to punish those hiding slaves and helping them escape from Florentine territory.[36] Sexual motives were at work here. So too in 1459 Genoa saw passage of a law declaring that anyone who married a *serva* without her master's permission had to pay him two hundred ducats as her price.[37] As a city containing a good number of female slaves serving largely as domestic labor, Genoa had to concern itself with sexual relations with slaves and consequent effects on the slaves' market value.[38] In 1481, to counter overcrowding in its foundling homes, Genoa's legislators ordered all pregnant slaves or servants be registered and bound by oath to keep and raise their children.[39]

Florentine bastards faced diminished legal personhood and substantially reduced rights not only within the family but outside it as well. "Florence was by no means unique in this. The histories of many medieval communes betray an unpleasant though comprehensible distrust of bastardy, notably in connection with political rights and requirements for guild membership."[40] Actually membership in most Florentine guilds, at least originally, was unaffected by illegitimacy. The Arte di Calimala did not exclude bastards until 1414, when there was a general reform of guild statutes on the eve of civic statutory revision. The exclusion was, it must be admitted, as broad as possible—all those not born

35. Statuta 1415, book 3, rubric 186: De sclavis et servis et eorum materia, 1:385–87 [ASF, Statuti di Firenze 29, fols. 153r–154r]. Cf. Umberto Dorini, *Il diritto penale e la delinquenza in Firenze nel sec. xiv* (Lucca, 1923), 53.

36. Statuti 29, fols. 388r–389v (13 April 1446 and 30 December 1452).

37. Geo Pistarini, ed., *Testi per lo studio del Medio Evo in Liguria* (Genoa, n.d.), 289–90.

38. Geo Pistarini, "Tra libere e schiave a Genova nel Quattrocento," *Annuario de estudios medievales* 1 (1964): 353–74.

39. Steven A. Epstein, *Genoa and the Genoese, 958–1528* (Chapel Hill, N.C., 1996), 305.

40. Martines, *Lawyers and Statecraft,* 99.

legitimate.[41] Other guild statutes I consulted carried no such prohibition.[42] The oil merchants *(oliandoli)* in their statutes of 1414 even included bastards in rules extending liabilities among male agnates who worked in the same shop.[43] The Arte dei Giudici e Notai, on the other hand, excluded illegitimates from its ranks.[44] Exclusion of bastards from the notariate spoke powerfully of both presumptions about them and the nature of law. Much legal activity was encoded in and depended upon formally notarized documents. The notary was a certified witness and scribe.[45] His trustworthiness had to be above reproach. He had to be someone fully in the mainstream of society, or else there was no trust. Bastards, suspect in person from the situation of their generation and birth, were inherently suspect, as were Jews, who were also excluded from the notariate.[46]

A jurist such as Angelo degli Ubaldi could maintain that *spurii* could fulfill the function of *tabellionatus* (a mere recorder of events) because, though it was public service, it was a "vile" office and their *instrumenta* deserved full credence, unless they otherwise sullied their *fama*.[47] A century or so later Filippo Decio could easily agree with Angelo that the notariate was a "vile officium" and not a "dignitas" such that even a *spurius* could be a notary.[48] Of course, the safest step, especially if they

41. Arte di Calimala, 5, fol. 110v: "quod de cetero nullus qui non sit sua origine natus ex legiptimo et vero matrimonio et toro legiptimus procreatus possit suo vel alieno nomine habere, tenere, facere, vel modo aliquo exerceri aliquod officium in dicta arte sub pena librarum mille."

42. These were Medici e Speziali 5, Lana 8, Cambio 5, Vinattieri 1, Fornai 1, Albergatori 3.

43. Steven A. Epstein, *Wage Labor and Guilds in Medieval Europe* (Chapel Hill, N.C., 1991), 211–12.

44. Martines, *Lawyers and Statecraft,* 28; Santi Calleri, *L'arte dei giudici e notai di Firenze nell'età comunale e nel suo statuto del 1344* (Milan, 1966), 31.

45. Cf. Armando Petrucci, *Writers and Readers in Medieval Italy: Studies in the History of Written Culture,* ed. and trans. Charles M. Radding (New Haven, 1995), 152–57; M. T. Clanchy, *From Memory to Written Record: England 1066–1307,* 2d ed. (Oxford, 1993), 304–8.

46. Cf. Mario Montorzi, *Fides in rem publicam: Ambiguità e tecniche del diritto comune* (Naples, 1984), 90–93. Bologna had parallel provisions: see Giorgio Tamba, ed., *La società dei notai di Bologna* (Rome, 1988), 106.

47. Angelo, *cons.* 284, *Consilia,* fol. 198rb: "Et si virtutibus pollet et fama, suis instrumentis fides adhiberi debet plenarie: ut d. § spurios versi. cessantibus. Si autem fama denigrata est, aliter quam per nativitatis ortum, tunc licet instrumenta ab eo confecta subsistant, non tamen eis est fides in dubio adhibenda: sed veritas instrumentorum eius in dubium revocatur."

48. Filippo Decio to l. Si quis asserat, De mandatis principium (C. 1.15.1), *In primam et secundam codicis partem commentaria* (Venice, 1568), fol. 113ra.

sought to be more than a mere *tabellio* and gain the *dignitas* of being a *iudex ordinarius* (who also officiated at acts with legal *auctoritas*), was to be legitimated formally by imperial or papal authority. As a rule Florentine notaries were *iudices ordinarii* and thus needed legitimation to transcend the limitations of their birth status; and the guild's exclusion of bastards from its ranks was broadly consistent with the situation in *ius commune*.

The silence of most guild statutes regarding illegitimacy as a bar on membership does not necessarily mean that it did not matter. Bastards might be members but not be allowed to hold guild offices. Indeed, as we will see shortly, a law was passed making that the case for all the city's guilds. But to prohibit bastards from the guilds, while having the effect in Florence of political disenfranchisement, would be to preclude their earning a livelihood, to make them recipients of charity, or push them into criminal activities. Guilds in Ghent and some areas of Germany took a decidedly tough moral stand on illegitimacy—refusing membership to those born out of wedlock, revoking membership from those who married a bastard or known bastard-begetter, and adamantly refusing to allow any form of ecclesiastical or secular legitimation to change things. They stood for a particular view of marriage and the purity of descent that shut their trades off from not only the social groups below them but from the illegitimate sons of nobles and priests who might otherwise seek their livelihood in the company.[49]

At least twice Florentine legislation hit legitimated persons with *gabelles* that legitimate persons did not have to pay. The first occasion was in 1374, when all bastards who inherited as a result of legitimation by civic councils or by paternal testament had to pay twelve denarii on the lira (5 percent) just as any *extraneus* to whom a portion of an estate fell. The law seems to have been intent on closing some fiscal loopholes and raising revenues, but it is interesting to see where it looked.[50] It may well also have been provoked by a case in which Angelo degli Ubaldi determined that by Florentine law *naturales* born of a kept concubine were exempt from inheritance *gabelles*.[51] A second, more inclusive law passed in early 1414 (the same year the Calimala banned bastards). All

49. Knut Schulz, "Die Norm der Ehelichkeit im Zunft- und Bürgerrecht spätmittelalterlicher Städte," in Schmugge, *Illegitimität im Spätmittelalter*, 67–83; Nicholas, *Domestic Life*, 183.

50. ASF, Provvisioni registri 62, fols. 2r–v (28 March 1374).

51. Angelo degli Ubaldi, *cons.* 30, *Consilia*, fols. 18vb–19rb.

bastards, even those legitimated by whatever means, had to pay the *gabelle* on inheritance or legacy from their fathers or paternal uncles.[52] This may have been again a simple revenue-raising measure—a sort of fifteenth-century "sin tax" hitting a group who seemed to have a weaker moral, if not legal, position. However, it may also be that around that time, as a result of actions by counts palatine, there were a few Florentines who were taking advantage of legitimation and thus attracting attention.[53]

When the catasto was instituted in 1427, bastards were accorded full value as personal deductions.[54] Consequently Florentines were willing to claim and report illegitimate children in their tax declarations, and the catasto records prove to be an important source of information allowing us to identify hundreds of bastards. Here bastards were indeed accepted as family members for whom there were expenses just as for legitimate children. However, the catasto officials retained a healthy scepticism in the face of deduction claims for bastards. In January 1458, Florentines were ordered to specify which of their dependents were illegitimate. By February the catasto officials declared that deductions for illegitimates would be given only after they had satisfied themselves that it was a true deduction. Apparently the noted ingenuity of Florentines at lessening their fiscal exposure had led some to claim fictitious bastards.[55] In 1469's renewal of the catasto the administering officials stated that no deduction for an illegitimate would be allowed without their deliberation and approval by nine votes out of ten.[56] Even in 1480, when the government decreed not a true catasto but an assessment of real property, without deductions for dependents, the officials still wanted a listing of household members with the illegitimates so designated.[57]

In allowing deductions for illegitimates, those who managed Flor-

52. ASF, Provvisioni registri 102, fols. 164r–165r (22 February 1413 [1414]): "quod omnes et singuli qui non sunt nati orriginaliter et vere et ab initio de legiptimo matrimonio etiam qualitercunque legiptimati vel quocunque modo, forma, causa, vel vigore legiptimati vel legiptimi facti aut effecti hactenus vel qui fierent aut efficerentur in futurum teneantur et debeant solvere communi Florentie pro gabella contractuum."

53. In 1513 Antonio Strozzi considered a case that raised the question whether the legitimate son of a *legitimatus* was liable for gabelles. Cf. ASF, Carte strozziane, 3d ser., 41/9, fols. 3r–4v.

54. Otto Karmin, ed., *La legge del catasto fiorentino del 1427* (Florence, 1906), 27–28.

55. Elio Conti, *L'imposta diretta a Firenze nel Quattrocento (1427–1494)* (Rome, 1984), 253, and on fraud, passim.

56. Ibid., 272.

57. Ibid., 284, 286.

ence's fiscal affairs (who were also the class most active in producing bastards) recognized their familial membership, but they also retained a suspicion about them. Another Florentine fiscal instrument, the *monte delle doti,* similarly recognized family membership when it expressly allowed deposits for illegitimate girls. However, in a revealing method of accounting, deposits for bastard daughters were usually permitted to attain a value of no more than half the maximum allowed for legitimates. By a law of March 1451/52, legitimate daughters could have a matured dowry of twelve hundred florins; illegitimates could have as much as five hundred; legitimate girls from the contado and distretto four hundred; illegitimate *contadine* could not have dowries; foundlings could have a fifty-florin dowry established in their behalf by the Innocenti. In 1479 bastard girls were allowed six-hundred-florin dowries, as against twelve hundred for their legitimate sisters.[58] Over the life of the fund into the mid–sixteenth century, around four hundred illegitimate girls had deposits opened for them by their families, including less than one hundred funded at modest levels by the Innocenti.[59]

Illegitimate birth was also a consistent source of political disabilities in Florence. A law passed in 1404 specified that no one who was born illegitimate could sit in the major executive and legislative councils, as consul of any guild, or in a variety of other posts, including vicariates of the more important subject cities.[60] That on occasion some, however, managed to do so becomes clear in the face of legislation of 1428 that set a five-hundred-florin penalty on any illegitimate who accepted and exercised an office despite the disability of birth. The expressed intent of this legislation was to prevent fraud.[61] It passed by a wide margin (220 to 47 in the final council) and was followed a year later by legislation ordering the registration of ages of politically eligible males and demanding the

58. Cf. the authoritative study of the fund, Anthony Molho, *Marriage Alliance in Late Medieval Florence* (Cambridge, Mass., 1994), 52–53. ASF, Provvisioni registri 170, fols. 26v–28r (12 May 1479); Provvisioni 148, fols. 176v–177r (28 May 1457).

59. Molho, *Marriage Alliance,* 93–107.

60. ASF, Provvisioni registri 93, fols. 100r–101r (6 October 1404). The first part of the *provvisione* enunciated similar prohibitions on those who had not resided in the city and paid *prestanze.* On the legal problems created by that aspect of the law, see Julius Kirshner, "Paolo di Castro on *Cives ex Privilegio:* A Controversy over the Legal Qualifications for Public Office in Early Fifteenth-Century Florence," in *Renaissance Studies in Honor of Hans Baron,* ed. Anthony Molho and John A. Tedeschi (Dekalb, Ill., 1971), 227–64.

61. ASF, Provvisioni registri 120, fols. 3v–4v (4 February 1428). It concerned "fraudes in publicis legibus que quandoque perversa via ad nota quorundam succedunt impunitatem sibi promictentium."

names of underaged Florentines be removed from the purses from which the names of officeholders were extracted.[62] Here the intent was to avoid wasting time going through ineligible names, but the conjunction of the two laws suggests as well that some Florentines may have been eager to keep hold of some sort of office and power within the family through the use of offspring.

Other cities similarly restricted civic participation to the legitimately born. Illegitimates were notably excluded in Venice, which city also (in 1422, contemporary with Florentine legislation) sought to remove those whose mother's family did not carry patrician status.[63] The patrician fathers ultimately went to the point of registering patrician births (1506) and later even marriages (1526) in their concern to keep the civic bodies from being contaminated by illegitimacy. They were aware that Venetians considered bastards to be part of the family and were quite willing, at least in the absence of legitimate children, to use them to maintain a presence in the halls of power. Registering marriages circumvented the presumptions in *ius commune* regarding the marital status of a cohabiting couple. Whatever their actual marital status, failure to register meant sons could not hold office; and this seems a consistent stance for a patriciate that since at least 1376 had revealed itself disinclined to accept legitimation by subsequent marriage as enabling offspring for council membership and officeholding. Venetian fathers' presentation of bastard sons to the councils for approval spurred this legislative reaction.[64] Matters did not go that far in Florence, but they did get to the point that 1421 saw an unsuccessful attempt to forbid unmarried men from holding office, "the unstated assumption of this measure being that men not prepared to produce their own legitimate offspring should not be allowed to carry the weight of political responsibility."[65] Perhaps because this law would have dumped the merely unmarried into the same status as the illegitimate, it did not pass.

The Conservatori delle Leggi were created in 1428 with specific com-

62. Provvisioni—registri 120, fol. 462r–v. The underaged were not removed, in fact, if only because to be *veduto,* even if not *seduto,* still carried a degree of honor. Cf. David Herlihy, "The Rulers of Florence, 1282–1530," in Molho, Raaflaub, and Emlen, *City-States,* 197–221.

63. Cf. Stanley Chojnacki, "Marriage Legislation and Patrician Society in Fifteenth-Century Venice," in *Law, Custom, and the Social Fabric in Medieval Europe: Essays in Honor of Bryce Lyon,* ed. Bernard S. Bachrach and David Nicholas (Kalamazoo, Mich. 1990), 167.

64. Cf. Crescenzi, *Esse de Maiori Consilio,* 343–48, 354–69, 407–8, 423.

65. Molho, *Marriage Alliance,* 7.

petence over all matters of eligibility for officeholding—fiscal obligations, age, and legitimacy.[66] Establishment of a registration of birth dates settled most questions regarding ages, but there was no such registry of marriage for legitimacy. Anonymous denunciations against personal political enemies caused proceedings inquiring into legitimacy for some Florentines. Andrea Zorzi has discovered that accusations and charges of illegitimacy were especially prominent in the highly charged atmosphere of competition for office in the middle and minor guilds. Accusations were based on little or no evidence, and the Conservatori delle Leggi were able to see through many of these thinly disguised vendettas.[67] In any case, whatever the reasons and motivations, the legal prohibition against bastards holding office was not a dead letter. It was known, used, cited. Citizenship of bastards, even if recognized by fathers of distinguished parentage, was diminished and passive in the same way their family membership was diminished.

The prohibition on illegitimates in office was repeated in the Savonarolan reforms of 1495, which also extended ineligibility for office to those whose fathers or grandfathers had not been legitimately born.[68] Also, when the Signoria and advisory councils on rare occasion provided a form of legislative legitimation of bastards, they did so with clear statements as to whether the illegitimates also gained political rights. Almost without exception political rights were not granted, an exception being a Pratese, previously legitimated by rescript, who had been serving in various offices for years before a new law of 1461 removed his eligibility to his loss and shame.[69] In one instance where political rights were accorded, conflict predictably arose. In 1445 Niccolò di Dardano di Niccolò Acciaiuoli was specifically conceded an exemption from the laws of 1404 and 1428 and allowed to be extracted for office.[70] In 1498, however, Niccolò's sons faced loss of political rights on the grounds that their father had not been born legitimate (as the law of 1495 demanded).[71] After reviewing the relevant legislation and taking the advice of two jurists, Guidantonio Vespucci (143[?]–1501) and Antonio Malegonelli

66. ASF, Provvisioni registri 120, fols. 7v–11r (11 February 1428).

67. Andrea Zorzi, "I fiorentini e gli uffici pubblici nel primo Quattrocento: Concorrenza, abusi, illegalità," *Quaderni storici* 66 (December, 1987): 733–35. His work is based on records of the Giudici degli Appelli.

68. ASF, Provvisioni registri 186, fols. 140r–142r (26 November 1495).

69. ASF, Provvisioni registri 152, fols. 140r–141r (25 August 1461): "quod sibi non tantum dampnum quod parum existimat sed verecundiam affert."

70. ASF, Provvisioni registri 136, fols. 104v–105v (29 July 1445).

71. Cf. Martines, *Lawyers and Statecraft,* 99–100.

(1451–1506), the Signoria and the advisory colleges ordered the *cancellarius extractionum* to place the names of Dardano and Francesco di Niccolò in the purses.[72] Here at least the later government decided to follow on the consequences of a predecessor.

The role played by the city's governing councils in relation to political and civic dimensions of kinship is indeed interesting. The city acted to consecrate abjurations of kinship on the part of branches of a lineage seeking to avoid magnate status or consequences of the misdeeds of a kinsman. In officially registering the rejection of rights and obligations of vendetta, the government declared not that these rights and obligations were situationally or temporarily suspended but that it was "as if" the bonds of kinship never existed. The same fiction was employed, to opposite effect, when the city endorsed legitimations, seemingly grafting to an existing lineage a new (future) branch. Christiane Klapisch-Zuber likens this civic definition and redefinition of kinship to the role of the church in sacramental acts.[73]

The government, of course, could not unilaterally erect or abolish kinship; it was "consecrating" forms of social fusion or fission brought to it and justified in formulaic terms. It also provided mechanisms to care for fatherless children, like foundling homes. There was also from 1393 a civic magistracy, the Ufficiali de' Pupilli, who cared for those whose fathers had died intestate and were thus not left under the control of *tutores* or of those whose nominated *tutores* (including possibly the mother) or close paternal kin refused the burdens of guardianship.[74] The Ufficiali appointed and supervised *tutores,* investigated their handling of the resources left to the *pupilli* under their care, and excused or replaced them as needed. As only those under *patria potestas* could have *tutores,* illegitimates were not under the protection of the officials, unless they had been legitimated.[75]

72. Signori e Collegi, Deliberazioni fatti in forza d'ordinaria autorità 100, fols. 38v–39r (29 April 1498).

73. Christiane Klapisch-Zuber, "Kinship and Politics in Fourteenth-Century Florence," in *The Family in Italy from Antiquity to the Present,* ed. David I. Kertzer and Richard P. Saller (New Haven, 1991), esp. 223–28.

74. See Francesca Morandini, ed., "Statuti e ordinamenti dell' Ufficio dei pupilli et adulti nel periodo della Repubblica fiorentina (1388–1534)," *Archivio storico italiano* 113 (1955): 522–51; and my "Social Processes and Legal Processes in the Renaissance: A Florentine Inheritance Case from 1452," *Quaderni fiorentini per la storia del pensiero giuridico moderno* 23 (1994): 365–96.

75. For a rare example of *tutela* over a *legitimata,* see Notarile F 298 (1420–21), 10 February 1421/2, the daughter of Gabriele di Bartolomeo Panciatichi of Florence.

3
Honor and Illegitimacy

Florentine bastards and their parents faced the prejudices of a culture of honor in addition to those inscribed in *ius commune* and local legislation. These prejudices ran parallel, but it is also the case that the demands of honor did not merely isomorphically map those of law. Honor could be lost or redeemed independent of legal means and definitions, most apparent in vendetta. Further, even though both honor and law can be described in terms of constituent rules, in neither case can knowledge of rules be said to explain, much less describe, behavior. Rules, such as those regarding legitimacy of persons, and strategies adopted in social interactions by people or groups are not fixed things. It is easy to reify them, to forget that codes of conduct were and are not solely coercive; social actors used and use them.[1]

Honor has received extensive attention from anthropologists of Mediterranean societies.[2] Historians have begun to extend these anthropological insights to Florence and other places.[3] At its base, honor is both a reputation accorded to individuals and families by society and an intense subjective experience on the part of those who would lay claim to

1. Michael Herzfeld, *Anthropology through the Looking Glass: Critical Ethnography in the Margins of Europe,* (Cambridge, 1987), 83, 113, and 183.

2. Important are J. G. Peristiany, ed., *Honour and Shame: The Values of Mediterranean Society* (Chicago, 1966); Julian Pitt-Rivers, *The Fate of Shechem: Essays in the Anthropology of the Mediterranean* (Cambridge, 1977), esp. 71–93; Jane Schneider, "Of Vigilance and Virgins: Honor, Shame, and Access to Resources in Mediterranean Societies," *Ethnology* 10 (1971): 1–24; J. K. Campbell, *Honour, Family, and Patronage* (Oxford, 1964); Juliet du Boulay, *Portrait of a Greek Mountain Village* (Oxford, 1974); and du Boulay, "Lies, Mockery, and Family Integrity," in *Mediterranean Family Structures,* ed. J. G. Peristiany (Cambridge, 1976), 389–406.

3. Kuehn, *Emancipation,* 60–69 and the literature cited therein; Ronald F. E. Weissman, *Ritual Brotherhood in Renaissance Florence* (New York, 1982), 26–40; Kent, *Household and Lineage,* 43–117, 199–201; Julius Kirshner, *Pursuing Honor While Avoiding Sin: The "Monte delle doti" of Florence* (Milan, 1978), 2–15.

honor.[4] Those whose behavior transgresses the rules (the "code" of honor) are honorless and rightless. Bastards commonly fall into this category.[5]

As the site of social reproduction, family is the group within which personal honor (in relation to one's peers) could link with a sense of honor tied to the prerogatives of social class.[6] The wealth of the family consists of both its possessions and its people, and honor bound them all together, circulating from generation to generation in patrilineal forms, but also vitally circulated and reproduced through women.[7] Bastards arising from women not within those ideologically masked patrilineal bounds complicate or misdirect this social reproduction. Another way to look at it is that male honor is active (requiring labor, courage, cunning) and female is passive.[8] Honor thus both operates to exclude people from a group and to unify the group. Genealogies can be one expression of this process of inclusion and exclusion.[9] Blood is a social, not just a biological substance. Filiation is not only natural but legitimate, as the language of legal documents and other texts indicates. Honor yields a deep stratum of moral colorations touching the mother primarily, but also the father. The illegitimate child is not the result of a union negotiated between two honorable families, linking them in bonds of kinship; rather an illegitimate is much more likely to be a cause of enmity between families and a constant reminder to one family of its failure to maintain its honor and the shame of its women—the most forceful image of which is the cuckolded husband. If anything, then, the illegitimate falls heir not to honor but to dishonor.[10]

The inheritance of family honor was a vital element of Florentine soci-

---

4. See Pitt-Rivers, *The Fate of Shechem,* 77; du Boulay, "Lies, Mockery," 390–91, 405.

5. Frank Henderson Stewart, *Honor* (Chicago, 1994), 38–39.

6. Ibid., 59–60.

7. Jean-Marc Mariottini, "'Il corredo e lo legittima,'" in *Femmes et patrimoine dans les sociétés rurales de l'Europe méditerranéenne,* ed. G. Ravis-Giordani (Paris, 1987), 163–68; Bruno Martinelli, "Matrimoine et patrimoine: Sur les fonctions successorales des femmes dans quelques exemples provençaux," in *Femmes et patrimoine,* 75–87.

8. Julian Pitt-Rivers, "La veuve andalouse," in Ravis-Giordani, *Femmes et patrimoine,* 263.

9. Di Bella, "Name, Blood, and Miracles," 155.

10. On shame and adultery, Julio Caro Baroja, in Peristiany, *Honour and Shame,* 118. Two examples of shame brought on by female sexual misconduct can be found in Gene Brucker, ed., *The Society of Renaissance Florence: A Documentary Study* (New York, 1971), 42, 218–22.

ety. Those who begot bastards, but above all those who were bastards, brought dishonor or disgrace and met with exclusion—from the home and not just from genealogical memory. They did not conform to the image Paolo da Certaldo, a fourteenth-century compiler of proverbial wisdom, claimed to derive from Cicero:

> Tullio says that certainly he who is the legal son of the man he considers his father, and is not a bastard, loves and fears and honors and obeys his father, be he young or old or poor or rich or healthy or sick, and there always comes from him a great sense of kinship. And that it is thus stands to reason, for existence is the most noble thing; and if the father and mother were not, the son would not have been. Thus it is that you must love your father and mother and honor them rather than yourself.[11]

Bastardy, even though it too resulted in *l'essere,* was not accompanied by the call to honor and obey parents (and would one know who they were?).

For Florentines, honor attached to legitimate marriage. To marry a woman, especially with a dowry, was "condurre ad onore"—to lead her to honor.[12] It was to unite not just two individuals but two honorable families. Legitimate offspring of their blood would inherit their honor. The humanists of fifteenth-century Florence, moreover, gave precise and self-conscious expression to this marital ideology. According to Matteo Palmieri, what distinguished the natural inclination to procreate among humans, as opposed to animals, were the human powers of reason and expression. Friendship, kinship, and civic life were possible on this basis; the honorable and the useful could then be identified.[13] *Onore* and *utile* were certainly closely paired when looking at marriage.[14] Bastards fathered outside marriage and, in all likelihood, on women of lower sta-

11. Paolo da Certaldo, *Il libro di buoni costumi,* ed. Alfredo Schiaffini, in *Mercanti scrittori: Ricordi nella Firenze tra Medioevo e Rinascimento,* ed. Vittore Branca (Milan, 1986), 52.

12. Kirshner, *Pursuing Honor,* 2–15; Diane Owen Hughes, "From Brideprice to Dowry in Mediterranean Europe," *Journal of Family History* 3 (1978): 284.

13. Matteo Palmieri, *Della vita civile,* ed. Felice Battaglia (Bologna, 1944), 52.

14. Leon Battista Alberti, *I libri della famiglia,* ed. Ruggiero Romano and Alberto Tenenti (Turin, 1969), 107–8. Also cf. David Herlihy and Christiane Klapisch-Zuber, *Les toscans et leurs familles* (Paris, 1978), 543–51.

tus represented a statement about paternal status and virility and about sexual passion rather than calculated social alliance.[15]

Honor, household, progeny, and patrimony were all interrelated, and they were human and civic, not merely natural. They rested on control of sexuality. In Alberti's *Della Famiglia,* the illegitimate Battista points out that lust (nature) is a force that can overcome reason (honor). "Yet," Battista goes on, "I don't know how, but not rarely one finds a woman to whom a strange lover is more pleasant than her own husband."[16] Lionardo responds to Battista's clever arguments, using terms reminiscent of jurists who placed marriage in a chronologically developed hierarchy of "natural" laws. Reason dictates that friendship and family should overcome lust, that fathers tirelessly bend all their efforts to enriching their families.[17] Giovanni Gherardi da Prato, another fifteenth-century Tuscan moralist, warned that a man who followed "inordinate desires and unrestrained passion" [la inordinata voglia o lla isfrenata iracundia] made the queen, Reason, subject to a servant and traded enduring "fruit" for "vituperative and weak loves" [vituperosi e fragili amori].[18] Paolo da Certaldo warned men not to become enamored of women other than their wives, as all dishonors, shames, sins, expenses, and enmities derived from women.[19] One struck by inordinate love lost concern for all human values and was reduced to the level of an animal, where no honor was possible. As one popular preacher made clear to his audiences, lust made one a brute, "stained" the soul, and "made of the member of Christ the member of a woman."[20] Peasants and women, as well as bastards, were likened on occasion to animals by their social superiors.[21] To call someone a bastard, therefore, was a great insult; it

15. Jane Fair Bestor, "Bastardy and Legitimacy in the Formation of a Regional State in Italy: The Estense Succession," *Comparative Studies in Society and History* 38 (1996): 557.

16. Alberti, *I libri della famiglia,* 108.

17. Ibid., 113–15; Alberti's *De iciarchia,* in *Opere volgari,* ed. Cecil Grayson, 2 vols. (Bari, 1966), 2:198–99, 225–26. Also on *ragione,* see Christian Bec, *Les marchands écrivains: Affaires et humanisme à Florence, 1375–1434* (Paris, 1967), 323–25.

18. Giovanni Gherardi da Prato, *Il paradiso degli Alberti,* ed. Antonio Lanza, *I Novellieri italiani,* ed. Enrico Malato, vol. 10 (Rome, 1975), 52–53.

19. Da Certaldo, *Libro di buoni costumi,* 29.

20. Jacopo di Benvenuto, "Giardino di consolazione," in *Prosatori minori del Trecento: Scrittori di religione del Trecento volgarizzamenti,* ed. Giuseppe de Luca (Milan, 1954; rpt. Turin, 1977), 3:496–97.

21. Joyce E. Salisbury, *The Beast Within: Animals in the Middle Ages* (New York, 1994), 79, 96–98, 153–55.

was to call him a lout or a bumpkin, to label him as beneath honor, subhuman, no better than a "dog" or a "mule."[22] Accusations of bastardy or dubious parentage were frequent forms of insult and, in consequence, actionable in court.[23]

It was the promiscuity of women that met with moral disapproval.[24] Fornication, adultery, and *disonore* were linked conceptual opposites to honor.[25] An illegitimate child was the result, then, of a shameful act on the part of the woman casting dishonor on the men upon whom her protection was incumbent, or, in the case of poor women or slaves (frequently, in fact, the mothers of Florentine bastards), those who had no men to protect them. Palmieri put everything in place in discussing adultery in his work on *vita civile* (civic life):

> The greatest and principal guardian must be the wife, and not only about getting involved with another man, but avoiding all suspicion of such sad wickedness. This mistake is the great shame to reputation [*onestà*]; it takes away honor, disjoins the marital union, brings in uncertainty about the children, makes families infamous and hateful and divided among themselves, and dissolves every tie. Nor does she deserve any longer to be called a married lady but a corrupt woman, and worthy of public disdain. Yet the husband should not be so light in taking his seed elsewhere, nor spill it in some woman so that he lose his dignity and bring infamy to the children not born legitimate.[26]

Adultery threatened family substance and both domestic and social order. If the bloodline was disturbed by adultery, its virtue was compromised in transmission. Fornication could mix a "good" blood with a

22. Jacob Black-Michaud, *Cohesive Force: Feud in the Mediterranean and the Middle East* (New York, 1975), 233 n. 12. Franco Sacchetti, *Il trecentonovelle,* ed. Antonio Lanza (Florence, 1984), Nov. 143, 319–21, crafts a tale around the theme how "per essere affigurato d'essere mulo, si scornò in forma, che sempre fu nimico di chi gli lo disse."

23. Daniel R. Lesnick, "Insults and Threats in Medieval Todi," *Journal of Medieval History* 17 (1991): 71–89; Martin Ingram, *Church Courts, Sex, and Marriage in England, 1570–1640* (Cambridge, 1987), 292–319.

24. Iris Origo, "The Domestic Enemy: The Eastern Slaves in Tuscany in the Fourteenth and Fifteenth Centuries," *Speculum* 30 (1955): 343–44; Herlihy and Klapisch-Zuber, *Les toscans,* 559, mention a story presented by Giovanni Dominici of a woman who refashioned the features of the offspring of an adulterous liaison to deceive her husband.

25. Kirshner, *Pursuing Honor,* 10–11.

26. Palmieri, *Della vita civile,* 133–34.

"bad" or simply confuse relationships.[27] The illegitimate, morally "stained" in conception, could thus be presumed to be morally corrupt. Important and interesting is the jurist Angelo degli Ubaldi's description of the liaisons that produced bastards and that dictated, therefore, that they stood outside fundamental kin relationships.

> It is established that those we call bastards are not blood relatives, because they are vulgarly conceived, either from those serving maids who daily traverse through cities and villages, or from those vile women whom we call domestics, to both of whom very much so, although not publicly and openly, access may be had easily and in secret, as we see them daily and touch them. Therefore those born of such women, access to whom is had by various men, are properly what we call commonly *begotten* . . . in that they cannot point to a certain father because of the variety of men who had the capacity of mingling with these women.[28]

Such was the stereotype of the mothers of bastards and their relationships. These liaisons took place in the shadows, whereas legitimate marriage was at the center of peaceful and productive relations.[29] Who

27. Daniel E. Bornstein, in his excellent study *The Bianchi of 1399: Popular Devotion in Late Medieval Italy* (Ithaca, N.Y., 1993), 199–200, gives an example of a warning against false priests and false sacraments that would mean there was concubinage where it was thought there was a marriage and, in consequence, bastards would seek the inheritance.

28. Angelo degli Ubaldi, *cons.* 191, *Consilia,* fol. 125ra: "Constat autem illos, quos bastardos appellamus, non fore consanguineos: quoniam sunt vulgo concepti, vel ex fantellis illis, que quotidie per civitates, et vicos discurrunt: vel ex illis mulieribus vilibus, quas casalingas appellamus: ad quas forte, licet non publice, neque palam, cum de facili saltem et in occulto habeatur accessus, ut videmus quotidie et palpamus, nati ergo ex talibus mulieribus, ad quas per diversos habetur accessus, sunt proprie illi, quos appellamus vulgo quesitos: ff. de sta. ho. l. vulgo. [D. 1.5.23] eo quod patrem certum demonstrare non possunt, propter diversitatem virorum, qui cum talibus mulieribus habuerunt potestatem commiscendi."

29. As Palmieri: "Dopo i figliuoli si stimano e debbono essere utili i nipoti e qualunque altro nato di nostro sangue: comprendesi in questi prima tutta la casa, e poi multiplicati e non attamente in una medesima casa ricevuti, si diffundono le schiatte, le consorterie e copiose famiglie, le quali, dando e ricevendo legitime nozze, con parentadi e amore, compreendono buona parte della città, onde per parentela coniuncti caritativamente si subvengono e fra loro medesimi conferiscono consigli, favori et aiuti, i quali nella vita recano attitudini, commodità e abondanti frutti" (*Della vita civile,* 136).

would want to marry a bastard girl, heir to the dishonor and "virtue" of her mother?[30]

Concubinage met with disapproval in Florence. The *capitoli* of the Misericordia, which cared for abandoned children, in 1490 and 1501 forbade *publici concubinarii* from becoming members of the *compagnia* (usurers, sodomites, blasphemers, and gamblers were also forbidden).[31] People knew the difference between a wife and a concubine and took steps to clarify which situation they—and their children, as a result—were in.[32] At least in 1480, for example, Mariano di Piero di Mariano, who with his brother had gone bankrupt and fled to Casentino to escape creditors, admitted to Florentine catasto officials that his two children were illegitimate and that Angnola was his concubine.[33] That same year the elderly Antonio di Domenico di Bonafe said his three young children were not the progeny of his fifty-year-old wife but "sono nati di ququbina [*sic*]." Belfredello di Niccolò dello Strinato Alfieri, however, may have confused matters when he termed his donna Maria "a foreigner who is in my house with me" [foristiera la quale è in chasa meco mia], mother of his two *naturali*.[34]

The implications for familial and personal honor of illicit sex and illegitimate birth are perhaps best seen in the moralizing novelle of writers like Giovanni Boccaccio, Franco Sacchetti, and Giovanni Sercambi of Lucca. In a number of novelle Sercambi, for example, clearly links illicit sex with dishonor. Having fallen for a roguish member of the powerful Panciatichi family, Antonia Virgiliesi eagerly accepted a feigned "marriage" ceremony and his amorous advances. When later she sued before the bishop to have the "marriage" declared valid, the young scoundrel, having long since lost interest in her, declared that he had never intended to marry her and had simply "used her like any whore." All the Virgiliesi were thus dishonored by her; and Antonia "in her shame left the court and never again had honor."[35] Sacchetti reversed this theme for comic

30. Cf. Julius Kirshner and Anthony Molho, "The Dowry Fund and the Marriage Market in Early Quattrocento Florence," *Journal of Modern History* 50 (1978): 425–26 and n. 44.

31. *Documenti inediti o poco noti per la storia della Misericordia di Firenze (1240–1525)* (Florence, 1940), 63, 94.

32. Ruggiero, *The Boundaries of Eros,* 30; Tamassia, *La famiglia italiana,* 222.

33. Catasto 1022, fol. 99r.

34. For these examples, Catasto 818, fols. 1053v–1055^{bis}r; Catasto 825, fols. 113v–114v.

35. Giovanni Sercambi, *Novelle,* ed. Giovanni Sinicropi (Bari, 1972), novella 30. See also my "Reading Microhistory: The Example of *Giovanni and Lusanna,*" *Journal of Modern History* 61 (1989): 512–34.

effect in a tale in which a wife reproves her husband for sexual adventures with whores during her illness. He counters that she had previously had her own sexual adventures; but she replies that she had done it "for the good of the house with our laborer" to make him loyal and honest, whereas her husband's actions had only been "in danno della casa."[36]

When sexual misadventures resulted in procreation of a child, it was naturally much harder to keep an affair from becoming public knowledge. Tales in which outraged men kill, or threaten to kill, deflowered daughters or faithless wives alternate with tales in which abortion is attempted or birth kept secret, with the child sent quietly away to be raised.[37] Fornicating priests complicate the world of the novelle, as they "are not shamed to have filled sacred places with concubines and the children born of such dissolute *luxuria.*"[38] The consequences of illegitimate birth from adultery were seen as particularly disturbing. If the husband never learned of the affair, he was seen as the worst of cuckolds, simple and foolish, unwittingly raising another's child.[39] If the husband found out, however, his revenge fell on the child as well as the wife. In one tale of Sercambi, a man who catches his wife in the act kills their four children (all in fact legitimate, according to the author) because he can no longer trust their descent.[40] Sercambi also wrote a variant of the "child of snow" tale, in which a man sells into slavery the love child of his wife, conceived and born while he was away on business, so obviously illegitimate.[41] Again Sacchetti reversed this sense to comic effect in a brief tale in which Pope Boniface VIII confronts the octogenarian *cavaliere* Rossellino della Tosa of Florence. Boniface is amazed at the almost daily revelation that della Tosa has had another child. But the Florentine simply reveals that he claims whatever is born where "the ram" has roamed and he does not care beyond that. Sacchetti concludes by noting that there are those who will admit they cannot prove paternity of their children, or heirs who cannot prove descent from the deceased, but della Tosa made things certain.[42]

36. Sacchetti, *Il trecentonovelle,* 237–39.

37. Ibid., novella 60; Boccaccio, *Decamerone,* ed. Vittorio Branca (Turin, 1980), novella V, 7.

38. Sacchetti, *Il trecentonovelle,* 58–59.

39. *Decameron,* III, 8; Sercambi, *Novelle,* novella 149.

40. Sercambi, *Novelle,* novella 83.

41. Sercambi, novella 127. On the "snow baby" tale, see also Robert Hellman and Richard O'Gorman, *Fabliaux* (New York, 1965), 17–21 and the literature cited 20–21.

42. Sacchetti, *Il trecentonovelle,* 280–81.

The relationship between honor and social position was nicely spelled out by the Venetian patrician Francesco Barbaro, whose *De re uxoria* of 1416 was addressed to the Florentine Lorenzo de' Medici:

> It is certain that legitimate marriage is appropriate in order to have children born in an honorable estate, important for educating them and best for eventually making them useful citizens, for whom a great city will be more valued in justice to its friends and more terrifying in military valor to its enemies. For that great teacher experience has established well the fact that those who are conceived illegitimately in uncontrolled love-making often turn out to be inferior and infamous and are much more prone to immorality. The light of paternal glory does not permit the well-born to be mediocre; they understand that the image of their parents is more of a burden than an honor unless they prove themselves by their own virtue worthy of the dignity and greatness of their ancestors.[43]

By implication, those who were truly "mediocre" had little or nothing to prove. One anthropologist found that twentieth-century Tuscan sharecroppers had less concern about fornication and illegitimacy than villagers, who looked to dowry size and household skills.[44] The illegitimate represented a labor resource rather than an inheritance claim. On a larger, less overtly functional level, families with an undoubtedly prestigious name and social rank could withstand a degree of scandal. A woman of undeniable aristocracy might even transgress sexual rules with impunity.[45] For most people in the middle social ranks, it was the vital combination of male and female honor that was needed and worked in a dynamic tension. "It is therefore an error to regard honor as a single constant concept rather than a conceptual field within which people find the means to express their self-esteem or their esteem for others."[46]

---

43. Francesco Barbaro, *De re uxoria,* ed. A. Gnesotto, *Atti e memorie della R. Accademia di scienze, lettere ed arte di Padova,* n.s. 32 (1915): 6–105. Translation here is from Benjamin G. Kohl and Allison Andrews Smith, eds., *Major Problems in the History of the Italian Renaissance* (Lexington, Mass., 1995), 277–78.

44. Sydel Silverman, "The Life Crisis as a Clue to Social Function: The Case of Italy," in *Toward an Anthropology of Women,* ed. Rayna R. Reiter (New York, 1975), esp. 317–20. Tommaso Astarita, *Village Justice: Community, Family, and Popular Culture in Early Modern Italy* (Baltimore, 1999), 193, found a similar situation in an eighteenth-century Calabrian village.

45. Di Bella, "Name, Blood, and Miracles," 156.

46. Peristiany and Pitt-Rivers, *Honor and Grace,* 4.

Illegitimacy might shame one group but be a form of boasting for another. Lauro Martines has pointed to the existence of bastards among the elite as a flaunting of social and moral conventions that paradoxically was a claim to honor of such magnitude that the usual norms did not apply. The truly powerful had a social strategy that turned on the point of honor, leading to vendettas at times, in which bastards were included, "which even allows them to erase, if necessary, the stigma of their bastardy."[47]

Only the extraordinary sacrality of the king of France could permit elevation of royal bastards ahead of more distant but legitimate kin, and even then not without at least covert protest.[48] Only the power and connections of the Este of Ferrara could accomplish the legitimation of a succession of bastards as heirs not just to property but to political office and the ducal title.[49] No fifteenth-century Florentine family could claim such charisma. In patrician families bastards were highly unlikely to acquire the true substance of the family's social position. They would gain enough to place themselves socially, however, and possibly better off than the average. Hence the understandable fear of illegitimacy by the middle and lower social orders, who had reason to be worried about the social and economic competition of bastards above.[50]

Abandonment of bastards to a foundling hospital was the extreme expression of embarrassment and concern for honor, the mother's family's or the father's, while the leaving of some sign of recognition with the abandoned child indicated hope for later recovery of the child, thus denying the reality of abandonment.[51] It did nothing for the child's honor, especially in contrast to those children who were not abandoned. Because abandonment protected family honor, the extended kin were not a likely reservoir for bastards and may even have pressed for abandonment.[52] It seems justified to conclude that many families kept bastards only reluctantly; that they saw bastards as another set of claims on limited resources.[53]

47. Di Bella, "Name, Blood, and Miracles," 164.

48. See Emmanual LeRoy Ladurie, "The Court Surrounds the King: Louis XIV, the Palatine Princess, and Saint-Simon," in Peristiany and Pitt-Rivers, *Honor and Grace,* 51–78.

49. Bestor, "Bastardy and Legitimacy."

50. Cf. Willoweit, "Von der natürlichen Kindschaft," 64–65.

51. Kertzer, *Sacrificed for Honor,* 28, 113.

52. Ibid., 180–81.

53. De la Roncière, "Portraits," 2:161, 260.

Florentines revealed their embarrassment at the presence of illegitimates in less dramatic ways. To cite one example, Guido Baldovinetti related in his *ricordanze* how he helped his friend Jacopo di Pagolo Niccolini quickly put a bastard infant to baptism and to nurse, to avoid scandal ("per fuggire loro i schandoli").[54] Another, more celebrated *ricordanza,* that of Giovanni di Pagolo Morelli (himself father of a bastard), recorded his reluctance to name illegitimate relations because they were not honorable ("perchè non è onesto si fatta ischiatta"), even when the mother had come from a good family.[55] Christiane Klapisch-Zuber takes Morelli's interruption of genealogical continuity as the occasion to remark that

> illegitimacy at Florence certainly would merit an extended study; at least the genealogists who do not systematically ignore the bastards of their blood show that this stain, in its turn rendering an honorable marriage problematic, is hardly compatible with the perpetuation of the lineage or the foundation of an independent line. For the rest, disapproval strikes the bastard himself less than the progeny issued from him; hence they are neglected if they exist.[56]

Elsewhere in his *Ricordi,* in fact, Morelli made clear how damaging was the stain of illegitimacy. He advised his sons to choose wives of good *parenti:* "Let them be of an old family in your city, let them be honored by the Commune and be Guelfs, and let them not have any stain, as being descended of a traitor or thief or murderer or bastard, or of any other thing that is cause for rebuke or shame."[57] An illegitimate line of descent was as bad as having a murderer, thief, or traitor in the family.

The *ricordanza* projected the lineage as a community in time. Reference to illegitimacy in such writings validated a sense of family by shar-

54. ASF, Acquisti e Doni 190, insert 3, fol. 28v.

55. Giovanni Morelli, *Ricordi,* ed. Vittore Branca (Florence, 1956), 162–63. The mothers were a slave and "una donna assai da bene." The children were said to be "di buona condizione assai, secondo loro essere." He, in fact, named the three boys, but not the two girls, just a few paragraphs later (164–65). He had no qualms earlier naming Morello's bastard daughter, Cietta (137).

56. Christiane Klapisch-Zuber, "Les généalogies florentines du xive et du xve siècle," in *Le modèle familiale européen: Normes, déviances, contrôle du pouvoir* (Rome, 1986), 121–22.

57. Morelli, *Ricordi,* 208–9: "Sieno antichi nella città tua, sieno onorati dal Comune e sieno Guelfi, e non abbino alcuna macula, come di traditore o di ladro o di micidio o di bastardo discesi, o d'altri cose che sono di rimprovero o di vergogna."

ing its secrets, but also exposed its shame if examined too closely. Dishonorable acts or bad fortune, such as bastardy, could lead Florentines to slight the memory of a branch of the lineage. Morelli, in fact, was more forthcoming than other Florentines who, says Klapisch-Zuber, probably covered over bastardy with simple remarks to the effect that there were no legitimate descendants.[58] On the other hand, Florentines were anything but reticent at moments. So, for one example, although the sons of Giovanni di Francesco Spina did not live with their bastard brother Vangelista, we know he resided with their maternal grandmother because they saw fit to try to claim him as a deduction in the 1458 catasto.[59]

Indeed, the catasto is another interesting source for Florentines' attitudes about bastards. There one finds others who shared Morelli's reluctance to name a bastard.[60] Some tried perhaps to excuse the presence of an illegitimate in their midst by calling it a "love child" *(figliuolo d'amore)*. This designation pointed to the irrational state that had overcome the father. That it somehow pointed to an emotional relationship seems clear when one finds it used in connection with premarital sex and extramarital affairs.[61]

Perhaps most indicative of embarrassment from bastards, however, is the total failure of many Florentines to be honest about the birth status of their offspring, or of themselves. To discover such bastards obviously requires turning up more than one reference to them, which is not easy. We can begin a few examples with one of the most evident, that of Salvadore di Niccolò da Uzzano, illegitimate and only son of one of Florence's wealthiest and most powerful citizens in the first third of the fifteenth century. In his catasto declaration Niccolò failed to say his son was either illegitimate by birth or legitimated (in 1419). On the other hand, Niccolò carefully noted that his deceased brother's daughter was illegitimate.[62] Another powerful and wealthy contemporary, Luca di Maso degli Albizzi, did not designate his son Masetto illegitimate,

58. Klapisch-Zuber, "Les généalogies florentine," 121.

59. Catasto 798, fols. 117r–121r.

60. Giovanni di Barduccio Cherichini admitted he had given a *podere* to his nine-year-old illegitimate son "e per meno male non dicho il nome" (Catasto 64, fol. 83v).

61. One child "d'amore" might have been by a slave, that of Carlo di Marco Strozzi (Catasto 76, fol. 406r). Other examples from 1427 are Catasto 65, fol. 403r; Catasto 69, fol. 325v and 539r; Catasto 73, fol. 4v; Catasto 76, fols. 310v and 374v; Catasto 79, fols. 411v and 490v.

62. Catasto 64, fol. 83v. The legitimation is in Notarile 9039 (1417–21), fols. 190r–194v (10 April 1419).

although his age and order of appearance in the catasto declaration gave away his status tacitly.[63] Rosso del Boneca de' Rossi gave no indication in his catasto report that any of his household were not legitimate. But not only did he list two children under one year of age, seven months apart, with a fifty-year-old wife, but we know he legitimated his three eldest sons.[64] Likewise Neri di Giovanni Corsini failed to call Sandro illegitimate, when other Corsini knew him to be a "bastardo."[65] Others were even less eager to associate themselves with their bastards. Bartolomeo di Verano Peruzzi, with three legitimate children including a young son at home, placed his adulterine bastard in a female cousin's home.[66] More harsh was Pagolo di Zanobi da Diacceto, who said of his six-year-old "he will not return at present and he does not want to be in my house for good reason" [no torna al presente e no vole in chasa mia per buona chagione].[67]

Of course prejudices against bastards could surface most plainly when one was involved in some sort of crime that only seemed to confirm suspicions. Lorenzotto Soderini was condemned and executed by the Podestà of Florence for forgery and other crimes. He was a bastard brought to Florence and raised as part of his father's *casa,* but always in a lesser standing to his legitimate half-brother Francesco. Lorenzotto was eventually legitimated by the Signoria in 1390 but cut out of his father's will in 1400.[68] His mother lived in Avignon, and, according to the court records, he confided to her his anger at what his father, one of Florence's wealthiest citizens, planned to leave him. He hoped to find a way to keep from being effectively disinherited. So he had a marriage contract carefully forged that said his mother had been married to Thome. Not content with that, Lorenzotto also had drawn up a charter of emancipation and legitimation in Avignon. Despite the refusal of some Florentine lawyers to take his case, following his father's death, he returned with the

63. Catasto 80, fol. 52v. Masetto had an ecclesiastical career and was a Florentine canon. That he was illegitimate is confirmed by Michael Mallett, *The Florentine Galleys in the Fifteenth Century* (Oxford, 1967), 198. Because he was not directly labeled illegitimate, his status was not picked up by Herlihy and Klapisch-Zuber, *Les toscans.*

64. Catasto 65, fol. 237v; Notarile 9040 (1422–29), fol. 301r (28 June 1427).

65. Compare Catasto 66, fol. 350r–v, and *Il libro di ricordanze dei Corsini,* ed. Armando Petrucci (Rome, 1965), 129.

66. Catasto 72, fol. 58v.

67. Ibid., fol. 196v. Pagolo had an infant son and young wife.

68. Paula C. Clarke, *The Soderini and the Medici: Power and Patronage in Fifteenth-Century Florence* (Oxford, 1991), 16. Record of the legitimation is in ASF, Manoscritti 433, p7.

forged marriage charter and a bull obtained in Avignon. He did not win a judgment, but he kept petitioning various courts, because "he was bound by diabolical chains to this evil plan and crazed foolishness." He was also actively and effectively opposed by Niccolò da Uzzano, paradoxically father of a bastard of his own, who was guardian for the legitimate Soderini children.[69] The court that condemned Lorenzotto termed his actions harmful to his father's memory and deleterious and infamous for his legitimate children "against law and justice and all humanity."

The larger irony is that Lorenzotto was legitimately married and had two sons. Even though his widow had to sell their small house to Francesco Soderini and return to live with her kin, it would be Lorenzotto's sons, Niccolò and Tommaso, who would become the most prominent, wealthy, and successful Soderini in the course of the fifteenth century, mainly from political allegiance with the Medici.[70] Ultimately Tommaso would acquire their grandfather's house and thus, in defiance of their aloof collaterals, seem the true descendant of Soderini fortunes in Florence.[71] To many Florentines the marginal judgment of the bastard at the outset of the court record, that he was a man capable of falsehood, of bad condition, opinion, life, and reputation, may have been an understatement.[72] When, against expectations, a bastard turned out to be of "good" character and morals, Florentines felt themselves compelled to note that extraordinary fact.[73] Otherwise it was in the nature of things for illegitimates to be disruptive of the proper, legitimate order of things.[74]

The Soderini case was a celebrated incident that arose within the range of criminal proceedings. On a more mundane level was the civil case that arose around the middle of the fifteenth century and drew the attention of four Florentine jurists: Otto Niccolini (1410–1470), Salustio

69. Clarke, *Soderini and Medici,* 17.

70. Clarke, *Soderini and Medici,* 17–18. Tommaso would himself have two bastards by slave women and would not give them treatment equal with the legitimate children from what Clarke calls his "traditional" sense of family (128–29). Niccolò had a bastard before his marriage and treated him with affection, finding him a good church position and later establishing him in a successful legal career (129).

71. Clarke, *Soderini and Medici,* 131.

72. ASF, Podestà 4038, fols. 57r–62r (27 and 28 August 1405). A partial translation can be found in Brucker, *Society of Renaissance Florence,* 162–66.

73. Klapisch-Zuber, "Les généalogies florentines," 121 n. 69.

74. Cf. Roger Sablonier, "The Aragonese Royal Family around 1300," in *Interest and Emotion: Essays on the Study of Family and Kinship,* ed. Hans Medick and David Warren Sabean (Cambridge, 1984), 210–39.

Buonguglielmi (1373–1461), Tommaso Salvetti (1390–1472), and Zanobi Guasconi (1397–1464), acting at the behest of one party. Their *consilium* concerned a bastard's claim to be legitimate in fact and, as a consequence, his father's heir.[75] The father, Damiano d'Antonio di Santi, resident in Siena, left his property by testament of 1424 to two brothers, although by 1447 it had fallen by arbitration to a third brother, Baldassare, who lived in Florence. Damiano had an illegitimate son Niccolò, offspring of an adulterous liaison with a *monna* Tessa, wife of maestro Nigio Alfani, "although the marriage had not been consummated" [non tamen matrimonio consumato]. Slandered by his uncle Cosimo, who called him a bastard, Niccolò brought suit in the court of the Podestà of Florence alleging, with some sort of proof, that he was legitimate and that Cosimo should cease defaming him. When, following a summons, no one came forth to contest Niccolò's claim, the Podestà issued a judgment in contumacy that legitimacy had not been disproved and the defamation of Niccolò's reputation should stop.[76] Niccolò then sued for his share of his father's property. Baldassare—ironically himself also father of an illegitimate girl[77]—countered with two arguments. The first was that the Podestà's judgment was invalid because matters of matrimonial status belonged to ecclesiastical and not secular courts. The second was that, even if the judgment in contumacy stood, it should not affect him because he had not been specifically cited to appear in court; and he was obviously an interested party who should have been summoned.

Niccolini found more than enough support in Bartolo da Sassoferrato, Baldo degli Ubaldi, and Antonio da Butrio for the assertion that a secular judge was not competent to determine legitimacy. Even if the Podestà's ruling held, it was not clear that it affected others. Legitimacy was a public matter to be treated analogously to personal freedom, where it was not fitting that one be considered free in relation to some people and slave to others. He also hastened to second Baldassare's allegation

75. BNF, Magliabechiano xxix, 193, fols. 34r–40v. This is, in fact, one of three original *consilia* in the same manuscript dealing with inheritance problems in this family. I have now discussed all three as a group in my "Vicissitudini di un patrimonio fiorentino del xv secolo," *Quaderni storici* 88 (April 1995): 43–61.

76. On defamation using the term *bastard,* see R. H. Helmholz, *Roman Canon Law in Reformation England* (Cambridge, 1990), 63. Generally on the subject see Francesco Migliorino, *Fama e infamia: Problemi della società medievale nel pensiero giuridico nei secoli xii e xiii* (Catania, 1985).

77. This according to his 1427 catasto, Catasto 79, fols. 159v–160v.

that he should have been specifically called to court, so that even if the Podestà's sentence could affect everyone it could not prejudice his interests, which were directly involved. Finally he added a thinly disguised moral accusation:

> I might also touch upon another item, namely that there may have been some collusion, which for the sake of respectability I will not bring up, because the aforesaid [arguments] are so clear that deservedly it seems that justice overflows for the party seeking *consilium* from me.[78]

Buonguglielmi next argued that the judgment against Cosimo could not touch Baldassare, as the inheritance rights had been ceded to him before the defamation case ever arose. Buonguglielmi also pointed out, as had Niccolini, that the sentence against Cosimo had been rendered in contumacy because of his nonappearance, but a firm principle of law held that a decision in contumacy, because it was not a real judgment on the facts of a case, could not harm others. Tommaso Salvetti agreed that even a valid judgment of legitimacy could not affect those "whose interest is primary and must specifically be summoned lest harm be done to legitimate persons without them knowing."[79]

Niccolò seems to have lost his case. Whatever else was alleged by Baldassare's side, the Podestà's judgment was not valid and Niccolò's birth status had never been tested in court. Certain presumptions of legitimacy could favor Niccolò if he were able to demonstrate certain things about how his parents treated and talked about him and each other.[80] That he was not named as heir in his father's testament was telling evidence against him. The jurists had protected family property from a bastard, giving legal form to the prejudices against bastards within the law and without.

---

78. Magliabechiano xxix, 193, fol. 36v: "Possem et attingere articulum unum, videlicet quod fuerit quodammodo collusum quod gratia honestatis non attingo, quia predicta sunt adeo clara quod ex eis merito patet pro parte querenti consilium a me superabundare iustitiam."

79. Magliabechiano xxix, 193, fol. 40r: "ne legitimis quorum principaliter interest et debuerunt in spetie vocari fiat preiudicium ipsis ignorantibus."

80. ASF, Carte strozziane, 3d ser., 41/9, fols. 306r–307v, contains an *allegatio* in Antonio Strozzi's hand on a case arising before the Podestà of Pisa in 1515 in which filiation was at issue. Among the arguments he raised were "quando pater tractat aliquem ut filium constituitur ille in quasi possessione filiationis, que operatur ut presumatur filius nisi contrarium probetur," and being named heir was a good example. Simply being called *filius* by one's *pater* before others also created a useful presumption.

PART TWO

Lives

4
The Social Place of Florentine Illegitimates

Perhaps the most extensive surviving critical description of a Florentine bastard is that of Rinieri di Luigi Guicciardini penned by his famous cousin Francesco, who is best known to posterity as a statesman and historian but who was also a practicing attorney well versed in the legal prejudices against bastards. In his family *ricordi* Francesco recalled the character of his ancestor messer Luigi in tones that evoked a sense of scandal: "He was a most randy fellow toward the ladies, even as an old man, and he would be inclined to play around with his servants and to joke around even in the streets with any evil woman he might meet, without any respect for either his age or his dignity."[1] Luigi's only son was the bastard, Rinieri, fathered on a slave girl during a sojourn in Pisa. Luigi had his son made a priest and, by rescript and during a term on the board of Florence's university, enabled him to become a doctor of canon law.[2] Francesco Guicciardini did not hide his dislike for Rinieri, who, though he had been sent to Pavia and Pisa to study, wasted his time at various amusements and gained little from his studies.[3] More to the point, Rinieri's acquisition in 1502 of the bishopric of Cortona cost over four thousand florins—far too much for a post that returned little more than three hundred a year. Francesco ended his discussion of Rinieri with negative assessments of his character and circumstances: "His habits were evil, because he was much too dedicated to luxury, especially with boys." Then, in a rather perverse argument, Francesco claimed that Rinieri's prosperity was the result of his bastardy: "Because he was a bastard and

1. Francesco Guicciardini, *Ricordi, diari, memorie,* ed. Mario Spinella (Rome, 1981), 55: "Fu libidinosissimo *etiam* vecchio circa le femine, e sarebbesi posto a scherzare colle sue fante, ed a motteggiare *etiam* per la via con qualche vile donna avessi riscontro, sanza rispetto alcuno o della età o della degnità sua."

2. Cf. Jonathan Davies, *Florence and Its University during the Early Renaissance* (Leiden, 1998), 102–3.

3. Guicciardini, *Ricordi,* 70.

did not have education or virtue, he pursued such benefices and dignities that before the episcopacy he had an income of more than one thousand ducats; and all were given him not by his industry and hard work but by the effort and authority of his father Luigi." Finally Francesco unleashed a vicious judgment from the perspective of a legitimate scion of the lineage.

> Concerning spending he was liberal and magnificent in clothing, in holding a good and honorable court, in entertaining often and well, but avaricious in distributing his income in works of charity; thus in all that which could become useful and beneficial to his kin, with whom he always wanted to be closely involved, he was never useful, neither in life nor in death.[4]

In Rinieri's success and Francesco's dyspeptic resentment we see perhaps most clearly the sorts of ambiguities bastards embodied in society, in its families. Continual seething tensions and occasional overt conflict could mark the life of any family; they were not incompatible with positive senses of belonging and interaction, although positive moments may have been fewer with illegitimates. If it is true that both the "language of property" and the "language of sentiment" mediate relationships within families, then the relations circulating around bastard children seem to heighten and intensify both languages.[5]

Institutionalized Abandonment

Undeniably the simplest and most direct way to minimize tensions and ambiguities clustering around a bastard was to abandon him or her at birth or soon thereafter, if not to kill the child outright. Infanticide and abandonment were extreme steps but, if not detected, effective. Infanti-

4. Ibid., 71–73: "perché essendo bastardo e non avendo lettere o virtù, conseguitò tanti benefici e tanti degnità, che innanzi al vescovado aveva di entrata più di mille ducati; e tutti gli furono dati non per industria e fatica sua, ma per opera ed autorità di messer Luigi suo padre"; and "Circa allo spendere fu liberale, e magnifico in vestire, in tenere buona ed onorevole corte, in convitare spesso e bene, ma avaro nel distribuire le sue entrate secondo le opere della pietà, cosí in tutto quello che tornassi utile e beneficio a' parenti, co' quali volle sempre vedere le cose minutamente, in modo che né in vita né in morte non giovò mai loro."

5. Cf. Hans Medick and David Warren Sabean, "Interest and Emotion in Family and Kinship Studies: A Critique of Social History and Anthropology," in Medick and Sabean, *Interest and Emotion,* 10–13.

cide and abortion, however, were consistently condemned and prosecuted. Samuel Cohn has observed that infanticide cases prosecuted in the Florentine countryside generally involved "adulterous, often incestuous" relationships, suggesting that these relationships were too shameful. He goes on to argue that infanticide (especially to the disadvantage of females) should be viewed as rational family planning.[6] Whatever else it was, it was a much rarer alternative to abandonment. Abandonment was not condemned.[7] As John Boswell remarked, "no one urged that children had an essential right to a place in the family into which they were born."[8] The church formulated rules not to prevent the practice but to regulate it.[9] To observe that abandonment was not prosecuted criminally does not mean that it was not generally decried as a rejection of duty and blood relationship. The secrecy surrounding abandonment yields a historical silence that, nonetheless, speaks volumes.[10]

Provision of an alternative to infanticide was one of the expressed reasons for the founding of the Innocenti in the fifteenth century.[11] The Ospedale degli Innocenti was directed to aid "those whose fathers and mothers, against nature's laws, are deserters, namely the little ones who in vulgar speech are called *i gittatelli*."[12] Prior to the Innocenti other institutions, the Bigallo, the Misericordia (these two consolidated in 1425 with responsibilities limited to care of abandoned children and orphans), Santa Maria della Scala, and San Gallo all took in foundlings, though not exclusively; and they continued to do so even after the Inno-

6. Samuel K. Cohn Jr., *Women in the Streets: Essays on Sex and Power in Renaissance Italy* (Baltimore, 1996), 100, 106, 158–60.

7. James R. Farr finds a similar situation in France in his *Authority and Sexuality in Early Modern Burgundy (1550–1730)* (New York, 1995), 131.

8. Boswell, *The Kindness of Strangers,* 91.

9. Ibid., 334–35.

10. Lucia Sandri, "Modalità dell'abbandono dei fanciulli in area urbana: Gli esposti dell'ospedale di San Gallo di Firenze nella prima metà del xv secolo," in *Enfance abandonnée et société en Europe, xive–xxe siècle,* Collection de l'École Française de Rome 140 (Rome, 1991), 994–95.

11. Cf. Richard Trexler, "Infanticide in Florence: New Sources and First Results," *History of Childhood Quarterly* 1 (1973): 98–116, esp. 101, 112 n. 23; Mary Martin McLaughlin, "Survivors and Surrogates: Children and Parents from the Ninth to the Thirteenth Centuries," in *The History of Childhood,* ed. Lloyd deMause (New York, 1974), 120–22; and an example from Florentine judicial records in Brucker, *Society of Renaissance Florence,* 146–47.

12. The *provvisione* of 1419 authorizing the Arte di Por Santa Maria to establish the Innocenti is printed in Luigi Passerini, *Storia degli stabilimenti di beneficenza e d'istruzione elementare gratuita della città di Firenze* (Florence, 1853), 942–46.

centi began operating in 1445.[13] Also some Florentines had children carried to foundling homes elsewhere, like that of San Gimignano, just as people outside Florence brought babies there on occasion.[14]

Abandonment was widely perceived in Florence to be the fate of many illegitimates. Honor helped define family membership, support its identity, attract members' loyalties, and determine the activities of the head of the family in pursuit of its interests.[15] A bastard was without honor and so lacking in essential social attributes and more easily left at the mercy of nature or in the hands of institutions that could at least see to the good of its soul.[16] "Just look at the foundling hospitals!" shouted Boccaccio's misogynistic interlocutor in the *Corbaccio*.[17] As a bastard himself and the father of five illegitimates,[18] Boccaccio may have been sensitive to the fate of such children; nonetheless, Florence was home to a growing population of abandoned children in the fifteenth century. The hospital of Santa Maria della Scala held 151 children in 1428; San Gallo had 150 by 1448; and the Innocenti housed 700 by 1469.[19] The children in these hospitals were thus pushed to the institutionalized margins of society, away from kin and family, to meet their death in many cases or, if lucky, to struggle to find a modest social position.

If only under the influence of present heated debates on contraception and abortion, there has been a notable upsurge of historical interest about abandonment and foundling hospitals. We now have excellent studies of the Innocenti and San Gallo in Florence, as well as comparable work on charitable institutions elsewhere, ranging chronologically from the late Middle Ages through the nineteenth century. The effect of foundling homes was to shield parents from responsibility for the chil-

13. Philip Gavitt, *Charity and Children in Renaissance Florence: The Ospedale degli Innocenti, 1410–1536* (Ann Arbor, Mich., 1990), 13–15.

14. Cf. Lucia Sandri, *L'ospedale di S. Maria della Scala di San Gimignano nel Quattrocento: Contributo alla storia dell'infanzia abbandonata*, Biblioteca della "Miscellanea Storica della Valdelsa," vol. 4 (Florence, 1982), 75–78.

15. See my "Honor and Conflict in a Fifteenth-Century Florentine Family," *Ricerche storiche* 10 (1980): 287–310, reprinted in *Law, Family, and Women*, chap. 4.

16. Cf. Campbell, *Honour, Family, and Patronage*, 187; Jacob Black-Michaud, *Cohesive Force: Feud in the Mediterranean and the Middle East* (New York, 1975), 181, 226–27.

17. Giovanni Boccaccio, *The Corbaccio*, trans. and ed. Anthony K. Cassel (Urbana, Ill., 1975), 28, in a context of discussion of the dangers of adultery and fornication.

18. Vittore Branca, *Boccaccio: The Man and His Works*, trans. and ed. Dennis J. McAuliffe (New York, 1976), 71.

19. John Henderson, *Piety and Charity in Late Medieval Florence* (Oxford, 1994), 376, 380.

dren they abandoned. Use of the wheel (a rotating door through which the child could be placed and spun to the inside without detection) to place the abandoned child in the hospital functioned to shield parental anonymity. Yet in the nineteenth century, under pressure of new notions of motherhood and childhood, the wheels were removed and women, but not men, made to take some responsibility for their offspring, who now had to be solely illegitimate to be in a foundling home.[20]

Although the conventional image of the abandoned child stressed illegitimacy as the motive for abandonment, before the nineteenth century there were always a number of legitimate children abandoned as well, under stress of poverty.[21] Legitimates tended to be older on average when abandoned and were more likely to be adorned with signs or objects by which they might be recognized and reclaimed; but they too had been marginalized.[22] Both legitimates and, more so, the usually younger illegitimates experienced heavy mortality in abandonment, so, though parental consciences may have been assuaged, abandonment could be said to amount to "un infanticide différé." Past biological survival, "the child abandoned is, more than a bastard, promised a sort of 'social death,' that of the 'child of no one.'"[23] It is worth noting that, at least according to Baldo degli Ubaldi, foundlings were legally classifiable as *spurii.* Not only were they born "quasi sine patre" like other *spurii,* they were essentially "sine matre."[24] He also posed, using the example of an illegitimate birth involving a student and a servant girl, that an infant, once exposed, could not be reclaimed by the servant's master, unless he had repaid all expenses of those who had taken the child in.[25] Some sort of parental alimentary responsibility had to be acknowledged to retrieve a child.

The Innocenti in Florence was founded with a one-thousand-florin bequest from the wealthy Pratese merchant Francesco Datini. Datini had

---

20. See Kertzer, *Sacrificed for Honor;* Carlo A. Corsini, "'Era piovuto dal cielo e la terra l'aveva raccolto': Il destino del trovatello," in *Enfance abandonnée et société,* 81–119.

21. Graziella Pagliano, "Il motivo dell'infante abbandonato in letteratura: Considerazioni su alcuni testi italiani," in *Enfance abandonnée et société,* 879–95.

22. Volker Hunecke, "Intensità e fluttuazioni degli abbandoni dal xv al xix secolo," in *Enfance abandonnée et société,* 27–72.

23. Pierre Dubuis, "Enfants refusés dans les Alpes occidentales (xive–xve siècles)," in *Enfance abandonnée et société,* 573.

24. Baldo, *additio* to l. Vulgo, De statu hominum (D. 1.5.23), *Opera omnia,* vol. 1, fol. 33rb.

25. Baldo to l. Si invito, C. De infantibus expositis (C. 8.51[52].1), *Opera omnia,* vol. 8, fols. 180rb–va.

no legitimate children, but he did sire an illegitimate daughter on a slave, who at one point had been secretly placed at the hospital of Santa Maria Nuova in Florence. In his life Datini would see to her marriage, with a one-thousand-florin dowry, bequeath her another one thousand florins and promise five-hundred-florin dowries to all her "legitimate and natural" daughters.[26] Establishment of a foundling home, it was put to him, would assure him a sort of earthly immortality denied him otherwise for want of legitimate sons.[27] Others among the earliest benefactors of the new institution also were parents or relatives of bastards.[28]

Prior to the actual opening of the Innocenti in its famous Brunelleschian building in 1445, the hospital of San Gallo, just outside the city's walls along the road to Bologna, took in most foundlings. Tomoko Takahashi counts 1,452 infants (853 girls, 599 boys) taken in there between 1395 and 1463, with the numbers peaking in the 1430s and 1440s.[29] At San Gallo some 62 percent of *trovatelli* were from the contado. The abandoned infants were *illegitimi* of all sorts (children of young unmarrieds, clerical children, children of servants or slaves), but also *legitimi* whose parents were likely to be hard pressed. Children of domestic servants and slaves, categories of persons for whom family solidarity was situationally impossible, were most frequent among abandoned illegitimates at San Gallo, most notably so after 1440.[30]

The abandonment of bastards to these institutions is indicative of abiding prejudice against them, as well as fear of social disapproval that would result from recognizing and raising such children. They were often deposited at night so the parent eluded detection; or intermediaries brought the child, thus shielding the parents. When able, hospital

26. Gavitt, *Charity and Children,* 44–45, 50.

27. Gavitt, *Charity and Children,* 36–37.

28. Gavitt, *Charity and Children,* 64, 113–14.

29. Tomoko Takahashi, "I bambini abbandonati presso lo spedale di Santa Maria a San Gallo di Firenze nel tardo medioevo (1395–1463)," *Annuario dell'Istituto Giapponese di Cultura* 24 (1990–91): 62.

30. Sandri, "Modalità dell'abbandono," 1000, 1003, 1006; Takahashi, "San Gallo," 67–68, 71, 76–77; David Herlihy, "Medieval Children," in *The Walter Prescott Webb Memorial Lectures: Essays on Medieval Civilization,* ed. Bede Karl Lackner and Kenneth Roy Philip (Austin, Tex., 1978), 118; David Nicholas, "Childhood in Medieval Europe," in *Children in Historical and Comparative Perspective: An International Handbook and Research Guide,* ed. Joseph M. Hawes and N. Ray Hiner (New York, 1991), 31–52; cf. Richard Trexler, "The Foundlings of Florence," *History of Childhood Quarterly* 1 (1973): 266–67; and Sandri, *L'Ospedale,* 78–85.

officials would question those who brought children to learn the identity of the parents and if the child had been baptized. No matter how secretly and anonymously left, usually children carried some indication as to their baptismal status.[31] But some parents left signs for later recognition or even identified themselves, although fathers' identities were usually withheld.[32] In examining evidence for causes and motivations behind abandonments to San Gallo, Takahashi finds that poverty and death of parents were constants, as was illegitimacy.[33] Notes left with children released to the Innocenti, as at San Gallo, specifically mention fear of scandal or shame, although there were undoubtedly other motives at work in the abandonment of illegitimate children. Lucia Sandri found that priests and monks were willing to reveal their identity with an abandoned baby, but the shame for nuns was total, as also for married women or even the unmarried.[34] Abandonment to a foundling hospital may have saved a child's life (or merely prolonged it), but mainly it saved a woman's reputation. Slave women's children were abandoned from a sense of shame at the mother's lowly social status and foreign provenance or because abandonment made the slave mother available for remunerated service as a wet nurse to someone else's infant.[35]

Those who abandoned children sired on slaves were from wealthier families who could afford slaves. However, families that harbored slaves had to be concerned with the disruptive effects of slaves' sexual activities, be those with their masters, outsiders, or other slaves and servants.[36] When Giuliano di Salvestro da Campi brought a fifteen-day-old boy to San Gallo in 1439, he revealed that the boy's father was a "buono cit-

31. Sandri, "Modalità," 1008.

32. Gavitt, *Charity and Children,* 187–88, sees these indicators as marks of diffidence on the part of abandoning parents.

33. Takahashi, "San Gallo," 68–70, 72–74, 77–78.

34. Sandri, "Modalità," 1001–2. She notes that cuckolded husbands had an interest, paradoxically, in revealing the adultery and that the abandoned child was not theirs.

35. Cf. Kertzer, *Sacrificed for Honor,* 28; Christiane Klapisch-Zuber, "Parents du sang, parents du lait: La mise en nourrice à Florence (1300–1500)," *Annales de démographie historique* 20 (1983): 43, now translated in her *Women, Family, and Ritual in Renaissance Italy,* trans. Lydia G. Cochrane (Chicago, 1985), 132–64; Trexler, "The Foundlings of Florence," 271; Sandri, *L'Ospedale,* 91–95. Passerini, *Storia degli stabilimenti,* 704, notes a piece of legislation from 1456 that attributed the growth of the Innocenti's population to the abandonment of slaves' babies.

36. Cf. Dennis Romano, *Housecraft and Statecraft: Domestic Service in Renaissance Venice, 1400–1600* (Baltimore, 1996), 53.

tadino" whose wife "does not want to see him because he is the son of his slave."[37] But illegitimacy was its own stigma, no matter the mother's status. Another Florentine who turned over a child to San Gallo explained that he did so not because of poverty or an unwillingness to care for the infant, "but it is much more fear of scandal that could take shape if such a thing were known."[38] Of course, within this grid of illegitimacy and slavery, infants were also more liable to be abandoned simply for being female, and Takahashi has uncovered explicit confessions to this effect.[39]

Abandoned children had a miserable survival rate. Lucia Sandri found that of 362 children taken in by the Scala hospital of San Gimignano in the fifteenth century 251 certainly died and the fate of 58 others remained "unknown."[40] Of the dead, one-quarter died in the first thirty days; 40 percent more did not see their first birthday; 22 percent more did not see their third; and another 13 percent did not reach the age of six.[41] Giuliano Pinto found that only 32 percent of those taken in by San Gallo saw their fifth birthday, while Sandri found for the same institution that 58 percent of *trovatelli* died, 88 percent of them in the first two years of life during wet-nursing and just after.[42] Even the relatively favorable survival rates among the Innocenti's foundlings in its early years were quickly reversed as it took on greater numbers and its resources were stretched.[43] The very presence of the Innocenti, argues Richard Trexler, encouraged more abandonment.[44]

The children left to the Innocenti did not substantially differ in their parentage from those left elsewhere, with slave children being around 60 percent of the total, many of them fathered by wealthy Florentines.[45] The great majority of the Innocenti children were less than three weeks of age on admission and hailed largely from the contado.[46] In his research Philip

37. Takahashi, "San Gallo," 74.

38. Ibid.; and Tomoko Takahashi, "I bambini e i genitori-espositori dello spedale di Santa Maria degli Innocenti di Firenze nel xv secolo," *Annuario dell'Istituto Giapponese di Cultura* 25 (1991–92): 55.

39. Takahashi, "San Gallo," 74; Sandri, "Modalità," 1001, 1003; Trexler, "Infanticide in Florence."

40. Sandri, *L'Ospedale,* 188, and the mortality percentages she offers, 161–62.

41. Ibid., 161.

42. Giuliano Pinto, "Il personale, le balie e i salariati dell'Ospedale di San Gallo di Firenze negli anni 1395–1406: Note per la storia del salariato nelle città medievali," *Ricerche storiche* 2 (1974): 127; Sandri, "Modalità," 1009–10.

43. Trexler, "The Foundlings of Florence," 275–78.

44. Ibid., 268; Sandri, *L'Ospedale,* 129, finds reason to support him.

45. Gavitt, *Charity and Children,* 190–97, 207.

46. Ibid., 188, 206.

Gavitt investigates the relative weight of poverty as a motive for abandonment in comparison with other factors of a noneconomic nature, such as shame for illegitimacy. He argues that increasing admissions to the Innocenti (less than one hundred per year 1445–54, one hundred to two hundred 1455–66), an increase from 4.8 percent of baptized infants in Florence in 1451 to 8.9 percent in 1465, during which period grain prices also increased, shows economic pressures, but nothing on the order of eighteenth-century figures.[47] As with other hospitals, girls were more likely to be abandoned and more likely to die while under the hospital's care.[48] If, however, the Innocenti encouraged abandonment, as some contemporaries believed, it still cared for a much smaller portion of the child population than eighteenth-century hospitals, leading Gavitt to speculate that high plague-related infant mortality, truncated households, and labor shortages "combined to make children valuable and less vulnerable to abandonment."[49] Tomoko Takahashi, however, finds that the opening of the Innocenti seemed to have encouraged greater abandonment of male infants born in Florence. Abandonment of children of slaves seems also to have been increased in consequence of the Innocenti's opening, so the Innocenti seems to have encouraged treating slaves as sexual servants and then transforming them into wet nurses by removing their infants.[50]

Some abandoning parents promised remuneration for expenditures on a child, and by the 1460s the Innocenti, ever strapped for cash, worked out written payment schedules with some of them. Some provided money for a nurse, even directly—thus showing a continual involvement with the abandoned child, and prompting a sense that for them the Innocenti functioned as a referral service or broker for nurses.[51] But for others these hospitals were a social garbage heap on which were tossed the human refuse spoiled in its generation. Thus Boswell concludes that institutionalization of abandonment was a worsening of things for such chil-

47. Ibid., 207–10. See also Giuliana Albini, "I bambini nella società lombarda del Quattrocento: Una realtà ignorata o protetta?" in *La famiglia e la vita quotidiana in Europa dal '400 al '600: Fonti e problemi,* Atti del convegno internazionale, Milan, 1–4 December 1983 (Rome, 1986), 23–50.

48. Gavitt, *Charity and Children,* 210–12.

49. Ibid., 226.

50. Takahashi, "Santa Maria degli Innocenti," 44, 56–57, 60–61.

51. Gavitt, *Charity and Children,* 199–201; but also see Claudio Povolo, "Dal versante dell'illegitimità: Per una ricerca sulla storia della famiglia: Infanticidio ed esposizione d'infanti nel Veneto nell'età moderna," in *Crimine, giustizia e società veneta in età moderna,* ed. Luigi Berlinguer and Floriana Colao (Milan, 1989), 89–163.

dren.[52] Is it that simple, however? Not all the evidence is negative. For one thing, there is the very existence of these hospitals to account for. For another, there are the behavior and attitudes of Florentines in conjunction with them. Takahashi importantly notes that no Florentine hospital made use of the wheel, and places like the Innocenti had multiple functions and were not just holding tanks for socially undesirable children. They were operated in continuity with medieval charitable traditions and were not a new and harsher form of disposal, rather than treatment.[53]

The hospitals were intended to prevent infanticide of these children and thus secure divine favor for Florence. They provided opportunities for citizens to practice charity, as in testamentary bequests to the hospitals.[54] They also played a social function by raising some of those children.[55] As places where legitimate children were also put, they allowed the survival of family units and valuable members of the community during times of crisis. Return of such children to their families was one goal.[56] *Trovatelli* were also taken in by some families as servants or in other, low-paid capacities.[57] In sum, then, as David Herlihy has pointed out, along with education and apprenticeship, foundling homes and orphanages were indicative of a social investment in children.[58] This investment seems to have been more used in the fifteenth century, especially in its second and third decades. The Innocenti's founding in 1419 came in a context that included the Misericordia's proposal in 1407 to record baptisms, the Conservatori delle Leggi's recording of birth dates of politically eligible males beginning in 1429, the registration of emancipations with the Signoria in 1421, the establishment of the *monte delle doti* in 1425, the merging of the financially strapped Bigallo with the Misericordia in the same year, and the catasto's project to survey the population.[59] Only in the fifteenth century did hospitals arise dedicated

52. Gavitt, *Charity and Children,* 21–22, criticizes Boswell on this.

53. Takahashi, "Santa Maria degli Innocenti," 62.

54. Trexler, "The Foundlings of Florence," 260.

55. Pinto, "Ospedale di San Gallo," 127.

56. Cf. Howard Saalman, *The Bigallo: The Oratory and Residence of the Compagnia del Bigallo e della Misericordia in Florence* (New York, 1969), 10.

57. Herlihy and Klapisch-Zuber, *Les toscans,* 434.

58. Herlihy, "Medieval Children," 122.

59. On the Misericordia, Passerini, *Storia degli stabilimenti,* 461–62; on emancipations, Kuehn, *Emancipation,* 37–39; on the dowry fund, Julius Kirshner and Anthony Molho, "The Dowry Fund and the Marriage Market in Early Quattrocento Florence," *Journal of Modern History* 50 (1978): 403–10; on the Bigallo, Saalman, *The Bigallo,* 5–6.

solely to care of foundlings.[60] It has become customary to associate these institutions with the new educational emphases of humanism as expression of a new, more modern sense of childhood.[61] Without reopening that stale issue, it is certainly possible to say that—beyond a concern with numerical accuracy—those responsible for such measures were concerned with economic well-being, the prevention of fraud, the fiscal state of the government, and the perpetuation of households and patrimonies as the basic units of society. They faced an era in which Florence's population was unstable and at a nadir, and the city's economy was shaken.[62] In that context it is interesting to note that after 1447 fines collected from convicted sodomites (who by their sexual behavior had acted to preclude procreation, legitimate or not) were used to fund the former prostitutes of the Convertite and later the abandoned children of the Innocenti.[63] Procreation and marriage were moral, political, and economic imperatives.

Yet the existence of these institutions added a greater element of choice to the recognition and raising of bastard children. Perhaps more parents (the father, or the mother acting alone or with her kin) were willing to avail themselves of the new opportunities to remove the shame from their midst, but it is striking that some did not. Those who have studied foundlings have consistently remarked that "with the exception of slave and clerical parentage, illegitimacy does not seem to have furnished sufficient moral or material justification for abandonment."[64] This insight is confirmed by the fact that parents still had some sense of obligation to these children.[65] One has the sense that abandonment by some couples was provisional, until they could recover economically, whereas for others hiding conception and shame meant that abandonment was definitive.[66] Proportionally more often boys were restored to their father's home, as more often than girls boys arrived at foundling homes with some sign by which they could be rec-

60. Sandri, *L'Ospedale,* 73–74.

61. Herlihy and Klapisch-Zuber, *Les toscans,* 570.

62. Essential here is Herlihy and Klapisch-Zuber, *Les toscans,* 165–88, 209–15, 241–66.

63. Michael Rocke, *Forbidden Friendships: Homosexuality and Male Culture in Renaissance Florence* (Oxford, 1996), 53.

64. Trexler, "The Foundlings of Florence," 271.

65. Ibid., 273; Sandri, *L'Ospedale,* 100–109.

66. Povolo, "Dal versante dell'illegitimità," 111.

ognized.[67] It was more often the wealthier parents of bastards who left their name or some sign, even for their children by slaves.[68] In a survey of 1452, Innocenti officials learned that 6.3 percent (34) of 534 children had returned to their parents (10 percent of boys, 3 percent of girls). "[T]his suggests that one of the hospital's social services was to provide temporary and respite care for children whose parents were ill or otherwise burdened with family cares."[69] Beyond misogyny, the matter of providing a dowry for a girl may have been a disincentive to reclaiming her.[70]

Occasional reclaiming of such children speaks to how powerful that sense of attachment, even to bastards, was. Luca di Matteo da Panzano fathered a child on a slave girl (after seventeen years of marriage and fifteen children to show for them). He abandoned the boy to the Scala but reclaimed him five years later (after his wife's death, indicating that she may have pushed the abandonment in the first place).[71] There were also numerous cases of *trovatelli* taken in by families not related to them and for which they became fostered children and domestic help.[72] Not only do these reclamations speak to some sort of modification of Boswell's judgment, but they also remind us more forcefully that illegitimate children need not have been abandoned at all. Many, in fact, were not. They were raised at home, by their fathers, as part of a *famiglia* and *casa,* often containing legitimate siblings as well. It is to their stories that we must now turn.

Bastards in Households

A good proportion of bastards met with paternal recognition and care at some level. They are the historically interesting population of illegitimates, for all the ambiguities and uncertainties of illegitimacy came into play with them. They were to some extent part of a family, a kindred or lineage, and society. Their fates, as we will see, varied greatly. Some

67. Cf. Trexler, "The Foundlings of Florence," 265, 270–71; Sandri, *L'Ospedale,* 100–102, 171–75; Gavitt, *Charity and Children,* 196, Takahashi, "Santa Maria degli Innocenti," 65.

68. Gavitt, *Charity and Children,* 197–98.

69. Gavitt, *Charity and Children,* 204. However, he does not here indicate who counted as wealthy in his statement.

70. Gavitt, *Charity and Children,* 210–11.

71. Cf. Mazzi, *Prostitute e lenoni,* 53–54.

72. Takahashi, "San Gallo," 65.

gained little; for others there was a sort of material and personal salvation. Association with a male line of descent was the first step toward some form of social legitimacy, because it was a social identity.[73]

Family reconstitution is not possible for Florence in the fifteenth century. We are tied to Florentines' admissions of bastardy, so we must confront several problems and peculiarities in the sources. When illegitimacy was admitted, it was with reference to the father. Those most evidently illegitimate were those who remained among paternal kin. In only a few instances did a woman come forth to proclaim the illegitimacy of her offspring. Somewhat less rarely (mainly in the context of legitimation, the 1458 catasto, and the *monte delle doti*), the father or other kinsman might reveal the mother's identity.

The power of blood ties binding them to a family was such that bastards fathered elsewhere were at times tracked down by kin to be brought to Florence, cared for, raised, and eventually set up with a career and marriage. There are a number of good examples. Donato Velluti, in the fourteenth century, retrieved his brother's bastard daughter from Sicily.[74] Francesco di Ridolfo Peruzzi did the same in the fifteenth with the son of his deceased brother Antonio.[75] Alessandra Macinghi negli Strozzi welcomed a bastard girl sent from Barcelona by her son. She assured him, "I hold her dear and will treat her like my own and gladly will be kind to her." Years later she succeeded in finding the girl a husband, a modest silk weaver, a good match "in view of her quality," and gave her all she needed "so that she might seem a girl of good quality because she will then be regarded much more so." Alessandra's son responded that she had indeed done "more than if she had been her daughter."[76] Such a girl was an expense, a bother, even an embarrassment; but she was a Strozzi. This is not to deny that this girl, like Maddalena Niccolini in a similar situation, probably received a smaller dowry and a much smaller wedding than if she had been legitimate.[77] But she

73. Cf. Christopher Boehm, *Blood Revenge: The Enactment and Management of Conflict in Montenegro and Other Tribal Societies* (Lawrence, Kans., 1984; rpt. Philadelphia, 1987), 129.

74. Donato Velluti, *La Cronica domestica di Messer Donato Velluti,* ed. Isidoro Del Lungo and Guglielmo Volpi (Florence, 1914), 147–50; also Tamassia, *La famiglia italiana,* 231.

75. Catasto 805, fols. 700r–701v.

76. Alessandra Macinghi negli Strozzi, *Lettere di una gentildonna fiorentina del secolo xv ai figliuoli esuli,* ed. Cesare Guasti (Florence, 1877), 111, 145, 163.

77. Cf. Ginevra Niccolini di Camugliano, *The Chronicles of a Florentine Family, 1200–1470* (London, 1933), 164–66.

got something. The power of the blood is perhaps more evident with Giovanni Bonsi, who raised along with five legitimate children a mentally impaired bastard son whose mother was a slave and who cost more than the others.[78]

Florentines' catasto declarations betray rare expressions of love for an illegitimate. Giusto di Francesco Coverelli put his son Alamanno to wet nurse in Campi, but later moved him to the Mugello when an epidemic broke out at Campi and later still brought the boy to live with him in Florence.[79] Perhaps also in this context belongs the comment of Brancazio di Francesco del Rosso regarding his sixteen-year-old, Ginevra—"her mother was named Giovanna from Florence and stayed with me several years [before his marriage, it would seem], and she was raised in our house so her mother might nurse her."[80] The actions of Niccolò Soderini in 1465 were also taken to be the product not solely of political maneuvers against Piero de' Medici but as an expression of his "immoderate" love for his bastard son, messer Geri, whom he treated like his legitimate sons.[81]

Evidence is plentiful of at least a matter-of-fact acceptance of some bastards. Their presence in the family was reported to catasto officials by Florentines who were at least eager to claim the allowed deduction. Their births and deaths were noted along with those of legitimates.[82] One of the most forthcoming was Bernardo Salviati. He recorded the births of three children, two boys and a girl, by two different slaves. He also recorded whom the slaves later married and how large their dowries were. He married off the bastard girl with a sizable dowry. All this was set down apparently without undue discomfort:

> I, Bernardo di Marco di messer Forese Salviati, make record how I had on 2 December 1447 from Gianna, our Russian slave, a male child to whom we gave the name Piero. And we married the said Gianna and she had 225 lire as dowry, that is 225 lire Genoese at Rhodes and Vico

78. Strozzi, *Lettere,* 122.

79. Catasto 790, fols. 520r–523v.

80. Catasto 816, fols. 311r–315r: "la madre ebbe nome mona Joanna da Firenze, istette mecho parechi anni e alevala in cha' perchè la madre gli dette la popa."

81. Mark Phillips, *The "Memoir" of Marco Parenti: A Life in Medici Florence* (Princeton, N.J., 1987), 173; also see Clarke, *Soderini and Medici,* 129.

82. Strozzi, *Lettere,* 507; Elizabeth Swain, "Faith in the Family: The Practice of Religion by the Gonzaga," *Journal of Family History* 8 (1983): 187; Guido dell'Antella, "Ricordi," ed. F. L. Polidori, *Archivio storico italiano,* 1st ser., 4 (1843): 13; also ASF, Carte strozziane, 5th ser., 1750, fol. 184v.

Peruzzi, our associate in Rhodes, paid the said 225 for me as appears in the red book on folio 114.

She died at Rhodes on [blank in text] November 1465, may God have mercy on her soul if it pleases him.

I make record of how on 14 August 1448 the above-said Gianna our slave made us a girl child, and we named her Marietta from reverence for Our Lady that God and the Madonna may make her good, as appears in the record book, folio 114.[83]

He was not as precise or forthcoming with these children, however, as he was with legitimate ones. Note the following entry in contrast:

> I make record how by the grace of God and the Virgin Mary, I, Bernardo Salviati, have had on this 26 October 1467 a male child [born] at six and a half hours at night on the twenty-fifth by Lucrezia di Pellegrino Chattani, my wife, who was baptized by ser Antonio, priest of Sant'Erbalmo of Camerata and ser Rigoglio di Solo di Rigoglio, chancellor of the Mercanzia, and Bartolomeo di ser Benedetto Fortini and monna Lodovica, wife of Fruosino da Panzano, and we gave him the name Pellegrino and Ubaldo for the father of Lucrezia and for her uncle or grandfather that God by his grace may take consolation and make him live as it pleases his divinity and then at his end die in his grace and as much through his grace and mercy.[84]

83. Acquisti e Doni 302, insert, on a folio numbered 95r (I thank Elaine Rosenthal for bringing this text to my attention):

> Richordo chome io Bernardo di Marcho di messer Forese Salviati ebbi insino a dì 2 di deciebre 1447 della Gianna nostra schiava rossa uno fanciullo maschio al quale ponemo nome Piero, e maritamo la detta Gianna ed ebbe di dota lire 225, cioè lire 225 di Rodi a gienovese, e per me paghò detti l. 225 Vicho Peruzzi nostro chompagno a Rodi apare al quaderno rosso di Rodi 114.
>
> Morì a Rodi a dì di novembre 1465 a Rodi, dio abbia auto misericordia dell'anima sua, s'è di suo piacere.
>
> Richordo chome a dì 14 d'aghosto 1448 la sopradetta Gianna nostra schiava ci fecie una fanciulla femina, iponemola nome Marietta per riverenza di nostra donna che dio et madonna gli facia buoni apare al detto quaderno rosso 114.

Compare this to his declaration: Catasto 810, fols. 753r–756r.

84. Ibid., fol. "96r": "Richordo chome per la grazia di dio e della vergine Maria, io Bernardo Salviati ò auto questo 26 d'ottobre 1467 uno fanciullo maschio a ore 6 1/2 di notte a dì 25 detto della Lucrezia di Pellegrino Chattani e mia donna, el quale battezò ser Antonio prete di Sant'Erbalmo di Chamerata, e ser Righoglio di Solo di Righoglio e chancelliere della Mercatatia, e Bartolomeo di ser Benedetto Fortini, e mona Lodovicha donna di Fruosino da Panzano e ponemoli nome Pellegrino e Ubaldo pel padre di detta Lucrezia e

Unfortunately the final prayer was only partially answered; Pellegrino died within a year. Yet Salviati did not pray similarly for his bastards.

Another Florentine, Francesco di Matteo Castellani, had two bastard sons by a woman who was probably a servant. The birth of the first was not recorded, but there is a record of his transfer to a wet nurse and subsequent expenses for his upbringing elsewhere. The later birth of a legitimate son met with copious expressions of concern that he grow "always in God's grace a good and virtuous servant and worthy man as is our wish," record of his baptism, and—unfortunately—his death one month later.[85] Paliano Falchi, however, did not record illegitimate and legitimate births in a different manner. He had three children by a Perugian widow prior to his first marriage. The birth of the first, Antonio, in 1382, was described with the names of the godparents, expenses (three lire), and the expression of hope that God be merciful to him. Terms with a wet nurse were also recorded. Unfortunately the boy died less than six months later, and Paliano recorded his place of burial and "and for this reason I cancel here as a paid account" [per detta ragione cancello qui per paghato]. The record of the birth of a sister in 1389 gave just her name. The birth of a brother, Bartolomeo, in 1387, like that of Antonio earlier, met with a listing of the godfathers' names and the same hope for good moral and physical growth. The death of the sister, along with her mother (who had been Paliano's concubine for at least eight years) in 1390, was recorded in the same terms as Antonio's.[86] Following a barren first marriage (1390–99) terminated with the death of his wife, Paliano remarried early in 1401 and over two years later finally was able to write down a legitimate birth, a daughter, who was baptized and for whom he expressed the same hope for good growth. Where this legitimate birth seems to have made a difference is that Paliano three years later canceled the will he made in 1400 when he was a widower with one illegitimate son.[87]

The naming of these bastards is also indicative. In some societies the

---

per zio di detta overo avolo che dio per sua grazia cie ne presi consolazione e facilo vivere quanto piacie alla sua divinità e poi alla sua fine morire nella sua grazia e quanto per la sua grazia e misericordia."

85. Francesco di Matteo Castellani, *Ricordanze,* vol. 1: *Ricordanze A (1436–1459),* ed. Giovanni Ciappelli (Florence, 1992), 113: "sempre nella sua gratia bon suo servo virtuoso e valente homo quanto sia nostro desiderio"; and 171.

86. ASF, Carte strozziane, 2d ser., 7, fols. 2v–3r, for the events recounted here.

87. Ibid., fols. 124v (birth), 58v–60v (will), 61r (cancellation).

illegitimate receives the mother's family name.[88] Those who came through foundling homes were named by the hospital, which invented surnames often distinctively labeling a child with suspicious origins (e.g., Innocenti, Esposti, del Prete). In Milan between 1475 and 1825 foundlings were given the surname Colombo.[89] Florentine bastards recognized and raised at home faced no such marking but received a paternal and patrilineal identity. We have seen how jurists had to resolve the question of the rights of bastards to a family name. Generally they conceded such rights to *naturales* only. The foremost student of Florentine naming practices, Christiane Klapisch-Zuber, has said that Florentines were willing to use names that overtly tied their bastards to the legitimate kin. The examples she uses are Luigi Curiani naming a son Curiano and Luca Firidolfi da Panzano naming a son Ridolfo. One could cite in addition Giandonato d'Altobianco Giandonati or Altovito di Mariano Altoviti.[90] They became involved in a network of material and symbolic interests that bound them to the lineage's past members.[91] Bernardo Salviati, however, was not quite so obvious, choosing names that were general in the society but not usual in his branch of the Salviati lineage.[92] The same can be said for Bartolomeo di Tommaso di Federigo Sassetti, who named his illegitimate son Ventura, which he later changed to Sandro.[93]

Clearly, in a society very aware of symbolic statements, naming even illegitimate children was not a casual matter. One finds fathers using names on their bastards that were infrequent and not usually saints' names: Amoretto di Guido Baldovinetti (a revealing name, perhaps), Peracino di ser Francesco da Romena, Altavilla di Spinetto Pitti, Urbano di Marabottino Rustichi, Sinibaldo di Taddeo Magaldi, Achille d'Ormanno Foraboschi. But for the most part Florentine bastards bore names just like those found throughout the society. They too were Antonio,

88. As in contemporary Andalusia, cf. Julian Pitt-Rivers, "La veuve andalouse," in Ravis-Giordani, *Femmes et patrimoine,* 265.

89. Cf. Kertzer, *Sacrificed for Honor,* 119–22.

90. Both in Catasto 811 (1458), fols. 41r–44r and 157r–162v. Also Chacinno di Galeotto di Michele del Caccia (Catasto 810, fols. 614r–615v) and Cavalcante di Giovanni Cavalcanti (Catasto 790, fols. 237r–240r).

91. Christiane Klapisch-Zuber, "Le nom 'refait': La transmission des prenoms à Florence (xive–xvie siècles)," *L'Homme* 20, no. 4 (1980): 100–101 (translation in *Women, Family, and Ritual,* 283–309).

92. Cf. Hurtubise, *Une famille-témoin,* 121–22, 297.

93. ASF, Carte strozziane, 5th ser., 1750, fol. 184v.

Giovanni, or Francesco, Ginevra, Bartolomea, Francesca or, revealingly often, Madalena. Nor were their fathers always wary of giving them names worn by legitimate members of the family. Lorenzo di Francesco Segni, whose only surviving legitimate progeny was a ten-year-old daughter, "remade" his father in his nineteen-year-old bastard Francesco.[94] Piero di Bartolomeo Rossi first "remade" his father in an illegitimate son but then, seven years later when he had a legitimate son, again used the name Bartolomeo, though the first recipient of the name was still a member of his household.[95] Jacopo di Giurozzo Bardi named both an illegitimate (age twelve in 1458) and legitimate (age one in 1458) daughter Caterina.[96]

Nonetheless, one cannot escape the impression that names in the direct paternal line, or even names of brothers, were rarely used for bastards.[97] The "new" names given them would instead set them off. Any branch descended from them would then be designated at least partly by the recurrence of different names. Magnate branches seeking *popolano* status had to change their names.[98] Perhaps it was even easier or necessary with bastards and their weak sense of reputation. Countless times one finds patterns like the following: Giannotto di Domenico di Bartolo Ottavanti, who had brothers named Bartolomeo and Priore, named his legitimate son Bernardo, while his brother Bartolomeo named his illegitimate son Galeotto.[99] Tiere di Lorenzo di Tieri named his legitimate sons Piero, Niccolò, Lionardo, Querino, Lodovico, and Giovanni; the illegitimate was named Tommaso. Niccolò, in turn, named his bastards Ghismondo and Sforza.[100] But it is hard to say, in the end, that the naming process was much different for them than it was for younger children. If the goal of the family head was some sort of assimilation of the bastard into patterns of family life and a playing down of the illegitimacy, a truly distinctive name would not have been a good strategy. Cultural presumptions about the similarities between parents and offspring—similarities not merely contingent or coincident but substantial, in the blood—

94. Catasto 788 (1458), fols. 651r–652v.

95. Catasto 788 (1458), fols. 791r–793r.

96. Catasto 786 (1458), fols. 57r–64r.

97. Cf. Bernard Vernier, "Putting Kin and Kinship to Good Use: The Circulation of Goods, Labour, and Name on Karpathos (Greece)," in *Interest and Emotion,* 43.

98. Christiane Klapisch-Zuber, "Ruptures de parenté et changements d'identité chez les magnats florentins du xive siècle," *Annales* 43 (1988): 1205–40; also Michael Herzfeld, *The Poetics of Manhood,* 237.

99. Catasto 816 (1458), fols. 194r–197v.

100. Catasto 818 (1458), fols. 273r–274r.

meant that care had to be exercised in naming and handling an illegitimate. Repetition of names was an assertion of continuity in the bloodline, as was the careful framing of even physical resemblances in portraits. The portrait of the illegitimate Duke Federigo da Montefeltro with his young son Guidubaldo by Justus of Ghent insists on associating the two in succession to rule in Urbino.[101] Resemblance of behavior was even more important. Lorenzo de' Medici himself began a vernacular tale, "Giacoppo," with the statement that "since they say a good son resembles his father, perhaps the sons, not wishing to bring shame upon their fathers, endeavor to behave in such a way as not to seem to be bastards."[102] Clearly the opposite also applied; bastards, whose fathers had behaved badly, were expected to be bad.

Catasto Data

Whether loved as much as legitimates or not, Florentine bastards were listed in households in the catasto. Family members, kin, and neighbors could all have an interest in perpetuating the stigma of illegitimacy and use of the label in that record, although sometimes they got away with dropping it. In the course of my research I surveyed the volumes of the catasto for 1427, 1458, and 1480, limiting myself to the city of Florence alone. These volumes yielded information on almost 1,000 bastards: 174 bastards in 1427, 557 in 1458, and 255 in 1480 (table 1). There is very little overlap in these figures (i.e., same person named in two surveys). The first problem is to confront the variations in numbers, especially the large number for 1458.

The demographic import of the 1427 figures has already been explained by David Herlihy and Christiane Klapisch-Zuber in their magisterial study, *Les toscans et leurs familles.* They found the impossibly small total of only 206 bastards for all of Tuscany, 171 in Florence (174 by my count).[103] As Florence had fewer than 40,000 souls, against over

101. Patricia Simons, "Alert and Erect: Masculinity in Some Italian Renaissance Portraits of Fathers and Sons," in *Gender Rhetorics: Postures of Dominance and Submission in History,* ed. Richard C. Trexler (Binghamton, N.Y., 1994), 166.

102. In Lauro Martines, ed. and trans., *An Italian Renaissance Sextet: Six Tales in Historical Context* (New York, 1994), 141.

103. My figure varies from theirs because they neglected to count a son added in 1428 (Catasto 64, fols. 35r–36r), counted as illegitimate a legitimate younger brother (Catasto 67, fols. 208v–209r), counted two girls as males (Catasto 74, fols. 180v–181r and Catasto 72, fols. 404v–405r), missed a four-year-old brother labeled "bastardo" (Catasto 76, fols. 99v–104r) and a twenty-two-year-old also so labeled (Catasto 79, fols. 490r–v) and a ten-year-old girl (Catasto 79, fols. 159v–160v).

TABLE 1. Ages and Sex of Florentine Bastards

	Sex					
	Male			Female		
Age	1427	1458	1480	1427	1458	1480
0–1	20	23	5	7	21	5
2	7	20	4	4	20	2
3	6	23	5	3	10	4
4–5	10	34	7	1	29	9
6–10	28	77	26	16	52	34
11–15	23	64	46	9	40	19
16–18	2	26	18	0	9	6
19–25	20	39	24	1	2	2
26+	10	41	17	1	2	7
Unknown	3	15	8	3	10	7
Total	129	362	160	45	195	95

Source: ASF, Catasto

250,000 for the whole of the Florentine domain in Tuscany, there seems clearly to have been serious underreporting of illegitimacy in the countryside and subject cities, if not in Florence itself. To give greater precision to this vague sense, limiting ourselves to bastards under age thirteen, the 140 (of the 206 total) amount to only 0.16 percent of the total population of Florentine Tuscany in that age group (87,484 in total). The 114 bastards under thirteen in Florence itself, on the other hand, amounted to 0.91 percent of their age group in the city's population (12,562).[104] Against the findings of demographic historians, these percentages appear too low. Even the low percentages (1–3 percent) of so-called traditional societies show how low the figures from the catasto were.[105] The illegitimacy ratio was also likely to be higher yet in a city like Florence. Neithard Bulst has suggested (working from figures from the baptismal register of 1451 supplied to him by Klapisch-Zuber, which showed 22 illegitimates among 1,871 children, or 1.17 percent) that the illegitimate birth rate in Florence was around 3 percent, taking into account the

104. Cf. Herlihy and Klapisch-Zuber, *Les toscans,* 339 n. 46, 434 n. 25, and tables 1 and 2 and appendix V, along with my own investigation offered below. I here acknowledge gratefully the generous assistance of the late David Herlihy in furnishing me with a printout of the declarations listing illegitimates. This sort of gesture, in addition to the imposing scholarship, is why he is so sorely missed.

105. Cf. Demonet, Dupâquier, and LeBras, "Repertory of Stable Populations," 298; Laslett, *Family Life,* 109.

trovatelli. Allowing for the skewed sex ratio among bastards in the catasto, he even surmises that the rate may have been as high as 10 percent—a figure reached in Siena between 1530 and 1550.[106] The latter figure seems far-fetched, if only because not all bastards in Florence were born there and not all born there remained there.

There are two other relevant figures to consider. Herlihy and Klapisch-Zuber estimate a total population of 1,500 to 2,000 in Tuscan hospitals, some of whom were abandoned illegitimate children.[107] From other sources we know the Scala took care of 150 children in 1396 and was taking in about 15 children each year a couple of decades later. In 1456 the Innocenti had 318 children; just ten years later it had 657 under its care.[108] The 1427 catasto also listed 216 *trovatelli* (137 girls, 79 boys) taken into households as an act of charity or to gain a needed laborer.[109] Some of these probably were illegitimate.

Clearly a number of illegitimates were not disclosed to be such to the catasto authorities. The shame of illegitimacy was perhaps enough incentive for Florentines and Tuscans to withhold from those nosey outsiders any mention of illegitimacy. It becomes intriguing rather, especially in view of catasto law and administration, to speculate why anyone would bother to reveal illegitimacy in the family. Illegitimacy was no bar to claiming a child as a deduction, so there was no fiscal penalty to admitting it. The head tax *(testatico)* gave Florentines an incentive to disguise sex or to deflate ages, but it hardly mattered if the child was illegitimate.[110] On the other hand, the personal deduction was not allowed outside Florence (except in Pisa, where it was set at only fifty florins). In rural Tuscany, then, illegitimates might have been hidden or not acknowledged so as to avoid the *testatico.* This could begin to explain the differences in the willingness to enroll children as illegitimate between the city of Florence and the rest of Tuscany.

Illegitimacy data from the 1480 catasto has been recently analyzed by Anthony Molho. He found 252 bastards (155 men and 97 women) in the

106. Neithard Bulst, "Illegitime Kinder—viele oder wenige? Quantitative Aspekte det Illegitimität im spätmittelalterlichen Europa," in Schmugge, *Illegitimität im Spätmittelalter,* 30–31.

107. Herlihy and Klapisch-Zuber, *Les toscans,* 160.

108. Passerini, *Storia degli stabilimenti,* 668, 682, 703–5; Gavitt, *Charity and Children,* 204–15.

109. Herlihy and Klapisch-Zuber, *Les toscans,* 331.

110. Cf. Herlihy and Klapisch-Zuber, *Les toscans,* 334–36.

total Florentine population of 40,874, in 8,414 households.[111] There were half again as many bastards in 1480 as in 1427, but the population had increased by only around 10 percent; and so the percentage of bastards in the total city population increased from 0.5 percent to 0.6 percent. These figures are generally in line with each other, and differences may be ascribed to the administrative changes in compiling the two surveys.[112]

The 1458 data, on the other hand, are well out of line. Five hundred fifty-seven bastards from a population spread between some 7,600 households, containing perhaps as many as 40,000 souls, works out to a percentage of around 1.4 percent. It would seem that a great deal of the difference must be ascribed to the document. For one thing this catasto survives only in the citizens' *portate,* not in the bureaucratically adjusted form of 1427 and 1480. I have thus been able to count all bastards identified by Florentines as such whether or not (and many were not) they were accepted as deductions by the officials. And this indeed is another aspect of the document—it is the first catasto to get tough about illegitimates and award the deduction only after deliberation by the officials. This, then, may have spurred a burst of honesty, including, as we will see, about the mothers of these children.[113] The recent opening of the Innocenti may have influenced both the administrative policies of the officials and the openness of the Florentines.

The overall sex ratios in all three catasti testify to the pronounced tendency of Florentines to abandon their daughters rather than their sons.[114] It is also notable that households with illegitimate girls, more so than those with illegitimate boys, tended to be bereft of other children, especially legitimate sons. It would seem that in the presence of legitimate siblings girls were more likely to be dispatched from the household as servants, wives, nuns, or even foundlings, especially younger girls born into

111. Molho, *Marriage Alliance,* 84, 177–78. My count differs slightly from his (255 vs. 252, 160 men and ninety-five women vs. 155 and ninety-seven).

112. Molho, *Marriage Alliance,* 277 n. 52, points out that in 1427 illegitimates could be claimed as deductions without a need to prove their illegitimacy, but in 1480 such children would count as deductions "only if they were legitimated." However, most of the 1480 declarations simply list the bastards as such—"naturale," "non legittimo," and so forth—without assertion of legitimation; and most of the bastards were certainly not legitimated.

113. Conti, *L'imposta diretta a Firenze,* 252–53.

114. Herlihy and Klapisch-Zuber, *Les toscans,* 339 n. 46 and 434; Molho, *Marriage Alliance,* 277.

households with older legitimate siblings. The 1427 catasto offers a very high ratio among the bastard population (287 to 100). Of the seven girls in 1427 with older legitimate siblings, three were only infants (one with an older illegitimate sister, both sired on the same slave, it seems), while three lived in a peculiar household that was home to eleven bastards as well as six legitimate children.[115] As Molho points out, this ratio of masculinity decreases to 159 men to 100 women in 1480. He goes on to note that at the lower end of ages (those less than thirteen), the 1427 masculinity ratio of 204 to 100 became 121 in 1480. The greatest imbalance in both catasti was at the upper end, over the age of twenty, where the masculinity ratio in 1480 was 276.[116] The 1458 data sit in between these figures with an overall masculinity ratio of 183, the ratio for those under thirteen being 137, and that for those over twenty being an incredible 1,540 (77 males to only 5 females), but in line with the 1427 ratio of 1,450 (29 men, 2 women). Another way to look at these figures is to say that while a small number of female bastards had passed their twentieth birthday, consistently over 20 percent of male bastards were over twenty years of age. One conclusion to draw here has already been sketched out by Molho and bears extensive repeating:

> one could reasonably argue that, once they passed puberty, women were able to assume stations in life which rendered their illegitimate status less evident. Many took monastic vows, a more substantial number married. In either case the stigma of illegitimacy was somewhat obscured, concealed in a new identity. Men, especially those born into distinguished lineages, had a smaller chance at marriage: because their offspring were bound to advance bothersome inheritance claims, it was better to prevent the proliferation of such spurious descendants. For this reason it is not uncommon to find a number of illegitimate sons of well-known fathers in the ranks of the Church,

115. The family with eleven bastards was that of Pagano di messer Cabrino Fondello (Catasto 80, fols. 633v–634v). The infants were in the families of Isau d'Agnolo Martellini (Catasto 67, fols. 63r–69r) and Niccolò di Maso Strinati (Catasto 79, fols. 323r–325r) with Antonio di Francesco Arrighi, who had a slave, showing a six-year-old and a six-month-old (Catasto 80, fols. 236v–238r).

116. Molho, *Marriage Alliance,* 278. He uses Herlihy and Klapisch-Zuber's published printout figures. My count yields eighty-two males to thirty-five females for a 234 masculinity ratio.

where they could attain social distinction without placing the material resources of their family in jeopardy.[117]

Married women certainly had no reason to carry illegitimate status with them into marriage. While illegitimacy might have some residual inheritance effect in one's family of origin (and thus lead them to keep a memory of it), in one's marital family it could only shame or even "contaminate" one's children. In all three catasti only one married woman is termed illegitimate; and because women moved into their husband's family, it is impossible to trace them from one catasto to the next. But by the same token male heads of household did not reveal their illegitimacy. It was not that illegitimacy went away with age. *Bastardi* in their fifties and sixties were revealed as such by the heads of household (often nephews). But having a separate household or being married relieved one of illegitimacy in some sense. Two examples prove the rule to some degree, though both were also legitimated at the time of the 1427 catasto. Andrea di Francesco di messer Arnaldo Mannelli was listed separately from his father, but his illegitimacy and/or legitimation was not mentioned.[118] Salvadore di Niccolò da Uzzano, married, legitimated, and a father, was listed in his father's household without mention of the irregular circumstances of his birth.[119] Nor did he bother to mention it in 1458.[120]

Households with Bastards

Herlihy and Klapisch-Zuber have noted that those households containing bastard children tended to be the wealthier and larger. In 1427 81.6 percent of bastards came from households with net worth of at least 400 florins.[121] Data culled from the catasto of 1458 regarding the wealth of households harboring bastards yield comparable results. If 400 florins is again employed as a benchmark, only about 10 percent of households with bastards fell below that mark. If the standard is raised to 600 florins, the percentage only doubles.[122] The poorer 20 percent of house-

117. Molho, *Marriage Alliance*, 278–79.

118. We know of his illegitimacy from an earlier paternal will: Notarile 9042 (1411–31), testamenti, fols. 15v–17v (30 March 1414).

119. Catasto 64, fols. 65v–84r.

120. Catasto 786, fols. 88r–91r.

121. Herlihy and Klapisch-Zuber, *Les toscans*, 434 and n. 25.

122. Based on 173 households distributed in six of the sixteen *gonfaloni*.

holds held 1.29 bastards on average, although the poorer 10 percent held 1.47—thus being more generous or more in need of children as assets (over a third of these children were female). The wealthier 80 percent housed 1.32 bastards on average. In comparison to 1427, more poorer households held onto bastard children, but they were still an obvious minority in relation to wealthier households with bastards.

Much the same situation held in 1480 also, although the preservation of the document makes recovery of the asset totals difficult or impossible in some cases. Of 203 bastards whose households' wealth we can speak to with some certainty, 64.5 percent lived in those with *sustanze* of 400 or more florins. Given differences in what was reported and subject to tax in 1480, however, a fairer demarcation line might be 300 florins, in which case the percentage of bastards rises only slightly to 66.5 percent.[123] That the percentage in poorer homes increased in 1480, however, is not due to more poor having bastards but rather to those poor who had bastards having or keeping more of them. Of the 51 households housing bastards with below 400 florins in assets, 11 had more than 1 bastard (2 had 6 each). The average number of bastards per household with wealth less than 400 florins (1.38) contrasts with that for households with wealth over 1,000 florins (1.16). Contrast that with averages in 1427 of 1.16 bastard children per household under 400 florins (18 with 21 children) and 1.4 per household over 1,000 florins (1.29 if one aberrant case is removed).

Wealth clearly was a major determinant in the fate of children—in this case the continued association of illegitimates with a household. "In the less advantaged classes," Herlihy and Klapisch-Zuber conclude, "the absence of children declared illegitimate suggests either that the notion of illegitimacy was not the same as among the rich or that illegitimacy was absorbed from birth by a systematic practice of infanticide."[124] That there were differences between rural and urban, poor and wealthy, households makes sense. The catasto, in extending certain fiscal privileges only to city dwellers, cemented some differences into the historical record. Herlihy and Klapisch-Zuber's judgment about differences in sexual practices and notions of marriage and legitimacy among social

123. Cf. Conti, *L'imposta diretta a Firenze,* 280–88.

124. Herlihy and Klapisch-Zuber, *Les toscans,* 339. This judgment is not found in comparable section of the English translation, *Tuscans and Their Families* (New Haven, 1985), 245, where it is simply asserted on behavioral basis "that more bastards were born into rich households, where susceptible, vulnerable women, servants and slaves, abounded."

groups is widely shared.[125] Premarital sex and informal pairing are taken to mark the lower classes, where dowries and other initial property settlements were absent or insignificant relative to effective partnership. Such people were either tolerant of bastards or did not even consider them as such.

Lucia Sandri, however, has expressed her doubts that the poorer folk had a different notion of legitimacy when infanticide and abandonment were clearly part of their world.[126] As she sees it, it was simply that the wealthy could afford their bastards. In the absence of evidence of expression of a different view of legitimacy, it makes more sense to see people making behavioral accommodations in view of their resources and circumstances. The wealthy could afford to maintain more children, bastards or not, as Herlihy and Klapisch-Zuber have demonstrated.[127] The wealthy may also have procreated more bastards because they had access to vulnerable women. None of those Florentines sporting bastards and less than four hundred florins total worth had slaves. So these poorer Florentine bastard-begetters generated their illegitimate offspring before marriage or simply in the absence of it.[128]

A similar picture can be painted for 1480. Of sixty-nine bastards from households under four hundred florins in wealth, twenty-six were attributed to fathers for whom no wife appears (some, of course, may have had a wife who had died or would go on to take a wife later), and another sixteen belonged to men who had wives but no legitimate children. Some of these married men might indeed later have had legitimate children, as had the fathers of another twenty-five for whom legitimate half-siblings can be identified. Only two of these bastards seem to have been adulterine (in that older legitimate siblings existed). Poorer Florentines fathered illegitimate children on poor women generally before marriage or without ever marrying.

Maria Serena Mazzi's excellent study of illicit sexuality in Florence

125. Cf. Ruggiero, *The Boundaries of Eros,* 153–58; Emmanuel LeRoy Ladurie, *Montaillou: The Promised Land of Error,* trans. Barbara Bray (New York, 1978); Barbara Hanawalt, *The Ties That Bound: Peasant Families in Medieval England* (Oxford, 1986), 103, 156, 195–96; Shulamith Shahar, *The Fourth Estate: A History of Women in the Middle Ages,* trans. Chaya Galai (London, 1983), 112, 114, 116.

126. Sandri, *L'Ospedale,* 97 and n. 71, 99.

127. Herlihy and Klapisch-Zuber, *Les toscans,* 432–35.

128. Seven of these fathers were certainly unmarried by the catasto's evidence; the others had legitimate children younger than the bastard(s), indicating, one presumes, the bastard resulted from premarital sex.

presents an illuminating event in this context. In 1460 two prostitutes ended up in litigation with a habitual client, a Giovanni del Chiaro. One of the women had given birth to a child of which Giovanni had recognized paternity. The legal problem was not with the child but with the "joke" the two women played out publicly by continually treating him as the husband of the mother. His suit was intended as an absolute denial of marriage, while freely admitting to frequent sexual congress. Whatever the dangers to his soul, his honorable standing was at stake; he had to deny the marriage, for all that he also thereby affirmed the child's bastardy.[129]

Having no honor and little hope of ever claiming much of it, the poor did not have to fear for their honor. But that does not mean they had a different sense of honor from that of the wealthy. They knew what honor was, just as they knew what legitimacy was. But they did not need to take cognizance of it in all things. The different behavior of the wealthy sprang from the same sense of honor. By acknowledging and raising illegitimates they were avoiding a more serious and damaging (for their reputations and their souls) implication of abandonment. They could even be declaring that their honor was so firmly established as to be beyond challenge. Luca da Panzano recorded an illegitimate within his lineage, born in an adulterous affair of an agnate who was also a priest at the time. The child was passed off as the legitimate offspring of the mother's cuckolded husband.[130] Premarital sexual liaisons could also produce regular contacts and valuable friendships.[131] One has to suspect that it was mainly those toward the middle of the social hierarchy who most powerfully felt the control of honor's demands. They faced both expense and dishonor in raising an illegitimate and were more likely to practice denial and deception regarding illegitimacy, even in the face of neighborhood knowledge and gossip.[132]

One is left with the impression that legal reasons also impelled some Florentines to confess illegitimacy to the catasto officials. As the status

129. Mazzi, *Prostitute e lenoni,* 349.

130. Carlo Carnesecchi, "Un fiorentino del secolo xv e le sue ricordanze domestiche," *Archivio storico italiano,* 5th ser., 4 (1889): 166–67.

131. At least that was one way Alberti explained them, and the directness of his reference to Genoa may excuse his own illegitimacy: "finsi amare una quale fra l'altre stava in bellezza e gentilezza celebratissima fanciulla; e con questa licenza me tragittai fra gli altri nobili dati in quella età all'ozio amatorio, appresso de' quali principai notizia e familiarità a me e a' miei fino in questa età utilissime" (*I libri della famiglia,* 364).

132. Du Boulay, "Lies, Mockery," 398–406.

TABLE 2. Households with More than One Bastard

	1427	1458	1480
Households	28	112	32
Bastards			
Male	53	169	46
Female	21	92	32
Total	74 (2.64 per house*)	261 (2.33)	78 (2.44)

Source: ASF, Catasto.
*2.33 without one house containing 11 bastards

involved inheritance, when there were also legitimate children, which was the situation faced by the majority of Florence's acknowledged bastards, there was reason to keep status straight. Could failure to designate a bastard as such in the catasto be used in court to create a presumption of legitimacy against legitimate heirs? Some Florentines may have decided not to risk that possibility.[133] And those fathers without legitimate offspring—at least the younger among them—would have wanted to keep legitimacy straight in anticipation of future legitimate children. Where more wealth was at stake, there was more riding on maintaining legal categories. The wealthy did not necessarily have a different sense of legitimacy or even a more exact knowledge of the law, just a heightened awareness of its greater potential impact on their lives, and on the devolution of their patrimonies and bloodlines. Having made a conscious decision to recognize paternity, take the child from its mother and raise it, Florentine bastards' fathers (more rarely in the catasto their brothers, cousins, or others) could equally consciously hang the label on their progeny (table 2). Finally, it must be kept in mind that the catasto had its safeguards. *Portate* could be checked against testimony of neighbors, who had financial interests (both in direct monetary rewards and in more equal sharing of fiscal burdens) in keeping others honest.

On the other hand, it is hard to say whether Florentines had a precise sense of the legal distinctions between types of illegitimates. One did not have to be a jurist to know the differences.[134] And Florentines used all the

133. Cf. Anthony Molho, "Deception and Marriage Strategy in Renaissance Florence: The Case of Women's Ages," *Renaissance Quarterly* 41 (1988): 193–217.

134. The one good example I have found, however, comes from the Ragusan merchant Benedetto Cotrugli's *Della mercatura et del mercante perfetto* (Venice, 1573), fol. 99v, where he accurately distinguished *naturali* from *spurii* or *bastardi.* I thank Susan Mosher Stuard for bringing this to my attention. Tamassia, *La famiglia italiana,* 224, claims there was no legal precision in popular language.

terms. In the catasto one finds illegitimates labeled *illegitimo, naturale, bastardo, spureo,* or more vaguely *non è legittimo.* How precisely they were meant, however, is open to question. What is one to make of a married man's newborn "naturale" when he had a 36 year-old wife?[135] Can we believe that a thirty-year-old deserved the harsh term *bastardo* when his eldest legitimate brother was only fifteen, though his father's wife was fifty?[136] In this case the wife would have been nineteen or twenty when the bastard was conceived. Here, as in other areas of life, one is entitled to entertain the suspicion that Florentines were perfectly precise when they needed to be. Giovanni di Notto de' Bardi, married, called his thirty-year-old son *bastardo,* when the best guess is that this son was conceived before his marriage. Arnolfo, his unmarried brother, called his daughter *bastarda.* But Simone, another brother, with a twenty-four-year-old wife, called his nine-year-old daughter *spurea,* perhaps to indicate adulterous circumstances.[137]

This occasional terminological care may reveal that its absence was no less deliberate. Keeping or abandoning a bastard was a conscious decision; so was attaching a label to one. To understand this part of the story of Florentine bastards and the legal difficulties to which they gave rise, we have to look at their parents and the sorts of factors that weighed in their minds when they procreated, kept, or abandoned their illegitimate progeny.

135. Catasto 788, fols. 15r–17r.
136. Catasto 74, fol. 158v (Giovanni, Simone, and Arnolfo di Notto de' Bardi).
137. Catasto 74, fols. 157r–158v.

5
Bastards and Their Kin

Fathering Bastards

Precise legal status seems to have influenced decisions to keep or abandon bastards. We cannot identify all the types of bastards that were specified in the *ius commune.* Offspring of clergy do not figure in the catasto, and I have found only one admission of an incestuous relationship behind a bastard birth. These circumstances were just too painful and shameful to admit to. Adulteries were also rarely acknowledged. Otherwise, one can attempt to reconstruct the status of bastards from correlating information on household relationships and ages in the catasto. To do so requires some firm assumptions, based mainly on demographic data about ages at first marriage and differences in spouses' ages, as well as ignoring the unknowable (deaths of previous spouses or children).

Bastards may be classified as adulterine (the father being married) by one of two indexes. Either there were older legitimate siblings or their father was married and the wife's age was such that (assuming marriage coming between sixteen and twenty for her) the child's birth in all probability came after marriage.[1] Otherwise, where there was no wife or where legitimate siblings were younger and the wife's age fit the profile, bastards are assumed not to have been adulterine. The numbers reveal that the proportion of bastards adulterously procreated and kept with the family decreased steadily through the fifteenth century (from over 28 percent in 1427 to a bit more than 13 percent in 1480) (table 3). It seems that it became rarer for Florentines to keep adulterine bastards in the presence of legitimate progeny, especially older. The largest category of

1. Balerino Nerli may have engendered his two bastards before and after a second marriage: cf. Catasto 67, fol. 489v; and Zacheria di Giovanni Vannicelli may have sought solace after his wife's death: Catasto 66, fols. 418r–419r. Giovanni di Pagolo Morelli had a child in the absence of his wife who had left him six years before with a legal separation agreement (cf. Catasto 72, fols. 130v–131v).

TABLE 3. Legitimate Half-Siblings

	No Siblings			Female Only		
Bastards' Status	1427	1458	1480	1427	1458	1480
Adulterine	3	15	11	1	7	4
Not Adulterine	71	253	109	1	20	16
Uncertain				1	4	3

	Male Siblings					
	Younger			Older		
	1427	1458	1480	1427	1458	1480
Adulterine	3	3	2	42	95	17
Not Adulterine	44	142	89	1	2	
Uncertain	5	13	4	2	1	

Source: ASF, Catasto

bastards (consistently at least two-fifths) were those not born in adultery and retained in their father's or his kin's home in the absence of other legitimate siblings. As the father might later marry and have legitimate sons, the bastards would move into the category of nonadulterine bastards with younger legitimate siblings, which is indeed consistently the second largest category (one-quarter, becoming over one-third in 1480). The proportion of bastards retained in the presence of only female legitimates, though always small, also increased through the fifteenth century.

In addition to wealth, then, the father's marital status affected both the procreation and keeping of bastards. In examining the catasti, we find that the fathers of illegitimates were themselves of various ages when their children were born. They clustered between twenty-five and thirty-four, though there were still a good number spawning bastards when they reached their late thirties and forties. With an average age of males at first marriage of 27.9 years in 1427,[2] the ages of fathers of bastards indicate a degree of adulterous activity on their part. Men, however, married across a broader spectrum of ages than did women, whose ages at first marriage clustered close to the average of 18.9. If we look at the ages of all their offspring, we find a strong presumption that the largest category of bastards resulted from premarital sex for the men. Less than one-quarter of bastards were younger than their oldest legitimate sibling. Those bastards without legitimate siblings were usually the result of pre-

2. Herlihy and Klapisch-Zuber, *Les toscans,* 396.

marital sex. Only ten of their fathers in 1427, for example, are known with certainty to have been married, and the relatively young age of five of their wives gives rise to the presumption that they had only just married.[3] So the experience of Goro Dati, who fathered an illegitimate child during business travel before marriage and later brought her back to Florence, was not atypical from that of other Florentines of his class who fathered bastards.[4] Of course, the circumstances of some bastard-begetters could be quite extraordinary. To bring up one example at this point, Lorenzo di Ghirigoro Lenzi completed a catasto report for his brother Giovangualberto in 1480, listing his forty-five-year-old brother and his wife and children and then confessing "he has more children, male and female, legitimate and not, of whom I do not know their names nor their ages, and so I do not know them in particular." This was because Giovangualberto "has met with defeat in the world and remains and lives in Ferrara without taking stock of or thinking of any of his interests, I must see to it that he belongs here and that he does not remain worthless and that he and his sons not lose the benefit of their country and their city."[5]

To rely once again on an anthropological perspective (but one also found in Machiavelli), in an imperfect world one could not gain resources and friends by always being perfect. By turns one had to be an animal, a trickster, a real "bastard."[6] As Florentine men, particularly among the city's elite families, typically waited into their late twenties before marrying for the first time, if at all, there was a period of premarital sexual activity for young bachelors, an "environment in which unauthorized sexual activity of all sorts flourished." Some of this pent-up youthful energy was directed into male-on-male sexual activity, which

3. Forty-four fathers showed no wife in 1427. Of the married, Antonio di Niccolò had a twelve-year-old bastard and an eighteen-year-old wife (Catasto 66, fol. 167v); Tommaso di Matteo di messer Luca da Panzano had only married in January (Catasto 69, fols. 245r–247r); Francesco Villani's son was twenty-one, his wife thirty (Catasto 69, fols. 326r–328r); Bertoldo Gianfigliazzi had an eight-year-old, his wife being only sixteen (Catasto 75, fols. 141v–145v); Jacopo di Francesco Buonaparte had a seventeen-year-old wife (Catasto 77, fols. 95r–96r).

4. Gene Brucker, ed., *Two Memoirs of Renaissance Florence,* trans. Julia Martines (New York, 1967), 112. Lippaccio Bardi fathered a child in Genoa and his brother had two in Venice (ibid., fols. 437r–446v), while another Florentine had two children in Lisbon (Catasto 790, fols. 265r–268v).

5. Catasto 1006, fol. 347r: "A ppiù figliuoli maschy e ffemine legittimi e non legittimi de' quali io non so i loro nomi né ll'età e pperò io non gli so partichularmente," and "lui inabbi disfatto del mondo e stassi e abiti a Fferrara sanza stimare o ppensare a nnessuno suo interesso, ho debito che ssi gli appartengha di qua e perché egli non rimangha biancho e perché egli non perda il beneficio lui e figliuoli della patrya e della città sua."

6. Cf. Herzfeld, *Anthropology through the Looking Glass,* 46.

led to a variety of concerns on the part of city fathers (a doubly meaningful term in this context).[7] Otherwise it was directed at females, and civic concern (distinct from ecclesiastical) was to channel it away from honorable women. The city's brothels were supposed to direct those sexual drives toward a pool of sexually receptive females who were beyond the pale of discourse about honor. But a young well-to-do Florentine had an even vaster "terreno di caccia," "composed of socially inferior women, servants, slaves, peasants, poor widows of dubious repute, wives and daughters of humble laborers already gossiped about by neighbors for a suspected disapproved behavior."[8] Fornication with such women carried little danger of social disruption and loss of honor; indeed sex with these women expressed the prepotent prerogatives of the elite.

Business travel or political exile for a young patrician male could also result in seeking the comforts and companionship of a woman. Leon Battista Alberti was conceived during a period of political exile in Genoa. Lorenzo di Filippo Strozzi had two children by his Neapolitan concubine, and he brought the children with him to Florence and kept them even after his marriage to a Florentine.[9] How often were other such children left behind? We simply cannot say. There may have been real fear in losing track of such children—not just the fears of unwitting incest that clustered around foundlings in literature but the problems of unexpected claims on inheritance. Lorenzotto Soderini, after all, was one such foreign-born bastard.

Adultery by married men upon easily available servants and slaves was condoned (though hardly praised) socially—if not by their wives.[10] Servants and slaves were considered devoid of scruples and moral principles and thus were fair game for the males of the household, their relatives and guests, even total strangers.[11] The legendary easy virtue of slaves and servants left them open to men other than their employers or owners.[12] A

7. Cf. Rocke, *Forbidden Friendships,* 29, 113–14.

8. Mazzi, *Prostitute e lenoni,* 51–52.

9. Cf. Lorenzo Fabbri, *Alleanza matrimoniale e patriziato nella Firenze del '400: Studio sulla famiglia Strozzi,* Quaderni di "Rinascimento" 12 (Florence, 1991), 48.

10. Mazzi, *Prostitute e lenoni,* 87.

11. Ibid., 118, and regarding peasants, 123–26.

12. For an example, cf. D. V. Kent and F. W. Kent, *Neighbours and Neighbourhood in Renaissance Florence: The District of the Red Lion in the Fifteenth Century* (Locust Valley, N.Y., 1982), 110; Michael Goodich, "*Ancilla Dei:* The Servant as Saint in the Late Middle Ages," in *Women in the Medieval World,* ed. Julius Kirshner and Suzanne F. Wempel (Oxford, 1985), 120–23; Martines, *Power and Imagination,* 165; Jacques Heers, *Esclaves et domestiques au Moyen Age dans le monde méditerranéen* (Paris, 1981), esp. 212–16, 225–32. Mazzi, "Il mondo della prostituzione."

man like Paolo di Lapo Niccolini, a patriarch surrounded by offspring of two wives and two mistresses, was "openly and unblushingly immoral."[13] Gene Brucker and others have spoken of a sexual double standard by which men faced no stigma for their relations with women other than their wives.[14] One historian has speculated that males of the Florentine elite may have sired entire satellite families, not recoverable from legal records; some clearly did so with their slaves, and not only in Florence.[15] The wealthy and noble could flaunt sexual conventions and keep their bastards around them as indications of how far they were above the moral rules for others. Sigismondo Malatesta and his bastard heir, legitimated, Roberto, provide excellent examples of such an attitude, especially in the latter's actions in regard to his own bastard, Troilo.[16] Cosimo de' Medici's bastard son Carlo was recorded for posterity in the Gozzoli fresco adorning the walls of the chapel in the Medici palace (though notably with darker skin and an exotic headdress, on foot and behind the mounted figures of his father and the eldest legitimate son, Piero), as well as in a portrait by Mantegna; and he was prominently paraded past all of Florence in the funeral processions of his father and brother (fig. 2).[17] The Medici clan as a whole seems to have had a small enclave for bastards.[18] Later Michelangelo supposedly suggested making

13. Ginevra Niccolini di Camugliano, *Chronicles of Florentine Family,* 110.

14. Gene Brucker, *Renaissance Florence,* rev. ed. (Berkeley and Los Angeles, 1983), 107, and his *Giovanni and Lusanna: Love and Marriage in Renaissance Florence* (Berkeley and Los Angeles, 1986), 78–80; Jacques Heers, *Family Clans in the Middle Ages: A Study of the Political and Social Structures in Urban Areas,* trans. Barry Herbert (Amsterdam, 1977), 65–66; and his *Esclaves et domestiques,* 212–32; Dorini, *Il diritto penale,* 66–67; Tamassia, *La famiglia italiana,* 221–22, 231–32; Origo, "The Domestic Enemy," 342–45.

15. Julius Kirshner, "Some Problems in the Interpretation of Legal Texts *re* the Italian City-States," *Archiv für Begriffsgeschichte* 19 (1975): 21; Ruggiero, *The Boundaries of Eros,* 30–41; Susan Mosher Stuard, "Urban Domestic Slavery in Medieval Ragusa," *Journal of Medieval History* 9 (1983): 155–71.

16. Cf. Daniel Bornstein, "The Wedding Feast of Roberto Malatesta and Isabetta da Montefeltro: Ceremony and Power," *Renaissance and Reformation,* n.s. 12 (1988): 101–17.

17. Rab Hatfield, "Cosimo de' Medici and the Chapel of His Palace," in *Cosimo "il Vecchio" de' Medici, 1389–1464,* ed. Francis Ames-Lewis (Oxford, 1992), 235 and 236 n. 70; and on the painting and the artistic patronage of Cosimo de' Medici in general, see now Dale Kent, *Cosimo de' Medici and the Florentine Renaissance: The Patron's Oeuvre* (New Haven, 2000), 316 and passim.

18. G. Caroci, "Notizie e curiosità storiche fiorentine," *Arte e storia,* 3d ser., 18 (1899): 131–35, where he quotes from the 1469 catasto declaration of Piero di Cosimo de' Medici that three *casette* in via de' Pucci were inhabited by his brother Carlo, by Giovanna, the mother of the bastard Guerrino di Lorenzo, and by the bastard Mariotto di Averardo. None of these bastards, however, were designated as such in 1458.

Fig. 2. *The Procession of the Magi,* detail, by Benozzo Gozzoli. Palazzo Medici Riccardi, Florence, Italy. (Courtesy of Alinari/Art Resource, NY. Reprinted with permission.)

a piazza from Medici holdings to be called Piazza dei Muli.[19] As a surrogate term for bastards, *muli* interestingly raised both their half-breed origins and the sterility that (the legitimates hoped) marked their future. In a similar vein, while one finds that Giovanni di Giovenco Bastari had his bastard daughter living elsewhere and did not give her name to catasto officials, she lived in a house "sul Canto de' Bastari" and so, in some vague way, remained part of the family.[20]

Illegitimate daughters, even if recognized and fostered by their fathers, were not good marital catches, any more than poor or kinless women.[21] The illegitimate girl would arrive on the marriage market with a perhaps crippling lack of relationships, a smaller dowry, and in all likelihood without the trousseau normally put together by her labor and that of female relations.[22] For the men honor was played out in an active political and economic domain, so the male's exact marital value could not emerge to view until at a later age he had gained some sort of stable social position.[23] The male bastard might never be able to overcome social and economic handicaps. And legitimation—at least by means of subsequent marriage—was doubtful.[24] One historian has argued that it must have been rare

> because in most cases Tartar, Circassian, and Slavic slaves would have become wives to their too tender patrons. It was necessary, therefore, only to attenuate the consequences for the children without upsetting the bases of the family, which could not be rebuilt with feminine elements, sufficiently removed from our customs.[25]

This remark ignores the fact that legitimation could be had by means other than marriage. Still a good many relationships involving unmarried men might indeed have thus been beyond consideration.

In view of the demands of honor, what is surprising is not that Florentines abandoned children but that in a number of cases the fathers did

19. F. W. Kent, "Palaces, Politics, and Society in Fifteenth-Century Florence," *I Tatti Studies* 2 (1987): 61, 67.

20. Caroci, "Notizie e curiosità storiche fiorentine," 134.

21. Fabbri, *Alleanza matrimoniale,* 37–41, 79.

22. Cf. Agnes Fine, "A Consideration of the Trousseau: A Feminine Culture?" in *Writing Women's History,* ed. Michelle Perot, trans. Felicia Pheasant (Oxford, 1992), 118–45.

23. Fabbri, *Alleanza matrimoniale,* 120.

24. Marino Berengo, *Nobili e mercanti nella Lucca del Cinquecento* (Turin, 1965), 37.

25. Tamassia, *La famiglia italiana,* 243.

not, while nonetheless not hiding the fact of illegitimacy. That married men could keep bastards fathered on their slaves and servants (hardly an honorable social parentage) seems surprising every bit as much as that unmarried men would try to raise a child. Wives were not always happy at the prospect of raising the result of their husbands' indiscretion with a slave. There could be no question of their contesting the prerogatives of the *capo di famiglia,* and there usually was not a problem with dishonor. But there were the prerogatives of one's own, legitimate children and the matter of jealousy or betrayal.[26] But for fathers there were also at play powerful cultural presumptions regarding blood, itself a substantial element of honor, and a sense of obligation to one's offspring. There was the addition of a member to the household—and perhaps an exceptionally loyal one who recognized that in his or her regard family ties had a more voluntary and contingent quality to them. A legitimate son who dishonored his family might well be incarcerated at his father's request or even disinherited, while an illegitimate son such as Boccaccio or Alberti might prove to be a considerable asset to his father and family.

James Casey claims that in the Mediterranean, where lineage was the basis of social organization rather than household, it was easier to tolerate illegitimacy. Then honor and family continuity in symbolic terms gave bastards a function that could not, he claims, be accorded where property mattered in primary form, as in English households.[27] While it is difficult to downplay the importance of material resources, against which bastards represented potential claims, it is essential to retain an awareness of the cultural connotations of property. Wealthier Florentines could better shoulder such costs. For them there was some likelihood that they would recognize paternity and raise bastards, especially those fathered in their youth, prior to marriage. These children were not rejected, but they also were in an inferior position, always faced with the possible later birth of legitimate brothers or sisters.

Bastards' Mothers

One factor, then, that could greatly influence decisions to keep bastards was the identity and social status of the mother. It is not a simple matter to determine who these women were. Of course, one did not need to own

26. Cf. Mazzi, *Prostitute e lenoni,* 54–55.

27. James Casey, *The History of the Family* (Oxford, 1989), 105, 112.

the slave to sleep with her. Filippo d'Ardingo de' Ricci, who had an illegitimate son according to the 1427 catasto, had already fathered two other bastards six years earlier on a slave belonging to Giuliano di Cattaneo di messer Cristiano. We know of them because his paternity was alleged in the notarial instrument of her manumission.[28] Beyond slaves the usual presumption is that wealthy males preyed on young servants and other women of poor, and perhaps rustic, backgrounds. The only firm attribution of motherhood in the 1427 census came from Francesco di Cambio da Siena, who lived in concubinage with his servant, Nencia, and had six children by her.[29]

The 1480 catasto is equally reticent about mothers, yielding the following bits of information. Santi di Giovanni dal Borgo said his son was fathered on a former servant.[30] Mariano di Piero di Mariano said that Angnola was the concubine by whom he had two young children, and Giuliano di Angnolo Benciatti had his infant by monna Antonia, "who stays in my house" [sta mecho in chasa].[31] Giovanni di Taddeo dell'Antella admitted that he had a son by his *serva* Caterina. Antonio di Bonaccorso Soldani had three children by a Marconchetta di Matteo. And Ruberto, son of the lawyer Giovanni Migliorati da Prato, himself studying canon law in 1480, reported his son, who had been legitimated and was studying grammar, was born of Camilla, a *serva*.[32]

The 1458 catasto, however, is an exceptionally rich source of information on illegitimate maternity, which gives us some statistical basis to substantiate more occasional evidence. Catasto officials required, in order to back the claim to paternity and a consequent deduction, that the mother's identity be disclosed. That a good number of bastards were not given a deduction indicates that the numbers resulting from this catasto may be inflated, but generally failure to gain the deduction only means that it was not approved.[33] In any case, with a possible deduction at

28. Notarile 9039 (1417–21), fols. 197r–v (21 April 1419), 333v–334v (2 April 1421). Ricci's catasto declaration is Catasto 81, fols. 464r–465r. A second example is the manumission by Giovanni di Lorenzo of a slave Pacetta, "nate olim ex Jannina Gheza olim sclava et serva ipsius Johannis et filie, ut asseruit dici, olim Stefani Pacetti de Venetiis" (Notarile 7942 [1423–27], fol. 23r–v [21 August 1424]).

29. Catasto 65, fols. 326v–327v.

30. Catasto 1014, fol. 266r–v.

31. Catasto 1022, fol. 99r; 1003, fol. 488r.

32. Catasto 1002, fols. 210r–211r; 1005, fols. 41r–42r; 1007, fol. 345r–v.

33. To give an example, an official appended the following to the statement of Marco di Marco di messer Forese Salviati: "Metteglisi in chonto due bocche oltra alla sua, cioè la dompna del figluolo e la Lisabetta sua figluola, e Francesco non si mette perché non è ligiptimo et non fu aprovato" (Catasto 809, fols. 72r–73r).

TABLE 4. Bastards' Mothers, 1458

Bastards	Mother's Status			
	Slave	Serva	Fante	Free or Unknown
Male	83	45	9	124
Female	58	24	6	58
Total (n = 407)	141	69	15	182

Source: ASF, Catasto

stake, Florentines' reticence broke down. Of 557 illegitimates, identity of the mother (at least her first name in most cases) was given for 407. Of these, 141 (34.8 percent) were the children of slaves (eighty-three sons, fifty-eight daughters) and a further 84 (fifty-four male) were by a servant *(serva* or *fante)* (table 4). One gets a clear indication of the degree of exploitation of younger women of little or no status or honor within households not of their birth.

One has to suspect that many unnamed mothers were also slaves or servants. Some of these *schiave* or *serve* were also later let go or sold off, showing, perhaps, that sharing the master's bed was not always the ticket to easier treatment. Jealous wives, after all, might not want such women around.[34] But the jealous wife could also be avoided by bedding someone else's slave or servant. An astounding number of mothers of bastards were slaves or servants in the households of people other than the child's father. Forty-five bastards in 1458 (twenty-eight men, seventeen women) were fathered on others' domestics. We have already encountered a notorious example in Rinieri di messer Luigi Guicciardini, whose mother was a slave of Bindo Galetti of Pisa.[35] Lionardo di Zanobi del Recha, a forty-two-year-old with no wife or legitimate children, raised his two-year-old by the slave of Pagolo da Diacceto, as Vieri d'Antonio Davanzati raised his son by the slave of Andrea dello Stufa. Francesco di Giovanni Strozzi owned the distinction of having two bastards by the slaves of others. Bettino d'Antonio Ricasoli took advantage of what the fortunes of war threw his way; a young girl from Volterra had stayed with him as *fante* and paid for the experience by leaving behind a child.[36] Ser Marchione di ser Marchione Donati seems to have fallen for the teenage slave Madalena, who belonged to Stoldo Frescobaldi. After having a daughter

34. Cf. Catasto 786, fols. 43r–45r; 788, fols. 565r–568v; 790, fols. 23r–24v; 801, fols. 1092r–v; 813, fols. 276r–277v; 814, fols. 46r–48r.

35. Catasto 788, fols. 302r–306v.

36. Catasto 798, fols. 315r–318v.

by her he obtained her freedom, and thereafter she lived with him and he called her his *donna*.[37]

The treatment of Madalena shows that some slaves and servants did get preferential treatment. While the children of servants, as we will see, were at times themselves treated as servants in their father's home or that of relatives, their mothers may have hoped to gain other favors from their patrons by sharing their beds; although they were never really secure, even if they did not have to fear the reaction of the mistress of the house.[38] Freedom was one thing that could accrue to slaves who gave birth to bastards. The slave Lucia who bore Filippo di Jacopo Tani in 1440 had been manumitted by 1458, but remained in Tani's house.[39] Giovanni di Luca Ubertini's slave gave birth in 1449, was manumitted in 1452, and remained with Ubertini to give birth again in 1454.[40] The widow of Corsino di Jacopo Corsini made it clear that she freed her slave girl because she gave birth to a daughter by Giovanni di Corsino.[41] Girolamo di Nichola Bonciani freed the mother of his daughter when he later married, which may have been a concession to his spouse.[42] Tommaso di Piero Giovanni freed the mother of his little girl when, at the young age of thirty-five, he thought he was about to die, and because she had borne him two children.[43]

The mother's virtue, however, could be restored in some sense by finding her a normal and honorable marriage. Several Florentines reported that their *schiave* or *serve,* mothers of illegitimates, had been married off. Tommaso Biliotti's marriage to the former slave Caterina, mother of his son Piero, but property of his cousin Giovanozzo, meant that "from shame I will remain silent" [da vergho' traschò sordo].[44]

37. This and other examples are Catasto 804, fols. 336r–v; 814, fols. 489r–490v; 816, fols. 776r–v; 832, fols. 394r–395v.

38. See Piero Guarducci and Valeria Ottanelli, *I servitori domestici dell casa borghese toscana nel basso Medioevo* (Florence, 1982), esp. 22–24, 72–76, 88, 90–91.

39. Catasto 821, fols. 130r–133v.

40. Catasto 790, fols. 541r–544r.

41. Catasto 791, fols. 207r–v, 210r–v.

42. Catasto 811, fols. 542r–543v.

43. Catasto 816, fols. 466r–467v: "La chagione e ragione della sua Liberttà ne fu chagione che del detto mese per malattia ch'io ebi e istavo male e perché di lei avevo avuto 2 figliuoli ed era grossa, per remedio dell'anima mia la liberai chome di sopra v'è detto e per ischriture me potrete essere ben chiari." There is a general discussion of slave manumissions (often legally incorrectly labeled emancipations) in Steven A. Epstein, *Speaking of Slavery: Color, Ethnicity, and Human Bondage in Italy* (Ithaca, N.Y., 2001), 86–93.

44. Catasto 790, fols. 60r–62r.

Lionardo di ser Piero Doffi married off his slave to a *famiglio* of the Arte degli Speziali; Francesco di Giannozzo Alberti put his *serva* with a cook in the Mercato Vecchio.[45]

A goodly proportion of the mothers of bastards were not slaves or servants. These were women for whom generally some indication of their paternity was given. They were the victims of sexual aggrandizement beyond the household in a variety of circumstances. Where names alone are given, one cannot be sure of the social status of such women. Lorenzo del Chiaro said the mother of his son's bastard was Piera d'Andrea. Who was she?[46] For other mothers, however, more information was given. Some were from and remained in other cities, where they met the peripatetic Florentine father.[47] Many of these women were from the countryside. It is not clear if the fathers met them in Florence or in the course of *villeggiatura*. Piero di Simone Orlandini had an illegitimate brother from a woman in Piombino and a son by a woman from the Mugello.[48] But it seems safe to say that exploitation of such women was not far removed from that of slaves and servants. One finds among mothers of bastards Appollonia d'Antonio of Impruneta, Madalena d'Antonio del Poguzoli from Cerrida near Poggibonsi, Tana di Pagolo di Giovanni da San Casciano, Gemma di Marchione da Castel Nuovo, Mea d'Agnolo da Casentino, and Mea da Quarantola.[49]

Florentines did not have to leave the city to reach across class lines for a mother of a bastard, although one imagines more potential for conflict if they too blatantly pursued women in other households, however humble. Still one finds a few situations like that described in the catasto declaration of Antonio di ser Paolo della Camera. He had a bastard by a woman from Fighine, while his brother ser Jacopo fathered one on Caterina d'Andrea di Tome, daughter of a weaver.[50] Uberto di Giovanni degli Albizzi fathered one son on a slave (who received no deduction) but an

45. Catasto 800, fols. 259r–261r; 805, fols. 577r–581r; with further examples in 809, fols. 274v–275r and 387r–391r; 818, fols. 273r–274r.

46. Catasto 832, fols. 347r–349r.

47. A few examples: Catasto 785, fols. 16r–18r; 788, fols. 791r–793r; 790, fols. 265r–268v; 800, fols. 281r–283v and 620r–621v; 804, fols. 267r–276r; 805, fols. 518r–519v and 700r–701v; 809, fols. 77r–85r; 816, fols. 1021r–1022r; 825, fols. 185r–187v.

48. Catasto 804, fols. 956r–957v.

49. Catasto 790, fols. 51r–54v; 791, fols. 65r–69r and 119r–120v; 798, fols. 537r–538r; 825, fols. 229r–231r; 829, fols. 637r–638r. Other examples are Catasto 825, fols. 92r–94v; 832, fols. 939r–940v.

50. Catasto 801, fols. 1290r–1293r.

older one on the daughter of a blacksmith of Cortona (who did).[51] Frusino d'Ugolino Cuicci found in the daughter of a *tintore* the live-in mother of two children. He even legitimated the boy, despite the fact that he had an older illegitimate son by a woman from Anghiara.[52]

Such women might have met the legal definition of a concubine (if both were unmarried), especially where they bore more than one child by the same man. We have already encountered the case of Paliano di Falco, whose *ricordi* disclose the births of three children by a Perugian widow between 1382 and 1389.[53] Here was a long-standing relationship, and it is interesting to note that Paliano does not appear to have looked to marry a Florentine woman until after his concubine died. Ghita di Nanni di Bonsi da Montespertoli lived with Bernardo di ser Orlando di Giovanni in his villa and bore his three children.[54] Giovanni di Piero da Meleto had three illegitimate children by a Piera d'Andrea who lived with him for ten years; Belfredello di Niccolò Alfieri had two by a Maria, a "forestiera" who lived with him even after his marriage.[55] Apparently, after Francesco di Bartolomeo Baldovini's wife died giving birth to a son, he took up with a Giora di Giovanni da Romagna, who gave him three children over an eight-year span.[56] On the other hand, Francesco di Bonaiuto reported that his eldest son Bonaiuto (age thirty-one) had had two daughters by a woman named Giovanna di Marcho who lived in the Via del Mero.[57] Her separate residence would have precluded her categorization as a concubine, and her children's as *naturales,* in a strict sense, even if she otherwise was a "kept woman."

On the other end of the spectrum, some men had bastards by more than one woman. Antonio di Goro d'Antonio had two eleven-year-olds by different women. Piero di Giovanni di Ciragio had two sons in his younger days—one by Agnesa di Corsica and one by Maria, who was living with Biagio da Vinci.[58]

Some of these women were also vulnerable as widows. At least six mothers of bastards were so designated.[59] On the other hand, I uncov-

51. Catasto 828, fols. 390r–391r.

52. Catasto 804, fols. 492r–493v.

53. ASF, Carte strozziane, 2d ser., 7, fols. 4v–5r.

54. Catasto 788, fols. 689r–690r. Also ibid., fols. 183r–184v; 825, fols. 648r–649r.

55. Catasto 801, fols. 1283r–1287r; 825, fols. 113r–114v.

56. Catasto 832, fols. 651r–653v.

57. Catasto 810, fols. 535r–536v.

58. Catasto 791, fols. 287r–288v; 801, fols. 726r–729v

59. Catasto 785, fols. 318r–321r; 795, fols. 256r–258v; 801, fols. 1153r–1159r; 809, fols. 256r–259r; 811, fols. 475r–476v; 813, fols. 240r–242r.

ered instances where the mother was said to be married, but none of these can be taken as conclusive of adultery on her part. The mother of Leonardo da Vinci, for example, was said to be married "al presente" to a fellow from Vinci, implying that she was not married when the then five-year-old was conceived.[60] The married woman whose bastard was twenty-two in 1458 may also have been single at the time of conception.[61] In the case of Tommaso di Marco di Tommaso, however, adultery may lie behind the two-year-old twins he had from monna Maddalena, wife of Pippo, a poor *farsettaio*.[62]

One must also consider the instances where Florentines did not reveal the mothers' names. At times, relatives confessed, they just did not know her name because the father was long deceased and the mother lived elsewhere, or something of that sort.[63] But at other times Florentines made it abundantly clear that they would not reveal her identity. Emblematic here is the following statement by Niccolaio di Piero da Meleto, who otherwise had willingly revealed that two bastards were by Caterina da Rossia, a slave subsequently liberated: "Of the other children, because it would be necessary to name the mother, this I have not done because their honor should not suffer and be what it can."[64] Similarly Bartolomeo di Puccio and Geri di Poldo de' Pazzi cited honor *(onestà)* as the reason for not revealing a bastard's mother's name.[65] *Onestà* only applied to mothers who had not been slaves or domestics. Filippo di Filippo Tornabuoni did not hesitate to disclose the name of the slave mother of his nine-year-old, who was younger than his legitimate children; but he invoked a sense of *onestà* for not telling who the mother of the thirty-year-old Giovanni was.[66] Ruggieri di Taddeo di Ruggieri Crucci operated with a finer sense of *onestà:*

> And the aforesaid Lisa, not legitimate, her mother was the slave of my brother Giovanni, whom he later sold, and she [Lisa] is without a dowry. And my illegitimate Francesco, his mother is alive and is named monna Papera, daughter of Cienni Cienini, a laborer, and her

60. Catasto 795, fols. 502r–503r; see also 788, fols. 487r–493v.

61. Catasto 814, fols. 602r–603v.

62. Catasto 804, fol. 266r–v. See also 788, fols. 651r–652v.

63. As Catasto 785, fols. 16r–18r; 828, fol. 327r–v.

64. Catasto 801, fols. 1230r–1266r, at 1247v: "D'altri figliuoli, perché bisognia nominare la madre, questo non ò fare ché nolle patisce l'onestà e ssia chome si può."

65. Catasto 816, fols. 448r–450r; 832, fols. 859r–863r.

66. Catasto 818, fols. 1045r–1048v.

husband is a laborer, and for the sake of honor I do not write [his name].[67]

He gave the mother's name but not her husband's, while also showing how his eldest (his legitimate eldest brother was only twelve, whereas Francesco was eighteen) lived and worked.

Finally, we can corroborate these data about mothers from another source, the records of the *monte delle doti*.[68] Fund records yield indication of the girls' mothers in 298 cases. Fifty-four of these mothers are designated as slaves or former slaves, twenty-six as *serva,* two as *fante,* and the rest (217) either specifically or vaguely as free women not in some form of domestic service (although some of them may well have been). None of the Innocenti girls had a mother attributed to her, so these numbers undoubtedly underrepresent the slaves and domestics as mothers. The *monte* may overrepresent the slave-owning class, but the percentage of girls in the dowry fund with slave mothers was less than the percentage of such girls in the 1458 catasto, an indication of a greater reluctance to fund even a modest dowry for the daughter of a slave.

On rare occasions slave women took the initiative in admitting maternity of an illegitimate in order at the same time to make a declaration/accusation of paternity. One, Maddalena, at the time wet nurse to a neighbor's boy, "wanting to exonerate her conscience and soul so that the truth might be established and made known," confessed that her two-year-old son was conceived in her owner's home by a Pisan, Cristofano d'Antonio da Saiano. She specified the time of the conception (November 1424) and swore that "afterward she had nothing to do, no concubinage, with anyone else."[69] Sandro Rondinelli's slave likewise revealed that her pregnancy was the work of Bartolomeo, a *cambiatore,* son of Barduccio.[70] Giovenco di Giuliano de' Medici's slave girl asserted that her pregnancy resulted from several encounters ("quamplures habuit agens") with Giovenco and ser Piero di Domenico Mazzinghi of Florence.[71]

67. Catasto 800, fols. 376r–379v: "E la Lisa sopradetta non ligittima la madre fu schiava di Giovanni mio fratello, la quale di poi vendò e sanza dota. E Francesco mio non ligittimo la madre vive e à nome mona Papera figluola di Cienni Cienini lavoratore, ed è marito uno lavoratore per onestà no lo scrivo."

68. I thank Anthony Molho for sharing with me this information regarding deposits for illegitimate girls.

69. Notarile 682 (1425–29), fol. 322r–v (15 December 1427).

70. Ibid., fol. 360r (17 April 1428).

71. Notarile 687 (1440–42), fol. 346r (12 May 1442). In 1449 Giovenco left a dowry of 140 florins to an illegitimate daughter Giovanna, who may have been this slave's child

These confessions were easy to make or easily forced, because there was no need to worry about the slave's reputation. The men's reputations were less at issue than was monetary support for the child and compensation, by statute, for damage/depreciation to the slave. Paternity was one matter where a slave had standing in the law.[72]

I have found one example only of a practice Nino Tamassia claimed occurred with some regularity—namely, a wife's confession that someone other than her husband was father of her child.[73] In a notarial charter containing a long preamble about clearing one's conscience and having children raised by the proper father, Lena di Giovanni di ser Benedetto di Neri, wife of Benedetto di Piero, swore on the Gospels that her infant son Filippo had been fathered by Francesco di Bartolo Bischeri, who admitted his paternity. Bischeri seems to have taken over raising the child and twenty-two years later claimed him as a catasto deduction, correctly reporting the mother's identity, though suppressing any mention of her marriage.[74] I have also located an interesting example to the opposite effect. The wife of Fascello di Matteo di Fascello Petriboni, in the presence of the archbishop Antonino and others, including her confessor and her husband, in 1454, countered gossip and rumors about her marital fidelity by asserting that her son belonged to her husband. She did not exactly say that she had not committed adultery.[75] There was a double

(Notarile 690 [1447–50], fols. 205r–207v [26 June 1449]). Two other examples are Notarile 6253 (1450–54), fol. 200r (5 May 1456) and fol. 311v (16 December 1456).

72. Cf. Laura Balletto, "Stranieri e forestieri a Genova: Schiavi e manomessi (secolo xv)," in *Forestieri e stranieri nelle città basso-medievali,* 263–83.

73. Cf. Tamassia, *La famiglia italiana,* 227–29.

74. Catasto 832, fols. 347r–349r; Notarile 3374 (1433–44), fol. 187r (21 October 1435).

75. Notarile 13501 (1447–59), fol. 78r (7 October 1454): "dixit et sponte affirmavit tam pro sue conscientie exoneratione quam veritate delucidanda, et pro omni scandali quod aliquo unquam tempore exoriri posset materia tollenda et restanda . . . et ad preces et complacentiam dicti Fascelli eius viri hec fieri potentis, et pro tolleranda et abicienda de mente dicti Fascelli omni dubietate si quam haberet quod infrascriptus Aldobrandinus non foret ipsius Fascelli filius legitimus et naturalis, pro eo maxime quod ad ipsius domine Vaggie notitiam devenerat quod aliqui ipsam diffamare voluissent, quod ipsa non fuisset continens et honesta et matrimonium violasset, que omnia dictus Fascellus etiam dixit audivisse et ad sui notitiam devenisse, et tandem in predictorum reverendorum patrum et testium dictique sui viri ac mei notarii presentia in verbo veritatis dixit et iuramento firmavit quod Aldobrandinus filius suus quem peperisse dixit die tertio mensis maii anni incarnationis dominice mccccxlviiii fuit et est filius legitimus et naturalis suus et dicti Fascelli eius legitimi mariti conceptus ex dicto Fascello eius marito." See Carol Lansing, "Gender and Civic Authority: Sexual Control in a Medieval Italian Town," *Journal of Social History* 31 (1997–98): 33–59.

irony here. For all her efforts, the paternity of the child, who was five, ultimately did not matter because he seems to have died young. Fascello's will of 1470 named as his heir his sister. The further irony is that the same will contains legacies to Petribono and Caterina, Fascello's *naturales.*[76] Nothing was said in the will about the identity of the children's mother(s). We also do not know what became of his "honest" wife.

Taken all together the evidence regarding the mothers of bastards from these sources is fairly consistent. A fair proportion of these women were slaves (34.8 percent by the catasto, 18.1 percent by the dowry fund). Others were domestics (20.8 percent in the catasto, 8.6 percent in the fund). The largest category of mothers was always that of relatively poor and vulnerable women, including foreigners either resident in Florence or more often met with by Florentine men in their travels. In a few cases these women had enjoyed prolonged relationships with the fathers. For most, however, we cannot with confidence make any such claim.

The somewhat longer period of celibacy experienced by the average Florentine male as the fifteenth century progressed may have encouraged more illicit sexual conduct and consequent illegitimacy.[77] The slight increase in the proportion of bastards born or conceived before the father married, if he ever did, is testimony to that, as well as, perhaps, the increase in the overall number of illegitimates. But do these numbers also reveal in some way a change of concern about these children? a "golden age" of bastards? To answer such questions we must progress to examining their social and economic treatment.

Bastards and Their Families

Once a Florentine father had decided, for whatever reason, to raise his bastard, he had to determine how to treat the child and how much to invest in him or her. Here, as in so much else revolving around illegitimates, there was no single script to follow. Treatment could range from relatively harsh (little better than a servant or slave) to roughly equivalent to a legitimate child, especially if there were no legitimate children. But beyond the treatment meted out to a bastard by his father, there was also

76. Notarile 14715 (1469–71), fols. 43v–44r (28 May 1470).

77. Klapisch-Zuber, "Déclin démographique et structure du ménage," in *Famille et parenté dans l'Occident médiéval,* ed. Georges Duby and Jacques Le Goff (Rome, 1977), 255–68; David Herlihy, "Vieillir à Florence au Quattrocento," *Annales* 24 (1969): 1338–52.

the question of the attitudes and behavior of other kin. No matter how favored paternally, agnatic reception was something else.

The example of Jacopo della Seta of Pisa can serve to set up these themes. Jacopo della Seta was a particularly well-treated bastard. As the jurist who wrote a *consilium* in the appellate stage of his case, the renowned Milanese Giason del Maino, was moved to remark, paternal blessings were undoubted, "for from witnesses produced in both courts it is sufficiently proved that the father had twelve legitimate and natural children but treated said Jacopo, a *spurius,* like the other legitimate and natural children, although in Pisa, as the witnesses deposed, others who have legitimate and natural children are accustomed to treat *spurii* as servants and slaves." Jacopo had been sent to school and apprenticed in the wool trade, having been long a master in the guild himself. Finally, and perhaps most conclusively, Jacopo had been legitimated and made an heir with the others—that being worth seven hundred florins.[78] It was the transfer and acceptance of paternal obligations and liabilities toward the bastard that met with resistance from the heirs.

Specifically, Jacopo had been left legacies by Agostina, his paternal grandmother, which legacies he had formally given his father, Pietro. When, following his father's death, Jacopo attempted to get them back, he had to go to court against the heirs of his father and against Gabriele, son of Pietro's brother, Niccolò. Jacopo lost in the court of first instance, and the Milanese jurist reviewed the case materials for the appeals court and quickly affirmed, "I think the lord judge of the appeal should side with confirming the sentence in favor of the sons and heirs of Pietro and Niccolò, and so we pronounce the case well judged and badly appealed."[79]

First, as a *spurius* Jacopo had not been in his father's *potestas,* so the gift was valid. Further, because the gift was made "propter innumerabilia beneficia" received from his father, del Maino struck down Jacopo's

78. ASF, Carte strozziane, 3d ser., 41/3, fols. 414v–415r: "Nam ex testibus productis in utroque iudicio est sufficientia probatio quod Petrus habens xii filios legittimos et naturales, tamen tractabat dictum Jacobum spurium prout alios filios legittimos et naturales, quamvis ibi Pisis prout testes disponunt alii qui habent filios legittimos et naturales soleant tractare filios spurios tanquam famulos et sclavos. . . . Item facit eundem Jacobum adiscere literas et sic legere et scribere ad quod tamen pater non tenetur erga filium spurium. Item fecit eum adiscere artificium artis lane et fieri magistrum dicte artis lane. . . . Item dictus Petrus immediate post donationem factam de predictis legatis fecit ipsum Jacobum legittimari ut apparet ex instrumento legittimationis post donationem factam. Item instituit eum heredem equaliter simul cum aliis filiis legittimis et naturalibus."

79. Ibid., fol. 418r.

claim that the gift was legally revoked in view of the fact that Jacopo had since had children of his own. Although the subsequent appearance of direct heirs did lead to revocation of gratuitous gifts according to Roman law, a gift for *benemerita* was not revocable in law.[80] It was possible to enumerate the benefits Jacopo had received.

Giason del Maino came to a conclusion that hurt an illegitimate, keeping that gift in the patrimony where, in inheritance, it had to be split with the other twelve siblings. The effect of the conclusion was that, in the end, Jacopo would indeed be treated equally with the other siblings as heirs, with no advantage of grandmaternal generosity to skew paternal provisions. Jacopo had been cared for, legitimated even, and left property by both his grandmother and his father; and for all that he probably lost his case. Other bastards encountered different results. How they were cared for, whether they were legitimated, what—if anything—they came to inherit and own, and how jurists respected and supported their claims or the competing claims of the kin who otherwise would have inherited and owned family property all varied.

A child represented an investment in familial survival.[81] Maintenance and education were costs that had to pay off. What did the men who took bastards into their homes provide them? An illegitimate's expenses would seem to represent an unwise investment. The contribution he or, less often she, could make to the family might not be much, and the biological and symbolic continuity a bastard might provide was at least open to question. While having no children was a disaster, families had to gamble with the dilemma of having too many children. They each represented cost, material and symbolic. It was difficult to cut these costs with legitimate children. Education was needed, some kind of dowry had to be provided. In inheritance, property had to be left to all sons, disinheritance being a very difficult proposition and requiring a statement of cause that itself could become an embarrassing admission of failure to measure up to a cultural model of familial comportment.[82] Taking on an illegitimate child was a risk, but for some Florentines it was not a high risk. Their education could be minimal; their dowries less; their inheritance

80. Ibid., fol. 412r. As this was, therefore, the jurisprudentially interesting point, he spent most of his energies here.

81. David Herlihy, "Family and Property in Renaissance Florence," in *The Medieval City,* ed. Harry A. Miskimin, David Herlihy, and A. L. Udovitch (New Haven, 1977), 3–24.

82. See *Enciclopedia del diritto,* s.v. "Erede e eredità (diritto intermedio)," by Manlio Bellomo, vol. 15 (Milan, 1966); Enrico Besta, *Le successioni nella storia del diritto italiano* (Milan, 1936).

small or nonexistent. On the other hand, investment in them might be realized to advantage, however small, with what they might earn or with whom they might marry. At a certain point, in other words, especially for wealthy families, bastards may have been a relatively cheap form of insurance for familial preservation. It is one of this chapter's goals to test this proposition, while facing the evidence of the catasto that the nature of that investment also changed across the fifteenth century.

A number of younger girls were placed in convents either to become nuns eventually or to await husbands.[83] Otherwise fathers or kin said nothing about girls in the catasto, except to note (especially in 1480) if there was a dowry for them (amounts rarely given). For boys there are occasional bits of information much more varied in nature. Niccolò di Marco Strozzi, for one, made it apparent that he wanted nothing to do with his illegitimate nephew.[84] In contrast, the young children of ser Bartolomeo di ser Nichola Schiattesi received equal treatment. The *legitimi*, Bartolomeo (age six) and Pieraccina (age seven), were placed with a woman at a rate of twelve florins each year for *alimenta*. Illegitimate Nencio was placed with a relative at the same annual rate.[85] We know of bastards learning the abacus, of one "alla squola," of one wandering about for employment ("ito per raghazo al soldo uno"), of several become monks, of one studying to be a priest, and of some become notaries (so much for guild prohibitions).[86] The illegitimate son of Giovanni di maestro Piero da Norcia, one of Florence's poorest doctors in 1427, eventually went to university and became a physician himself.[87] Cambino di Francesco Cambini sent Luigi to study in Perugia, which perhaps also got this twenty-five-year-old away from his older half brother and his children.[88]

Some bastards contributed nothing to the domestic economy or had nothing. In 1480 Francesco di Nicolaio Cavalcanti, for example, himself "senza alchuno aviamento," noted that his brother's bastard Andrea was

83. Catasto 995, fols. 152r–153v; 1001, fols. 351r–352r; 818, fols. 568r–569v, where we are told "la quale fanciulla perché inpari qualche virtù la tengho a uno munistero e persino si spuxa."

84. Catasto 1012, fols. 162r–163r.

85. Catasto 69, fols. 24v–25v.

86. Catasto 994, fol. 200r–v; 992, fols. 26r–27r; 1006, fol. 394r–v; 1011, fols. 151r–155v; 1021, fol. 79r–v; 1002, fols. 167r–169v.

87. Katherine Park, *Doctors and Medicine in Early Renaissance Florence* (Princeton, N.J., 1985), 156.

88. Catasto 826, fols. 380r–383v.

in the same position. In 1458 Lodovico Acciaiuoli, Giovanni di Jacopo Ventura, and ser Ambruogio Angeni said the same about their sons.[89] Guasparre di Lorenzo Guidetti was "sanza guadagno alchuno"; Lodovico d'Averardo Serristori was unemployed ("scioperato"); Bruto di Matteo Corsi "sanza exercitio"; and Alessandro di Vangelista di Brunetto "does nothing" [non fa nulla].[90] Often one finds mention of illegitimate sons away in other cities or regions, presumably on business.[91] In other cases, however, their fathers or relatives did not know where they were. "He journeys through the world" [va pel mondo] or "he goes in search of money" [va a soldo], they told catasto officials, who nonetheless listed such sons among the family's members, even if they did not usually give the deduction the family wanted.[92] Mariotto di Filippo di Parente simply said that his twenty-eight-year-old "returns to me when he wants" [torna mecho quando e' vuole]; Ugolino di Lorenzo Gherardini did not know where Matteo (age thirty) was.[93]

For the most part one assumes those bastards who saw their teens and twenties must have acquired some skills to earn at least a modest living. Some, of course, were able to do quite well, if not necessarily as well as their legitimate brothers. An outstanding example is Niccolò, the bastard son of Francesco di Matteo Castellani. Francesco's *ricordi* disclosed paternal expenses for this, his only son (there were four legitimate daughters). He bought his son a jacket, shoes and hose, just about every year, as well as a fee to be schooled on the abacus.[94] Here too is where we have to confront the evidence of Boccaccio's and Alberti's lives, as well as the successful ecclesiastical career of an Andrea di Francesco d'Alamanno Salviati in the fourteenth century and of Piero di Bernardo Salviati in the

89. Catasto 811, fols. 256r–257r; 818, fols. 167r–171v; 800, fols. 311r–313r. Zanobi di Tommaso Ginori explained that his Jacopo was "infermo continuamente" (Catasto 820, fols. 297r–300v).

90. Catasto 995, fols. 59r–60v; 1005, fols. 35r–36v; 1005, fols. 467r–468r; 1012, fols. 353r–354r. Also Catasto 1002, fols. 153r–154r; 1014, fol. 226r–v; 998, fols. 361r–362r; 1016, fols. 305r–306v.

91. Catasto 72, fols. 9v–14r; 79, fol. 490r–v; 80, fols. 18v–21r; 1006, fol. 394r–v; 801, fols. 696r–697r; 1005, fol. 78r–v.

92. Catasto 1008, fols. 65r–66r; 76, fols. 372r–373r; 74, fols. 15v–16v; 69, fols. 326r–328r.

93. Catasto 828, fols. 413r–414r; 798, fols. 378r–379r.

94. Francesco di Matteo Castellani, *Ricordanze,* vol. 2: *Quaternuccio e Giornale B (1459–1485),* ed. Giovanni Ciappelli (Florence, 1995), 57–58, 62, 79, 92, 115, 125, 127–29, 142, 163, 193, 197, 220.

sixteenth.[95] But the property interests of even these lucky bastards were not favored or protected. Niccolò Castellani faced an inheritance dispute.[96] We know Alberti had problems collecting the legacy left him by his father. That may not have been consistently the case for other bastards, but the fact that legacies for bastards were entered among the assets and liabilities of households in the catasto does not mean that they were later paid.[97] And illegitimates were not covered—formally at least—by the guardianship *(tutela)* that safeguarded legitimate children after their father died (though *legitimati* could have a *tutela*).[98]

In this context one cannot neglect the life and career of the bastard Carlo di Cosimo de' Medici. Born of a Circassian slave, Carlo was early on destined for an ecclesiastical career. With his family connections he obtained a doctorate in canon law and participated in the affairs of the Florentine college of doctors of law; he also secured the post of rector in Prato (where he persuaded Filippo Lippi to complete his frescoes); and later became an apostolic protonotary.[99] Carlo gained a reputation of sorts for scholarly interests and gathered coins and manuscripts for his father. Bastard or not, he had an active role in his father's funeral procession and in the wedding celebration at Rome when his nephew Lorenzo married Clarice Orsini.[100] The Medici would build on the Roman ecclesiastical connections Carlo gave them with Giovanni and Giulio (also illegitimate) later.

In this connection it is worth noting Giorgio Vasari's treatment of

95. Hurtubise, *Une famille-témoin,* 121–22, 297, 344, and 318–19.

96. Castellani, *Ricordanze,* 2:10–12.

97. Cf. Catasto 75, fols. 156v–157v; Catasto 80, fol. 569r and 156v–157v, where one finds the following notation: "E per lascio per testamento a Simone sopradetto [illegitimate brother] fi. cc in fino ad primo d'Ottobre 1427 non n'ànno paghato nulla per rispetto delli ghravezze."

98. To cite examples, a *tutela* for Zanobi and Antonio di Filippo di Niccolò Macinghi with no mention of the illegitimate Berto who lived with them in 1427 (Notarile 682 [1425–29], fols. 78v–79r [10 March 1425/6]); for Domenico d'Antonio di Bartolomeo di ser Santi without mention of two older illegitimate brothers listed with him in 1427 (Notarile 684 [1431–33], fols. 141v–143r [10 March 1431/2]); for six children of Francesco di Marco Bartoli, all born after 1427, but not for Catalano (Notarile 686 [1436–40], fols. 24v–26v [22 February 1436/7]).

99. Cf. Jonathan Davies, *Florence and Its University during the Early Renaissance* (Leiden, 1998), 100, 130, 164.

100. Lacy Collison-Morley, *The Early Medici* (New York, 1936), 36, 65, 114–15; Sharon Strocchia, *Death and Ritual in Renaissance Florence* (Baltimore, 1992), 182; Kent, *Cosimo de' Medici,* 248, 342.

Carlo in the context of his discussion of the works and career of Filippo Lippi, himself a bastard and father of one. Vasari considered Lippi's talents to have in some way excused his origins and his eccentric lifestyle.

> Fra Filippo was indeed so highly estimated for his great gifts, that many circumstances in his life which were very blameable received pardon, and were partly placed out of view, in consideration of his extraordinary abilities. In the work just described [Prato frescoes] is the portrait of Messer Carlo, natural son of Cosimo de' Medici, who was rector of the church wherein it was executed, which had received large benefactions both from him and his house.[101]

Carlo de' Medici received no such favor; his bastardy was clearly noted, for all that he was obviously acting within the framework of a family. When Vasari later revealed that Lippi supposedly turned down an offer of a papal dispensation to regularize his relationship with the Florentine woman whom he had seduced from one of the city' convents, his refusal was attributed to his desire "to retain the power of living after his own fashion, and of indulging his love of pleasure as might seem good to him."[102] Unlike Carlo de' Medici, Lippi was unattached and uncontrolled.

Another bastard worth mentioning is Bernardo Machiavelli, father of the famous political theorist Niccolò, who was legitimated by his father, Buoninsegna, on his deathbed. Bernardo received a legal education and had connections in literary circles, though only a modest patrimony. In these regards it is all the more interesting how in his *Ricordi* Bernardo Machiavelli maintained silence about the circumstances of his paternity and yet became incensed when a male relative impregnated his servant girl.[103]

Notarial evidence regarding activities of illegitimates is extremely rare. I take this less as an indication of a lack of property and interests to transact than as a consistent failure to label themselves as illegitimate or legitimated where the status was not legally relevant. Filippo di Piero Lippi

---

101. Giorgio Vasari, *Lives of the Most Eminent Painters, Sculptors, and Architects,* 2 vols., trans. Jonathan Foster (London, 1878), 2:82–83.

102. Ibid., 2:86.

103. Cf. Sebastian de Grazia, *Machiavelli in Hell* (Princeton, N.J., 1989), 5; and on him see my *Law, Family, and Women,* chap. 2.

admitted legitimation in appointing *procuratores.*[104] This is a rare instance where the label was used. Yet even where one has another source like the catasto to reveal the identity of bastards, they still appear seldom. Their fathers are not hard to find in notarial records, nor are their legitimate siblings. But they just were not associated with them.

The few examples include Luca di Matteo da Panzano, who in 1444 gave two *poderi* to his brother Tommaso, who received them also in the name of his son Luigi. No mention of Luigi's illegitimacy was made in the notarial charter encapsulating the gift.[105] A few years later Bernardo d'Antonio de' Medici formally acknowledged receipt of forty florins loaned by him to Lancilotto di Giovanni d'Andrea d'Alamanno de' Medici. Lancilotto was illegitimate, though, again, one would not know it from reading in the notarial text.[106]

Family investment in bastards would also be evident in what happened to them across their lives, but the main historical problem is that it is very difficult to follow most Florentine bastards through their lives. With annoying regularity bastards disappear into the mists of history, leaving little paper trace. In the absence of a computerized index of all catasti, tracing bastards remains a hit-or miss-proposition, mainly miss. For a high proportion of bastards it proved difficult even to find their families in catasti thirty or so years later, leave alone to find them. As the age table reveals, only fifteen of the 1458 bastards were over thirty, of an age, that is, to have appeared in the 1427 catasto. Many, of course, were still there, but were no longer labeled as bastards, being, one assumes, out on their own—their fathers, for the most part, having died. Similarly the 1480 catasto shows only twenty bastards old enough to have been listed in the earlier survey of 1458.[107]

One assumption made in trying to trace bastards was that the family's place of residence remained constant—that is, in the same *gonfalone*—

104. Notarile 14712 (1458–63), fol. 121v (8 January 1461/2); the legitimation is in Provvisioni—registri 144, fols. 39r–40r (23 October 1453).

105. Notarile 688 (1442–45), fol. 196r (27 January 1443/4) and Catasto 69, fols. 245r–247r.

106. Notarile 690 (1447–50), fol. 27r–v (17 May 1448) and Catasto 79, fols. 255v–258r.

107. Use of intervening catasti, such as those of 1446 and 1469–70, would reduce the time frame, of course, but the huge effort to do so would not change the overall problem to be explained—namely, that after a time Florentine bastards disappear from the catasto (or at least from where one would expect to find them).

from one survey to the next. My attempts to locate 1427 bastards and their families in 1458 yielded paltry results. Eleven of the 1427 bastards turned up in 1458 (and thus account for most—but not all—of the 1458 bastards with reported ages over thirty); but households or their full or partial successors that had previously housed some bastards yielded no more information about them. In fact, it was difficult merely to track these fiscal households over thirty or so years. Vagaries of scribal practice between surveys, making identification from one to another difficult, and a certain amount of morbidity and mobility in the population must account for the missing households.

Between 1458 and 1480 I ran a tight comparison of three administrative districts, *gonfaloni* (Chiave and Drago in San Giovanni quarter, Bue in Santa Croce). Again, given the age profile of the bastard population, one could expect only a handful from 1458 to show up in 1480. For Chiave I located households that held sixteen bastards in 1458, six of whom still appeared (another sixteen households with twenty-three bastards did not show up in the same *gonfalone*); for Drago, of fourteen households located, five bastards emerged (another twenty households with twenty-seven bastards missing); for Bue twenty-four households yielded only two bastards (seventeen more from fifteen households were lacking). In none of these cases were the bastards who also turned up later female. One expects that they were married or in a convent. One also finds bastards in a later catasto whose age indicates that they should have been, but were not, in the earlier one. The thirty-one-year-old Piero d'Albano Frescobaldi, for example, was old enough to have appeared in 1427, and Giovanni di Piero di Giovanni di Nofri was old enough in 1480 to have been recorded as an illegitimate in 1458.[108] These bastards either were elsewhere during the earlier survey or their bastardy had not been disclosed.

These numbers propel us to conclude that Florentine bastards melted into the social world in one way or another. Women, we assume, were assimilated either into another household by marriage or into a convent. There are some odd cases of older women in their natal households. We know Giovanni di Pollito della Casa's sister, Mattea, was illegitimate. In 1427 she was said to be sixty-five, living with her brother's family and possessing nothing.[109] We know of one girl, a cousin, sent out to the

108. Catasto 816, fols. 639r–640v; 1019, fol. 239r–v. The mobility of Florentines may account for a good deal of this.

109. Catasto 79, fols. 235v–237v.

home of a peasant.[110] Was she to work for him or also later become his wife? Gieri de' Bardi took in the thirty-six-year-old illegitimate daughter of his brother.[111] Giovanni di Piero da Meleto reported that his eighteen-year-old was in the convent of San Jacopo in Florence.[112] Fruosino d'Ugolino Ciucci kept a twenty-two-year-old girl and her legitimated twenty-six-year-old brother.[113] Datino di Pacino di Datino in 1458 tried to claim a deduction for his twenty-six-year-old bastard daughter even though she was married.[114] Niccolò d'Antonio Amadori housed an older (then age fifty-six) illegitimate sister.[115] Benedetto di Lorenzo d'Antonio said his thirty-two-year-old bastard daughter was widowed.[116] The sons of Bernardo di Buciello Bucielli reported that all six sisters, including the two illegitimates aged thirty-two and twenty-six, were in a convent in Pistoia.[117] Giovanni di Luigi Altoviti reported that his son of thirty-five was a monk and his daughter of thirty a nun.[118] More surprisingly, Polito di Jacopo di Simone admitted that his wife was the bastard daughter of Antonio di Lipaccio de' Bardi.[119]

It was possible to find some of the men. Those of wealthier or more stable lineages possessing a *cognome,* could be traced more easily across catasti. Many of them could not.[120] For men diverse possibilities existed. In 1458 Sandro di Jacopo Deti continued to live, unmarried, in a household with his younger legitimate brothers, their mother, wives, and children. Tommaso di Giovanni Mannelli still lived with his father, who had since married and listed six children; Bernardo di Giovanni di Simone dell'Antella still lived with his uncle as he had back in 1427, even though Ruffilo was now married with seven children and Bernardo's younger

110. Catasto 994, fols. 398r–399r.
111. Catasto 785, fols. 514r–515r.
112. Catasto 801, fols. 1283r–1287r.
113. Catasto 804, fols. 492r–493v.
114. Catasto 832, fol. 1188r.
115. Catasto 993, fol. 167r–v.
116. Catasto 1002, fols. 80r–81v.
117. Catasto 1005, fol. 446r–v.
118. Catasto 1008, fols. 273r–274v.
119. Catasto 788, fol. 891r.
120. By way of example: In 1427 Francesco di Marco Bartoli had in his household only a twelve year-old bastard, Catalano. In 1458 his household consisted of himself, a wife, a son who had a wife, another son, and a son of the first son, named Catalano (for the missing illegitimate uncle?). (Compare Catasto 75, fols. 78v–79r to 813, fols. 335r–336v.) In 1480 Guidantonio di messer Domenico di ser Mino no longer reported a bastard daughter (at age nine in 1458, well past marriage in 1480) but was married to her mother. (Compare Catasto 801, fols. 915r–917r to 1003, fols. 558r–559v.)

brother Lorenzo was no longer listed. Francesco di Priore di Jacopo Risaliti was still with his father in 1458, when he was about forty, but he was no longer in the household (probably dead), by then in the hands of his three younger legitimate brothers, in 1480. By 1480 Filippo di Filippo Tornabuoni had established a separate household from his brother and cousins, but he kept Giovanni with him and a second bastard, only nine, by a slave, although he was married with eight legitimate children. Domenico di Niccolò di Maso dello Strinato Alfieri was not listed as illegitimate in 1427, although his infant sister Lena was termed *bastarda.* She is not found in the Alfieri household in 1458, but Domenico was still there, now termed *naturale,* along with a younger illegitimate brother named Marco and three legitimate brothers, as well as a woman sent to them when pregnant from Ferrara by Belfredello Alfieri, who gave him two *naturali* he listed along with his young wife in his declaration in 1458. Domenico, married with five children, no admission of illegitimacy, had his own household and work as a shoemaker according to the catasto of 1480.[121]

Most of those who turned up in the later catasto and were unmarried were still in their father's household, or that of his legitimate heirs.[122] Others lived apart. Francesco di Giovanni di Tedice degli Albizzi, an illegitimate in 1458, in 1480 appeared as sole member of his household, with *sustanze* of 209 florins, including one-fourth of a palazzo and *podere* where he lived and part of a *casa* shared with three brothers.[123] The illegitimate son and daughter (ages twenty-five and fourteen respectively) of messer Tommaso Soderini were listed as a household apart in 1480, with assets of 419 florins, and a 500-florin dowry on deposit for Lisabetta. The catasto officials were also told that they had not been listed among the mouths in the 1470 catasto because they were not legit-

121. For Deti: Catasto 785, fols. 179r–181v, and 64, fols. 151r–152r; Mannelli: Catasto 790, fol. 342r–v, and 66, fols. 119v–120r; dell'Antella: 798, fols. 283r–286r, and 68, fols. 185v–186r; Risaliti: 800, fols. 580r–581v, and 69, fols. 222v–224v, and 1004, fol. 27r; Tornabuoni: 818, fols. 1045r–1048v, and 77, fols. 383r–390r; Alfieri: 825, fols. 116r–118v and 113r–114v, and 79, fols. 323r–325r, and 1018, fol. 289r.

122. Examples are 811, fols. 287r–288r with 74, fol. 105r–v; 813, fols. 536r–538v with 75, fols. 159r–160r; 818, fols. 1100r–1102v with 77, fols. 51r–53v; 832, fols. 505r–506v with 81, fols. 464r–465r; 1004, fols. 20r–22r with 800, fols. 408r–412v. Also compare Catasto 790, fol. 342r–v with 66, fols. 119v–120r; 800, fols. 580r–581v with 69, fols. 222v–224v; 1022, fol. 390r–v with 828, fols. 390r–391r.

123. Catasto 829, fols. 687r–689r, and 1021, fol. 64r.

imate.[124] On the other hand, Tommaso di Tieri di Lorenzo, who appeared as a household of one with assets of 257 florins in 1480 at age fifty, did not mention his illegitimacy in admitting that he had a life interest of 18 florins annually from his brothers in accordance with an arbitration of 1468. It was the brothers who, in including this obligation in their catasto declaration, revealed that Tommaso was their illegitimate brother.[125]

There were bastards who had married and ran their own households. A number of these were also legitimated. And, if there is one distinction of a chronological nature to be drawn, they were more numerous in 1480 (if only because we have so many bastards from 1458 to track). Of the 1427 bastards only Salvadore di Niccolò da Uzzano and Luigi di Tommaso di Matteo da Panzano appeared as heads of their households in 1458. Both were aided by the fact that their fathers never had legitimate sons. In 1427 Luigi di Tommaso was three and his father had just married. Thirty years later Luigi, still living with his father, was married and the father of seven children. By 1480 Luigi was dead and his three sons and widow had his patrimony of 1,910 florins and were about to begin their own families.[126]

Examples from 1458 include Antonio di Giovanni del Magnio, then a child living with his thirty-seven-year-old legitimate brother Luigi, who in 1480 was married with two daughters.[127] Francesco di Giovanni di Tedice degli Albizzi, who lived with a legitimate brother in 1458, in 1480 had a fourth of a palazzo as his home and was assessed alone in the catasto.[128] Giovanni di ser Antonio Ughi was likewise on his own in 1480 but not in great financial condition. He had obligations to furnish a chapel in his father's memory, and he was in debt for over 300 florins.[129] Luigi di Cambino Cambini, who had been sent by his father to study in Perugia, was legitimated in 1458 and in 1480 was a practicing notary with a wife, a son, another child on the way, a *serva,* and no *sustanze.*[130]

124. Catasto 1000, fol. 133r: "nogli furonsi condotte ne boche nel catasto del 1470 per non essere legittimi."

125. Catasto 1014, fols. 106r–v and 274r.

126. Compare Catasto 1003, fols. 348r–350r with 801, fols. 743r–746r, and 69, fols. 245r–247r.

127. Catasto 1020, fol. 79r with 829, fols. 53r–54v.

128. Catasto 1021, fol. 64r with 829, fols. 687r–689v; also see the case of Cleofe di ser Niccolò della Casa: Catasto 1018, fol. 233r with 825, fols. 548r–551v.

129. Catasto 1018, fol. 491r–v with 825, fols. 92r–94v. See also Domenico di Francesco Gherucci: 1020, fol. 443r–v with 828, fols. 80r–82r.

130. Catasto 1019, fol. 114r with 826, fols. 380r–383v.

Marriage

Marriage could make the illegitimate the progenitor of legitimates. Separate residence with his own patrimony also left him with no one immediately around him who had an interest in keeping the public aware of illegitimacy. It is a very odd situation to encounter a head of household, Andrea di Jacopo di Giorgio Bardi, who in the 1480 catasto described himself as "non legittimo." A poor scion of this large patrician clan, with *sustanze* of less than eighty-nine florins, Andrea revealed that his major asset was a *poderuzzo* near San Miniato al Tedesco purchased by his father by means of his mother's money (forty florins). The Magistrato de' Pupilli, who oversaw the estate for the legitimate children, awarded him the small farm after they examined his father's books.[131] In a more boastful manner, Luigi di Giovanni di messer Stefano Buonaccorsi, descendant of a lawyer, listed himself as "ligittimato" in 1480 as he presented a household consisting of assets worth 1,868 florins, a wife, his four children, and the twelve-year-old son and widow of his also legitimated brother Michele.[132]

Luigi da Panzano later married and had children of his own, as did Martino d'Antonio di Bartolomeo di ser Santi, despite being left out of the *tutela* over his legitimate siblings.[133] These two bastards thus began a new family branch such as that of Piero di Niccolò Baldovinetti, celebrated in a genealogical history constructed in 1731.[134] Social integration may have most effectively begun with marrying a Florentine woman. Anthony Molho suggests that marriage to a foreigner, especially by an illegitimate, was indicative of a *déclassement*.[135] The main problem is that we cannot gain any systematic vantage point on the marriages of Florentine male illegitimates, and even anecdotal evidence is spotty.

Sandri's suggestion that there was a fear lest bastards in one generation bear bastards in the next recalls Laslett's notion of a "bastardy prone subsociety."[136] If there was such a phenomenon in Florence, it is

131. Catasto 992, fol. 87r.

132. Catasto 825, fols. 628r–629r, and 1019, fols. 33r–34r.

133. Notarile 14716 (1472–74), fol. 24v (17 June 1472) carries a transaction by "Frusinus olim Loisii." Notarile 691 (1450–54), fols. 112v–113v (10 October 1451) contains the *aditio hereditatis* to his father by Niccolò di Martino.

134. Acquisti e Doni 190. Piero was a "naturale natoli d'una contadina per nome Domenica" in 1506.

135. Molho, *Marriage Alliance,* 242–43.

136. Laslett, *Family Life,* 147; Sandri, *L'Ospedale,* 181, 187.

likely it flourished among those classes of people who did not record births as illegitimate. To exist, such a subsociety would have to be tolerant within and reticent toward outsiders. I have discovered only one bastard who himself turned around and had bastards of his own (beyond the notable examples of Petrarch and Boccaccio). Piero d'Albano di messer Castellano Frescobaldi by age thirty-one had two bastards himself by the family's slave. He was not married, and his father, it seems, had had no legitimate children of his own.[137] On the other hand, there were plenty of close relatives of bastards who had bastards. People sharing a patronymic also shared the experience of fathering or living with a bastard.[138] There were three cases I have found of a bastard's brother, who must have had a close awareness of the disadvantages or differences of illegitimacy, who, nonetheless, fathered a child out of wedlock. Perhaps their fathers had set an example of good treatment.[139] There was Luigi d'Agabito d'Ardingo de' Ricci who, when he was thirteen, saw a bastard brother come into the world and later had a daughter himself.[140]

In any case, bastards themselves, if they had children, seem to have made sure that they did not pass the status, and all its disadvantages, on to their own progeny. They did not need the encouragement of the positive reevaluation of marriage that Herlihy and Klapisch-Zuber attribute to fifteenth-century civic humanism. This reevaluation itself interestingly involved bastards. The fourteenth-century figures cited as seeing marriage as a negative (getting in the way of intellectual and literary pursuits) included two bastards who begat bastards, Boccaccio and Petrarch. In addition to their scholarly ambitions, why would they not disparage the institution that left them at some social disadvantage? In the fifteenth century, however, Alberti played up the values of conjugal love, though he also retained a more forbiddingly patriarchal sense of marriage than did, perhaps, other humanists like Lionardo Bruni and Coluccio Salutati.[141] But Alberti did not have bastards himself; he did not even marry.

The consistent disappearance of bastard girls from the later catasto

137. Catasto 816, fols. 639r–640v.

138. As an example, the 1427 catasto shows six Bardi households with bastards.

139. Bernardo di Piero di Cambino Cambini fathered Nicholazzo and had an illegitimate younger brother Papi (Catasto 66, fols. 89r–91r and 996, fol. 146r–v). Carlo di Ruberto dell'Antella had an illegitimate older sister and later fathered a child on a slave (Catasto 68, fols. 279v–280r and 798, fol. 166r–v).

140. Catasto 81, fols. 18r–19r and 832, fols. 717r–718r.

141. Cf. Herlihy and Klapisch-Zuber, *Les toscans,* 586–88, and English translation, *Tuscans and Their Families,* 228–31.

declarations of their fathers' households argues for their eventual marriage or monacation. In a few instances we learn what happened to them from notarial and other evidence. We know Lisabetta di Luigi di Zanobi Gaddi married Simone di Michele Tucci and had a son.[142] Francesco di Giovanni di messer Niccolò Strozzi married his illegitimate daughter to a humble man without a surname and with the appropriately humble dowry of eighty-five florins.[143] We are much better informed about the marriages of bastard girls where there were institutional interests at stake. Placement in a convent did not necessarily result in a miserable life.[144] But the likelihood was that the lives of illegitimate girls were not as fortunate as those of their legitimate sisters. The most systematic evidence we have on this score comes from the Florentine *monte delle doti.* The registers of this fund were carefully kept and so yield the historian accurate evidence on the marriages, monastic vows, and deaths of bastard girls in the fund. Illegitimate girls' dowries were smaller on the average (by law they had a ceiling of half the allowed value for legitimate girls), ranging usually between a quarter and a third of what the same father would arrange for a legitimate girl. Those bastard girls who died before marriage did so at a slightly younger age, on average, than legitimate girls; and bastards were more likely to end up in a convent.[145] And these girls were married down the social scale. Lauro Martines suggests that Florentine bastard girls were married to *contadini* "expecting the country to absorb them and forget."[146] Evidence from the 1458 catasto would seem to bear him out, not with regard to daughters themselves (for nothing generally was said about a married daughter), but with their mothers. The stigma of illegitimacy may have attached more permanently to girls, through their mothers. To leave such girls in the ambiguous situation of being neither married nor placed in a convent, where gossip and suspicion could arise, may have been intolerable.[147] Molho found illegitimate girls were twice as likely as legitimate girls to end up in

142. Notarile 19078 (1462–64), fols. 379v–380r (21 June 1463).

143. Heather J. Gregory, "Chi erano gli Strozzi nel Quattrocento," in *Palazzo Strozzi,* 20.

144. Hurtubise, *Une famille-témoin,* 120.

145. Julius Kirshner and Anthony Molho, "The Dowry Fund and the Marriage Market in Early Quattrocento Florence," *Journal of Modern History* 50 (1978): 429–30.

146. Martines, *Power and Imagination,* 165.

147. Sandri, *L'Ospedale,* 187; da Certaldo, *Libro di buoni costumi,* 83–84.

TABLE 5. **Illegitimate Girls in the *Monte delle Doti***

	Illegitimates	Foundlings	Total
Married	225	44	269
Died	56	25	81
Convent	29		29
Unknown	21	17	38
Total	331	86	417

Mothers	Married	Died	Convent	Unknown	Total
Slave	40	7	2	4	53
Serva	18	7		1	26
Fante	2				2
Free or unknown	146	36	25	11	218

convents, and in the years between 1480 and 1530 were three times as likely to monacate, and at younger ages.[148]

Molho's book tells us 394 bastard daughters had accounts in the *monte delle doti* in its history, 260 registered before 1480 and 100 of the 394 coming from the Innocenti. In a variation of the pattern for legitimate girls, not only were the deposits for *bastarde* smaller but they were made later in life. Illegitimate women who married with the aid of a *monte* dowry overwhelmingly married lower on the social scale, as Molho painstakingly measures it, and the men who married them did not admit the illegitimacy.[149] Working from Molho's data, I can add the following observations (while coming up with slightly different numbers) (table 5). Of 417 illegitimate girls—a few from the contado but far and away the majority Florentine—with *monte* accounts from the fund's founding until the 1530s, 269 married, 29 entered convents, 81 died before marrying, and the fate of the remaining 38 is unclear. Included in these 417 were 86 foundlings whose fund dowry was arranged by the Innocenti. Of those girls 44 married, 25 died, while the fate of 17 is unclear. None of the foundlings ended up in a convent, which seems instead to have been the refuge of girls from good fami-

148. Anthony Molho, "*Tanquam vere mortua:* Le professioni religiose femminili nella Firenze del tardo Medioevo," *Società e storia* 43 (1989): 1–44.

149. Molho, *Marriage Alliance*, 93, 105–6, 144, 279.

lies.[150] The foundlings thus married in lower proportion than the population of bastard girls associated with a household (51.2 percent to 67.2 percent) but died in higher proportion (29.1 percent to 17.2 percent) or more often met with a fate left unclear in the records (19.7 percent to 6.4 percent). Still it is revealing how many of these girls found husbands of some sort.[151]

Florentines who kept bastards, who could "afford" it in economic and cultural currency, had a talent pool available to them and a "blood bank" of last resort. Illegitimacy was still a stigma. Bastards, even legitimated ones, did not get full benefits of membership in their family. Their status was as tainted, and artificial, as that of those who had acquired citizenship by some manner other than the normal mode of birth by citizen parents.

The utility of these bastards to their families was also related to keeping their illegitimacy before them. Certainly those Florentines who admitted to having illegitimates (few of the latter are ever seen admitting to it themselves, and then usually as legitimated) had them by and large before marriage and by women who were easy prey. Some seemed to have developed genuine affection for their offspring and their mothers; all took care of them in some way if they chose not simply to abandon them. Illegitimate children who were older than their legitimate siblings may also have helped bridge the generational age gap between fathers and offspring (a position otherwise filled by the wife and, as David Rheubottom has recently pointed out, her kin).[152] They found some sort of place in their families (though not in all instances), and some of them succeeded in marrying themselves. As we have seen from time to time, some were even legitimated, and for all there were possible questions of inheritance.

150. Names like Gondi, Covoni, Tornabuoni, Pazzi, Martelli, Albizzi, Soderini, Altoviti, and Portinari are found among those who ended up in convents. Of the mothers of these girls, only two were known to have been slaves; twenty-five were not (two more unknown).

151. Molho, *Marriage Alliance,* 279, states the number of illegitimates who married was 309, which is the number married and the number whose fate is unclear and without allowance for three duplicate records.

152. David B. Rheubottom, "Genealogical Skewing and Political Support: Patrician Politics in Fifteenth-Century Ragusa (Dubrovnik)," *Continuity and Change* 9 (1994): 369–90.

6
Legitimation

"Per ovviare che la famiglia non declini"

Marino Berengo has advanced the thesis that the keeping of bastards and their legitimation was due to a preoccupation to preserve the family name, add to the "potenza della casa," and maintain biological continuity.[1] One of the pressing worries for Florentines in an era of plagues and wars was the fragility of family survival.[2] Family preservation was a dominant value. Failure to preserve family lines was tragic. This was a "truth" acknowledged by jurists[3] and is the theme that began Palmieri's *Vita civile.*[4] Alberti's dialogue on the family notes how many formerly great Florentine lineages had disappeared and was overtly intended to show how his lineage and others might avoid such a fate; and the popularity of his work shows he struck a chord with the city's elite.[5]

For a family threatened in its survival in the male line, a bastard might prove to be its salvation. However, the illegitimate had to have been accepted and recognized, probably many years before it became apparent that no other children would be born or that none had survived. Families that kept illegitimates may have been taking on an expense, but they also could be said to have made an investment. The fathers of these bastards need not have been looking for sexual adventures, much less for children,

1. Berengo, *Nobili e mercanti,* 35.

2. On this theme, see Kuehn, *Emancipation,* 55–71; Herlihy and Klapisch-Zuber, *Les toscans,* 165–88, 548–49; Paolo Cammarosano, "Les structures familiales dans les villes de l'Italie communale, xiie–xive siècles," in Duby and Le Goff, *Famille et parenté,* 193.

3. As Angelo degli Ubaldi, *cons.* 68, *Consilia,* fol. 45rb–va: "Secundo ratione cuiusdam publicae utilitatis, quae exposcit, facultates suas singulis agnationibus conservari, ut familiarum salva sit dignitas et honestas, quae absque divitiis non conservatur . . . quia interest Reipublicae per digniores et ditiores regi, et non pauperes et abiectos."

4. Alberti, *I libri della famiglia,* 11–12.

5. Cf. Judith Ravenscroft, "The Third Book of Alberti's *Della Famiglia* and Its Two *Rifacimenti,*" *Italian Studies* 29 (1974): 45–53.

but once faced with an illegitimate birth, they may have decided to seize upon a potentially useful asset, as well as avoid scandal and embarrassment of abandonment or worse. But it is also true that, in a larger sense, lineage encompassed several lines of male descent, and the failure of one did not diminish the others. Florentines' genealogies also tracked their collaterals. Rather than leaving property to an illegitimate (even legitimated), a Florentine with no legitimate son could leave his patrimony to a brother or cousin. Many did.

Of course legitimation of bastards was not the only legal means to preserve family continuity. There was adoption. However, it seems that for Florentines and many others in late medieval and Renaissance Italy, blood connection removed most ambiguity or provided more certainty than law alone. They were notoriously reluctant to adopt.[6] Fostering or apprenticing were different matters. Those relationships were frequent in Florence. Many people spent parts of their formative years in homes of people other than their parents. Filippo di Piero Lippi reported to catasto officials in 1480, for example, that his eldest daughter was living with his wife's brother (Marco d'Ugolino Bonsi) "as his daughter and so he treats her as his own and has to feed and marry her as it suits and pleases him."[7] The Innocenti placed its boys and girls in Florentine homes.[8] Fostered children were to be taught a trade and given moral upbringing; the girls were to be married with a modest dowry. Only in rare instances were these children legally adopted.[9] As I have pointed out elsewhere, when the illegitimate Leon Battista Alberti mentioned adoption as a remedy for childlessness in his *Della Famiglia,* he can plausibly be taken as referring to legitimation of bastards because adoption was in fact so seldom used.[10]

Legitimation was relatively more frequent and familiar in Florentine life. In theory legitimation was the height of legal assimilation for a bastard. One would assume, as well, that fairly full social and economic

6. See Giulio Vismara, "Adozione (diritto intermedio)," *Enciclopedia del diritto,* vol. 1 (Milan, 1958), 583–84; Pietro Torelli, *Lezioni di storia del diritto italiano: Diritto privato* (Milan, 1947), 98; Pertile, *Storia del diritto italiano,* 3:396; Tamassia, *La famiglia italiana,* 244–46; and the interesting remarks of Natalie Zemon Davis, "Ghosts, Kin, and Progeny: Some Features of Family Life in Early Modern France," *Daedalus* 106, no. 2 (1977): 104–5; McLaughlin, "Survivors and Surrogates"; my "L'Adoption à Florence."

7. Catasto 999, fol. 476r: "per sua figluola e chosì lui la tiene per propria figluola e alla a nutrire e maritare chome a lui pare e piacie."

8. In that sense Gavitt, *Charity and Children,* 243ff., errs in using the term *adoption.*

9. As Gavitt, *Charity and Children,* 246–47, for one example.

10. My *Law, Family, and Women,* chap. 6.

assimilation would precede or follow on legitimation. Bastards whose fathers produced no legitimate progeny would seem especially likely to have experienced legitimation. But in fifteenth-century Florence legitimation too was not all that frequent when we consider how many *illegitimi* (and thus potential *legitimati*) there were. If we begin again with the catasto, we find some reference to legitimated bastards, but not many—only thirteen of the almost one thousand bastards uncovered in that source: Niccolò di Neri di Bivigliano de' Medici, Giuliano di Francesco Quaratesi, Bonaiuto and Domenico di Mariotto Lippi, Antonio di Fruosino Ciucci, Francesca and Zanobi di Benedetto di Durante, Maria Lisabetta di Cambio d'Antonio de' Medici, Giovanni d'Antonio di Matteo de' Ricci, Luigi Buonaccorsi, Franceschino di Francesco d'Antonio di Tomaso Nori, Giovanni di Ruberto di messer Giovanni Migliorati da Prato, Antonio di Goro d'Andrea Martignoni.[11] If we limited ourselves to catasto evidence alone, then, we might have to conclude that legitimation was only slightly less rare than adoption, that one who was legitimated felt no need to reveal bastard birth, or that legitimation did not really change things in people's minds, so no distinction was drawn and such bastards remained that. Leon Battista Alberti, whose father never had legitimate children, was nonetheless not legitimated. His fate was not so aberrant in comparison to other Florentine bastards in the supposedly golden age of bastardy.

The statutes of the city did not concern themselves with legitimation, so the rules that applied were those worked out in the *ius commune;* but the city did make legitimation available by act of the Signoria and governing councils. Legitimation by rescript was also available to Florentines by means of the counts palatine who happened to reside there, including the archbishop since 1364, and, of course, by subsequent marriage of the parents. Legitimation could provide an appropriate strategic compromise, retaining a sense of "natural" blood relationships while maneuvering practically and legally around the principle of legitimacy for the sake of family interests.[12] But legitimation also implied much more than inheritance, and the use of legitimation did not necessarily result in inheritance.

11. Catasto 79, fols. 160v–163r; 785, fols. 157r–162r; 791, fols. 625r–628r; 804, fols. 492r–493v; 814, fols. 593r–594v; 825, fols. 626r–627r; 832, fols. 494r–498r; 1019, fols. 33r–34r; 1005, fols. 609r–613r; 1007, fol. 345r–v; 1017, fol. 658r.

12. Alberto Tenenti, "Famille bourgeoise et idéologie au Bas Moyen Age," in Duby and Le Goff, *Famille et parenté,* 437.

Barring computer-aided studies of marriage and birth statistics, our knowledge of legitimation by subsequent marriage can only be impressionistic. No subsequently married parents disclosed to catasto officials the illegitimate birth of their children, as opposed to those instances of continued extralegal concubinage. A few examples have turned up. In 1418 Francesco d'Antonio di Cambiozzo appeared before a notary and reported that after years of living together his parents had finally married, with a formal dotal instrument. Francesco was recording his consent to legitimation arising from this marriage. His father, it seems, had waited on marrying the woman, Caterina di Filippo del Buono, until he was about to die, for that same day she took over as her son's *tutrix*. A few days later Antonio's two sisters, who had been named as executors in his will, tried to have the *tutela* voided, without success.[13] In the context, one can see from what quarter questions were raised about the child's consent. The mother, however, eagerly used the law, having a judge of the Podestà oversee the expression of consent and Nello da San Gimignano, a jurist, oversee the formation of the *tutela*. These very practices of deathbed marriage and filial consent to it were of lively interest to jurists.

In a closely parallel event from 1436, Giovanni di maestro Cocco de' Casciatelli da Perugia, living in Borgo San Sepolcro, and his wife, Giovanna di messer Jacopo de Panna, asserted that years before they had married by the terms of canon law and had consummated their marriage and procreated children, although no notarial charter of the marriage had been drawn up. So as a precaution they publicly enacted a wedding before Giovanni had his testament drafted. In it he named as universal heirs, ser Antonio, son by his first wife, and Francesco, son by Giovanna.[14] Technically this was not a legitimation of Francesco by subsequent marriage, unless, of course, his parents were lying, in which case one anticipates that his coheir, if he could mount an effective proof, would have challenged his succession.

Otherwise, when we know of legitimation, it is legitimation by imperial rescript or by act of Florence's governing councils. We will not consider dispensations to clerical orders, most of which concerned the sons

13. Notarile 10452 (1410–49), fols. 45r–51r, 51v–54v (10 and 19 February 1417/8).

14. Notarile 7046, testamenti (1420–62), 21 April 1436. I must thank Elaine Rosenthal for this reference.

of clergy.[15] The language employed in notarial charters of legitimation by rescript is instructive. The imperial privilege to the count palatine (often reproduced in full) first asserted the emperor's prerogative to grant to the count such power

> that you can legitimate bastards, *manzeres, nothos, spurios,* and whatever others procreated from illicit or unapproved coitus, in life or death of their parents and return them to legitimate rights and take from them all stain of birth, so that they might hold any offices and be admitted to all acts, public and private, in the image of others who are derived from legitimate marriage.

When faced with a proclaimed illegitimate kneeling before him, the circumstances of whose birth and parentage were spelled out, the count proceeded to make him "nil a legitimis differendo."

> We restore you to the true and ancient free birth and legitimate rights and place you under the power of said N. your father, and in and for all we legitimate and make and establish you legitimate, differing in no way from legitimate children or making a difference, and wiping away and fully abolishing any mark, stain, defect, or impediment of your birth, and by the same authority we restore and enable you fully to all legitimate rights and to you we concede, want, settle, and order that just as one born legitimate and from legitimate marriage, in all property, paternal and maternal and of other ascendants and descendants, collaterals and transversals, cognates and agnates, allodial and feudal and of whatever sort acquired or to be acquired, by testament or intestacy, you can succeed so that by this legitimation may not be prejudiced other children and descendants of your parents if they do or will survive, but you may succeed to an equal portion just as you would succeed by rights otherwise if the defect of birth did not withstand and as if you were procreated from legitimate marriage; and you are made and are established agnate and cognate to the agnates and cognates of your parents in whatever degree, and reciprocally they are to you; and

15. One example of dispensation involves two young Florentine bastards, Francesco di Giovanni di Vanni and Giovanni di Bernardo Salviati: cf. Notarile 13504 (1452–60), fol. 145v (17 July 1457). Federico R. Aznar Gil, "Die Illegitimen auf der Iberischen Halbinsel im Spätmittelalter," in Schmugge, *Illegitimität im Spätmittelalter,* 171–206.

> also to all public and civil acts, offices and honors, if occasion should arise, you are admitted and may be admitted and you can pursue your action in all matters whatever, stain of illegitimate birth not withstanding.[16]

On paper everything seemed aimed at removing any distinction between legitimate and legitimated in moral and legal status. Legitimation would seem to have resolved all ambiguities and uncertainties regarding the bastard's status.

A contrast between the language of legitimation and that of legal emancipation is instructive. Legitimation was all about putting one under *potestas;* it concerned removal of defect and rights to inherit. Conversely, emancipation dissolved *potestas;* its language concerned not status and future inheritance but active capacities—"without obtaining paternal power's leave to act, contract, obligate, be and stand in court, testate, make a codicil, and do and exercise all things and everything, in court as well as out, that any paterfamilias and *homo sui iuris* can do and exercise"—and the transmission of at least the *peculium,* if not a more specific *praemium* (gift) as a material portion on which those capacities could be exercised.[17] Legitimation was about being a *filius;* emancipation was about becoming a *homo sui iuris.*

Legitimation by the Florentine Signoria, in contrast, was not full legitimation. Consistently the records specified that the father could henceforth, by whatever means, bequeath property to the child(ren) "as if born of a legitimate marriage," but "that by the aforesaid or any of the aforesaid or anything depending on them in any way [the son] will obtain or have no benefit or ability of accepting or exercising any office of the commune or on behalf of the commune of Florence." These acts were consistent with legislation that excluded bastards from civic offices. Typically the fathers approached the governing councils (the Priors, the sixteen *gonfalonieri,* the twelve *buonuomini*) and stated that they had no legitimate children but had one or more illegitimate, disclosing something in most cases about the status, if not the identity, of the mother. These fathers usually included a statement to the effect that they loved the child, who was virtuous, respectful, obedient—in short, a good family member and a good Florentine. To quote the language of one: "And therefore he greatly loves said Filippo his son and especially as he shows himself of

16. Cf. Notarile 9037 (1408–11), fols. 373v–376r, reproduced in the appendix.

17. See the appendixes in my *Emancipation.*

sufficiently good character in appearance in his childhood and he stays obedient to him and very good natured."[18] These civic legitimations carried no language to the effect that they removed stains of birth or established agnation.

Legitimation made one an heir, but it also accorded rights of membership and participation in kindred and community. It removed the "stain" of illegitimacy—the dishonor; so it had a wider range of uses. How else to explain the legitimation of girls, which occurred rather more often than one might anticipate?[19] On the other hand, it is clear that the mother played no role whatsoever in legitimation. She could not legitimate her child; only the father could. Her desires for her child or even her consent were not given expression in legitimation (except in her marital consent). "She could not pretend to any right over the child whom the father, by legitimating, had inserted into his own legal family, into his own sphere of interests, into the exclusive sphere of his own existence."[20] By means of legitimation children of women of humble status or foreign extraction, children of transient and illicit unions might enter fully into society. The exercise of imperial privileges and *ius commune* by counts palatine thus benefited various segments of society by providing heirs and by cloaking ambiguous persons with social, moral, and legal legitimacy. But it could not remove the fact that the child had not, in fact, been fathered in marriage and that the mother, in all likelihood, was not of the social (or even ethnic) status to be married appropriately to the father. The quality of blood that flowed in the child's veins was one thing specifically not affected by legitimation.

On the local level the illegitimate could not remain a legal abstraction. At this level, both the sense of attachment, obligation, and even love for the illegitimate, and the sense of fear, prejudice, and even hatred were more apparent. The resulting tension issued in greater discretion in the treatment of bastards. At least the choices to be made with these children were more evidently encountered and treated as such. Alberti even tried to turn this into an advantage, noting that by "adopting" one could

18. Provvisioni—registri 144, fol. 39v.

19. Tamassia, *La famiglia italiana,* 242; Airaldi, "Bastardos," 324–25, see it solely as a matter of inheritance. Berengo, *Nobili e mercanti,* 35–37, treats legitimation less as securing an heir than as "l'assorbimento nella vita domestica." However, Ann Twinam, *Public Lives, Private Secrets,* 279, remarks that legitimation of a woman resolved issues of honor and thus strengthened the traditional perquisites of patriarchy, whereas legitimation of a man "could radically disturb the present and the future status quo."

20. Airaldi, "Bastardos," 324.

choose one's son in a way not possible when tied to legitimate offspring.[21]

Yet legitimation itself came only after various other decisions had been made about an illegitimate—to recognize paternity, to label the child illegitimate. There were also certain advantages to be had from the lack of *patria potestas* over a bastard—advantages that also operated in the emancipation of legitimate offspring.[22] In this way they prolonged the uncertain status of the illegitimate—a member of the family, but not entirely; a possible heir, but not yet. At the same time, illegitimates might be active in the family's interests, adding to or protecting its property and prestige. A papal dispensation might prove to be a wise investment here, but it was not a legitimation.

Legitimations by the Florentine Signoria had more immediate but limited social and legal efficacy. We possess a unique source by which to measure the frequency of legitimations in Florence by legislative decree. Sometime around or after 1676 an unidentified ducal bureaucrat compiled a listing of all illegitimates (in fact, he was not thorough) legitimated by act of the Florentine legislative councils as contained in the books of *provvisioni* from 1357 to 1572.[23] In fact this manuscript contains a series of lists culled from other sources also (with each entry numbered consecutively), and there is also a final list of "quelli i quali nati o espuri o naturali."[24] Fifty-five of the first eighty-four *legitimati* come from the period between 1357 and 1513, and of the seventy-four illegitimates in the final list, the first thirty come from the republican period of Florentine history (and include the Medici bastards Giovanni "delle Bande Nere," Alessandro, and Ippolito). Of those fifty-five legitimated before 1513, the first thirty-eight were legitimated by the councils between 1357 and 1390. A number of these legitimated bastards (fifteen of thirty-eight) carried surnames of illustrious Florentine lineages.[25] The rest were the children of men listed as *merciaio, notaio, vinaio, albergatore, vinattiere,* or of no profession, or whose foreign origins were betrayed (da Freggiaia, di Mugello, including a "nobil uomo Guidone di Franze"). These thirty-eight legitimations affected fifty-seven children,

21. Alberti, *I libri della famiglia,* 152–53.

22. See Kuehn, *Emancipation,* 71–75, 156–60.

23. Manoscritti 433, titled "Spurii legittimati."

24. Entries 85 to 199 from the books of the ghabelle on contracts from 1539 to 1568 and entries 200–401 from the same source by leave of the grand dukes, ending in 1676.

25. Guicciardini, Buondelmonte, Giugni, Forese, Bardi (twice), Donati (twice), Baldovinetti, Riccardi, Rucellai, Obriachi, da Castiglionchio, Morelli, Soderini.

eight of whom were girls. Legitimations in the fifteenth century were much more sporadic: one in 1414, one in 1435, the remaining fourteen between 1460 and 1491 (ten in the 1460s, seven of which were between 1464 and 1468), and a final legitimation of five sons of Andrea di Francesco di Filippo Bardi in 1513. Leaving aside this latter, the sixteen legitimations recorded for the fifteenth century were by eleven fathers with surnames, to the benefit of nineteen sons, no daughters.[26] In broad terms the chronological picture is that there were periods of no legitimations by legislative councils in the 1370s, 1390s and the first decade of the fifteenth century, the 1420s and 1440s. But our bureaucratic compiler, who may have had some particular purposes at hand not otherwise recoverable from this list, missed some legitimations in the interims and even in the self-same volumes he consulted. I found legitimations from 1404, 1453, and 1457, as well as one from 1410.[27] Even in 1363, where he found the legitimation of Appollonio di Puccio di Filippo, he missed the earlier legitimation of Giovanni and Soldo di Matteo di Federigo Soldi.[28]

What does not emerge from these lists but does from an examination of some of these legitimations themselves, is that there was no set form for this infrequent procedure. Age of the child to be legitimated, identity of the mother, exact legal status of the child (*naturalis, spurius,* and so forth) might or might not appear. Those of the fifteenth century dispensed with ages at times but—in keeping with the catasto of 1457/8—were concerned to know something of the mother and the marital status of the father at the time of the conception. Of eight legitimations of ten sons, from families of some wealth and prominence, mothers were *solutae* (five) and *servae* (three), and a married woman. None were said to be slaves. Fathers, some of whom were married when they brought the child to the Signoria, claimed, with two exceptions, to have been *soluti* when the child was conceived.[29]

The one terminological consistency in these council-granted legitima-

26. Bonciani, Bartoli, Ricci, Mellini, Soderini, Tigliamochi, Lippi (twice), Buoni, Buonamici, Tornaquinci.

27. Provvisioni—registri 93, fol. 140r (27 September 1404); 99, fols. 78v–79r (28 June 1410); 144, fols. 39r–40r (23 October 1453); 148, fols. 25v–26v (23 February 1456/7).

28. Provvisioni—registri 51, fols. 9r and 59v–60r.

29. Provvisioni—registri 155, fols. 134r–135r (5 October 1464); 156, fols. 66v–67v (20 June 1465); 159, fol. 238r–v (16 January 1468/9); 166, fols. 142v–143v (5 September 1475); 178, fols. 49v–50r (20 April 1486); 182, fols. 28v–29r (28 April 1491), as well as four listed in previous note 28.

tions is the recourse somewhere to the language of fiction—"ac si essent filii legitimi et naturalis"—and concession of a right to inherit in the absence of legitimate children. That these legislative councils could craft such a fiction would not have seemed inconsistent, as they also worked the opposite magic at times, dissolving kinship for branches of magnate clans who thus regained political rights while symbolizing their new identity with an approved change of name.[30] Bastards were rarely enabled to hold political office. Dardano di Niccolò Acciaiuoli explained in 1445 that his seventeen-year-old Niccolò, whom he greatly loved ("valde diligit"), had been conceived when he was single on a young girl, Rosa of Ragusa. The boy was "good," "always obedient to him and showed him due honor and reverence" [semper sibi obediens ac debitum honorem et reverentiam exhibuit], and so Dardano asked for a full restitution of legitimacy to hold office, specifically exempting him from the terms of the disabling legislation of 1404 and 1428.[31] On the other hand, eight years later when Piero di Chino Lippi sought legitimation for Filippo, for whom there were similar expressions of love and testimony of good character, it was expressly said that he would enjoy no benefits of officeholding.[32]

There was also the bizarre reversal notoriously worked out by the sculptor Lorenzo Ghiberti. His mother had been married to Cione Ghiberti of Pelago, but had left him and moved to Florence to live with the goldsmith Bartolo (or Bartoluccio) di Michele, whom she married in 1406 following Cione's death. Lorenzo had grown up with the benefit of Bartolo's tutelage in his craft but had otherwise claimed to be the legitimate son of Cione. He had exploited this paternal duality until 1444, when as one of the *Dodici,* he was secretly denounced to the Conservatori delle Leggi as ineligible on grounds of illegitimacy. Two witnesses knew his background in great detail, claiming that Ghiberti's several rejections of the office of guild consul were due to his knowledge that he was ineligible and that his birth status was common knowledge among fellow craftsmen and neighbors. Ghiberti had only paid fiscal duties to Florence since 1420, thanks to claiming legitimate descent from Cione, so even if legitimate he did not have a family citizenship tradition. Faced with a fine of five hundred florins, Ghiberti countered that he was Cione's legitimate son, only treated like a son by Bartoluccio. His parents had

30. Klapisch-Zuber, "Ruptures de parenté."

31. Provvisioni—registri 136, fols. 104v–105v (29 July 1445).

32. Provvisioni—registri 144, fols. 39r–40r (23 October 1453).

been married and together at the time of his birth in 1378 (marriage instruments were produced), and in 1413 he had pursued legal inheritance from Cione. He conceded that he had posed as Lorenzo di Bartoluccio at times. He also allowed as how he had paid taxes only since 1420 as Lorenzo di Bartoluccio. Convinced by his arguments and evidence, on 29 April 1444 the Signoria reduced his fine to fifty lire, adding that, as he was better known as Lorenzo di Bartoluccio than as Lorenzo di Cione, in the future when extracted for office as Lorenzo di Bartoluccio he could exercise the office with impunity "as if said Bartolo or Bartoluccio truly were his legitimate and natural father."[33] In effect Ghiberti was declared legitimate for purposes of officeholding to a man he said was not his biological father.

In terms of the *ius commune* legislative legitimation was a *legitimatio per oblationem curiae.* It resulted in agnation and inheritance rights between father and child only. The peculiar disabilities that concerned Florence's rulers were those involving officeholding and exemption from gabelles. The only illegitimate I have found who was said to result from incest experienced such a legitimation. This was Daniela, daughter of Gabriele di messer Bartolomeo Panciatichi, who was legitimated to inherit by the governing councils of Florence along with a half brother and two half sisters in 1410. It was her *tutores* who in 1422 revealed the incest, which may have been nothing more than a relationship within the canonically prohibited degrees.[34] Obviously Gabriele Panciatichi did not marry this woman, even if *soluta.*

The mode of legitimation one encounters most frequently in notarial records is legitimation by imperial rescript. This was a visible public legitimation, duly notarized, but not above challenge. This too was hardly the most frequent judicial act. I have found twenty-nine (one being a double instance) from the fifteenth century (ranging from 1412 to 1484). That I found even that many can be credited to the fact that one notary, ser Francesco di Piero Giacomini, worked closely with the counts palatine Niccolò d'Alessio Albizzi and Antonio di Tedice Albizzi in the 1410s and 1420s (thirteen of the legitimations come from his books and precisely in

33. Cf. Richard Krautheimer, *Lorenzo Ghiberti* (Princeton, N.J., 1956; rpt. 1982), 3–4, and the documentary appendix, 391–94.

34. Notarile 7384 (1420–21), 10 February 1421/2, where it says "quod dicta Daniella tempore sue conceptionis et postea usque in dicta infrascripta legiptimatione fuit spurea et nata ex incestuoso coytu ipsius Gabrielis tunc temporis habentis uxorem." Provvisioni—registri 99, fols. 78v–79r (28 June 1410).

a period when legislative legitimation was very rare). Other counts palatine who officiated at legitimations were Giovachino da Montedolio, Stefano di Benedetto degli Avogari, Antonio Roselli (author of the treatise that figures so prominently in the first chapter), Bernardo di Filippo Giugni, Zanobi Guasconi (jurist), Benedetto di Bartolomeo Fortini, Maso di Luca Albizzi, Jacopo di Piero Guicciardini, Tommaso Salvetti (jurist), and Benedetto di Paolo Benzi. The archbishops Amerigo Corsini, Antonino di ser Niccolò Pierozzi, and Orlando Bonarli were also active in legitimations.

The fathers in these legitimations were not all Florentine. The count palatine's authority was not a matter of territorial jurisdiction; it was voluntary and available to anyone. Conversely, just as some foreigners gained legitimation in Florence, some Florentines may have had legitimations performed elsewhere. Of those who legitimated children in Florence, some came from very prominent and privileged backgrounds: Niccolò di Jacopo del Palagio, Francesco di messer Arnaldo Mannelli, Stefano di Giramonte Bardi, Bernardo di Marco Salviati, Niccolò di Lorenzo di messer Tommaso Soderini, and Niccolò da Uzzano. Fates of some substantial patrimonies were implicated.

For legitimation by rescript the legal status of the child had to be revealed, thus disclosing the mother's identity or at least her relationship to the father. Of the thirty-eight bastards legitimated by rescript, the category of illegitimacy is unknown for only one.[35] For eighteen, one parent was married (making them adulterine). In ten of these instances the father was married. The mother of the bastard was a slave in only two of these, a *serva* in two more (one mother is unknown). The other bastards to be legitimated were fathered on women of the community. Rosso del Bonecca de' Rossi legitimated three sons by Verdiana, whom he termed wife of Martino di Pietro da Ulignano; but in his catasto report of 1427, Rossi listed her as his own wife.[36] Lorenzo di Lionardo Raffacani legitimated five children, all conceived on Nanna di Goro, widow of a ser Giovanni. His affair with her began well before his marriage. The oldest, a girl, was conceived before Lorenzo married but while Nanna's husband was still alive, and the oldest son came in the interim while she was a

35. We can tell nothing regarding the second participant, Matteo di Jacopo Villani, in a unique double legitimation by the archibshop (Notarile 13501 [1447–59], fols. 183r–185v [28 June 1456]).

36. Notarile 9040 (1422–29), fol. 301r (28 June 1427); Catasto 65, fols. 235v–237v.

widow and he was yet unmarried (and so was the only one of the five not technically adulterine). The other three came after his marriage.[37] Then there was also Niccolò di Jacopo di Giovanni di Bindo del Palagio, who disclosed to the jurist Antonio Roselli, as count palatine, that

> while he was single many times he knew carnally a woman by the name of monna Piera, daughter of the late Nuto di Grazia Cingatti of Poggio in the podestaria of Terra Nuova . . . and wife of Vanni di Dino of San Clemente in said podestaria, serving for a long time in Niccolò's house, and from said coition with said monna Piera is conceived of said Niccolò you, Salice, today over seven years of age and also from the impeded coition with said Niccolò said monna Piera conceived you, Luciano, who were later born in the year 1430 in April; and that said Niccolò at these times and throughout them and before and always and continually had been and was and was reputed and today is and is reputed to be unmarried; and that said Niccolò for the past twelve years and more kept said monna Piera and keeps her in his house, absent and separate from her husband Nuto [*sic*], and that said Niccolò at present lacks legitimate progeny.[38]

A few months later he declared that he owed Piera the hefty sum of 304 florins "by reason of her salary as servant and in nursing the sons of Niccolò and his brother Francesco." Niccolò further specified that none of this money could go to her husband.[39] Del Palagio and Raffacani cer-

37. Notarile 9039, fols. 319v–321v (17 February 1420/1).

38. Notarile 9039, fol. 201v (31 May 1419); Notarile 9040, fols. 249r–250v (26 July 1426); ibid., fol. 301r (28 June 1427); Notarile 685, fols. 123v–126v (16 August 1435): "dum esset solutus pluries et pluries carnaliter cognovit quandam mulierem nomine dominam Pieram filiam condam Nuti Gratie Cingatti de Podio potestarie Terre Nove vallis Arni superioris comitatus Florentie et uxorem Vannis Dini de San Clemente dicte potestarie iam diu famulantem in domo dicti Niccolai et ex dicto coitu sic cum dicta domina Piera habito concepit ex dicto Niccolao te Salicem hodie maiorem septennio etiam deinde ex intecato coitu sic cum dicto Niccolao habito dicta domina Piera concepitur te Lutianum qui postea natus fuisti in anno domini mccccxxx et mense Aprilis, et quod dictus Niccolaus dictis temporibus et per dicta tempora et ante et semper et continuo fuit et erat et seu reputabatur et hodie est et reputatur solutus, et quod dictus Niccolaus dictam dominam Pieram iam sunt anni duodecim et ultra retinuit et eam retinet in domo proprie habitationis ipsius Niccolai ipso Nuto viro et marito dicte domine Piere absente et separato existente habitante separata a dicto suo marito, et quod dictus Niccolaus ad presens caret legitima sobole."

39. Notarile 686 (1436–40), fol. 20r–v (13 February 1436/7): "occaxione sui salarii famulatis et in lactando filios dicti Niccolai et Francisci fratris."

tainly fit the profile of sexually predatory wealthy Florentine males, although both these men were relatively monogamous.

Nineteen legitimated bastards, then, were presented as the product of a relationship between a *solutus* and a *soluta.* Whether these were casual or long-standing relationships cannot be said for every case; though clearly for all there was ultimately no marriage. Some of these women had more than one child by the same man, which might indicate concubinage. Pasqua di Domenico Mistici d'Arezzo had two children by a Bastina de' Chiareni, having years earlier fathered another son on a Lucia from Genoa.[40] Otherwise these wealthy Florentines picked on wives of poorer men who were in no position to cause them harm. Cere di Frusino da Verrazzano kept Filippo's mother as concubine, but he did not use marriage to this woman of Montaguto to legitimate their son.[41] Another possibility, of course, was that the wealthy Florentine may have married his concubine off to someone else. That is what Francesco d'Arnaldo Mannelli did with the woman "he retained as concubine before he took a wife and whom he later married to Nuto d'Agostino da Fibiana."[42] We know that Antonio di Cambiozzo eventually married his concubine Caterina di Filippo del Buono, mother of Francesco.[43] These were "honest" women of "good" families. It is striking how many had family names with a place designation. Those recently come to a strange city may have been more vulnerable. Otherwise mothers of these nineteen bastards included two slaves, two servants, two widows (one unnamed "ex honestate"), two termed *concubina,* and the rest simply *soluta* (one of whom we know from Bernardo Salviati's *ricordi* was really a *serva,* but she and four others were unnamed in the legitimations).

In her study of Genoese legitimations, Gabriela Airaldi found that the children's mothers were generally slaves or non-Genoese.[44] The Florentine evidence reveals only three women who gave birth to bastards were slaves, five others *serve.* Six women came from outside Florence (Venice, Genoa, Cortona). Of those who can be said with any certainty to have been Florentine, four were certainly married. For the rest, if they did not originate in the city, it still does not seem that they came from far away.

40. Notarile 10194 (1484–88), fol. 38r (9 December 1484).
41. Notarile 9634 (1476–77), fols. 57r–59v (8 November 1476).
42. Notarile 9042 (1411–31), testamenti, fols. 15v–17v (30 March 1414).
43. Notarile 10452 (1410–49), fol. 45r (10 February 1417/8).
44. Airaldi, "Bastardos," 331.

In general, then, those bastards favored with legitimation were those whose mothers were a socially better class than slaves and household servants. Certainly the children of slaves, in view of the catasto, were underrepresented among the *legitimati.*[45] Airaldi also argued that the relatively advanced ages of *legitimati* were an indication, in conjunction with the frequent declarations by the fathers that they had no legitimate heirs, of an interesting attempt to procreate heirs outside marriage.[46] Whether such was so at Florence is hard to say. Only nine *legitimati* had ages attributed to them in the act of legitimation, and of these five were legally *infantes* (under the age of seven). As such they could not consent to a legal act, so the necessary consent was being made up for, as also in emancipation of *infantes,* by the imperial rescript.[47] In two legitimations the child was absent, so his consent was thus still pending.[48] More problematic judicially were legitimations enacted at the initiative of the son. I have turned up two examples. The palatine Bernardo di Filippo Giugni legitimated the notary ser Pietroniccolò di Pietro di Domenico, born in adultery.[49] Ser Domenico di messer Anastagio da Castel San Giovanni was legitimated at his own request (his father was alive, but his presence not noted). The titles in this case indicate seemingly well integrated members of society. The notarial charter also begins with a preamble about the blamelessness of children.[50]

That these legitimations were usually made with an eye to inheritance is made clear by several different features. For one thing, not surprisingly, legitimation was basically reserved for boys. Only five rescript-legitimated bastards were girls. They were the eldest of five by Lorenzo Raffacani in 1421; Bilia di Filippo Ticci by his slave, who could "succeed by testament only to what he should want to leave her etc. and she cannot

45. See Helen S. Ettlinger regarding the favoring of bastards in fifteenth-century princely families: cf. "Visibilis et Invisibilis: The Mistress in Italian Renaissance Court Society," *Renaissance Quarterly* 47 (1994): 270–92.

46. Airaldi, "Bastardos," 329.

47. Kuehn, *Emancipation,* 16.

48. Notarile 13501 (1447–59), fols. 183r–185v (28 June 1456); Notarile 10188 (1473–75), fol. 252v (17 April 1475).

49. Notarile 6209 (1462–65), fols. 17v–23r (30 June 1462).

50. Notarile 3372 (1425–28), fols. 90v–91v (3 December 1426): "Cum humane nature dilectio in universi orbis non solum licite prolis circuitu homines procreaverit sed ab ipsa etiam et quasi inlicitorum copia procedat profetto quidem divini numinis providentia tales minime culpabiles procreatos considerans propriis annuens cogitationibus sinceri affectione remediis providere opportunis talibus exoptans apud romanorum nationes."

contest the testament"; the slave-born daughter of Bastiano di Chirico del Ghiotto da Seccomo; Bernardo di Marco Salviati's daughter Marietta; and Angela di Pasqua Mistici.[51] These girls account for three of the eight bastards fathered on slaves or servants. Other than Angela di Pasqua, the others had brothers, legitimate or legitimated, so perhaps they mainly gained in terms of marriage prospects and dowry claims from having the "stain" of illegitimacy removed.

Most of the time fathers stated that there were no legitimate children. Fathers were supposed to do this, although it was the count's prerogative to legitimate even if there were legitimate heirs. We know, on the other hand, Francesco di Arnaldo Mannelli had two legitimate younger daughters when he legitimated Andrea, but they were not mentioned in the notarial text.[52] Giovanni di Jacopo Banchi declared that he had a legitimate son, Jacopo, when he had Michele legitimated. Michele's legitimation had an apparent purpose other than that of securing an heir, however. He was also immediately made a notary by imperial (not guild) privilege. As ser Michele di Giovanni di Jacopo Banchi he would appear at others' legitimations as witness, though he did not record any legitimations himself before dying, it seems, only a few years later.[53] Cessino di Salvestro Cessini also became a notary following his legitimation.[54] Niccolò Soderini had been married to Ginevra di Filippo Macinghi almost four years when he legitimated Geri.[55]

Even as heirs, *legitimati* faced testamentary restrictions. Paolo Morelli's legitimation of his four-year-old Giovanni carried the stipulation that he could not inherit more than five hundred florins.[56] Niccolò di Giovanni del Bellaccio was not prepared to give up his freedom of testation, and so laid on Carluccio a prohibition from contesting his will.[57]

51. Notarile 9039 (1417–21), fols. 319v–321v (17 February 1420/1): "quod ex testamento succedat solum in eo quod sibi relinquere voluerit etc. nec possit testamentum querelare"; Notarile 9040 (1422–29), fol. 107r (10 July 1423); Notarile 685 (1432–40), fols. 153v–157r (13 October 1435); Notarile 10187 (1469–72), fol. 182r (16 April 1470). Cf. Airaldi, "Bastardos," 324–25.

52. Notarile 9040 (1422–29), fol. 31r (7 August 1422).

53. Notarile 9039 (1417–21), fol. 70r (13 March 1417/8) and repeated fol. 114r–v (20 July 1418). He was present to witness a legitimation, ibid., fol. 188r (7 April 1419). His only volume of papers is Notarile 1505 (1418–26), containing only seventy-eight folia.

54. Notarile 9037 (1408–11), fols. 373v–376r (5 February 1411/2). As did ser Luigi di Cambino di Francesco Cambini, who had legitimate siblings: Catasto 826, fols. 380r–383v with Notarile 13504 (1452–60), fols. 175r–177r (3 January 1457/8).

55. Notarile 10444 (1428–41), fol. 191r (14 April 1437), 213v–214r (17 June 1438), 331r–v (20 February 1440/1).

56. Notarile 9039 (1417–21), fol. 173r (13 February 1418/9).

57. Notarile 9040 (1422–29), fol. 182r (10 March 1424/5).

Bartolomeo di Giovanni Giani's legitimation of his son was set up for inheritance purposes, at least in that in his will drawn up twelve years later he named his son as his universal heir, noting that he had also secured consent of the Signoria to his legitimation.[58]

What the *legitimatus* might claim was perhaps less a problem than the obstacles others might present to his inheritance. One measure was for the father to have his brother, whose inheritance rights were being postponed in favor of the nephew, present at the legitimation.[59] Another was to name at least all the relatives who had potential inheritance interests. Niccolò di Jacopo del Palagio carefully named those whose rights were affected by the legitimation of Salice and Luciano. These included both the del Palagio line and the Bardi from whom they sprang.[60] When Niccolò da Uzzano had Salvadore legitimated in 1419, he carefully disclosed that he had a legitimate daughter, Bonda, then married to Giovanni di Niccolò Soderini, who had three sons and a daughter; that his deceased daughter Ginevra, who had been married to the late Piero di Bartolomeo Capponi, had had three sons and two daughters, and that he had a brother Agnolo.[61] Francesco d'Antonio Neri made sure his brother Benedetto was present when his son was legitimated.[62] Citation of *agnati* by means of a herald to appear at the legitimation and learn that they were having their possible inheritance claims prejudiced by it was an appropriate precaution. When Mariotto di Dinozzo di Stefano Lippi came before Archbishop Antonino to have his little boy Bonaiuto legitimated, a herald was dispatched to summon any agnates or cognates, "and by name monna Teghiaia, blood sister of Mariotto." When she failed to appear, Mariotto petitioned that she be held in contumacy and the legitimation proceed, which is what happened.[63]

Legitimation approximates Pierre Bourdieu's idea of a rite of institution or incorporation. Such rituals separate those who have undergone them not only from those who have not but especially from those who cannot and never will. In this light a circumcision ritual, for example, is not about boys becoming men but the line between male and female. "The institution of an identity, whether a title of nobility or a stigma.

58. Notarile 3374, fols. 347r–348v (10 June 1440).

59. Notarile 10188 (1473–75), fol. 252v (17 April 1475); Notarile 9037 (1408–11), fols. 373v–376r (5 February 1411/2).

60. Notarile 685 (1432–40), fols. 123v–126v (16 August 1435).

61. Notarile 9039, fols. 190r–194v (10 and 11 April 1419).

62. Notarile 10188, fol. 252v (17 April 1475).

63. Notarile 13498 (1439–82), fols. 260r–265r (9 and 12 August 1449).

. . . is to signify to someone what he is, and to signify to him that he must comport himself in a certain manner in consequence."[64] The ritual of legitimation signified the comportment of a legitimate person, which, in the abstract, encompassed the entire range of legal possibilities. It was also about paternity—something women could not experience, obviously—but also something that could not be experienced by *vulgo quaesiti* or foundlings or anyone else for whom firm biological paternity could not be socially and legally imputed or acknowledged.

Florentine families were fields in which various tensions were present, and those tensions were managed, understood, and played out—quietly or explosively—with the terms and mechanisms of law.[65] Included in these might be the fate not only of one's legitimate children but of illegitimates as well. Florentine bastards may almost always emerge to our sight from the documentary base as objects of the actions of others, and as lesser persons in that light, but we need not take that as an inaccurate or deceptive sense of the personhood of bastards, of their possible agency in family and social events.

Inheritance by Illegitimates

We have to remain aware that "there is a great risk in talking about a culture's sense of personhood, or sense of self or individualism. The risk is to assume that all people within a culture are governed by the same view. This is not so, even among us."[66] Certainly the bastard in Florence was not accorded the degrees of honor, respect, and property that came to legitimate persons, but just as surely those bastards raised by their fathers (or their families) had something more than those who were abandoned, and some of these bastards had much more than legitimate folk of more modest social circumstances. Those legitimated had much more—in status if not in property. Still the bastard carried a deep, even indelible stain of dishonor. How were legitimate descendants and heirs, whatever their relationship to the bastard bearer, to get along with the illegitimate, even

64. Pierre Bourdieu, "Rites as Acts of Institution," in Peristiany and Pitt-Rivers, *Honor and Grace,* 83.

65. Cf. My "Il diritto di famiglia e l'uso del diritto nelle famiglie fiorentine nel Rinascimento," in *Palazzo Strozzi,* 108–25.

66. William Ian Miller, *Humiliation: And Other Essays on Honor, Social Discomfort, and Violence* (Ithaca, N.Y., 1993), 226 n. 28.

if legitimated? And even if they could coexist on a daily basis, disputes could arise at inheritance.[67] Legitimation did not obviate disputes with kin about status and inheritance. It was merely a fiction; and this fiction might be exposed by someone interested in realizing the real rights claimed by a *legitimatus*. Escaping the ambiguities of illegitimacy, even when armed with the sweeping language of a charter of legitimation, was not easy. The point at which social, cultural, and legal prejudices against bastards, legitimated or not, were most in evidence was in inheritance. It was the inheritance claims of bastards that were most feared in culture and law. It was the lack or limitation of inheritance claims that perhaps most clearly demarcated illegitimate from legitimate. Even legitimation, which legally erected inheritance rights, did not triumph over such prejudices unchallenged. If anything, legitimations—much like testaments—by changing expectations, only made disputes more likely. With tangible interests on the line and tangled legal concepts in operation, only trained jurists could hope to provide a way out. Let us consider one nice example here.

Toward the later decades of the fifteenth century, the Capitano of Sarzana, subject to Florentine rule, handed a case to three Florentine jurists: Bernardo di messer Giovanni Buongirolami (d. 1484), Angelo di messer Otto Niccolini (d. 1499), and Antonio Malegonelli (1451–1506).[68] Parties to the suit were a ser Aloisio, acting in his wife's name, and ser Giovantonio de' Grisi, acting on behalf of Francesco de' Giandolfi. The jurists isolated one central problem: whether Francesco's legitimation was effectual in making him heir to his father, Andrea, a priest, while thus excluding the wife of Aloisio, who was Andrea's sister.

Francesco's legitimation rescript contained only a general derogative clause, "not withstanding any law," instead of mentioning the specific texts of the civil law being set aside. The failure to insert that clause opened the door to extensive speculation whether the emperor, here through his count palatine, had sufficient *voluntas* to allow this legitimation of the son of a priest. Also, Aloisio argued, there had been no mention of the statute of Sarzana by which even a *spurius* could be left one-fourth part of a patrimony by testament; this failure was taken as

67. This reverses Berengo, *Nobili e mercanti,* 35, who believes fictitious sales, gifts, and so forth from the father could take care of illegitimates and "rendono inconsuete le liti tra legittimi e illegittimi sulla tomba del capofamiglia."

68. ASF, Carte strozziane, 3d ser., 41/5, fols. 1r–23v.

indicative that "the emperor does not seem to have consented" to legitimation in this place, because the legitimation was not necessary for something to be left to the child. The count had not been told that there were no other children, and no mention had been made of *agnati.* Those *venientes ab intestato*—including, one presumes, the priest-father's sister—had not been summoned. All these facts seemed to militate toward classifying the legitimation as evasive or deceptive *(surreptitia),* as did the fact that the child was not explicitly labeled son of a priest and the woman who gave birth to him was not a kept concubine. One could not infer the count knew the status and conditions of the persons before him and, therefore, wanted to legitimate such a child.[69] All these arguments aimed at invalidating the legitimation in its entirety rather than simply trying to challenge its results.

The arguments in favor of the legitimation were certainly more powerful. "All doctors" agreed that the emperor could legitimate *spurii,* including a priest's son.[70] Also, in distinction to emancipation, legitimation was not performed by the father. It only required his consent. It was in fact an act of the imperial power.[71] The general clauses "not withstanding" rules of *ius commune* in the rescript were also sufficient, judged Buongirolami and his colleagues. The argument about the statute was countered by declaring it contrary to *ius commune* and so not valid. This argument was backed up with a sweeping assertion of the universality of imperial power, even to the point of denying legitimacy to the de facto powers of a monarch like the king of France.[72]

More pointedly and appropriately, the jurists said that an assertion to the effect there were no other children was not required, nor was the summoning of *agnati* or of intestate heirs. Failure to lay out all the aspects of the circumstances of Francesco's birth was insufficient to invalidate the legitimation: "although he who asked to be legitimated did not plainly state all his defects, still from the 'not withstanding' clause it seems the intent of the legitimating person was that he wanted to legiti-

69. Ibid., fol. 8v: "Nam ex hoc non infertur necessario quod comes per hoc sciat et intelligat istum natum esse ex constituto in sacris, nam potest quis nasci ex soluto et soluta laicis et tamen dici de illicito et damnato coitu natus, scilicet ibi illa mulier non fuit vera concubina quia forte deficiebat aliquod ex requisitis ad legitimum concubinatum."

70. Ibid., fol. 11v.

71. Ibid., fols. 2v and 11v–12r: "Nos autem sumus in legitimatione que non est actus patris sed principis et potest fieri absente et ignorante patre, dummodo etiam ex intervallo ratum habeat."

72. Ibid., fols. 16v–17r.

mate even if greater defects were revealed."[73] Similarly failure to be specific about the mother did not vitiate the act. The fact that the child was called *naturalis* simply reflected the *usus loquendi,* of which the count palatine was aware.[74] From all this, therefore, followed a directed finding to the Capitano of Sarzana

> that said legitimation is valid and so the role of the lord Capitano is to pronounce among these parties in the following manner: by absolving said Francesco from the charges and imposing perpetual silence on ser Aloisio about the estate of said messer Andrea and to absolve the parties from the expenses of litigating this case as a result of the various opinions of jurists and *consilia* produced for both sides . . . not withstanding the statute of said land that commands the vanquished be condemned to pay the victor's expenses, because it should be understood according to *ius commune.*[75]

Thus the jurists admitted to the complexities and uncertainties of jurisprudence. But their decision upholding the legitimation was firm and in line with that arrived at around the beginning of the century by Signorino degli Omodei in the case of Simone di Domenico. There too the legitimating powers had been questioned; the summoning of *agnati* or *venientes ab intestato* had been at issue. The answers then had been about the same as Buongirolami and his colleagues offered, though they betrayed no awareness of the earlier *consilium.* It was unlikely, it seems, that jurists would strike down a valid legitimation, even on technicalities of not being honest with the count. But upholding legitimation and the status it conferred was one thing. Making it effective with regard to inheritance was something else.

If we turn to a frequent source for our inquiry, we find that the catasto provides interesting evidence regarding inheritance by bastards.

73. Ibid., fol. 21r.

74. Ibid., fol. 21v.

75. Ibid., fol. 22v: "dittam legitimationem validam esse et propterea partes domini capitanei esse in pronumptiando inter dictas partes hoc modo, videlicet: dictum Franciscum absolvendo a petitis et imponendo dicto ser Aloisio dicto nomine perpetuum silentium super dicta hereditate dicti d. Andree ex causa successionis ab intestato et absolvere partes ab expensis propter istam causam litigandi resultante ex variis oppynionibus doc. et ex consiliis pro utraque parte in causa productis. . . . Et non obstat statutum dicte terre quo dicitur disponi quod victus victori in expensis condepnetur, quia debet intelligi secundum ius comune."

Carlo di Meo Altoviti noted that he possessed a *podere* that had belonged to an illegitimate brother, Lancilotto, but he had died, and the farm reverted by the terms of the paternal testament to Carlo.[76] The legitimated Maria di Cambio de' Medici was owed 1,443 florins by a Bartolo di Jacopo Canbiuzzi da Fornace di Mugello.[77] Matteo di Jacopo Villani, whose illegitimacy was not disclosed in the catasto but who was legitimated in 1456, was married (his wife was pregnant and soon bore a son) and had an infant daughter and *sustanze* totaling 1,706 florins, including a house where he lived, although he had only one-sixth and four of his brothers had the rest.[78]

Giovanni di ser Antonio Ughi reported that he earned nothing, and in the ledgers of the Mercanzia he was down for debts totaling 300 florins; and he had the obligation, being without children, to spend 200 florins on a chapel in San Lorenzo for his father's soul.[79] Giovanni di Bartolomeo Marsuppini, elderly cousin of messer Carlo Marsuppini, was owed expenses and clothing from his young cousins.[80] Andrea di Jacopo di Giorgio Bardi had the *poderuzzo* bought by his father from his mother's wages of service for 40 florins.[81] The five-year-old Lucrezia d'Andrea di Piero Petrini had the 500-florin dowry her father left her,[82] whereas Caterina d'Antonio di Filippo had no dowry but was taken in by her father's brothers "because it falls to us to lead her to honor [marry]" [perché a noi tocha condurla a onore].[83] Carlo di Salvestro Gondi took in the two sons of his brother Filippo and faced expenses "that we give them by virtue of testamentary obligations" [e quali diamo per incharichi per virtù di testamento].[84] The catasto thus informs us that some bastards did quite well, inheriting farms and other holdings or cash, while others were left with nothing or very little. We can also begin to see how important was the mechanism of the testament in directing property to illegitimates in the form of the bequest or legacy *(legatum)*.

Transmission of property need not await the death of the current

76. Catasto 811, fols. 503r–505r.
77. Catasto 825, fols. 626r–627r.
78. Catasto 826, fols. 542r–544r.
79. Catasto 1018, fol. 491r–v.
80. Catasto 1019, fol. 445r–v.
81. Catasto 992, fol. 87r.
82. Catasto 997, fols. 7r–8r.
83. Catasto 1001, fol. 422r–v.
84. Catasto 1013, fols. 204r–207r.

holder. Gifts were possible, and in fact a paternal gift while the giver was still alive was relatively unchallengeable. But fathers were not well advised to relinquish control of property too early, and those with only illegitimate children may always have waited in hopes of having a legitimate child. In any case, we only come across property transfers to bastards once in a great while. Antonio di Jacopo d'Uberto Arrighi, a legitimated son, was emancipated in 1476 in order to be given a house next door to his father in the Borgo degli Albizzi, the bed and other *masserizie* in his room in his father's house, and a farm in San Biagio to which his father retained usufruct.[85]

It is also important to keep in mind that many estates devolved by intestacy.[86] Although advice to draw up a will was commonplace, many Florentines either chose deliberately or neglected to do so. Intestacies are much more difficult to document and trace because there is no easily retrievable document, like a testament. One must rely on other sources (acceptances or repudiations of inheritance, court records, catasto records, and guardianship records) to locate intestate patrimonies and their heirs. But perhaps with regard to illegitimates one can conclude that "testamentary succession therefore can be considered the opposite of legitimate (i.e., *ab intestato*) succession precisely because it applied to illegitimate offspring; rather than being *ab intestato,* testamentary succession always required a will, and rather than being 'natural,' it always had to be artificially created."[87] A testament is something of a road map—an itinerary for the passage of property—drawn up before the trip. The actual path followed might vary a great deal. Although we might decode the legal formulas in one to a point where we think we understand the testator's intent (a jurisprudential polestar for navigating the text), we cannot—in the absence of other documentation—be sure that the intent was carried out by heirs or those who had hoped to be heirs, executors, guardians, or judges.[88] That said, testaments leaving legacies

85. Notarile 21151 (1476), fol. 90r–v (31 May 1476).

86. For now, see my "Law, Death, and Heirs in the Renaissance: Repudiation of Inheritance in Florence," *Renaissance Quarterly* 45 (1992): 484–516.

87. Linda Lewin, "Natural and Spurious Children in Brazilian Inheritance Law from Colony to Empire: A Methodological Essay," *Americas* 18 (1991–92): 360.

88. For one example of a dispute, where brothers contested the will of a childless brother who left his estate to the Innocenti, see my "'Nemo mortalis cognitus vivit in evo': Moral and Legal Conflicts in a Florentine Inheritance Case of 1442," in *The Moral World of the Law,* ed. Peter Coss (Cambridge, 2000), 113–33.

or even on rare occasion the entire patrimony to a bastard are found in the fifteenth century.[89]

Let us begin by considering what was intended for bastards who had not been legitimated. All the surviving wills providing for such bastards belonged to their fathers. There was surprising regularity. Most often those who had illegitimates named as their heirs in first instance legitimate sons, even if not yet born, or more rarely legitimate girls.[90] Even where the testator did not have other legitimate children or hope of them, he chose a more distant legitimate relative in preference to the bastard. These included nephews by brothers, sisters, a *consobrinus* (maternal cousin), paternal cousins, even the hospital of Santa Maria Nuova.

Only a few Florentines nominated illegitimates as their universal heirs. It is hard to envision any of these going unchallenged by other relatives. Antonio di Matteo di Guicciozzo de' Ricci, in a testament of 1474, named as his heir Francesco, termed *naturalis* though born of a slave. If Francesco died without issue, then Antonio's wife (Laudomina di Piero di messer Luigi Guicciardini) became heir—or *tutrix* if he died with legitimate children.[91] The only other person mentioned was the wife, indicating that there were no other close male relatives.

It was not always a good idea to reveal illegitimacy where it could harm one's honor or even the legal possibilities the illegitimate might enjoy. In his testament of 8 March 1471 Giovanni di ser Niccolò Pandiagoni referred to his son Pandiagone simply as "suo filio." But the substance of the testament betrays (as does the son's name) the son's illegitimacy. His father left him a specific bequest—namely, his rights in a mill near Vinci—with a firm command to remain content with that or lose it, if he tried to contest the will for more. As his *heredes universales* Giovanni named any legitimate and natural sons to be born of Pandiagone and his wife. The new legitimate line of descent would get the inheri-

89. Samuel Cohn claims that legacies to illegitimates appeared only in the late fifteenth and sixteenth centuries (see his *Death and Property in Siena, 1200–1800: Strategies for the Afterlife* [Baltimore, 1988], 248). I can neither confirm nor deny his findings, except to say that one finds such legacies in fifteenth-century Florentine testaments also.

90. In the wills I have found where illegitimates were not *heredes,* fathers or grandfathers left as heirs (before substitution) sons (ten), sons as yet unborn and unconceived (five), daughters (three), brothers (three), and others (nine).

91. Diplomatico Ricci, 27 July 1474 (another reference I owe to the generosity of Elaine Rosenthal). In his catasto portata of 1458 Antonio refused to name the boy's mother and claimed that he had been legitimated through the archbishop (Catasto 832, fols. 494r–498r).

tance.[92] In this legitimate progeny the bastard was linked back to his father's patrimony in a full manner and his illegitimacy overcome.[93]

Giovanni di Pagolo Morelli had legitimate sons, so he only left a legacy to his son Fruosino. Fruosino was to get some lands in the event he married and had legitimate children of his own. Otherwise, Morelli's inheritance strategy was to leave his property in the direct male line, "benefici" for the sons of Morello Morelli, and "assurance for the comfort of his daughter and bastard son" [assicurazione dell'agiatezza della figlia femina e del figlio spurio].[94] In a codicil Morelli left a thousand-florin dowry to the bastard daughter of his son Jacopo and a thousand florins in the *monte comune* to Fruosino for his alimentary rights. But Fruosino's line would never inherit, for if Giovanni's and that of his brother failed, the property would go to the Arte della Lana.

Few Florentines left any substantial property to illegitimates. The testators' concerns, almost universally, were to provide *alimenta* for their bastards and, in the case of girls, modest dowries. Indeed the desire to furnish a dowry to a girl—thus to marry her legitimately and preclude her following in her mother's misstepped footprints—was such that girls were about as likely as boys to be named in wills, even though they were by all accounts much less than half the population of recognized bastards.[95] Giovenco di Giuliano de' Medici left Giovanna a dotal sum of 340 florins and assured her of support and shelter until she married. His heir was his legitimate son Giuliano, with substitution, should he die without legitimate descendants, to Bernardo and Giovanni d'Antonio and Antonio di Giovanni de' Medici.[96] Piero di Domenico Lamberteschi left Gostanza 300 florins; Niccolò d'Andrea Benini left Mechera 200 florins.[97] Ghismondo di Nofri Busini left a legacy of 500 florins for her dowry and marriage expenses to Domenica, desiring that the money be placed in the *monte comune* for her. His other natural daughter Lena

92. Notarile 19832, testamenti, fol. 59r–v (8 March 1470/1).

93. In *The House That Giacomo Built: History of an Italian Family, 1898–1978* (Cambridge, 1985), Donald S. Pitkin reports an incident of a bastard girl's mother telling her, on the birth of her legitimate son, that the shame of her own birth was now lifted (23).

94. Leonida Pandimiglio, "Giovanni di Pagolo Morelli e la continuità familiare," *Studi medievali,* 3d ser., 22 (1981): 149.

95. I have found wills by men and women leaving something to twenty-one girls and to twenty-six boys, five of them by one father.

96. Notarile 690 (1447–50), fols. 205r–207v (26 June 1449).

97. Notarile 10198 (1456–96), testamenti, fol. 54r–v (8 September 1462), where the heir was his married sister Ermellina; Notarile 14663 (1407–30), testamenti, fols. 20r–23v (10 May 1411), where the heirs were three legitimate sons.

received 400 florins in similar manner. His heir was his brother Domenico.[98]

A grandmother, Cosa d'Ottinelli di Cino, saw to modest dowries for her son's daughters. To the *spuria* she left 35 florins, to the legitimate daughter only 25.[99] Her bias was unusual and perhaps allowable, as she was not the girls' parent and thus did not have primary responsibility for dowering them; she was only supplementing what the father should have provided. More in line with Florentine biases was Bernardo di Bartolomeo Gherardi's provision of 1,200 florins for the legitimate Vaggia and 600 florins for illegitimate daughters.[100] Geri de' Pazzi left his *filia naturalis* a *monte* dowry worth 600 florins along with rights to remain in his house before marriage and in widowhood and with yearly *alimenta* of 25 florins. To his bastard son Carlo he left *alimenta* of only 20 florins per year, as long as he should stay in and around Florence.[101] This will was later canceled, however, perhaps because, as revealed by the catasto of 1458, Geri had in the meantime married and had a legitimate son.[102]

Any sense that girls were favored in these wills must be tempered by the thought that the sons were capable of earning a living and probably had or could expect to have a "dowry" of skills and tools. But on paper illegitimate males were not usually left much more than *alimenta*. Giovanni di Simone Pecori had a child by his slave, whom he freed, and for the infant's *alimenta* he committed usufruct and all returns on a modest piece of vineyard. He hoped his three legitimate sons would take care of the boy.[103] Geri di Lorenzo di Niccolò di Geri allowed *alimenta* and residence in his house along with his legitimate male heirs to Benedetto, as long as "he acts well and lives honestly, otherwise he would deprive him of this bequest."[104] Cherubino di Piero Ghinozzi of Cortona left his houses and arms to his *naturalis* Jacopo "so that with them he could seek

98. Notarile 11877, 7 September 1417. Samuel K. Cohn, Jr., "Le ultime volontà: Famiglia, donne e peste nera nell'Italia centrale," *Studi storici* 32 (1991): 859–75, notes another instance from 1406 of a four-hundred-florin dowry left to an illegitimate Florentine daughter with the proviso that if she was not married by age sixteen the sum would revert to charity (865).

99. Notarile 16795 (1457–1518), testamenti, 28 April 1461.

100. Notarile 692 (1454–58), fols. 337r–343r (10 October 1457).

101. Notarile 691 (1450–54), fols. 140v–141v (15 December 1451) and 142v–144r (20 December). His heirs were his brother Alamanno and his descendants. This will was, in fact, later revoked: fol. 215v (18 April 1452).

102. Catasto 832, fols. 859r–863r.

103. Notarile 14663 (1407–30), testamenti, fol. 256r–257r (23 April 1424).

104. Notarile 16660 (1420–24), fols. 40r–43v (15 March 1420/1): "se bene habente et honeste vivente alias ipsum privaret dicto legato."

his support and nourishment."[105] Was he supposed to use them or sell them? Paolo di Lapo Niccolini spelled out the rights of his bastards to specified amounts of food. Girolamo and Carlo could live on a small farm in the Val di Pesa. Antonio had the right to live with his three legitimate brothers in Florence, and they in turn had to treat him properly "so that they not bring shame on the house."[106] Lionardo di Lorenzo Salvucci named a legitimate son, Pierfilippo, his heir; but he left to his illegitimate grandson ten *staia* of grain and four barrels of wine every year until the young Lorenzo turned eighteen.[107]

In an example arising in the contado, Antonio di Giovanni Muccii da Perugia left Guido, *spurio* of his late son Luca, *alimenta* for life and usufruct on a variety of properties in San Sepolcro and Perugia. These properties were to pass in full ownership to Guido's children, male and/or female, following his death. If he had no children, the property then passed to the children of his illegitimate sister Caterina. The universal heir was Antonio's legitimate daughter Angnola, married to maestro Jacopo di Francesco of Perugia.[108] Finally, Bartolomeo di Francesco di Matteo Castellani was left the legacy of a *podere* and use of a *castello* of Altafronte, while two other *poderi* and anything else were left to legitimate daughters and the palazzo in Florence went to Leone d'Antonio di Niccolò Castellani (to remain among the Castellani).[109]

On occasion fathers also provided for the mothers of these children. They freed their slaves, as Giovanni Pecori did. Or they left the mother, not a slave, some small amount. Pongano di Giovanni di Naldo Baldi was fairly generous to his longtime servant Margherita and their son Baldino. He gave them household furnishings and the yield of several pieces of land, substituting each for the other in case of predecease.[110] Pierantonio d'Onofri Cennini gave his *illegitima* a five-hundred-florin dowry; he gave her mother, Gostanza di Michele da Vinci, specified *alimenta* as long as she lived with her family or husband near Florence.[111] Few women were thus mentioned in wills. In all likelihood the relationship had been bro-

105. Notarile 10198 (1456–96), testamenti, fol. 364r–v (15 June 1482).

106. Ibid., fols. 350r–354r (15 April 1482) and Catasto 809, fols. 256r–259r.

107. Ibid., 19 August 1508.

108. Notarile 7046 (1420–62), testamenti, 25 February 1428.

109. Castellani, *Ricordanze,* 1:31.

110. Notarile 16795 (1457–1518), testamenti, 1 August 1497. His heirs were unborn legitimate sons, with substitution to his brother and nephew. His legitimate daughter received *alimenta* and a nine-hundred-florin dowry. Notarile 9655 (1484–1516), testamenti, fol. 269r–v (25 February 1511/2) provides another example.

111. Notarile 10198 (1456–96), testamenti, fols. 91r–92v (2 October 1464).

ken off prior to drawing up a will, and the testators had already assuaged their consciences by establishing some settlement on the woman.

Testators other than the fathers did not necessarily operate with a different agenda. Francesco di Michele Becchi, for example, wanted only to provide *alimenta* (fifty florins) to his son's bastard.[112] Giovanni di ser Thome Bracci provided one hundred florins toward the dowry of an illegitimate granddaughter, while also giving a son (not the girl's father) two hundred florins for restitution of his wife's dowry.[113] Once in a while women's wills directed property to bastards. One woman gave cash for dowries to illegitimate daughters of a son (three hundred florins) and of a brother (fifty florins).[114] Alessandra di Filippo, widow of Azino di Cristofano d'Azino, left one hundred florins each to her husband's two illegitimate sons while naming as her *heredes* her three brothers-in-law.[115] Hers is the extreme example in this small sample how women generally ignored bastards in their families of birth, versus in their affinal kin and procreative household.[116] Sandro Altoviti's mother (born a Gherardini) left his son a bed, while also leaving Alamanno Altoviti's illegitimate daughter some cloth.[117] Thus she took care of bastards in two different Altoviti lines while leaving her legitimate son as her universal heir. Another grandmother left fifty-two florins for a *monte* dowry for the *spuria* of one of her sons. If the girl died before marrying, the sum was to be used to dower three poor girls.[118]

These were all bequests from an ascendant generation. I found no examples of sisters or brothers leaving property to their illegitimate siblings. Whatever familiarity may have arisen from growing up in the same household, if they did, was apparently overcome by an understandable sibling rivalry in the division and securing of inheritance.[119] However, I did come across one instance of a man leaving *alimenta,* dowry, and widow rights to

112. Notarile 10198 (1456–96), testamenti, fols. 368r–370r (16 March 1483/4).

113. Notarile 16841 (1454–1505), testamenti, fols. 121r–122r (16 October 1479).

114. Notarile 10198 (1456–96), testamenti, fols. 228r–229v (10 July 1476).

115. Notarile 16841 (1454–1505), testamenti, fols. 143r–144r (14 June 1481).

116. Cohn, *Death and Property,* 131, however, finds a Sienese instance of a woman providing for an illegitimate brother.

117. Notarile 19167 (1470–1516), testamenti, #15 (3 June 1487). Sandro had no legitimate sons but two daughters, cf. Catasto 1008, fol. 509r–v and (for Alamanno) fol. 33r–v.

118. Notarile 14179 (1454–94), testamenti, fols. 103r–104r (22 September 1474), another reference I owe to Elaine Rosenthal.

119. To cite an example here, we know from the catasto that Domenico d'Antonio di Bartolomeo di ser Santi had two illegitimate brothers, but there was not a word of them in his testament (Notarile 688 [1442–45], fols. 236v–238r [2 April 1444]).

a brother's bastard daughter.[120] And there is another of a widow, Dianora di Francesco di Bellincione degli Agli, who had been twice married, leaving four hundred florins to a daughter and three hundred to the two *spurii* of her brother messer Bernardo. These boys were to receive the money within five years of her death, but if both were to die before reaching the age of twenty without legitimate male descent, or if they entered a monastery or holy orders, the bequest was canceled and remained with her named heir, the hospital of Santa Maria Nuova.[121] Thus Dianora exhibited her attachment to a family by marriage, family by birth, and church.

Last wills, finally, provide examples of a rare precision in legal language favoring illegitimates. Substitutions almost invariably specified legitimate birth as the condition obviating a substitution, and a number of legal cases turned on such language. In naming Sandro di Jacopo di Francesco Cambi as her heir, his grandmother specified a substitution to Santa Maria Nuova "if said Sandro, whenever he should die without legitimate and natural children, or just natural or *spurii* legitimated formally."[122] Lorenzo di Totto Gualterotti's wills of 1411 and 1416, which provided charitable sums for "indigentibus personis de domo de Bardis," established that, should his five sons all die without legitimate and natural sons, his daughters would receive increased dotal legacies and his patrimony would go to any "filius naturalis vel bastardus legiptimatus."[123] So when a woman named as heir her fraternal nephew and then set up substitution in case he died without legitimate or illegitimate descendants, one is forced to see that language as deliberate, especially when the more usual limitation of legitimacy for substitution was employed elsewhere in the same will.[124]

By and large Florentine substitutions worked to the benefit of legitimate persons, especially substitutions to illegitimates. Giovanni d'Antonio Perondini, in case he had no legitimate descendants, made a substitution to his natural son Benedetto of usufruct and *alimenta* and then, following Benedetto's death, ownership to his legitimate offspring.[125] Domenico di

120. Notarile 16841 (1454–1505), testamenti, fols. 64r–65v (3 December 1478).

121. Notarile 15790 (1480–1513), testamenti, 21 July 1491.

122. Notarile 9037 (1408–11), fols. 248r–249r (27 August 1410): "Et si dictus Sander quandocunque decesserit sine filiis legitimis et naturalibus vel naturalibus tantum vel spureis legiptimatis solempne legiptime tunc et in dicto casu legavit et reliquit hospitali sancte Marie nove."

123. Notarile 9042, fols. 3r–6v (26 June 1411) and 34v–39r (25 February 1416).

124. Notarile 16795 (1457–1518), testamenti, 9 April 1463.

125. Notarile 16660 (1420–24), fols. 40r–43v (15 March 1420/1).

Piero di Francesco Mellini, for all that he was legitimated to inherit by act of Florence's legislative councils, met with a similar fate in his father's wills.[126] And some fathers gave their executors great latitude in dealing with bastards, mainly, it seems, because they were too uncertain of the bastard's future character. Uberto di Giovanni Albizzi gave his executors total discretion even to give nothing to Vincenzo and Francesco.[127] Carlo di Ridolfo Boninsegni gave his mother full discretion regarding marriage, monastic vows, and dowering for his illegitimate daughter.[128]

The language of these substitutions must remind us that the testator's will was dependent for fulfillment on others. A man named Cambiozzo put together a testament leaving his three sons as heirs, with substitution if any died without legitimate and natural sons. As it happened, only one son, Antonio, left children, but his four sons were born of a concubine whom he finally married only as he was dying. By testament of their father, in turn, these four were named heirs and substituted for one another. Three of the four died, so Francesco d'Antonio, a minor, was left in sole possession of his grandfather's property. The two daughters of Cambiozzo, in the meantime, moved to secure their testamentary legacies by obtaining a decree from the Podestà of Florence evicting the young Francesco from the estate. A ser Guardino, as Francesco's *procurator,* appointed by his mother as *tutrix,* argued there was no substitution to these daughters because the legitimated sons precluded the substitution. But the daughters struck back with arguments of their own, through a *procurator.* The marriage was invalid, they claimed, because the mother, Caterina, was in fact a nun under vows, proof of which was offered in writing. Less telling arguments were that the parents had not been shown to have been able to marry and that the father, Antonio, had not kept Caterina in his house. Nor did the children ever ratify their legitimation. It is interesting, given the existence of doctrinal discussions of the validity of legitimation by marriage when on the verge of death, that no argument was offered on that score.[129]

126. Notarile 10198 (1456–96), testamenti, fols. 161r–163v (22 January 1470/1), fols. 165r–167r (9 April 1472), fols. 222r–225v (27 May 1476).

127. Notarile 10198 (1456–96), testamenti, fols. 246r–247r (8 July 1477).

128. Notarile 19167 (1470–96), testamenti, #85 and #86 (16 April 1510). Bernardo d'Ambruogio Mei left the discretion to Santa Maria Nuova (Notarile 684 [1431–33], fols. 47v–49r [26 July 1431]).

129. BNF, Panciatichiano 138, fols. 254r–259v. On Domenico da San Gimignano, see Domenico Maffei, *La donazione di Costantino nei giuristi medievali* (Milan, 1964), 277–79. Reference in the *consilium* to Antonio da Butrio as "recolende memorie" would put this case after 1408.

The court of first instance found for the daughters, confirming their taking of Cambiozzo's property, but the decision was appealed. In the appeal were produced valid tutelary documents initiated by the mother, a ratification of legitimation by Francesco, proof of concubinage and "singleness," and a rule of the convent requiring the superior to accept new professions, which was lacking for Caterina. So ser Guardino argued that even the secular court had to accept the proofs of legitimation and decide in their favor. The other side had not proved in ecclesiastical court that Caterina had taken vows, nor had they shown that Antonio knew of any such vows—then at least there was legitimacy resulting from a putative marriage. Ser Guardino further argued that no matter the legal rule regarding a professed nun as *tutrix,* Caterina had been confirmed as such by judicial decree.[130]

The appellate court transmitted the case to Domenico da San Gimignano (d. 1424), a canonist and a student of Antonio da Butrio, and Riccialbano di ser Gherardo of Florence, who added only his signature in agreement. The jurists had to determine the mother's monastic status and its effect regarding marriage as determined by a secular court, what effect it had on the husband and children, and whether judgment could proceed against a minor. Domenico da San Gimignano decided that the entire case was in the wrong court. Matters of legitimate status and especially the problem of the validity of the double marriage (one being the profession of vows) made this an ecclesiastical case. There was little reason, then, to delve into other matters. Not having seen the evidence regarding Caterina's alleged monacation, he could not judge but only point out that valid vows required age, consent, and a three-year probationary period. Also, as the legal presumption was of ignorance on Antonio's part (and so no illegitimacy for his children), the other side faced the burden of proof. For the rest, the presumption of ignorance bolstered Francesco's claims, as it should because "this matter of legitimacy that is done by marriage is favorable and should be enlarged."[131]

In this case there was only one surviving son, illegitimate *(naturalis)* by birth but legitimated and designated heir by paternal testament. And still his inheritance was contested by legitimate aunts. Just how much difference for inheritance did legitimation make? At least we can begin consideration of this problem by looking at a couple of examples where a child was named in wills written both before and after legitimation. Francesco

130. Panciatichiano 138, fol. 256r.

131. Ibid., fol. 259r: "hec autem materia legiptimitatis que fit per contractum matrimonii est favorabilis et amplianda. . . ."

di messer Arnaldo Mannelli first wrote a testament in 1414 when Andrea was only around fifteen. He left the boy seven-sixteenths of a mill on the Arno at Castelline. His heirs were any (as yet unborn) legitimate sons, with a complex set of substitutions to his brother's sons and other Mannelli.[132] In 1422, the day after Andrea's legitimation, Francesco had his will redrawn, this time leaving Andrea nineteen thirty-seconds of the same mill. In addition, if there were no legitimate sons, Andrea was to receive 500 florins, and he and his legitimate male descendants got Francesco's house, though he was still not substituted as a secondary provisional heir. Succession passed instead to a fraternal nephew and then other Mannelli.[133] Andrea's 1427 catasto declaration later showed him in possession of only 320 florins; the mill (worth 321) was still among his father's properties. But at least there were only two legitimate daughters and his father was not married at that time.

Another example involves Bernardo di Marco di messer Forese Salviati. Originally he gave rights to dwell in his house to his sister India, widow of Giovanni Baroncelli, to Mariotto, bastard of Piero Baroncelli, and to India's daughter Madalena.[134] To his bastard sons Giovanni and Piero he left the same domiciliary rights, and if he died without legitimate heirs an additional 25 florins per year. But he otherwise treated them differently. He gave "suitable food and clothing to said Giovanni, who worked in business with said testator's possessions. But to said Piero only food without clothing, those eaten and drunk, not clothing, because if he wants, he is more apt to do well than Giovanni and profit."[135] Piero was dead before the next two wills were drawn up. Eleven years later Bernardo Salviati had more legitimate children and had legitimated Giovanni, when he left him 400 florins in the *monte comune*. Roberto, Giannozzo, and Marco were named as heirs, and their father patched together a detailed division of assets between them to obviate conflicts.[136] A third will of 1481 did not change things for Giovanni or his legitimate half

132. Notarile 9042 (1411–31), testamenti, fols. 15v–17v (30 March 1414).

133. Ibid., fols. 100v–102r (8 August 1422).

134. In her earlier will India left bequests to Mariotto for *alimenta,* but she wanted Madalena to use up to three hundred florins to buy Bernardo's house as a residence for her and Mariotto: Notarile 10198 (1456–96), testamenti, fols. 66r–68v (19 December 1463).

135. Ibid., fols. 97r–99v (9 April 1465): "victum et vestitum condecentia dicto Johanni qui se exercet in negociis possessionum dicti testatoris. Dicto autem Piero solum victum sine vestitu hos esum et potum non autem vestitum quia si volet bene facere et lucrari est aptior ipso Johanni."

136. Ibid., fols. 237r–239v (25 October 1476).

brothers.[137] He would not inherit much, but he would survive. On paper what was left to him decreased, but in the intervening years he had gained wealth and experience.

For these *legitimati* inheritance did not mean becoming true legal social successors to their fathers. This was due in good part to the fact that there were legitimate children. Legitimation in these cases showed some concern or affection for the child, though not at the cost of fully inserting him into the family. In another instance, Ettore di Francesco degli Zamperlerii of Perugia legitimated a son by a slave and gave him habitation, alimentary, and vestimentary rights to age twenty; thereafter the estate gave him only eight florins additionally each year for food. Zamperlerii's heirs, his three legitimate sons, were strictly forbidden to expel their brother from the family dwelling. If they failed to observe the terms of the will, then, the testator added, the *legitimatus* was to be instituted as *haeres* and inherit equally with the *legitimi* and be substituted for them "as if the same Jacopo were a legitimate and natural son." Reference to the time and circumstances of Jacopo's legitimation can only have reinforced the meaning of this clause. Jacopo was also substituted as heir if all three *legitimi* died without issue, in which case he took half, the other half going to any unborn legitimate daughters, failing whom he got it all. Also interesting in this case is the fact that Ettore Zamperlerii left similar rights until age twenty to another illegitimate, Giovanmarco; but he did not legitimate this son or afford him the same guarantees of payment as he had for Jacopo. Giovanmarco, however, had been born after his slave mother had been sold out of the family. He had grown up elsewhere.[138]

Those fathers, like Zamperlerii, who sought to favor *legitimati* in the presence of *legitimi* had to worry that their heirs would not follow through. For those so favored with legitimation more safeguards were erected than for those just left in their fully illegitimate state. Jacopo d'Uberto Arrighi left a bequest of a house in the *popolo* of Sant'Ambruogio to the legitimated Antonio, as well as forty-four *staiora* of land and his *masserizie*. All was to pass back to the testator's legitimate sons and heirs following Antonio's death. Jacopo Arrighi also added a clause to the effect that any molestation of Antonio's rights was to be adjudicated through the Arte della Lana. It seems Jacopo anticipated trouble on this score, and

137. Ibid., fols. 347r–348v (10 January 1481/2).
138. Notarile 14713 (1464–65), fols. 60r–62r (14 June 1465).

he reaffirmed these terms in three subsequent testaments. Finally, however, he resorted to a more direct maneuver, emancipating Antonio and giving him the house as a *praemium.*[139] The same sort of tactic may have been adopted by Francesco d'Altobianco di messer Niccolò Alberti with the emancipation and *praemium* of his two legitimated sons.[140]

The most favorable treatment of *legitimati* who had legitimate male siblings was that accorded by Giovanni, son of the jurist messer Stefano Buonaccorsi, to his sons Michele and Luigi. They were named as *heredes* to one-third, the other two-thirds going to as-yet-unborn legitimate sons. Should none be born, then Michele and his legitimate son Antonio would get half and Luigi the other half.[141] There was no prevarication here.

Simply being the only surviving son, and legitimated, was no guarantee of full heirship. There remained something ambiguous about the *legitimatus,* as there was in the law about adopted sons. Take the example of Zanobi di Paolo di Stefano Bellandini. He set up a handsome legacy of three hundred florins, to be paid at age eighteen, for the legitimated Niccolò. But he did not make him *haeres,* even by substitution. If Zanobi did not sire legitimate sons or daughters, the *haereditas* was to go to his mother and to three paternal cousins.[142] Giovanni di Lorenzo dall'Ancisa made his two sisters, not his legitimated son Paolo, his heirs. He left him an ancestral house in Ancisa, the value of which was said to include the one hundred florins left to Paolo by his paternal grandmother. Paolo also received a piece of land and usufruct of two others annually. Perhaps most importantly Paolo was given unequivocal assurances that he could consult and keep his father's account books. In some important symbolic ways, then, Paolo was acceding to his father's position, though he shared it with his half sisters and their husbands.[143]

Even more revealing is the sequence of last wills drawn up for Piero di Francesco Mellini. His son Domenico had been legitimated by the Signoria in 1464. In a will of 1471 Piero left him usufruct on the estate, naming as heirs any yet-to-be-born *legitimi.* A little over a year later, for Domenico's *alimenta* and "lest being in need he be forced to commit a crime or do something shameful," a *podere* and a *poderetto* were set aside as his *legatum.* This time the *heredes* were to be Bernardo and Duc-

139. The testaments are in Notarile 21154 (1450–78), testamenti, fols. 135r–139v (17 July 1471), 140r–141r (15 September 1471), 142r–144v (5 May 1474), 145r–v (20 April 1475). The emancipation is in Notarile 21151 (1476), fol. 90r–v (31 May 1476).

140. Notarile 19118 (1434–35), 14 May 1434.

141. Notarile 693 (1459–62), fols. 73r–74v (17 May 1459), 78v–80v (8 June 1459).

142. Notarile 16795 (1457–1518), testamenti, 20 August 1467.

143. Notarile 9655 (1484–1516), testamenti, fols. 262r–266v (10 July 1511).

cio d'Onofrio di Duccio Mellini. Four years later the same two *poderi* were designated as Piero's wife's *legatum.* Domenico by then had three legitimate daughters, who were left *monte* dowries of eight hundred florins each. The *heredes universales* were Domenico's two legitimate sons, Francesco and Antonio, "yet with the burden that they be held to suffer Domenico, aforesaid son of said testator, for all his life to use and enjoy the property of said testator."[144] So Domenico never really figured as *haeres,* but his descendants carried a legitimate line; his real inheritance was getting married, in some sense. Another bastard who came out better than average was messer Luigi di Piero Guicciardini's *naturalis* messer Rinieri (denounced, as we have seen, by his cousin Francesco), who was legitimated and dispensed to receive orders and benefices. By a will of 1479 he was assured residence in the testator's *domus* along with the widow and all the *immobilia* bought by the testator in Rinieri's name.[145] By a later will of 1481 messer Luigi reaffirmed his widow's rights, as well as right of return in the event of widowhood for his three married daughters, and residence rights for messer Rinieri. In this will and the first, Luigi named as his heirs legitimate cousins—Piero di Jacopo and Oddo di Niccolò Guicciardini, adding in the second the sons of Braccio di Niccolò.[146] Although there were no legitimate sons, Rinieri gained little by the terms of the will. His "inheritance" came in the form of his education and purchase of dispensation and a clerical position. The real heirs, Piero di Jacopo and Oddo di Niccolò Guicciardini, would succeed in contesting Rinieri's rights and arranging an arbitrated compromise.

In the end, then, there are few examples recoverable from the vast archival treasures of Florence that depict a *legitimatus* simply and totally acceding as heir to his father. Even the prominent example involving the patrician statesman Niccolò da Uzzano did not result in the son's becoming heir in all respects. The process began on 10 April 1419 with a legitimation of Salvadore, according to the notarial text of which the son was to receive all benefits of inheritance, agnation, and civic honors available to him "not withstanding any stain of birth," with the exception of having no right to contest his father's will. If all we had were this text, we might assume that Salvadore was from that point Niccolò's heir. In the catasto of 1427 no mention was made of his illegitimacy or legitimation.

144. Notarile 10198 (1456–96), testamenti, fols. 161r–163v (22 January 1470/1), 165r–167r (9 April 1472), 222r–225v (27 May 1476).

145. Notarile 21063 (1440–81), testamenti, fols. 170r–172r (7 November 1479), repeated fols. 174r–176r.

146. Notarile 15790 (1480–1513), testamenti, 14 January 1481.

Salvadore had his own house, though he was carried on his father's declaration. He was married and had two legitimate children, including a son, Alessandro, then eight years old. His uncle Angelo had died, leaving an illegitimate girl living with Niccolò and his four legitimate daughters. So Salvadore did not have to fear major problems from legitimate male cousins.[147] And, of course, his father disposed of one of the largest patrimonies in Florence. Still, despite all this preparation, Salvadore did not become his father's *haeres universalis*. A few years later, in late 1430 and early 1431, the aged Niccolò made final arrangements for the disposition of his property. To Salvadore he left the house where he lived, all *immobilia* at San Cresci a Menzola in the Val di Greve, a *podere* near Lecce, another at Tobbiano purchased in Salvadore's name, and eighteen hundred florins in the *monte comune*—all of which Niccolò and his brother Angelo had given Salvadore years before. In addition, another legacy gave Salvadore four thousand florins, half in the *monte,* which could not be alienated but were to pass to his children, the other half of which was in cash but not to be spent without the consent of Bernardo d'Antonio da Uzzano and Bernardo Uguccioni. "And this the said testator did, fearing lest said Salvadore in administration of his patrimony be less diligent than he should be." So these two friends were bound in conscience to see that this sum was spent "in the use and useful and necessary utility for said Salvadore and his family" [in usus et utilitatem utilem et necessariam dicto Salvatori et eius familie]. If he died without legitimate issue, he could dispose of only half these monies as he wished; the other half went to Bernardo da Uzzano. Bernardo was Niccolò's universal heir, with, if he died without legitimate heirs, substitution to Salvadore. In a codicil Niccolò later stipulated that to Salvadore, and after him to one of his sons, went the right to bear arms accorded Niccolò by the city of Florence in 1403.[148]

It would seem that Niccolò had lost confidence in his son's ability to manage the patrimony. As he was dealing with a legitimated son, Niccolò da Uzzano was free to reduce his claims. That he reduced them in favor of Bernardo da Uzzano also may be telling evidence of social pressure to take legitimacy within the lineage in preference to illegitimacy within the direct line. Salvadore had his own children, but they were not made heirs either—except as spear-carriers where they might prove both useful and

147. Catasto 64, fols. 65v–75v.

148. Notarile 9042, fols. 168r–71v (27 December 1430), 172r–74r (4 March 1431), 174r–75r (7 April 1431).

expendable. One is left to wonder what might have been if his father had more confidence in him. Salvadore went on to have a relatively comfortable life. His *catasto* report of 1458 shows him with five children. He still held several farms and houses, including a residence in the *popolo* of Santa Lucia de' Magnoli; but his *sustanze* added up to only 1,146 florins. With two daughters to dower and three sons, Salvadore had some problems to face. He resurfaced in 1466 to name one of his half sister's sons, Niccolò di Piero Capponi, as *procurator,* and his new wife, Dianora di Giovanni d'Antonio, as *procuratrix* regarding the *monte* shares in his name. At that time he was about seventy-three, living on his lands in the Val di Greve. His sons Niccolò and Giovanni later also relied on a Capponi relation to act as their *procurator.*[149]

Summary

According to Gabriella Airaldi,

> The faculty of legitimation of bastards, which count palatines enjoyed, and its ample exercise on their part, were employed to the community's advantage. They offered a possibility of solution to difficult or emotional cases, and allowed to be reabsorbed into legality at least a part of so many who would be left marginal by a phenomenon—that of illegitimacy—that was universal but that became worse the more the custom of the age insisted on discrimination between children born within or outside marriage.[150]

She finds this functionality of legitimation especially opportune in a society like that of Genoa that contained a large number of slaves and an active merchant element whose members were frequently away on long trips. But it has to be wondered, in view of the foregoing, if legitimation contributed much in the way of long-term familial continuity, as opposed to social assimilation. It may be rather that, as has been argued for the French nobility in the fifteenth century, bastards constituted a reserve pool, available to be heirs if all else failed, but in any case capable of occupying positions of value to their family, of turning their talents to

149. Notarile 1844 (1466–69), fol. 61r (22 November 1466), fol. 312v (12 July 1469).
150. Airaldi, "Bastardos," 332.

good account, without being able to pretend to any more inheritance than the head of the family was willing to leave them.[151]

Anthony Molho has advanced and built on the working hypothesis that "starting in the late fifteenth century, Florentine society became more polarized; political honors, economic resources, social distinction, and symbolic rewards were more highly concentrated in the sixteenth century than in the fifteenth, with a smaller number of lineages more clearly in control of the city's destiny than earlier."[152] If Florence was indeed, as envisioned by Matteo Palmieri, a congeries of lineages linked in alliances and love by legitimate marriages, then bastards stood out for being at least partially unplugged. The lack of the ties of "blood-money-power" that moved through legitimate marriages made bastards expendable or usable in other ways.[153] The narrowing of the sense of lineage to a particular single line of descent, which Molho (among others) sees arriving in Florence in the sixteenth century, with the grand duchy and its nobility and use of *maggiorascato* (a form of primogeniture), may already have gained some focus in the contemplation of illegitimacy in the fifteenth century. The history of the actual use of substitutions in Florence has yet to be explored, but it is clear that they were a key legal component in the narrowing of descent and the congealing of noble patrimonies. Richard Goldthwaite pointed to a process of aristocratization by which Florentine patricians "invested heavily in landed estates to transform the family patrimony into a permanent dynastic possession for all time; and to assure that objective, they bound this patrimony with fideicommissa to prevent alienation and practiced primogeniture, if not in legal fact at least through the custom of limiting marriages to oldest sons."[154] Goldthwaite pursues the implications of this for changing and enlarging domestic patterns of consumption. R. Burr Litchfield has more broadly traced the consolidation of family wealth through use of fideicommissa, as well as marriage patterns and notions of nobility, through the grand duchy.[155] If nothing else, in that connection, it

151. Autrand, "Naissance illégitime"; Mikhail Harsgor, "L'essor des bâtards nobles au xve siècle," *Revue historique* 253 (1975): 319–54.

152. Molho, *Marriage Alliance,* 334.

153. Cf. Anthony Molho, Roberto Barducci, Gabriella Battista, and Francesco Donnini, "Genealogia e parentado: Memorie del potere nella Firenze tardo-medievale, il caso di Giovanni Rucellai," *Quaderni storici* 86 (August 1994): 365–403.

154. Richard A. Goldthwaite, *Wealth and the Demand for Art in Italy, 1300–1600* (Baltimore, 1993), 194. See also his *Private Wealth in Renaissance Florence* (Princeton, N.J., 1968), and Daniela Frigo, *Il padre di famiglia: Governo della casa e governo civile nella tradizione dell'* "economica" fra Cinque e Seicento (Rome, 1985).

155. R. Burr Litchfield, *Emergence of a Bureaucracy: The Florentine Patricians, 1530–1790* (Princeton, N.J., 1986).

is striking how frequently fideicommissary substitutions were employed in regard to bastards to assure that property went to legitimate progeny. Bastards were also the children about whom more deliberate and even cold-blooded or difficult decisions were first made, or more likely to be made: to be abandoned to a hospital, to be put in the church, to be married down the social scale, to be left a smaller portion of the estate.

The focal concern of Florentines was the preservation of patrimonies by their circulation among kin. In this circulation a whole constellation of factors—demographic survival, agnation and cognation, testacy and intestacy—came into play. For the movement of property through this maze of constructs, illegitimacy was a trapdoor that might spring open, dropping the goods into the hands of someone not otherwise in the direct line of succession. And where did it go from there? Property is and was a matter of rights between persons in relation to things charged with value. Illegitimacy and legitimation were legal conditions that helped set those rights, final determination of which was also shaped by testaments, gender, degrees of consanguinity. But would this latter constellation of factors have the desired effects when they were made to operate across the minefield of illegitimacy?

It was when the father left the scene that the bastard was most vulnerable. We can gain a sense of that vulnerability from provisions fathers stuck in their wills. Even legitimation had its effective limits in the face of hostility from kin and the rest of society. If it is true, and I believe it is, that

> the very fact that the bitter conflicts ran unabated for years, that claims and counterclaims to property could drag on for interminable court hearings—over the course of not just months and years, but even of decades—suggests how inextricably bound to each other members of these lineages were; how, often, these conflicts must have aroused and reinforced the knowledge of common, if temporarily divergent interests, and the consciousness of shared ancestry,[156]

then this could be so not only for disputes arising over dowry or marriage-related inheritance claims by legitimate persons but also in disputes involving illegitimates.

---

156. Molho, *Marriage Alliance,* 345–46, with the same exact sentiment in "Genealogia e parentado," 397.

PART THREE

Disputes

7

Disputes: Procedures and Jurists

Disputes and Settlements

The conjuncture of material and symbolic interests in inheritance with the ambiguity of illegitimacy gave rise to disputes, as we have already seen at several points. They were played out in procedures that ranged in Florence from legalized arbitrations to highly formal modes of adjudication. They took place on the streets, in the shops and houses of friends and family, and, of course, in courts of law. As "public" events they drew in friends, neighbors, and legal experts.

Anthropological study of dispute has highlighted the degree to which conflict is a normal social phenomenon and not just a pathological result of failure to observe rules.[1] It has made apparent, in a way that rule-centered study cannot, the various ways in which disputes can be handled. And, as it is rooted in fieldwork, anthropology can be contextual, drawing attention to the history of relationships between disputants, and the series of interactions that made up a dispute. Relationships characterized as variously multiplex, multivalent, or multifunctional (such as those among kin) are not easily susceptible to the zero-sum game played out where judgment is rendered for one side or the other, so compromise and mediation emerge as dispute processes in contrast to formal litigation.

The weight of social relations and interests relative to that of norms in settlement of a dispute is problematic.[2] A given society may witness the

1. Cf. Simon Roberts, "The Study of Dispute: Anthropological Perspectives," in *Disputes and Settlements: Law and Human Relations in the West,* ed. John Bossy (Cambridge, 1983), 1–24; John L. Comaroff and Simon Roberts, *Rules and Processes: The Cultural Logic of Dispute in an African Context* (Chicago, 1981), 3–20; Francis G. Snyder, "Anthropology, Dispute Processes, and Law: A Critical Introduction," *British Journal of Law and Society* 8 (1981–82): 141–80; Maureen Cain and Kalman Kulcsar, "Thinking Disputes: An Essay on the Origins of the Dispute Industry," *Law and Society Review* 16 (1981–82): 375–402.

2. Carol Greenhouse, "Looking at Culture, Looking for Rules," *Man,* n.s., 17 (1982): 58–73.

coexistence of a number of normative orders and indeterminateness of norms within and between those orders.[3] Rules—such as those governing illegitimacy—are also a form of knowledge, available in varying precision from different sources, by which an individual or group could recognize and frame interests. Disputes thus emerge as dialogues where communication "is essentially a process of negotiation over the social relational and justificatory meanings of normative statements."[4]

Legal anthropology has been constructed largely from study of societies without formal courts or written rules. Legal anthropologists have often framed their findings in terms of a dichotomy between stateless societies and the states of the modern West of limited utility to those who study Western societies before or during the formation of the modern state. In fact, any one society can sustain a variety of means of dispute resolution and of norms for each, and resolutions are not always and simply functional. Sometimes the parties were not satisfied with the results of a settlement procedure. Indeed, in some instances making one's claims and relationships public may have been the only outcome sought or truly attained.[5] The disputants could make bad choices and mount poor arguments.[6]

The notion of dispute itself, as an event between two autonomous individuals, seems to owe too much to legal ideology.[7] A complementary line of criticism is that a methodology concentrating on dispute processing is "incapable of arriving at a theoretical view of the apparent autonomy of law."[8] Rules cannot always freely be negotiated, and, at least within courts of law, a certain rough predictability of judgments holds, if only because certainty is one of the things law seeks.[9]

Florence was a city of written laws, teeming with notaries, jurists, and courts; it also had more informal means of disputing. The city's govern-

3. Cf. Sally Falk Moore, *Law as Process: An Anthropological Approach* (London, 1978).

4. Greenhouse, "Looking at Culture," 69–70.

5. Roberts, "Study of Dispute," 23.

6. Cain and Kulcsar, "Thinking Disputes," 395; Comaroff and Roberts, *Rules and Processes,* 130.

7. Cf. Cain and Kulcsar, "Thinking Disputes," 393–94, 397; Greenhouse, "Looking at Culture," 68; Snyder, "Anthropology," 161–63.

8. Snyder, "Anthropology," 163.

9. Goodrich, *Reading the Law,* 75, sees law lacking the rigor of science and logic but having the cogency of artistry and analogy. See also his *Oedipus Lex: Psychoanalysis, History, Law* (Berkeley and Los Angeles, 1995).

ment and legal apparatus—sophisticated as they were—were not those of a modern state, nor were they those of a stateless tribe.[10] To examine disputes here we must remain aware of both legal and social dynamics, of both the constraints and ranges of flexibility in the use of rules. For their own purposes or those of the court, disputants were compelled to frame their claims in a particular manner, thus creating a disparity between the documentary record and the "real substance of their conflict as they otherwise understood it."[11] Our dependence on the records of more formal and official institutions can too easily draw us into understanding and portraying disputes in a certain light.[12] We have to remember, above all, that in noncriminal matters definition of a dispute was, in the first instance and often throughout, in the hands of the disputants. They, or their representatives, set the normative referents and laid out the essential issues. Judges, arbitrators, and jurists called on by the court or the parties were bound within the grid the parties constructed.[13]

Arbitrations Involving Florentine Bastards

Francesco Guicciardini's *ricordi* reveal a dispute between the bastard messer Rinieri di Luigi and his father's other heirs and how Rinieri's inheritance was reduced without having to go to court. Jacopo Guicciardini claimed messer Luigi was mentally impaired by senility when he made his will, "importunato e stimolato" by Rinieri, whom Jacopo perceived as of a vicious nature and "having little love for his kin" [poco amorevole de' sua parenti]. Jacopo let it about that he intended to contest the will in court. So after much debate, Rinieri considered the benefits of keeping Jacopo happy and agreed to have only life usufruct on four properties, which would pass to the lines of Jacopo and Niccolò (Luigi's other brother) following Rinieri's death. The other few properties were divided

10. Cf. my "Antropologia giuridica dello stato," in *Origini dello stato: Processi di formazione statale in Italia fra medioevo ed età moderna,* ed. Giorgio Chittolini, Anthony Molho, and Pierangelo Schiera (Bologna, 1994), 367–80.

11. Cf. Roberts, "Study of Dispute," 22.

12. William L. F. Felstiner, Richard Abel, and Austin Sarat, "The Emergence and Transformation of Disputes: Naming, Blaming, Claiming. . . ," *Law and Society Review* 15 (1980–81): 631–54.

13. For a recent treatment of procedural developments, though concentrating on criminal cases, see Massimo Vallerani, "I processi accusatori a Bologna fra Due e Trecento," *Società e storia* 78 (1997): 741–88.

by them immediately. The payoff for Rinieri was that soon thereafter Jacopo helped him gain the post of archdeacon in Florence.[14] Here the threat of formal adjudication brought an extrajudicial settlement, perhaps because the ambitious Rinieri did not want people reminded of his illegitimacy (though he had been legitimated, dispensed, and left property). As he could not have legitimate sons of his own, in view of his reception of holy orders, he may well have contemplated the eventual passage of the properties to his Guicciardini relatives in any case. But in settling for usufruct, interestingly, he settled for an arrangement frequently used for widows, who also were not legitimate sons capable of full ownership by inheritance.[15] His position was weak, like the widow's. And although this matter was settled informally, the threat of law and litigation had been used. No matter the degree of informality, then, it always rested on a continuum that reached to law, which was never out of view.[16]

It is striking how rare are the records of arbitrations involving bastards. Arbitration was an enormously popular mode of handling disputes in Renaissance Florence—notably mandated by statute for disputes among kin, expressly including bastards. Arbitrations were also supposed to be about factual elements, not conceptual problems. Conceptual issues were matters of law, and those belonged to the courts, judges, and jurists. Arbitrators need not have particular legal expertise, though many times notaries served as arbitrators, but more for their also desirable neutrality and the ability to draw up the necessary papers. Illegitimates, however, seem inevitably to have raised legal conceptual difficulties along with material interests, so their cases were more appropriate for juristic treatment. Then again, their dubious family status may also have made kin more willing to risk the zero-sum game of formal litigation with

---

14. Francesco Guicciardini, *Ricordi, diari, memorie,* ed. Mario Spinelli (Rome, 1981), 70–71.

15. Cf. Giovanni Rossi, *"Duplex est ususfructus": Ricerche sulla natura dell'usufrutto nel diritto comune,* 2 vols. (Milan, 1996), esp. 2: 261–377.

16. Here note the parallel case of the bastard son of Cardinal Francesco Gonzaga of Mantua. The "Cardinalino" was legitimated and left property totaling two thousand ducats. But others among the Gonzaga were alarmed at the cardinal's plans to make the bastard his heir, and in the end the cardinal's younger brother became his heir. The Cardinalino gained specified properties with other Gonzaga as his guardians and "lived out his marginal and brutish life" involved in disputes over the property. Cf. D. S. Chambers, *A Renaissance Cardinal and His Worldly Goods: The Will and Inventory of Francesco Gonzaga (1444–1483)* (London, 1992), variously 24–25, 99–100, 130–31.

them. If, as both Florence's laws and modern legal anthropologists have it, arbitration worked to defuse conflicts and preserve multiform kin relationships, the highly infrequent recourse to arbitration when illegitimates were involved may be eloquent testimony either to the perceived lack of relationship to bastards or to the willingness to jeopardize any such relationship by taking a case to court.

For one illegitimate we have only the *compromissum* (the contract between two parties agreeing to submit to binding arbitration), and we have that not because illegitimacy was there admitted, but because it is known from another source. Lisabetta di Luigi di Zanobi Gaddi was listed as "bastarda" in the catasto of 1427. On 21 June 1463, as widow of Simone di Michele Tucci, she entered a *compromissum* with her son Michele.[17] That her illegitimacy was not mentioned is not surprising. For one thing it had not stood in the way of her marriage. Her illegitimacy was also in no way relevant to an arbitration with her legitimate son that probably concerned her dowry and widowhood rights.

Two arbitration settlements *(lauda)* involving illegitimates both concerned inheritance by a legitimated bastard. In one case there was an attempt to keep the matter out of litigation and within the family. The parties were Antonio di Manno di Giovanni degli Albizzi and Francesco d'Uberto di Giovanni degli Albizzi. In 1486 Uberto degli Albizzi had drawn up his will, naming Antonio his universal heir. The following year he had Francesco legitimated, although he did not change his will before dying some months later. Francesco pressed for a share of his father's estate on the grounds that the will had left it to the executor and arbitrators whether Francesco was to receive anything; and the arbitrators (three Albizzi men) found that the few assets in the estate were indeed being held in common between Antonio and Francesco. Declaring their desire to proceed by equity and not the rigor of law in order to avoid occasion for future conflicts, the arbitrators split the property by giving Antonio Uberto's farm and giving Francesco the furnishings *(masserizie)* and credits in Florence's funded public debt *(monte)* nominally totalling 2,522 florins (1,622 of which were security for Uberto's wife's 1,200-florin dowry). Antonio's earlier possession of one-quarter of a house in return for a 300-florin loan to Uberto was reaffirmed, while 720 florins of the dowry obligation were lodged against the farm, payable in two

17. Catasto 79, fol. 617v; Notarile 19078 (1462–64), fols. 379v–380r (21 June 1463).

months.[18] From the size of the obligation imposed on the farm, it must have been of considerable value. But without a more detailed accounting, it is impossible to tell how equitable the division was. What made arbitration the appropriate mechanism for this dispute was the lack of conceptual issues and the pressing material interests from the comingling of both Francesco and Antonio on Uberto's property and the involvement of other Albizzi as arbitrators as set up in Uberto's will. There was a relationship to perpetuate.

Another arbitration emerged as only one step in a protracted inheritance dispute that had moved well beyond the family. In 1461, Filippo di Piero Lippi, *legitimatus,* entered into arbitration with Marco d'Ugolino Bonsi, acting on behalf of his wife, Nera, daughter of Aloisio di Tommaso Alberti and widow of Piero Lippi. The arbitrator was the distinguished Florentine jurist Otto di Lapo Niccolini (1410–1470).[19] His presence is indicative of the relative complexity of the issues and this dispute's past litigation. The conflict was rooted in Filippo's father's will of 1454 and his widow's remarriage. Filippo had been named heir—something made possible for him by decree of Florence's legislative councils in 1453.[20] But Nera had been given a legacy of 1,000 florins as her dowry and made *usufructuaria* with Filippo as long as she remained a widow. After her marriage to Bonsi she had processed through the court of the Podestà a judgment for her 1,000-florin dowry. Filippo had countered by producing an inventory signed by her and her husband claiming she had been paid, and he demanded items on that inventory amounting to around 700 florins. But she won in the court of first instance and on appeal. On Filippo's side was the testimony of an unnamed friar who had been Nera's confessor and who broke the seal of the confessional to reveal her intent to defraud her late husband's bastard. Nera had responded to these claims, saying that Filippo's guardians, Nicola and Gino Capponi, had sold the various articles, that she had spent 220 *grossi* on Filippo's expenses, and that she was not bound for restitution on the farm or for the gabelles on it. In fact she claimed she was owed 1,000 florins by the will as well as the sums she had paid in gabelles and the expenses incurred in resisting Filippo's suit, a further 90 florins for

18. Notarile 10195 (1489–90), fols. 82r–86v (28 January 1489 [1490]).

19. Notarile 10184 (1460–62), fol. 233r (30 October 1461).

20. Provvisioni—registri 144, fols. 39r–40r (23 October 1453), wherein Filippo's birth was placed in November 1443 and his mother was said to be a Caterina di Filippo di Giovanni.

return on her dowry prior to remarriage, 600 florins in shares in Florence's public debt fund *(monte),* plus revenue from the *monte* and the sold farm (over 100 florins in total), and 100 florins she had supposedly loaned Piero.

Clearly Niccolini faced a tricky case, especially as it was hard to credit a notorious debtor like Piero Lippi with having the sorts of sums attributed to him. The breached confession revealed that Nera had indeed kept 220 *grossi* and several looms, but she had held them, though bothered in conscience, against the 100 florins loaned to Piero. Niccolini, while "wanting to deal humanely with said Filippo, especially in view of his age [eighteen]" [volentes cum dicto Filippo humaniter agere attenta maxime sua etate], affirmed her rights and gave Filippo two years to pay off the dotal legacy and the legal expenses he had caused her. She was conceded no further claims, however, and had to return whatever *masserizie* she had taken from Piero Lippi's home. She and Filippo gave their formal acceptances of Niccolini's judgment within a month and even before that began settling their financial affairs.[21] There seems to have been no love lost between this illegitimate son and his father's widow. This protracted dispute was also appropriate for arbitration because it was essentially a matter of accounting. As such it was far more appropriate for an arbitrator than for a formal court of law, which had already determined the legality of Nera's claims.

Florentine Jurists and Courts

When cases involving Florentine bastards came to court, they involved the city's practicing jurists. We cannot understand their role in cases involving bastards (or anyone else) without understanding the position and function of the legal profession in Florence and the control jurists had in judicial proceedings.

With few exceptions, Florentine jurists had pursued university legal studies to a doctorate in civil law (requiring seven to eight years after preparation in the arts), canon law (six years), or both laws, *utriusque iuris* (eight or nine years). Most studied in either Bologna or, after 1473, Pisa; but there were always a few who sported degrees from Perugia or

21. Notarile 10184 (1460–62), fols. 249r (30 November 1461) and 251r–254r (10 December 1461). On 14 December (fol. 260r–v) Filippo put a house to rent; on 30 December, the same day she ratified the *laudum* (fols. 262r–263v), Nera gave her husband four *poderi* that he then "confessed" as her dowry. Filippo ratified on 2 January (fol. 263v).

elsewhere.[22] They had learned grammatical, rhetorical, and dialectical analyses of texts crafted generations before. Most important was the mastery of the *pro-et-contra* technique of analysis that exposed legal points on both sides of a problem and yet also offered modes of resolution.[23] The best jurists were those who looked not for mechanical solutions but used the techniques of rational argument to forge modestly creative ways out of conceptual impasses and contradictions, hopefully adapted to practical realities.

Those realities included local features and twists of law for which their academic educations had only partially prepared them. The exact substance of local statutes and guild regulations and the exact functioning of procedure in local courts required on-the-job training. The intricacy of Florentine procedures and the accretion of authoritative, though not precedential, judgments in areas of private law are eloquently witnessed by the survival of two detailed glosses on the second book of the statutes of 1415. These were written by Alessandro Bencivenni (1385–1423) and Tommaso Salvetti (1390–1472).[24] Their work shows how Florentine jurists integrated *ius commune* with the statutes *(ius proprium)*. By training, if not by inclination, Florentine jurists accepted multiple sources of law with a hierarchy of rational methods to harmonize them.[25]

The costs of schooling were considerable, so the legal profession was socially exclusive. Those who entered it came from families that had already arrived at an elevated social and economic level, for whom a jurist in the family meant another sort of prestige and, quite often, good local political prospects.[26] Lauro Martines's pathbreaking study finds that between 1480 and 1530 forty-six jurists from Florentine families were active in the city, along with seven "outsiders." By those decades his distinction between families that were "new" in the ruling elite and those who were "old" was less meaningful than for the early fifteenth century, when there were only around two dozen native Florentines active but a

---

22. For this and so much else on Florentine lawyers, Martines, *Lawyers and Statecraft,* 81–82.

23. Cf. Manlio Bellomo, *Saggio sull'università nell'età del diritto comune* (Catania, 1979), 219–38; Montorzi, *Fides in rem publicam,* 217–28.

24. Bencivenni's is BNF, Principale, II, iv, 435, and Salvetti's is Principale, II, iv, 434.

25. Cf. Sbriccoli, *L'interpretazione dello statuto.* For an example of one jurist's career in that light, cf. Ingrid Baumgärtner, "Rechtsnorm und Rechtsanwendung in der venezianischen Terraferma des 15. Jahrhunderts: Die *Consilia* von Bartolomeo Cipolla," in *Consilia im späten Mittelalter,* esp. 93–96.

26. Martines, *Lawyers and Statecraft,* 68–70.

greater number of outsiders. The larger influx of Florentines, many from some of the city's most prestigious clans, seems to indicate either elevated professional opportunities by the end of the century or greater prestige in the law.[27] But outsiders came from the same sorts of social backgrounds as Florentines.

As a jurist himself, Francesco Guicciardini's professional advice to his nephew Niccolò in 1528 was that they were engaged in an "exercizio che ricercha lo stare fermo a bottega" (that is, a trade requiring constant presence in the "shop" or office). As Osvaldo Cavallar has demonstrated, this expression captured the essence of the practicing jurist when the center of jurisprudential prestige had shifted from the lecture halls to the private studies of jurists—evident in Florence when Antonio Strozzi forsook a promising academic career in Pisa to dedicate himself to consultative practice and an active political career.[28] Of course presiding judges were temporary and of foreign origin in important courts, so a local jurisprudential and procedural memory fell to the more permanent and learned jurists.[29]

Guicciardini's emphasis on consultative activity also marks a shift from personal intervention in proceedings to a more detached intervention in written form. Writing removed the *consulens* from the court. He received a written description of relevant facts, documents, and statutes (called the *punctus*) and the questions the court or the parties wanted him to address. He crafted his answer as advice to the court *(consilium),* and subsequently he could judge by the court's writing how much its decision was in conformity with his opinion. Juristic discourse took the form of a text, rather than an event in court, and these texts came increasingly to be larded with exhaustive authoritative citations. Mining of *consilia* for arguments and citations by later jurists only further abstracted these texts in copies they made or, finally, in those of the most authoritative jurisconsults whose *consilia* were printed.[30]

The establishment of the Rota in Florence and earlier judicial reforms of other courts, Mercanzia, Otto di Guardia, and the Podestà, made

27. Martines, *Lawyers and Statecraft,* 73–75.

28. On this see Osvaldo Cavallar, "Lo 'stare fermo a bottega' del Guicciardini: giuristi consulenti, procuratori e notai nel Rinascimento," in *Consilia im späten Mittelalter,* 113–44.

29. Ascheri, *Tribunali, giuristi e istituzioni,* 24–26.

30. Cavallar, "Lo stare fermo," 131; G. Nicolosi Grassi, "Analisi di manoscritti vaticani per uno studio dei 'Consilia' di Giovanni e Gaspare Calderini," *Rivista di storia del diritto italiano* 50 (1977): 127–49.

recourse to an expert *procurator ad iudicia* more necessary for Florentines dealing with these courts. *Procuratores* gained a power and control over proceedings that could rival that of *doctores consulentes;* they took charge of a series of procedural acts that crossed the line to submitting their own written briefs and arguments on some rare occasions. And they were cheaper to retain than *doctores.* But in general the controlling discourse in lawsuits was in the *consilium* or *allegationes* of jurists, and they controlled access to this discourse.[31] They had power and social contacts that their clients were aware of and wanted.[32] Aided by the attempts to reopen a *studio fiorentino* that could add a doctrinal dimension to their professional presence, aided even more by the willingness of Florentines to bring their disputes to the courts, and aided most importantly by a complex and confusing multiplicity of laws, jurists were in a prestigious and commanding position.[33] From that position they also attracted criticism, to be sure, but their high status and influence in local society were undeniable.[34]

These reasoned responses by jurists to legal problems that arose from practice were the meeting point between the jurisprudence of the universities, the local statutes and customs, and the interests and practices of the parties that came into conflict. The value of *consilia* as historical sources is immeasurable, even as they are consummately difficult materials.[35] In the face of the multiplicity of normative sources, jurists applied interpretive schemes that resolved antinomies and filled lacunae (both within statutes, in the doctrinal texts, and between the former and the

31. Cavallar, "Lo stare fermo," 136–38.

32. Ibid., 143.

33. For an incisive analysis of the state of law and legal consulting in the period, see Mario Ascheri, "Le fonti e la flessibilità del diritto comune: Il paradosso del *consilium sapientis,*" in Ascheri, Baumgärtner, and Kirshner, *Legal Consulting,* 11–53.

34. Cf. James A. Brundage, "The Medieval Advocate's Profession," *Law and History Review* 6 (1988): 439–64. For a Florentine example of criticism, in this case from a humanist, see Bartolomeo Scala's invective in his "Dialogus de legibus et iudiciis," ed. L. Borglia, *Bibliofilia* 42 (1940): 252–82.

35. Cf. Andrea Romano, "La giurisprudenza consulente e Paolo di Castro," *Rivista di storia del diritto italiano* 61 (1988): 141–70, esp. 153–54; Ingrid Baumgärtner, "Consilia: Quellen zur Familie in Krise und Kontinuität," in *Die Familie als sozialer und historischer Verband: Untersuchungen zum Spätmittelalter und zur frühen Neuzeit,* ed. Peter-Johannes Schuler (Sigmarigen, 1987), 43–66; Schuler, "Stadtgeschichte und Consilia im italienischen Spätmittelalter: Eine Quellengattung und ihre Möglichkeiten," *Zeitschrift für Historische Forschung* 90 (1990): 129–54; and the papers found in Baumgärtner, *Consilia im späten Mittelalter.*

latter), and adopted concrete solutions that "operate as 'political' choices that present the functioning of 'justice.'"[36] The *consilium* was presumed to embody not the personal viewpoint of its author but the *conscientia legalis,* assurance of which could be gained by submitting the issue to more than one jurist.[37]

It is important to remember that neither *consilia* nor the decisions based on them were in any sense binding precedents. In principle and in practice judges were not bound to prior decisions.[38] Certainly practicing jurists employed *consilia* as interpretive benchmarks. But they were also acutely aware that the statutes left the status of *consilia* in Florence the same as in the *ius commune:* to be followed they had to be legally sound and not just formally correct and procedurally enforced.[39] In point of fact, Florentine legislators repeatedly acted to deny legal force to *consilia* whose findings, howsoever much in conformity with *ius commune,* were contrary to what they saw as the clear intent and force of the laws they had cast.[40]

The character of juristic intervention depended on whether one was retained by one of the parties to the suit or approached by the judge. If employed by one of the parties, the jurist's intervention came early in proceedings, after jointure of the suit *(litis contestatio)* and preliminary arguments. Oral or written *allegationes* (presented orally by a *procurator* if written) were entered on behalf of one's client; or *responsiones* could be made to allegations and questions from the other party. Or a jurist could construct a more elaborate opinion on the entire case for his client's use, and this was one form of *consilium,* the *consilium pro parte*

---

36. Romano, "La giurisprudenza consulente," 147.

37. Cf. Julius Kirshner, "*Consilia* as Authority in Late Medieval Italy: The Case of Florence," in *Legal Consulting,* 107–40.

38. Gérard Fransen, "La valeur de la jurisprudence en droit canonique," *Ius canonicum* 15 (1975): 97–112; André Sergène, "Le précédent judiciaire au moyen âge," *Revue historique de droit français et étranger* 39 (1961): 223–54, 359–70; Biagio Brugi, "Sentenze di giudici antichi o opinioni comuni di dottori," in his *Per la storia della giurisprudenza e delle università italiane: Nuovi saggi* (Turin, 1921), 81–96.

39. Cf. Guido Rossi, *Consilium sapientis iudiciale: Studi e ricerche per la storia del processo romano-canonico* (Milan, 1958), 101–3; Bencivenni, Principale, 435, fol. 6r; Salvetti, Principale, 434, fols. 22v–23r.

40. Kirshner, "*Consilia* as Authority in Late Medieval Italy." In a parallel manner Florentine magistracies had concerns with statutes issued by communities under their dominion: see J. Black, "Constitutional Ambitions, Legal Realities," in *Florentine Tuscany: Structures and Practices of Power,* ed. William Connell and Andrea Zorzi (Cambridge, 2000), 48–64.

or *pro veritate.*[41] In theory, though retained by one party only, the jurist as a professional was to operate in the service of justice and to enlighten the judge about the law, not to serve only partisan interests and confuse the judge.[42] His *consilium* was intended to sway a court, although, of course, the other party too might have attorneys and their *consilia.* The party could use the *consilium* simply as pre- or extrajudicial advice or, more likely, submit it to the court as an authoritative reinforcement of one's case.[43] In the course of the fifteenth century this practice became more consistent and popular for litigants, and thus more of the energies of jurists went to them. Litigants sought to enlist the most prestigious jurists, if not as primary authors, then as cosignatories. Indeed, the more jurists who could subscribe to a *consilium* or contribute one to the same cause, the more *auctoritas* the party wielded.[44] The other party would be buried beneath a figurative avalanche of arguments, citations, and signatures.

Because they were designed to persuade, jurists kept and gathered *consilia pro parte,* especially those of renowned jurists but also, on the local level, those that had proven especially compelling. Facts of the case, however, were not of overriding meaning, even to the jurist who handled a case, and less so to subsequent jurists who wanted to mine a *consilium pro veritate* for their own purposes. *Consilia,* especially as recopied, began with facts only in the most generic fashion. Collections of *consilia* were "arsenals of 'possibility,'" in the words of Mario Ascheri—models and gatherings of citations.[45] Only with the great tribunals of the sixteenth century, with their educated professional judges, would court

41. Cf. Osvaldo Cavallar, *Francesco Guicciardini giurista: I ricordi degli onorari* (Milan, 1991), 207–25.

42. Romano, "La giurisprudenza consulente," 146 n. 5. On the *consilia pro parte* in general, see Lombardi, *Saggio sul diritto giurisprudenziale,* 132–39, 147. However, others have seen *consilia pro parte* as portals for venality, delay, and obfuscation in judicial processes or as a decadence in professional standards and development: cf. Ascheri, "Consilium sapientis," 561–65; Sbriccoli, *L'interpretazione dello statuto,* 391, 461; Manlio Bellomo, *Società e istituzioni in Italia dal medioevo agli inizi dell'età moderna,* 3d ed. (Catania, 1982), 475–81.

43. Romano, "La giurisprudenza consulente," 146 and n. 6. Also my "Social Processes"; and Peter Stein, "Civil Law Reports and the Case of San Marino," in his *The Character and Influence of the Roman Civil Law: Historical Essays* (London, 1988), 115–30.

44. Romano, "La giurisprudenza consulente," 151–52; Kirshner, "*Consilia* as Authority," passim; Peter Stein, "Safety in Numbers: Sharing of Responsibility for Judicial Decisions in Early Modern Europe," in *Character and Influence of the Roman Civil Law,* 101–13.

45. Ascheri, *Tribunali, giuristi e istituzioni,* 26–27.

decisions and reports of them edge aside *consilia* as the most authoritative usable form of legal knowledge.[46] At that point too the judges on the bench took a greater role, diminishing that of the *consulens.*

The political dimension of the jurists' work, including their social and economic ties to a city's ruling elite, can seem controlling of the decisions they reached. Still, as Luigi Lombardi insists, there had to be jurisprudential consistency in *consilia pro parte* for them to be persuasive to other professionals.[47] It was also true—beyond the tendency of legal histories to overvalue doctrines of *ius commune* and the capacity of jurists to intervene with respect to statutory law—that local statutes contained inconsistencies and formal deficiencies that opened the way to legal theory.[48] For our purposes this all means that we have to read *consilia* on two levels, or in two directions. We must remain aware of prevailing legal doctrines and how these were understood and used, and we must remain aware of interests being expressed through the law and how these were affected by judicial handling.[49] In Osvaldo Cavallar's terms these texts were iconic. They did not reproduce reality in all its details but in a simpler spatial and figural repertoire.[50] As Paolo Grossi has it, the jurists' power lay in the *interpretatio* that declared, integrated, corrected, and modified the legal texts, and it moved between them and the "facts."[51] It was not *ius commune* alone that gave these jurists their power and visibility. It was their ability to use it in conjunction with other norms that made them indispensable. Rule of law (to the degree it did) came to the streets and piazzas because jurists made the great ideas of academics come alive in courts and judicial institutions.

Legitimation and Litigation

The surviving Florentine *consilia* contain cases where illegitimacy was an issue. Most revolve, directly or indirectly, about inheritance (notably the

46. Ascheri, *Tribunali, giuristi e istituzioni,* 23–25, 91; Cavallar, *Francesco Guicciardini giurista,* 182–83.

47. Lombardi, *Saggio sul diritto giurisprudenziale,* 130–35; Cavanna, "Il ruolo del giurista."

48. Cf. Vito Piergiovanni, "Diritto e giustizia mercantile a Genova nel xv secolo: I *consilia* di Bartolomeo Bosco," in *Consilia im späten Mittelalter,* 65–78, esp. 72, where he modifies Ascheri's emphases.

49. Cf. Pierre Bourdieu, "The Force of Law: Toward a Sociology of the Juridical Field," *Hastings Law Journal* 38 (1987): 814–53, esp. 830–34.

50. Cavallar, "Lo stare fermo," 132–33.

51. Grossi, *L'ordine giuridico medievale,* 227, 230.

heading under which treatises on illegitimacy were grouped in the sixteenth-century *Tractatus universi iuris*), and most also involved legitimated bastards. Legitimation could strengthen a bastard's claims, but that may only have propelled recourse to the courts. Certainly legitimation made these cases more interesting for jurists as well as for litigants. We will examine in this chapter six cases, more or less in chronological order, that show us how jurists tried to make sense of the legal and social contexts we have examined to this point. We can see how these men used their expertise to construct a role for Florentine illegitimates and a meaning for illegitimacy that never gained so much specificity that its ambiguities were ever elided. The law could continue to mean legitimacy for legitimated bastards and their fathers while it could also continue to mean superiority and differences for the legitimately born. But we are also intent on understanding these cases as social disputes, where the identities and circumstances of the litigants also had meaning.

Case 1: A Hypothetical on Officeholding

A powerful assemblage of legal talent, some Florentine and some not, forcefully argued an interpretation of statutory law right about the time, 1414, when two of these jurists, Paolo di Castro and Bartolomeo Vulpi (ca. 1359–1435), were engaged by civic commission in revision of Florence's statutes. The issues in this case were lively and of broad implication. In the intervention of these jurists we see some of the influence they could have on shaping legislation in a direction compatible with a reading of *ius commune* beyond the social and political realities of Florence.

According to the *consilia,* this case arose at Siena. The legal problem was easily stated, not so easily solved. Was a son legitimated by marriage—here a Tizio di Francesco drawn for office as one of the Dodici Buon Uomini—eligible for office in view of legislation of 1404 barring "anyone who in truth of the matter really is not or had not or was not born in his origin and birth from a legitimate marriage" [aliquis qui in rerum veritate realiter non sit et seu non fuerit vel esset natus in sua origine et nativitate de legitimo matrimonio]?[52] Use of the Tuscan equivalent for the Latin *Titius,* a Roman law equivalent to *John Doe* in American legal writing, is one clue to the hypothetical nature of this case. But the father, Francesco, was given some fairly specific bits of history. He had

52. BNF, Panciatichiano 138, fols. 260r–263v.

lived with a concubine since before 1385 and continued to live with her following Tizio's birth in that year. Their marriage occurred in 1391. Perhaps, then, Tizio was a real person whose actual or easily imagined predicament was merely disguised behind that name. In any case, if the person and interests were not real and immediate, the larger political interests certainly were.[53] Although the case was said to be Sienese, the "law" of 1404 was, in fact, that passed in Florence in that year, when the problems of citizenship were much in the air.

In all, ten jurists' signatures adorned the final document. These included, in addition to the two revisers of Florence's statutes, Pietro d'Ancarano, the leading canonist of his day, who had written extensively on illegitimacy and legitimation in his commentaries, and Floriano da San Pietro (d. 1441) who was already gaining a reputation for his interpretations of civil and canon law concepts in vernacular. These four men were not Florentine. Paolo di Castro came from Imola, Vulpi from the town of Soncino, the other two from around Bologna.[54] The other six were not all Florentine, though their practices and reputations were largely local. One was from San Gimignano, one from Prato, one from Gubbio—three men who knew firsthand the problems of acquiring citizenship and, even more difficult, rights to hold office. Giovanni Buongirolami, for instance, had only received his doctorate and matriculated in the Florentine Arte dei Giudici e Notai in 1412. He was not yet a citizen at the time this "case" arose; that would come in 1416, and it would be two more decades before he was declared eligible to hold civic office (1434). These men were part of an influx of legal talent into Florence in the crucial first decades of the fifteenth century. But it was one of the true Florentines, Filippo di Tommaso Corsini (1334–1421), then nearing the end of a long life of prominence in the legal profession and Florentine politics, who wrote the lead opinion that all the others endorsed. Corsini, son of a jurist, was the scion of one of the older leading families of his

53. Its hypothetical nature comes through in Corsini's signature: "puto verum esse quod supra continetur et scriptum est et sic consulerem si dictus casus michi committeretur per me consulendus per alios qui commictere possent" (ibid., fol. 262r).

54. For almost all the jurists we will encounter there are at least brief profiles in Martines, *Lawyers and Statecraft*—here for di Castro (499–500), Vulpi (501), Corsini (482), Ridolfi (483), da San Gimignano (499), Buonaccorsi (483), Buongirolami (501), and Torelli (499). In addition, see Annalisa Belloni, *Professori giuristi a Padova nel secolo xv: Profili bio-bibliografici e cattedre* (Frankfurt am Main, 1986), for more on di Castro (283–92); and see Tommaso Diplovataccio, *Liber de claris iuris consultis, pars posterior,* ed. Fritz Schulz, Hermann Kantorowicz, and Giuseppe Rabotti, *Studia gratiana* 10 (1968): 328–30 for da San Pietro.

city, as were the other two Florentines, Lorenzo Ridolfi (1362–1443) and Stefano Buonaccorsi (1353–1433), men with whom Corsini shared many legal, political, and diplomatic moments. The combination of family background and a law degree gave him enormous political influence, which he used to advocate what Martines has called "close oligarchy" in Florence.[55] Yet his personal and professional integrity also led him at times to endorse legal conclusions at odds with prevailing oligarchic sentiments.[56] In the case of Tizio di Francesco he was clearly the man for the job.

The easy answer to the question of Tizio's eligibility for office would seem to have been that the legislative language that looked to condition at birth excluded Tizio, and that is where Filippo Corsini began his discussion. Amazingly he still managed to support the opposite conclusion. First, he argued, such a law that changed *ius commune* had to be narrowly construed. *Ius commune* did not look to birth when it spoke of legitimation, and, although the "Sienese" law said nothing explicit about legitimation, Corsini argued that it had to include legitimated bastards in some way or else it made no effective disposition beyond *ius commune*, which already excluded illegitimates from *honores*. He thus introduced a distinction from civil law between legitimation by marriage and other forms of legitimation that had no basis in the statute. The statute, he claimed, kept out all the others, but not those who were legitimated by marriage.

> Secondly a tacit intent about the condition in the statute leads to this restriction, for it is not probable that the condition would want to impede marriage and procreation, which would be the result because, on account of privation from offices fathers who otherwise would have contracted marriage, so their sons might be enabled for office, would withdraw from marrying their concubine, mother of their sons, especially as many of the men are noble and the women are not. Lest thereby good marriage be prevented said legislation is to be understood so that it does not apply to those legitimated by subsequent marriage.[57]

55. Martines, *Lawyers and Statecraft,* 45.

56. Ibid., 96–97, 150.

57. BNF Panciatichiano 138, fol. 261r: "Secundo hanc restrictionem inducit tacita voluntas condictionis, illud non enim est verisimile condictionem voluisse impedire contractum matrimonium et procreatum inducere quod esset quia propter privacionem officiorum patres qui alias ut ad officia habilitarentur filii contraherent retraherent a contrahendo matrimonio cum illa quam tenuit concubinam et filios habuit maxime cum ut plurimum viri sint nobiles et femine ingnobiles ne igitur impediatur bonum matrimonium dicta refformacio sic intelligenda est ut ad legitimatos per subsequens matrimonium non trahatur."

That local laws were not to discourage marriage (and, conversely, encourage sin) was a commonplace among jurists. The fact that those legitimated by marriage were able to become bishops or inherit fiefs, as Corsini claimed, were additional supports to this position. So he concluded that Tizio could hold office and signed off with the information that he had reached this conclusion in conference with his colleagues and with the affirmation that "so I would advise if said case were committed to me" [sic consulerem si dictus casus michi commiteretur].[58]

Paolo di Castro followed him and added briefly that those legitimated by marriage were truly, not fictively, legitimate, as the effects of legitimation by marriage were retroactive to the time of birth. Again, this was an element much debated and variously qualified by academic jurists, as we have seen. But here the debates were conclusively resolved by him in favor of the nonfictive view of legitimation. Thus the jurist actively engaged in statute revision, which was expressly intended to confront difficulties in existing laws to make the task of governance easier, allowed legitimation by marriage to enable *legitimati* for office despite the statutory language about birth condition.[59]

Lorenzo Ridolfi, who signed on 14 June 1414, Nello da San Gimignano (b. 1373), Stefano Buonaccorsi, Bartolomeo Vulpi, and Giovanni Buongirolami (1381–1454) added little but the weight of their signatures, not that that weight was not heavy. It said a great deal that Ridolfi, a canonist and member of an illustrious old lineage, merely confirmed the first two opinions. Vulpi, in fact, added the observation that legitimation by rescript was not as potent as that by marriage, which "cleanses all preceding acts" [purgat omnia precedentia] in a manner that a woman deflowered and then married to her seducer was said in canon law to have been married as a virgin.[60] The last three jurists to touch the case chose to expand, however modestly, on its substance. Torello Torelli argued that "one thus born [illegitimate] is legitimate by pretext of subsequent marriage such that he has that marriage in his origin by law."[61] Pushed too far, that idea could make legitimacy reside in the parental relationship outside marriage, but Torelli's point was that to dissuade people from marriage and procreation would not work to the *publica*

58. Ibid., fol. 262r.

59. Martines, *Lawyers and Statecraft,* 187.

60. BNF, Panciatichiano 138, fol. 262r: "et quia deflorata primo et postea desponsata dicitur in virginitate desponsata ut no. xxx q. v. c. qualis, licet de legitimacione principis dubitetur utrum retro trahatur que non est tante potencie."

61. Ibid., fol. 262v: "talis sic natus est causa matrimonii subsequentis unde habet a iure illud matrimonium in sua orrigine."

utilitas. Pietro d'Ancarano then amplified the argument that statutory intent was not to preclude marriages because to do so would illicitly "correct" civil and canon law. Also, he claimed, it was "absurd" to end up with a situation where *legitimati* could succeed as heirs and otherwise be legitimate but not hold office, although this absurdity would clearly continue, by his reckoning, for those legitimated by rescript. Lastly Floriano da San Pietro recalled the lesser evil status of children of concubinage and the powerful purgative effects of marriage on the stain of birth, as compared to the effects of a rescript on the deeper stain of *spurii*. By terms of the "primeval" *ius gentium* there was no distinction between legitimate and illegitimate. That distinction arose in positive law; and positive law could also remove it and reduce things to the primal natural legitimacy. In the end, "between the concubine and the wife the sole difference is in dignity."[62]

All these opinions were fairly brief and avoided citing frequently and broadly across the growing corpus of authoritative jurisprudential literature. The findings were simply motivated sufficiently to prove that there was a good basis (if not yet demonstrably the best basis) in law for this view. That this *consilium* was overtly hypothetical does not mean it was unimportant or not intended to have effects. The timing—on the eve of a new statute redaction—meant that it was aimed at raising interpretive problems and resolving them. In this same year, 1414, the Arte di Calimala rejected illegitimates for membership, and other concerns about citizenship were in the air.[63] Above all, real cases arose at times that dealt with matters of citizenship and officeholding. Just the next year two of these men, Torelli and Nello da San Gimignano, were involved in a case involving the fiscal obligations of a Pisan who had been granted Florentine citizenship. Corsini was at the center of heated debate in 1417 on the terms of eligibility for office.[64]

The general effect of these *consilia* was to protect the rights of children legitimated by later marriage of their parents, even at the cost of doctrinal consistency. Assertion of the greater power of legitimation by mar-

62. Ibid., fol. 263r–v: "Nam inter concubinam et uxorem in sola dignitate differentia est." In fact, of course, there were often substantial differences of social background and dowry between the wife and the concubine.

63. Cf. Julius Kirshner, "Paolo di Castro on *Cives ex Privilegio:* A Controversy over the Legal Qualifications for Public Office in Early Fifteenth-Century Florence," in *Renaissance Studies in Honor of Hans Baron,* ed. Anthony Molho and John A. Tedeschi (Dekalb, 1971), 227–64.

64. Martines, *Lawyers and Statecraft,* 415–16, 208–9.

riage, however, also raised the greater possibility, implied by Corsini, of regularizing some patrician misalliances. Their interpretation raised the question whether the lower blood of the mother weighed down the higher quality blood of the office-eligible Florentine father (precluding marriages with the lowest, i.e., slave, mothers).

Case 2: Paliano Falchi's Heirs

It took a number of Perugian and later Florentine jurists several *consilia* to dispose of the legal problems generated by the estate of the wealthy Florentine merchant Paliano Falchi, who died in 1412. In his testament he left a handsome legacy to his natural son Bartolomeo, whom he also substituted as heir for his legitimate daughters, should they die without legitimate issue. Paliano later legitimated Bartolomeo by rescript, using a *procurator* (the mother having died), and in the act of legitimation there was a standard clause that the boy swear fidelity to the Holy Roman emperor (with Paliano's longtime business partner, Ardingo de' Ricci, taking that oath). As Bartolomeo had not been present at the legitimation, he did not simply offer the oath then and there, and it is not clear if he was ever aware (before these events) that he had to do so.[65]

Bartolomeo had four legitimate half sisters, the youngest of whom, Caterina and Gostanza, were still under eighteen and unmarried in 1424. However, they would soon marry very well (to Andrea di Bindaccio Ricasoli and Benedetto di Marco Strozzi, respectively), as had their older sisters, Niccolosa and Margharita, both of whom succumbed to the plague in 1423. Margharita left a daughter by her husband, Priore di Mariotto Banchi. Niccolosa's husband, Niccolò di Bernardo Guadagni, also died; but it was his father as his heir—and thus heir to the one-thousand-florin dowry Niccolosa left to her husband by testament—who instigated legal action. He wanted his rights recognized by the court of the Podestà, which summoned as interested parties the children of Paliano, including Bartolomeo, who at the time was under communal ban, living in Perugia for over ten years for an undescribed murder. He was thus unable to appear to protect his interests; although Berto di Bonifazio Peruzzi came forth for him and argued that any case against his friend had to be pur-

65. For a more detailed examination of this case, see my "Inheritance and Identity in Early Renaissance Florence: The Estate of Paliano di Falco," in *Society and Individual in Renaissance Florence,* ed. William J. Connell (Berkeley and Los Angeles, forthcoming).

sued not in Florence but before the Podestà of Perugia.[66] It was probably at Bartolomeo's initiative, then, that the case was laid before the best legal minds of Perugia, men whose words would gain a respectful hearing from Florentine jurists.[67] They were Matteo Feliciani, Benedetto Barzi (the author of the treatise on illegitimates), Francesco Mansueti, Francesco degli Ubaldi, Alessandro degli Ubaldi, Giovanni da Montesperello (d. 1462), and Dionigi Barigiani.[68] Most of them were also teachers in Perugia's distinguished law faculty.

There were five questions for the jurists to address: (1) could the *naturalis* Bartolomeo succeed to his father by testament along with the legitimate sisters? (2) did legitimation remove the incapacity of his birth and give him capacity to succeed? (3) in view of the oath of loyalty to the empire that was never taken was the legitimation of any effect? (4) was the petition against him valid, as he was unable to appear in Florentine court? (5) was the procedure against him in Florence to be halted as he demanded? The first of three *consilia* confronted all these problems. All the jurists, except Barigiani, signed this opinion, and it is not clear to which of them we can attribute a primary authorship. This was very much a committee-written text. Whoever the author was, he found that the undoubted common conclusion of the glosses and commentaries was that a *naturalis* like Bartolomeo could inherit no more than one *uncia*. As a *naturalis* Bartolomeo enjoyed a better condition than that (termed "pessima") of *spurii,* for the relationship behind his birth was "non improbato nec approbato, tollerato tamen." This all was nothing more than a systematic rehearsing of all the distinctions and terms found in *ius commune;* but it all affirmed that Bartolomeo was entitled to something by a will written when he was only *naturalis*. Legally, if there were no legitimate children, he could have claimed it all. But legitimation also clearly removed any incapacity by removing the "stain" of birth and equating the *legitimatus* with the legitimately born.[69] Plenty of legal ammunition was fired in the form of supporting citations, to conclude

66. Peruzzi seems to have been a good friend of the entire family. He served as *mundualdus* for Gostanza when in 1426 she sought her dowry from her husband, Benedetto di Marco Strozzi, who was falling into bankruptcy: Notarile 9040 (1422–29), fol. 252r–v (3 August 1426).

67. BNF, Landau Finaly 98, fols. 155r–166r.

68. On some of these men, see Diplovataccio, *Liber de claris iuris consultis,* 342 (Francesco Ubaldi), 346 (Barigiani), 367 (Feliciani), 370–72 (da Montesperello).

69. Ibid., fol. 157v: "Talis etenim legitimatio omnem maculam abstergit et equiparatur legitime natus sit legitimatus."

Bartolomeo could succeed to however much was left him by testament (two thousand florins by the legacy in Falchi's will).

The objection that failure to swear the oath rendered the legitimation invalid was also dismissed. Here the jurists decided that such an oath was not procedural or formal. It was something that followed a formally completed act; it was not part of the act. There was no statement in the act of legitimation to the effect that failure to swear fidelity to the empire invalidated the legitimation. Bartolomeo's recovered legitimacy was fixed in his bones and not to be removed.[70] In any case, he could still offer the oath anytime.

The last two points were let go after brief consideration. Though in exile, Bartolomeo had a legal right to defend his interests; he could also operate through an agent *(procurator)*. In any case, the questions of jurisdiction were deemed unimportant because Bartolomeo clearly had a right to the legacy in his father's will.[71] Little was said here or anywhere of the realities of the lives this case touched. The jurists' concern had to be with the law and how they saw it operating to make sense of the conflicting claims in the dispute. They asserted Bartolomeo's right as *naturalis* to a portion of his father's estate, and they affirmed that legitimation broadened that successoral right. They denied that procedural or jurisdictional matters hurt him.

In the second *consilium* the jurists (this time minus Barzi as well) went back over the first three issues, this time stressing the fullness and validity of the count palatine's authority to legitimate and the restorative effects of that legitimation. The charter empowering the count palatine who officiated at Bartolomeo's legitimation was inspected, and the grant it contained *ex plenitudine potestate* was declared to allow legitimation of all sorts of illegitimates from *defectus natalium*. The failure to render the oath of loyalty did not matter because the oath was not something the count palatine had to demand according to his imperial charter of privileges.[72] The legitimation enabled Bartolomeo to acquire the testamentary legacy that exceeded what could be left to him as a *naturalis*. Finally Niccolosa's will leaving her dowry to her husband could not prejudice Bartolomeo's succession rights contained in the substitution in their father's will. Here finally the jurists touched on what was the crux of the case to the plaintiff, the husband's father, Bernardo Guadagni. This member of a

70. Ibid., fol. 158v.

71. Ibid., fol. 159r.

72. The second is fols. 160r–163r; here see 162v.

prominent old Florentine lineage faced Perugian, if not Florentine, jurists who told him, in effect, that his claims to his daughter-in-law's dowry fell before those of her illegitimate brother (a murderer in exile, as well), thanks to the substitution in his favor in Paliano's will.

A third *consilium* was authored by Dionigio Barigiani with the concurrence of the two Ubaldi, Mansueti, and Montesperello. It was the shortest of the three, and its efforts were largely spent on the problem of the unmade oath. Barigiani too did not want an unnecessary oath to strangle Bartolomeo's rights and status. But Barigiani also began with an interesting slant on *persona:*

> The act of an agent is ruled according to a dual personhood, namely according to the power of the one acting and the aptitude of the one receiving. . . . But the person acting was a dignity as appears in the letters of his privilege and from them is derived the authority attributed to the one legitimating, which is very broad and there are clauses of enlarged faculty.[73]

It was more the power of the count that was in question, but Barigiani certified the *persona* of Bartolomeo by his opinion. This was especially true in regard to the *procurator* who served as agent for both father and son. The desire of the empowered count to follow the father's wishes and establish the son's successoral capacity is what mattered.

A great deal of juristic effort went into the matter of the oath and the powers of the count palatine. It was the technical validity of the acts that excited controversy and concern. The jurists were defending the essence of acts embodying the intentions of the parties. In real terms they were also defending the claims of a legitimated natural son against those of an affine through a legitimate daughter.

The Falchi case did not end with these Perugians. They ably defended Bartolomeo's inheritance rights and the validity of legitimation, but they had not addressed the important jurisdictional issues. It does seem that by some route Bartolomeo and his heirs came into the property left him

---

73. The third *consilium* is fols. 164v–166r, quote at 164v: "Cum actus agentium reguletur secundum duplicem personam, scilicet secundum potentiam agentis et secundum aptitudinem suscipientis. . . . Persona autem agens fuit honus, ut patet in litteris sui privilegii et ex ipsis deprenditur autoritas attributa legitimanti, que est multum lata et sunt clausule ampliative facultatis."

by Paliano. We know that Antonio Roselli, Paolo di Castro, and Nello da San Gimignano later had a role in the eventual fate of this property. In a suit from the 1430s these Florentine practitioners did not have to deal with problems of exile and jurisdiction.[74] They instead directly confronted problems of inheritance to specific and sizable properties. All three jurists have been classified by Martines as outsiders in Florence. They might then have been more sensitive to the plight of illegitimates whose only hope was the law, but they might also have been more intent on currying favor with entrenched interests. Roselli, later grandfather of a bastard and long-since author of the treatise on legitimation, was the obvious choice to tackle the case.

In his testament Paliano had stipulated that the three *poderi* left to Bartolomeo, in case there were no legitimate male heirs, could not be sold or otherwise alienated except to Bartolomeo's own sons. If Bartolomeo had no sons, the properties passed to the daughters as *heredes.* In fact, Bartolomeo's sons were, as he had been, *naturales,* and they chose to sell off portions of their inheritance when the opportunity arose. Heirs of the legitimate sisters saw their chance. Could Bartolomeo "alienate" the property to these sons and could they, in turn, alienate it to *personae extraneae*?[75] The first problem for Roselli was to determine if these *naturales* excluded the substitution to the daughters. With regard to property they did, although not to dignities or honors, for which illegitimates could only bring shame.[76] One could not presume an intent by a testator to honor illegitimates with *dignitates.* But what was the intent of the testator, Paliano, whose testament governed these *poderi*? The presumptions of law were that the condition placed on Bartolomeo's succession ("decedere sine filiis") referred only to legitimate children. But this particular testator, in providing for Bartolomeo, was taking care of a *naturalis.* Paliano did not seem to fear any shame from a *naturalis* as heir, and, although the *moderni doctores* found it reprehensible, Roselli sided with Dino del Mugello in seeing a substitution phrased in terms simply of having children as including *naturales* in view of the testator's other wishes.

---

74. My dating rests on di Castro's death in 1441 and Roselli's departure for Padua in 1438.

75. BNF, Panciatichiano 138, fols. 263v–265v. One of the three farms was the ancestral "podere di Paliano."

76. Ibid., fol. 264r.

> Therefore, since the condition of children is placed here by a testator who made mention of a *naturalis* in his testament, namely of Bartolomeo, who he did not think would bring shame as his heir, although he was *naturalis,* the same reason applies to Bartolomeo's sons, although *naturales.* Whence I conclude these sons of Bartolomeo are such that Bartolomeo can alienate these farms to them.[77]

Here Roselli remained true to his youthful *Tractatus* in that the language of a testamentary substitution was looked to with care. No mention was made of legitimation. I suspect it would only have clouded the issue, as the essential problem was not succession of the legitimated Bartolomeo but of his natural sons.

The second problem was tougher. The testator had wanted the farms to remain in the family, so how could alienation by the *naturalis* to *extranei* be condoned? Roselli drew a distinction. Prohibition of alienation could fall *in personam* or *in rem.* A prohibition that fell merely on a person expired with him. So if the prohibition fell only on Bartolomeo as heir, it did not extend to his sons. A *prohibitio realis* forbidding the property to leave the *familia,* however, would remain in effect and have to be upheld. Roselli argued that the prohibition established by the testator fell only on Bartolomeo; he had not made a *prohibitio in rem* according to the testament's wording. So the sons were free to alienate the property to outsiders. There was a whole range of interests in this case, then, that are not recoverable, for the texts give no indication who these outsiders were. We cannot tell if the alienation was to the sons' benefit or not.

Paolo di Castro and Nello da San Gimignano affirmed Roselli's arguments. The former added the cautionary note that should Bartolomeo's heirs predecease him without heirs of their own, then the substitution in Paliano's will went into effect, as the alienation lasted only as long as Bartolomeo lived.[78] In thus giving some hope to the *heredes* of Paliano it would seem the jurist was also diminishing somewhat the value of the purchase made by the persons who acquired the farms. Certainly this is

77. Ibid., fols. 264v–265r: "Cum igitur condicio liberorum sit hic apposita a testatore qui fecit de naturalibus de suo testamento mentionem, videlicet de Bartolomeo, quem non reputavit sibi verecundiam habere subcessorem, licet foret naturalis, quod idem et eadem ratio est de filiis Bartolomei quamquam naturalibus per predicta. Unde concludo istos filios Bartholomei fore tales in quos Bartholomeus possit alienationem dictorum prediorum facere."

78. Ibid., fol. 265v.

the sort of thing that would make current real estate agents and mortgage lenders quake. We can only say that the jurists advised the court that the transmission of property from Paliano to Bartolomeo to his sons and on to others was legal and in accord with Paliano's will.

The patrimony of Paliano Falchi thus raised a complex set of issues and multiple disputes, occurring over a number of years. The case is also interesting as an object lesson in how a Florentine patrimony could dissolve into others' hands. Bernardo Guadagni tried to end up with his daughter-in-law's share; the other husbands or their children received dowries; unnamed others purchased at least part of the property of Bartolomeo's sons.

Case 3: Inheritance in the Covoni Family

In 1435 Palla di Bernardo Covoni wrote up his will. He gave a legacy of his interests in two farms to Scolaio di Tommaso Covoni, with the condition that Scolaio could not alienate them and they would pass to those who would have been the testator's intestate heirs. As his heir Palla named his illegitimate brother Ridolfo and after him, "if according to the statutes he cannot be his heir or does not want to be," the *venientes ab intestato*. By statute Ridolfo could not be heir, although in accordance with his father's (Bernardo's) will, Ridolfo was eventually legitimated by a count palatine. In any case he formally repudiated Palla's *hereditas*. It was probably not a very wealthy estate. In the 1427 catasto Palla and Ridolfo (then age five and *not* designated as illegitimate) had less than 400 florins in assets after deduction of liabilities (795 before deductions)—the main assets being three and a half farms.[79] Following Scolaio's death some *consanguinei* who would have been Palla's intestate heirs, had Ridolfo had been legitimated, laid claim to what Scolaio had held from Palla; but Ridolfo lodged a counterclaim that as legitimated he was able to succeed his brother. The case went (from the Podestà probably) to the jurists Otto Niccolini and Piero Ambrosini da Iesi (1403–1472), though the *consilium* seems to have been Niccolini's. Niccolini had only begun to practice in Florence in 1438 after getting his doctorate in Perugia; but he came from a rising family with wealth and connections and, in the case of his brother Paolo, its own bastards.

79. ASF, Catasto 72, fol. 252r–v. Scolaio owned land adjacent to one of these *poderi* and was listed as owing thirty-four lire to the boys, as did another relative, Matteo di Paolo Covoni. Palla was listed as fifteen years of age.

Ambrosini too began to practice in Florence around that time, but he was from a town in Umbria. The modest standing of the Covoni and their wealth is indicative of the level at which these two jurists worked at that point in their careers.[80]

These two determined first that in *ius commune* an illegitimate brother could not succeed on intestacy, but he could succeed by testament. Could he succeed on intestacy by the statutes of Florence? As a city recognizing no superior (a theme of government prerogative Niccolini would invoke in many of his *consilia*)[81] Florence could enact a statute "by which to even illegitimates succession may be referred since to treat of succession is to treat of positive law," although "he who is called to succession is not by this rendered legitimated."[82] Florence's statutes, however, did not seem to admit bastards to succession. *Naturales* were preferred only to the fisc. The statute would modify *ius commune* if bastards were allowed to succeed, so it did not seem permissible to read Florentine law that way.

> Yet I saw the contrary counseled by almost all the jurists of this city not four years ago, and there were all my teachers, among whom was first messer Bernardo di messer Giovanni Buongirolami, and by expanding and corroborating messer Pietro [Ambrosini himself, it would appear], Florentine advocate, described the situation and messer Tommaso Salvetti and many others and even other Italian jurists, and they were principally moved by the text where they say is a *casus* . . . where it appears that there is induced about successions, in an active sense, this is that someone succeeds another, in the same way is understood to be disposed also passively, this is that he may be succeeded to, and so when it is to be induced by statute that bastards are succeeded by relatives, in the same way it seems induced that those relatives are succeeded by those bastards.[83]

80. BNF, Panciatichiano 139, fols. 127r–132v. On Niccolini and Ambrosini, see Martines, *Lawyers and Statecraft,* 493, 503.

81. Cf. Martines, *Lawyers and Statecraft,* 209, 396, 417, 423, 433, 441.

82. BNF, Panciatichiano 139, fol. 127v: "per que referatur successio etiam non legitimus, cum tractare de successionibus sit tractare de iure positivo de quo sunt omnes successiones: videte quod per statutum liber civitas superiorem non recognoscens que talia statuta facere consuevit ut est civitas Florentie possit hoc disponi, licet ille qui ad successionem vocatur pro hoc non redderetur legitimatus."

83. Ibid., fol. 128r: "Sed tamen vidi contrarium consultum et quasi per omnes doc. huius civitatis non sunt iiii anni elapxi, et fuerunt omnes patres mei inter quos fuit primus d. Bernardus d. Johannis de Buongirolamis et descripxit ampliando corroborando d. Petrus

If relatives could succeed to *spurii, spurii* could succeed to them. A number of examples were then advanced of similar situations where a reverse equality in succession occurred, notably that legitimation *per oblationem curiae* did not make one legitimate to agnates and so did not make them agnate to him and that in *ius commune* men could succeed to women so equally that they could succeed to men.[84]

The counterargument was raised, to be sure. The statute need not concede illegitimates rights to succeed legitimates any more than by giving brothers rights to inherit from sisters, statutes gave sisters reciprocal rights. Here indeed was a powerful argument in the commentaries of Baldo that Niccolini dismissed ingeniously. There was a *diversa ratio* in each case.

> Nor withstands what Baldo noted . . . when a statute desires that a sister not succeed her brother that yet the brother succeed to the sister, and he proves by that text and what is recited there from the midst of jurisprudence, and so although the statute wants those bastards be succeeded to, it does not seem to want that they succeed to others, lest it compound an inconvenience. For one should be aware that, and in this consists the difficulty of this article, in the doctrine of Baldo is a different rationale, because that statute that a sister not succeed her brother seems to have in itself the rationale that dignity be kept in the family. But in this case a difference can be considered in this statute. For the aforesaid statute that called to succession of bastards did not consider the branch of a house but it only considered naturalness, which seems to be because it called to succession of bastards even those related by a woman, when it said "through those who are related to bastards by the male or female or paternal or maternal line." Consideration of the preservation of the branch of a house ceases when it deals with the female or maternal line. Therefore the statute considered naturalness, and the nature in relatives which is also in slaves, as appears of servile cognation, which is shown expressly by the statute's words when it adds "as if the bastards were legitimately

advocatus florentinus et d. Thome de Salvectis et alii plures et etiam alii doc. Ytalie, et moti sunt principaliter per tex. ubi dicant esse casum in dicto § filium vero in aut. qui. mo. na. effi. sui coll. vi<i> [A. 7.1.4], ubi patet quod inductum nihilominus circa successiones active hoc est quod quis succedat alteri eodem modo intelligitur dispositum et passive hoc est quod succedatur illi, et sic cum sit inductum per statutum ut bastardis succedatur per coniunctos eodem modo videtur inductum ut ipsi coniuncti succedantur ipsis bastardis."

84. Ibid., fol. 128v.

> born" and then adds that among them be observed that order and that prerogative which would be observed if the bastards were legitimately born. And so as the statute seems to return to primeval nature, bastards are of a nature common with others and do not differ from others.[85]

This return to *naturalitas,* it was argued, underwrote a reciprocity of inheritance rights to *naturales* and bastards and their descendants. Thus this *consilium* sided with all those Florentine jurists. Thus also Ridolfo Covoni was said to succeed his brother Palla.

The next step was to consider Ridolfo's legitimation, which came well after Bernardo's death, to see if he could succeed when there were *agnati.* Legitimation seemed to "reintegrate indifferently for all matters," which in this case meant fraternal succession. So Niccolini quickly affirmed that Ridolfo as *legitimatus* could succeed by testament as next in degree. But what of the intent of the testator with regard to this legitimation? When Palla spoke in his testament of the next in line, did he mean at the time of the drafting of the will or at the time of his death? The jurists first determined that the testator's language in the subjunctive looked to the future (time of death). It also betrayed ignorance of the law as to whether Ridolfo could be his heir, "for had he consulted even the least *iuris consulens* he would have been told that a brother could institute him as heir and leave him property."[86] Only a father was barred from leaving prop-

85. Ibid., fol. 128v: "Nec habet obstare quod no. Bal. ibi in pe. q. dum vult statutum quod soror non subcedat fratri quod tamen frater succedit sorori et probat per illum tex. et quod ibi recitatus de media iurisprudentia, et sic licet statutum velit subcedi ipsis bastardis non tamen videtur velle ut et ipsi succedant aliis ne sit multiplicare inconveniens. Nam advertendum et in hoc consistit difficultas huius articuli quia in doctrina Bal. est dare diversam rationem quia illud statutum quod soror non succedat fratri videtur habere in se illam rationem ut familiariter salva sit dignitas. Sed in proposito casu potest considerari ratio diversitatis in ipso statuto. Nam statutum prefatum quod vocavit ad subcessionem bastardorum non habuit rationem considerationis cippi domus, sed tantum consideravit naturalitatem quod patet quia vocavit ad successionem bastardorum etiam ex coniunctis ex femina, dum dixit per illos qui coniuncti essent bastardis ex linea masculina vel feminina seu paterna vel materna. Unde cessat consideratio conservationis cippi domus, cum tractetur de linea feminina et materna. Consideravit ergo naturalitatem statutum et ipsam naturam in coniunctionibus que est etiam in servis ut patet de servili cognatione, quod expresse ostenditur per verba statuti dum subditur per inde ac si bastardi legitime nati essent, et dum subditur quod inter illos servetur ille ordo et illa prerogativa qui servaretur si illi bastardi legitime nati essent. Et propterea cum statutum videatur redire ad naturam primevam bastardi sint communis nature cum aliis et ab aliis non differant."

86. Ibid., fol. 130r–v: "Iste autem testator non consuluit peritiores, nam si consuluisset quilibet etiam minimus iuris consulens ei dixisset quod frater poterat ei instituere et relinquere."

erty to a *spurius*. But in his legal ignorance Palla had larded his testament with subjunctive clauses and qualifications expressive of his doubts as to Ridolfo's capability to inherit from him. With those grammatical lessons and the observation that Ridolfo was clearly "predilectus," the jurists concluded that it was not absurd that the legitimated Ridolfo succeed on intestacy and at the same time gain the bequest left him by his brother's will. He even stood as intestate heir to the legacy left Scolaio Covoni. The legitimation seemed to coincide with the testator's wishes.[87] That was important because it became the basis to dismiss as invalidating the failure to summon the prospective heirs to a legitimation that occurred after the testator's death (and, surprisingly, unmentioned, well after the death of the bastard's father). Summoning of prospective heirs was called for by jurists because postmortem legitimation affected immediate material interests. But Niccolini and Ambrosini said no such immediate interests were involved in this case.[88] So there was no need to summon *venientes ab intestato*. Finally, Ridolfo's repudiation of the *hereditas* was judged not to preclude his acceptance of the *legatum* come to him from Scolaio. This finding too was said to be in accord with that of "many very famous doctors of this city."

Here then the jurists strove to advantage a brother as much as possible—a brother, moreover, who had grown up in the same house with the testator and who faced claims of fairly distant cousins. The jurists seem to have been successful in defending Ridolfo. Their *consilium* rested on framing a sense of a Florentine legal precedent and declaring itself therewith, but it was also a precedent kept in line with jurisprudence in general, as most of their citations were to the canonical texts of both laws and the authoritative commentaries of the leading jurisprudents.

Case 4: Giovanni d'Andrea Masi's Daughters

Several Florentine jurists had to wrestle with the rare legitimation of girls. The main opinion in the case was the work of Antonio Malegonelli, an important political figure during the turbulent 1490s when the case arose.[89] He was joined by four others, all working at the behest of mem-

87. Ibid., fol. 131r–v.

88. Ibid., fol. 131v.

89. ASF, Carte strozziane, 3d ser., 41/2, fols. 73r–78r. Vespucci died in 1501; Deti did not receive his doctorate until 1488, so the 1490s was the period when the case occurred. The copy in Antonio Strozzi's hand carries at the outset the notation "pro quibusdam de Businis." At the end Strozzi simply noted that Pepi, Deti, and Corsini had also signed the *consilium*.

bers of the Busini family, who had an interest in blocking the inheritance claims by these daughters of Giovanni d'Andrea Masi. Masi's girls were fathered on an unmarried woman (not a slave, it seems) prior to his own marriage. They had been legitimated but still had to go to court to assert their rights to their father's property against the daughter of Giovanni's sister. As legitimation had as a chief function enabling the bastard to inherit, and as inheritance from fathers was biased toward the male line, one would expect—and the historical record bears out—that it would be sons who were legitimated. Giovanni Masi had no sons or other close male agnates; but he did have his girls, who at least had to defend their inheritance only from the claims of another female.

Malegonelli and his companions on this case were all of prominent Florentine families.[90] They were the beneficiaries of patrimonies built up generations before and passed in the male line (along with the usual additions of enterprise, including marriages). In the inheritance of Masi's daughters they were encountering a situation they had to consider unfortunate, lack of male heir, here compounded by bastardy. There was also legitimation, testamentary substitution, and just the inevitable ambiguities of the law to complicate things. But they were also retained by the Busini to craft an argument denying the claims of Masi's girls.

Malegonelli began by asserting that the girls had to show proof of legitimation, because they did not seem to have been the issue of "concubina unica in domo retenta," which would have given them inheritance rights as *naturales*. But they had an instrument of legitimation performed through Bartolomeo Fortini as count palatine. So there was no doubt the girls succeeded to whatever their father had acquired in his life and whatever came to him from his father that was not subject to the fideicommissary substitution that graced Andrea Masi's testament. On behalf of the girls it was claimed the substitution was obviated by their legitimation and thus they were Giovanni's intestate heirs. Malegonelli thus posed that "the principal disputation must be aimed at the validity of the legitimation: about which can fall infinite doubts that the doctors raise in this matter, which, if we want to examine in detail, requires long commentary."[91]

90. Cf. Martines, *Lawyers and Statecraft,* 486 (Malegonelli and Pepi), 487–88 (Corsini), 488 (Deti), 494 (Vespucci).

91. ASF, Carte strozziane, 3d ser., 41/2, fols. 73r–v: "Quapropter principalis disputatio versari debet circa validitatem legiptimationis, circa quam cadere possunt infinite dubitationes quas faciunt doc. in hac materia, quas si sigillatim velimus examinare opus est facere longos commentarios."

Malegonelli laid out his approach in terms of efficient and formal causes (claiming there was no reason for looking into the material cause—the girls' illegitimacy). Under the heading of efficient cause he raised a number of questions without decisively solving them. He questioned the count's authority as coming from an emperor elected but not crowned. He moved quickly to question whether comital powers to legitimate included women as well as men. He raced on to question the count's actions in Florence, as a city not subject to the empire, and whether he could legitimate when there were *agnati* and *cognati* who could have inherited. Here especially he made reference to *consilia* of authoritative jurists, many of whom had been active in Florence (Paolo di Castro, Angelo degli Ubaldi, Pietro d'Ancarano, Raffaele Fulgosio [1367–1427], among others). But Malegonelli backed off all these points. Frankly, to concede them would effectively make all legitimations meaningless. The emperor's standing as elected but not yet crowned, for example, was common to all emperors in the fifteenth century, and to rest the case on crowning alone would leave all comital privileges invalid.[92] If all this put doubts in the judge's mind, that was fine. Malegonelli's real effort went into a fifth, narrower argument, to the effect that an emperor or count could not legitimate so as to prejudice *fideicommissarii.* Under this heading he pointed at several subissues: the meaning of the fideicommissary substitution with regard to legitimated *naturales* or *spurii,* the presumed intent of the testator who established the substitution, the failure to cite the fideicommissary heirs to the legitimation, the desire of the *legitimans* to prejudice those heirs, the problem whether the power to legitimate could remove the substitution. It was this last issue Malegonelli bit into and tore apart with juristic teeth. Here he mounted a citation campaign to the commentaries of Bartolo da Sassoferrato and Antonio da Butrio, to *consilia* of Pietro d'Ancarano, Paolo di Castro, and others. Lacking a specific clause in the empowerment of a count palatine to allow legitimations against the *spes succedendi* of fideicommissary heirs, one had to doubt the intent of the *princeps* to permit such because he should not act against legitimacy.[93] Malegonelli finally had to conclude that the emperor indeed had the power to legitimate to the disadvantage of probable fideicommissary heirs but that this power could not be used by a count to the harm of those, like Florentines, not subject to

92. Cf. *Law, Family, and Women,* 184. In fact, only Sigismund in 1433 and Frederick III in 1452 were crowned in the fifteenth century.

93. ASF, Carte strozziane, 3d ser., 41/2, fols. 75v–76r.

the empire, especially a count who had not specifically been given power to legitimate to the detriment of fideicommissary heirs.

Under the heading of the formal cause, Malegonelli pointed to the failure to make mention of these fideicommissary heirs in the course of the legitimation. Indeed, relying on others' *consilia,* he said a father burdened with such a *fideicommissum* had to do more than merely mention these probable heirs, he had to have them summoned to the legitimation. If it were only a matter of property whose disposition he was free to arrange, the father could have operated without reference to such heirs, but he was not free where a substitution was concerned. As to whether the legitimated offspring removed the substitution,

> I should think it can be said they do not, in view of our statute as set out in the facts of this case, for the main rationale of those holding the affirmative is based on this, namely because such a *legitimatus* differs in no way from a legitimate; but from the fact that by the statute there remains a difference between them, mainly in regard to succession, it seems that this rationale does not apply, and the words of the testament must be understood to mean one who is simply legitimate and natural and not according to something else.[94]

Juristic arguments thus had appealed to the statute as an indicator of intent of local testators, and Malegonelli had stuck to that approach. It could not be presumed that the testator—Andrea, not the girls' father, Giovanni—meant for *legitimati* to count. But, in any case, Malegonelli made it clear that his main argument was the logically prior consideration that this count palatine could not legitimate to the prejudice of those who stood to gain by the substitution, who should have been summoned to the legitimation in any case. Certainly we earlier saw Florentines take this precaution in their legitimations. Of course the property not subject to the *fideicommissum* was the girls', but Malegonelli found this not worth exploring.[95] He concluded the legitimation was invalid, and Guidantonio Vespucci (143[?]–1501) concurred, citing in support a *con-*

94. Ibid., fol. 77r: "putarem dici posse quod non stante statuto nostro de quo in puncto, nam principalis ratio tenentium partem affirmativam est fundata in hoc, scilicet quia talis legiptimatus nihil differt a legiptimo, sed ex quo per statutum restat inter eos differentia maxime in materia successionis, videtur quod cessat dicta ratio et verba testamenti debent intelligi de eo qui est legiptimus et naturalis simpliciter et non secundum quid."

95. Ibid., fol. 77v.

silium of Francesco Ramponi (ca. 1365–1401) and Roselli's *Tractatus*. Francesco Pepi (1451–1513), Ormannozzo Deti (b. 1464), and Luca Corsini (1462–1511) also signed the document, which is a good illustration of consultors' tendency to cite previous *consilia*, to develop arguments within the burgeoning literature of judicial practice.

Although Malegonelli insisted that he was investigating the validity of the legitimation, he was really concerned with its effects regarding the *fideicommissum*. It is hard to see the legitimation failing by reason of a lack of requisite comital power. It is also interesting to note what arguments were not used in this case, notably most of the counterarguments, which were only noted in passing. Succession by women, which was limited by statute, did not become an issue because the Busini claim lay through the sister. Also little in evidence here were moralistic tones regarding the illegitimacy of the girls as opposed to the legitimacy of the others. Instead the *consilium* took a technical tone, highly professional. It is worth recalling that in 1498 Malegonelli and Vespucci teamed up on another illegitimacy case, but that there they decided that a comital legitimation was sufficient to affect eligibility for office for two bastards of the powerful Acciaiuoli despite local statutes.[96] They were not opposed to legitimation, a viable institution in Florence and elsewhere, but they were seemingly out to limit its (unintended) effects. In that case we know that the ruling councils of Florence followed their advice and inscribed the Acciaiuoli on the lists of those capable of holding office. I have been unable to determine the outcome of the Busini-Masi case. The Masi girls had an uphill battle against such an array of jurists, but perhaps there were others who took their side.

Case 5: Rinieri Dei's Heirs

In his testament Rinieri Dei named as heir his legitimated son, Piero, leaving substantial dowries (three thousand florins each) to his daughters. Piero had been fathered on a woman named Peronetta back when Rinieri had been single. In effect he was treating Piero as fully legitimate, capable of excluding his sisters from further inheritance, in line with Florence's statute on intestate succession. Piero exploited his father's affection for him by seeking legitimation at the hands of the king of France in his father's absence, but Rinieri seems to have ratified this move, includ-

96. Martines, *Lawyers and Statecraft*, 99–100.

ing by his testament.[97] The girls brought suit—or their husbands or others for them—to strike down their exclusion to dowries. The relationship between Piero and these girls, born of his father's second wife, Maria di Piero Machiavelli, was a rocky one. When Piero returned to Florence after Rinieri's death, the widow and her girls were unable to live with him. She petitioned the Signoria for a separation of habitation and provision for support (had she just left, her widowhood rights from Rinieri's estate would have been forfeit and return of her dowry jeopardized). The Signoria turned to two lawyers, Antonio Strozzi and Ormannozzo Deti, who ruled against her. The case then went to the Florentine Rota in 1515, and Piero retained the services of Strozzi and Francesco Guicciardini to draft a *consilium* reiterating the earlier arguments revolving around the effects on the family economy if the widow and her property were to be separated.[98]

Unable to coexist with their half brother, the girls pursued a more forceful avenue—to have him removed from the patrimony. Filippo Decio (1454–1535), Matteo Niccolini (1473–1542), and Ormannozzo Deti wrote *consilia* supporting the girls, the crux of whose case was that Piero could not exclude them from inheritance because the statutory language specified exclusion only by those born legitimate.[99]

Decio was a Milanese whose reputation redounded through Italy in the years he taught at Pisa (1515–21), where he was when he signed his *consilium* in the Dei case, which was later printed in a collection of his opinions.[100] His argument that *legitimati* by rescript did not meet the meaning of legitimate birth in the statute was bolstered before the Rota not by referencing commentaries but by *consilia* by others and himself—"so I counseled at Florence along with preeminent Florentine doctors" [ita consului Florentie una cum primariis doctoribus florentinis]. He acknowledged that there were arguments to opposite effect but said simply that the language of the statute kept Piero from excluding his half sisters. The statute, however, dealt with intestacy, and in the Dei case there was a will that named Piero heir and a statutory provision that said girls could not con-

97. The facts of legitimation emerge in Antonio Strozzi's case notes in ASF, Carte strozziane, 3d ser., 41/10, fol. 323v.

98. Cf. Cavallar, *Francesco Guicciardini giurista,* 118.

99. I have already discussed Decio's and Deti's *consilia* in *Law, Family, and Women,* 252–54.

100. Cf. Martines, *Lawyers and Statecraft,* 505. The *consilium* in signed and sealed original is in BNF, Magliabechiano xxix, 193, fols. 182r–191r, reprinted in Filippo Decio, *Consilia, cons.* 383, vol. 2, fols. 42ra–43va.

test a paternal will. Decio's claim was that the statute concerned the wills of those who died with legitimate and natural male heirs, not with legitimated heirs. The girls retained a right by *ius commune* to contest a will that passed them over. So Decio concluded that as merely *legitimatus* Piero could neither exclude the girls on intestacy nor by testament.

The third concern Decio faced was whether legitimate fraternal nephews excluded the girls, and here he had to dance around statutory language that favored nephews over daughters. He took a paradoxical tack and said the nephews were not heirs because by testament Piero was. The girls and Piero were the only interested parties. Even though the statute mentioned nephews with no requirement that they in fact were heirs—their mere existence was enough—Decio insisted the statute was meaningless unless the exclusion of daughters was held to those who actually could be heirs. This was where a number of arguments from law and statute were produced and refuted. The *ratio statuti* did not hold if these males who excluded women did not themselves inherit.[101]

Deti's examination of the case was complete in its own right, for all that it took cognizance of its predecessors.[102] He did not deal with the issue of Piero's ability to exclude the girls. He took that as resolved and went instead to the issue of whether the girls could be termed *preterite* and as such possessed of a civil law right to break their father's will.[103] His conclusions were bolstered by frequent reference to *consilia.* He, like Decio, limited the Florentine statute to males born legitimate, and applied the same logic to legislation from 1486. He claimed to follow Bartolo da Sassoferrato in saying that

> a statute that excludes a daughter on intestacy when agnates exist takes place when the agnates are instituted as heirs; it is otherwise if *extranei* are instituted, as they were in our case, in which was instituted a legitimated son, and agnate nephews would not succeed.[104]

It is interesting how the legitimated bastard was here classified as *extraneus,* not even *cognatus,* despite the doctrinal body of opinion circulating

101. BNF, Magliabechiano, xxix, 193, fol. 189r.

102. I have been unable to locate Matteo Niccolini's *consilium,* whose existence is signaled by Deti at the beginning of his.

103. His *consilium* is BNF, Magliabechiano xxix, 193, fols. 1r–13v.

104. Ibid., fol. 5v: "quod stante statuto quod filia excludatur ab intestato extantibus agnatis procedit quando agnati sunt instituti: secus si sint instituti extranei prout erant in casu nostro in quo institutus erat filius legitimatus et nepotes agnati non succederent."

about the question of his agnation. It is all the more interesting given Deti's otherwise meticulous presentation of issues and exhaustive citation of texts. But his intent was to license greater inheritance shares by these girls without their having to deal with anyone other than their legitimated half brother Piero. Crucial here also was a *consilium* of another Florentine, Salustio Buonguglielmi (ca. 1373–1461), who had claimed that the sort of inheritance situation he faced (legitimate daughters, legitimated son, agnate nephews) was a *casus mixtus* not covered by Florence's statutes. So the rules of *ius commune* applied, and the girls would stand equally with their brother.[105] Deti was building up a sense of a precedent of sorts—a locally weighty line of interpretation about the statute. It was a line that saw a *legitimatus* as somehow *extraneus*. Piero di Rinieri Dei would enroll his six sons on the age lists for eligibility for office; he would have his life in Florence. But in these jurists' eyes he would not do so as his father's sole heir, for all that others had previously tried to safeguard the integrity of the patrimony against the departure of his father's widow. On the other hand, it appears that Antonio Strozzi, along with Marco degli Asini (ca. 1484–1575), in October 1522, wrote a *consilium* on the opposite side in that case—for the sons of Piero. Strozzi argued that male cousins would have excluded the girls on intestacy, so their inheritance was limited to the dowries, which they could not claim until their marriages, or otherwise make the object of testamentary provisions or dispose of before that time.[106] Strozzi otherwise spent time marshaling texts around various problems in Piero Dei's case circulating about the validity of his legitimation.[107] It was indeed possible for the jurists to argue both sides of an issue. We also see here how a succession of disputes went on. The issues changed but the antagonisms remained, especially among litigants possessed of the wherewithal to engage jurists.

Case 6: Inheritance in Cortona

Antonio Strozzi, in conjunction with Francesco Gualterotti (1456–1509), Giovan Vettorio Soderini (1460–1528), Niccolò Altoviti (1455–1518),

105. Ibid., fol. 12r.

106. ASF, Carte strozziane, 3d ser., 41/13, fols. 169r–180r, which is only a working draft. "Prima quod tempore mortis Rainerii testatoris extabant persone que secundum dispositionem statutorum repellebant eius filias a succedendo ab intestato" (fol. 180r).

107. ASF, Carte strozziane, 3d ser., 41/10, fols. 323v–324v, which includes some sweeping assertions of paternal power to dissipate property.

and Ormannozzo Deti,[108] all from prominent Florentine families, had to investigate a case from the subject city of Cortona. By statute daughters there could inherit without exclusion in favor of men, unlike Florence. If one died intestate without descendants, the ascendants in the male line succeeded along with any brothers. Mother and maternal ascendants were excluded in that case, unless the only other heir was a sister, in which case the mother could claim one-third. She could also get one-third if there were no brothers, sisters, ascendants, or descendants in direct male line. The other two-thirds were to go to the closest *agnati.*

Against this statutory situation was the inheritance in the family shown in figure 3.

In the genealogical diagram that accompanies Strozzi's *consilium* in manuscript, Tommaso is labeled *naturalis tantum* and Toccia *concubina.* However, in the *consilium,* Strozzi terms him *spurius,* born of a father then married *(uxorato)* and "some woman not kept in the house" [ex quadam femina in domo non retenta]. How the discrepancy arose is hard to say exactly. It may be that Gabriella sought to minimize Tommaso's illegitimacy, while in the course of preliminary argumentation the other side established his status as an adulterous bastard. Francesco invoked Tommaso's illegitimacy to claim his estate away from Gabriella, who claimed it as Susanna's mother. Here, while the family situation (no direct male heir, presence of illegitimacy) was not unusual in the experience of these Florentine jurists, they had to confront it in a statutory context different from that of Florence. Although Cortona was subject to Florence, it was only in administrative and governmental matters that Cortona's statutes were to be harmonized with Florence's.[109]

The case for Gabriella against Francesco had three strong components, each of which Strozzi fleshed out at some length. The first was that Francesco was not *agnatus.* Tommaso had been *spurius* from an adulterous and casual affair, and a *spurius* was not *agnatus.* In this regard, then, Gabriella could try to use her husband's illegitimacy to her benefit. Legitimation by rescript only established agnation between father and son, so Francesco was not helped by that either. Second, even if he were agnate, he was related in the fourth degree. The statute clearly stated that where there were no other heirs "then agnates of the deceased to the third

108. ASF, Carte strozziane, 3d ser., 41/14, fols. 607r–621v. Notes for *allegationes* by Strozzi in this case are in 41/10, fols. 298v–301r. For sketches of Gualterotti, Soderini, and Altoviti, see Martines, *Lawyers and Statecraft,* 487.

109. Martines, *Lawyers and Statecraft,* 220–32.

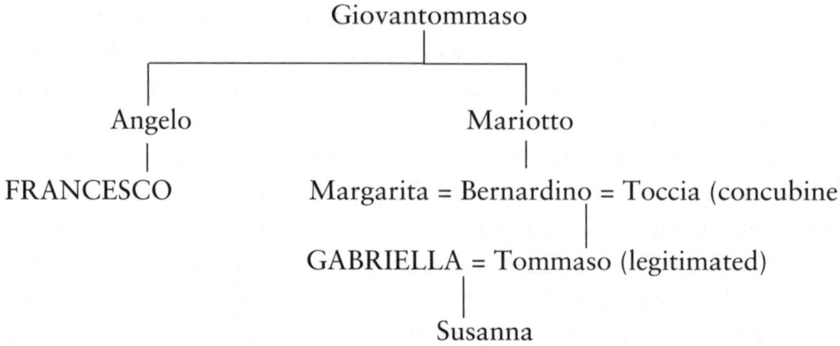

Fig. 3. Genealogy of Tommaso and Susanna

degree by canon law's computation exclude all *cognati* of the deceased of whatever degree and sex even though closer in degree to the deceased."[110] Francesco seemed to fall outside that wording. And it was also a commonplace that the statute excluding women was "odiosum" for them; therefore, it had to be construed as narrowly as possible so as both to harm them less and to "correct" *ius commune* less. Third, the paternal grandmother, Margarita, was still alive and, as her case was not covered by statute, it reverted to *ius commune*, by which she excluded the *agnati*. Strozzi here could cite a number of *consilia* where other jurists had interpreted similar statutes to put succession back in the realm of *ius commune*, thus bolstering female succession rights.

Strozzi and his colleagues, however, had been hired to construct a case in favor of Francesco's contention that he receive two-thirds of Susanna's property. His response to the first point was simple. Legitimation by rescript made Tommaso and his descendants agnate to all his father's agnates. A long list of references to *consilia* and commentaries by Angelo degli Ubaldi, Bartolo da Sassoferrato, Azo, Giovanni d'Andrea, Baldo degli Ubaldi, Paolo di Castro, Alessandro Tartagni, and unspecified *moderni* solidified the point. But there was some question about the legitimation's validity on two counts. One was that it was a surreptitious legal act

110. ASF, Carte strozziane, 3d ser., 41/14, fol. 607v: "tunc agnati persone defuncti usque in tertium gradum secundum ius canonicum numeratum excludant omnes cognatos defunte persone cuiuscunque gradus et sexus existente licet defunto proximiores sint in gradu."

in that the count palatine had not been told of the *spurius*'s right by another Cortonese statute to inherit one-sixth. The presumption underlying this argument was that the count would not have enabled Tommaso to receive the entire paternal estate had he known that the lad was already entitled to one-sixth by statute. There were indeed parallels in canon law where silence regarding a prior grant was said to negate a later, greater grant; and Strozzi obligingly cited them, as well as a *consilium* of Alessandro Tartagni.[111] But he deftly turned this argument on its head. Existence of this statutory provision would have made it easier, not harder, for the count to agree to legitimation, because it would not have been as great a favor. It was thus not necessary to have revealed the existence of this statute to the count. It would have been different, as in the case Alessandro Tartagni had handled, if the statute forbade inheritance by *spurii* and the *legitimans* had not been told that. Indeed, when he had faced a statute similar to Cortona's, Tartagni's decision had been unremittingly negative:

> For he counseled that such a legitimation of a *spurius* is not termed surreptitious without mention of that statute because such a statute permitting *spurii* to succeed to some part is not valid as conclude Bartolo, Baldo, Angelo, Giovanni da Imola and *moderni* . . . d. Federico da Siena, d. Jacopo Buttrigari, and messer Recupero da San Miniato etc. and d. Paolo d'Eleazari held this. . . . Pietro d'Ancarano held the same in a *repetitio* to c. i extra de constitut. cit. xvii in xi q. [X. 1.2.1], and they are moved principally by the fact that such a statute gives cause and occasion for doing bad and procreating *spurii.* Baldo [held] the same in l. i C. de summa trin. [C. 1.1.1] with many others to which for the sake of brevity it is not necessary to refer, but it is sufficient that all agree that this is the reason for the opinion that the statute is not valid. And so if the statute is not valid, no mention of it was needed, because it is not necessary to make mention of an invalid act . . . also this response to said statute is given by the famous doctors d. Bartolomeo Sozzini and d. Baldo de' Bartolini of Perugia, otherwise advising in contingent facts, who consulted on the same point: and so was also decided and concluded by three excellent Florentine advocates in contingent facts, namely d. Bernardo Buongirolami, d. Angelo Niccolini, and d. Antonio Malegonelli to whom was committed deciding the

111. Ibid., fol. 613v.

aforesaid case, on which had consulted d. Alessandro, d. Baldo, and d. Bartolomeo, in which was disputed a legitimation of a certain citizen of Sarzana with no mention of the statute of Sarzana disposing that to *spurii* may be left as much as one-fourth, concluding that as such a statute was not valid, it was not necessary to make mention of the statute, which decision falls right into our terms.[112]

This passage is offered at such length both to show in some detail what argumentation in *consilia* was like and, more pointedly, to show how Strozzi backed his negative judicial review of the statute with reference to others' *consilia*. Of course he had no power to abrogate a statute; it remained on the books.[113] But he notably set up a local precedent in the Sarzana case we encountered in discussing legitimations. In both cases the argument against the statute aimed to advantage the inheritance claims of someone who did not have illegitimacy in his line of descent.

The second objection to the legitimation was that Tommaso had been an *infans* at the time, and the count could not legitimate an *infans*

112. Ibid., fols. 614r–615r: "nam consuluit quod talis legiptimatio facta de spureo non dicitur subreptitia non facta mentione de tali statuto: quia tale statutum permictens spureos in aliqua parte succedere non valet, ut concludunt Bar. Bal. Angel. Imol. et moderni in l. iii ff de testamentis. Idem tenuit Bal. in l. i C. de iure aur. anul., hoc etiam consulendo tenuerunt Federicus de Senis, d. Jaco. But. dominus Recuperus de sancto Miniato et d. Paulus de Eleazariis, ut patet in consiliis Federici de Senis cclxxv *casus talis est statuto cavetur* etc. cum tribus consiliis sequentibus. Idem tenuit Petrus de Anca. in repetitione c. i extra de constitut. c. xvii in xi q. et moventur principaliter quia tale statutum dat causam et occasionem delinquendi et creandi filios spureos. Idem Bal. in l. i C. de summa trin. cum multis aliis quos causa brevitatis non est necesse referre, sed sufficit quod omnes concordant hanc esse rationem opinionis quod non valeat tale statutum. Si ergo non valet tale statutum nulla mentio erat necessaria de illo, quia de actu invalido non est necesse fieri mentionem in impetratione c. ex parte et ibi not. extra de rescriptis et glo. et doc. in c. ex tenore eo titulo, quam ad hoc allegat Imol. in l. iii ff de testamentis et est glo. ubi doc. in c. cum nostris extra de concess. preben., et tenet Bal. in l. i C. se contra ius vel uti p., hanc etiam responsionem ad dictum statutum alias consulendo in contingentia facta dabatur insignes doctores dominus Bartholomeus Sozinus et dominus Bal. de Bartolinis de Perusio qui super eodem puncto consuluerunt: et ita per predicta fuit etiam decisum et conclusum per tres excellentos advocatos florentinos in contingentia facti, scilicet per d. Bernardum de Bongirolamis d. Angelum de Nicholinis et d. Antonium de Malegonnellis, quibus fuit commissa decidenda causa predicta, super qua consuluerant dominus Alex. d. Baldus et d. Bartholomeus in qua disputabatur de quadam legiptimatione facta de quodam cive serzanensi, non facta mentione de statuto serzanensi disponente quod spureis possit relinqui usque in quartam partem: concludunt quod cum tale statutum non valeat non erat necesse fieri mentionem de tali statuto: que decisio cadit in propriis nostris terminis."

113. Cf. Thomas Kuehn, "A Late Medieval Conflict of Laws: Inheritance by Illegitimates in *Ius Commune* and *Ius Proprium*," *Law and History Review* 15 (1997): 243–73.

who could not consent to the legitimation. Strozzi's response was that the count could indeed legitimate; his rescript even made up for the incapacity of the *infans* to consent. Besides, consent could be given later, and it need not be explicit—simply a lack of dissent as indicated by one's actions. And by his behavior Tommaso certainly seemed to have consented: "in our case one supposes that there were many acts and deeds by Tommaso as a *legitimatus* and that he could not have done them unless he had been legitimated, so it seems in any case he tacitly ratified the legitimation."[114] It is interesting to see here how Francesco's case came down to upholding the validity of the legitimation of someone like Tommaso, otherwise so removed from him and not in direct line of relationship.

Strozzi then had to put real effort into expanding the meaning of the statute such that a fourth-degree agnate like Francesco could claim two-thirds of Susanna's estate, even though he was not within three degrees. Suffice it to say that Strozzi did so mainly by saying that the specification of third degree did not touch the other references to *agnati* in the statute. He dispatched the argument about the paternal grandmother by pointing out that she was excluded by the mother in *ius commune*. And other jurists—Bartolomeo Sozzini, Pierfilippo da Corgna (1420–1492), Giovan Battista da San Severino (fl. 1460–80)—had come to a parallel conclusion in a case dealing with the ramifications of Florence's statute. It was termed a "beautiful resolution that is very palpable."[115] With it Strozzi on this point also established something of a local judicial precedent.

Francesco got two-thirds, Gabriella one-third, Margarita nothing, as Strozzi saw it. Perhaps better than the other cases, this one shows how far legitimation's effects might go and yet how uncertain they often remained, as we hit the paradox that the bastard's descendants were best advised to play up his illegitimacy and argue against the legitimation. It was the fact that legitimation restored agnation that made it possible for Francesco to lodge his claim, as well as the fact that Cortonese inheritance statute favored men in ascendant lines against a mother.

---

114. ASF, Carte strozziane, 3d ser., 41/14, fols. 616v–617r: "cum in casu nostro presupponatur quod multa fuerunt facta et gesta per hunc Thommasium tanquam legiptimatum et que non potuissent facere, nisi legiptimatus esset videtur saltem tacite ratificasse dictam legiptimationem."

115. Ibid., fol. 620v, where he also said that Giovanbatista da San Severino was so taken with the beauty of this conclusion "quod nunquam voluit consulere pro opinione contraria."

Conclusions

Rules and relevant facts dominated suits; facts alone dominated the few arbitrations, where rules were not in question. In some cases, however, jurists found it expedient to soar beyond narrower rules to the realm of normative justifications, or even to the sorts of legal fictions that clustered around an institution like legitimation. The Covoni case as handled by Niccolini and Ambrosini did this. In arguing that Florence's statutes gave *bastardi* rights to inherit from other kin (which, in fact, it seems not to have done), the jurists reached to a different level where not the "branch of a house" but the "naturalness" of a relationship was said to be in view. In effect they were trying to make a new rule, and to do so they needed the tools of legal reasoning to extend analogies and forge distinctions. It helped them that there had been not only doctrinal development but previous practical judgment. They cited the case opinions of Buongirolami, Ambrosini, and Salvetti as corroborating theirs. Strozzi later also cited the *consilium* from the Sarzana case in his Cortona case, but to opposite effect.

Across all these cases, which range in time from the early fifteenth to the early sixteenth century, there are certain fundamental ambiguities of law. These were always available to be invoked by parties to litigation. Some were procedural—summoning of agnates in legitimation by rescript, expression of consent in all forms of legitimation. Some concerned the results of legitimation—for holding of office, for eligibility to inherit by the terms of statutes and of testamentary substitutions. The primary ambiguity was the equation of *legitimus* and *legitimatus*, the effect of the fiction "ac si de legitimo matrimonio natus." Near the beginning of the fifteenth century Signorino degli Omodei had dealt with the problem using imaginative metaphors.[116] Other jurists, then and later, were less imaginative and graphic, but they too had the same problem. There was no consensus.

In one sense ambiguity, it could be argued, persisted because it served jurists' interests. Disputes could keep occurring because arguments were available to both sides. Jurists could use the disputes as occasions to reassert their expertise, their power, as well as to collect fees for their services. But these ambiguities were real conceptual conundrums. Civil and canon law texts that formulated the fictional equation of *legitimus* and

116. Cf. Kuehn, *Law, Family, and Women,* 188–89.

legitimatus were still confronted by the "facts" of birth and the linguistic distinction that existed in both technical and "common" speech. The uncertainty of judgment regarding the effects of legitimation may well account for the fact that so many cases involved attacks on the validity of legitimation. Jurists fashioned, if not always determinacy and certainty, at least a viable line of reasoning to resolve these issues.[117]

The desire to uphold and give effect to a valid legal institution collided with the social prejudices against illegitimacy. Litigants themselves may have acted from no more than a visceral sense that they could, or even should, try to claim property away from a bastard. Some, however, may have had a more exact sense of the law; and relative ease of access to notaries, if not to jurists themselves, would allow their claims to be formulated in legal terms. Clearly there was awareness of some of the law's sticking points with regard to validity of legitimation. Also where bastards' inheritance arose, one was already in a more difficult situation than that of the simple normative model of father succeeded by sons. The sheer fragility of biological survival left gaps in family trees; distant relationships came into play. The rights of *legitimati* were not at stake alone; there were those related to and through them.

The distinction between illegitimacy and legitimacy, while rooted in marriage and sexual behavior, was couched mainly in terms of succession. As we have seen, jurisprudence, *ius commune,* and statutes were all directed at spelling out the limited inheritance rights (testamentary or intestate) of *naturales* to their fathers, the lack of such rights for *spurii,* or local modifications of these rules. Legitimation's effects and functions were also largely spelled out in terms of inheritance. Because of legitimacy, one inherited. It did not work the other way—that one had the *hereditas* first and as a result could lay claim to legitimacy.[118] But was it so simple in practice? How legitimate could one claim to be if one had little or no piece of the paternal estate? And in reverse could an *illegitimus* in possession of paternal property not claim to be more "legitimate" in some sense?

Certainly one cannot say that every bastard who inherited, under whatever terms, was challenged in court, though clearly many were.

117. Cavallar, "Lo stare fermo," 143.

118. Hostiensis to c. causam que, Qui filii sint legitimi (X. 4.17.7), *Summa aurea,* col. 1386: "non enim hereditas trahit ad se legitimationem, sed legitimatio hereditatem: unde non sequitur iste possidet hereditatem, ergo legitimus filius et heres est . . . sed bene sequitur legitimus filius et heres est, ergo iuste potest possidere hereditatem."

Some were successful in going through life "as if legitimately born." The preclusive jural definition of legitimacy, which could be easily maintained in a paper trail, as we have seen, prevented treating relationships as widely negotiable. But there was some room, even in a courtroom.

The negotiation of the meaning of legitimacy led to the intrusion of jurists. It cannot be said that their findings were predictable in social terms. In general they did not favor illegitimates, but they had to respect legitimation, at least in theory. That their decisions should have brought harmony, thus ending dispute and restoring social order is also true, but trivial. It is the sort of order they were contributing to that is of historical interest, and goes well beyond simple functionalist arguments about law and dispute processing. These jurists held to a vision of the family as the crucial element in society. Central to the family was a series of legitimate marriages. By that means the sexual capacity of sisters and daughters was used to contribute to social perduration and reproduction. By that means men identified their kin, especially males, and passed along property. The *legitimatus* could be an emergency stopgap to keep a family line going, but while he carried blood lines, he also did so in an irregular manner.

None of these *legitimati* simply stepped in as full heirs to their fathers, if only because they faced challenges a *legitimus* did not. Even where *legitimati* "won" (when their interests gained cogent juristic support), they shared with others. More legal and social bias lodged against those who had to go through the rescript procedure than legitimation by marriage. On the other hand, there was the memory of shared living arrangements and experiences, paternal solicitude and sense of obligation that singled out these sorts of bastards from among the nameless others. There were the undoubted constant threats to familial survival, the desire of men to have male progeny to carry on their name and patrimony. So jurists were not always or totally unfavorably disposed toward *legitimati* or bastards, even those whose birth had been under the most nefarious circumstances. These results were not predictable from academic law alone, as if it were possible to read Roselli and Barzi and know what the correct legal answer was.

Finally, although we have looked at only six cases in this chapter, a precariously thin basis on which to construct a chronological scheme, it does seem that earlier in the fifteenth century illegitimacy was less feared. At least the hypothetical Tizio would have held office, and Bartolomeo di Paliano Falchi and Ridolfo di Bernardo Covoni gained property. The earlier decades of the century were when the population was lower, the effects of plagues and wars more severe. But those were also the decades in which Florentine jurisprudence was powerfully influenced by an influx of outsiders who had a hand in the earlier cases. By the end of the century the cases involving illegitimates were falling into the hands of jurists of elevated and deeply Florentine social origin, like Strozzi, Deti, and Malegonelli. Their *consilia* tended to strike down inheritance by illegitimates, even legitimated. They built a body of opinion that went in quite the other direction from the expansive view of bastards' inheritance rights endorsed by Niccolini and Ambrosini in the Covoni case. By the end of the century population was rising and, as Anthony Molho and others have argued, a more aristocratic cast had arisen in Florentine families. Bastards were more often the fodder of foundling homes than paternal homes, and the wishes of fathers like Giovanni Masi and Rinieri Dei could be ignored or argued aside, as could the statutes of Sarzana or Cortona. The later jurists diminished the legal and social role of illegitimates, but they could not remove the essential ambiguity surrounding them.

Conclusion: The Illegitimate Person

In a world that did not know or conceive of DNA tests, presumptions of legitimate filiation rested on social observations. As Bartolo da Sassoferrato put it in a *consilium:*

> it is to be seen what results from the naming of said natural child [as heir] in a testament, about which it is to be said that, although the Authentica Item siquis, Codex De naturalibus liberis, disposes that if someone calls someone his son and does not add *natural,* then if he was of a woman with whom marriage could be contracted, he is understood to be legitimate, because those words "marriage could be contracted" must be understood honorably and according to the good customs of the city; whence if she was such a woman with whom there could not honorably be a marriage, but it would be shameful, with respect to wealth and dignity, for example if some honorable and noble citizen should have children by some servant who served him or another, then by those words he cannot say he is legitimate because marriage cannot happen with that woman, at least honorably.[1]

Here, no matter what a testator was willing to say, the social relationships that were or were not in play about the person of the child deter-

1. Vat. Lat. 8069, fols. 39v–40r: "Secundo videndum est quod operetur nominatio predicta facta in testamento de dicto filio naturali ad quod dicendum est quod licet auct. item siquis C. de na. li. [*C. 5.27.11 in c.] disponat quod siquis dicat aliquem suum filium esse nec adiciat naturalem, quod si erat ex muliere cum qua nuptie contrahi possent intelligitur legitimus quia illa verba 'nuptie contrahi possent' debent intelligi honeste et secundum bonos mores civitatis, unde si talis esset mulier cum qua posset esse matrimonium non honeste sed appareret cum verecundia, inspectis divitiis dignitatibus, puta si aliquis honorabilis civis et nobilis habuerit filios ex aliqua famula que sibi vel alteri famulabatur tunc ex illis verbis non poterit dicere se legitimum quia nuptie cum illa muliere constare non possunt, scilicet honeste."

mined legitimacy and all that flowed from it. But as Bartolo otherwise had to acknowledge, the father was still able to legitimate the child and leave him or her property, if he so desired. As we have seen in the course of this book, Florentine fathers treated their bastards better or worse in broad conjunction with the sense of honor in parentage expressed by Bartolo. Bastards fathered by men when single on women who were also single and, if not of elevated social position, at least not slaves or lowly servants, were more likely to gain inheritance in some form and to be legitimated.

James Casey has speculated that illegitimacy was more easily tolerated when and where a lineage sense of kinship held primacy and was, conversely, less tolerable where and when relations within the household were more prominent in people's minds and actions.[2] J. P. Cooper also sees a lineage structure as more accommodating to bastards. Throughout Europe there was a narrowing of the sense of lineage to emphasize direct descent in the male line in the course of the fifteenth century, so inheritance rules tended to favor daughters over collateral males or even illegitimate sons over legitimate collaterals.[3] But Bartolo's statement would indicate that the lineage-based sense of honor and shame was a more powerful deterrent to acceptance of the child than the household economy or paternal intent. We have seen hostility to bastards expressed by their cousins (as Francesco Guicciardini's acerbic comments about Rinieri di Luigi) and lawsuits initiated by cousins, siblings (often legitimate sisters), and other kin.

Can we say that the prerogatives of lineage or of household advantaged the bastard or tolerated him? The materials from fifteenth-century Florence speak with ambivalence to this. Regarding lineage, we have seen both how patrikin at times took in and supported bastards, but we have also seen them dispute inheritances, unswayed by a blood connection that was illegitimate and so disavowable. Regarding household we have encountered the entire range of behavior from swift abandonment to careful nurturing and legitimation, career and inheritance. As illegitimates were found more often in wealthier and larger households, which also more often had a greater sense of lineage and numerous kin, it is difficult to say whether household or lineage did more to help those who were not fully members of either one.

2. Casey, *History of the Family,* chap. 5.
3. Cooper, "Patterns of Inheritance," 302.

As honor and power in Florence concentrated into the hands of fewer lineages by the sixteenth century, Florentines of the elite adopted strategies to preserve patrimony in a direct line.[4] It strikes me that any such aristocratic narrowing of lineage would function, in effect, to minimize the distance and difference between household and lineage—to reduce lineage to household. But any such narrowing in Florence does not seem to have contributed to any greater tendency to legitimate bastards and make them full heirs of a household's fortunes and its place within a lineage. Perhaps the number of legitimations recorded by the ducal official in the seventeenth century is indicative of a movement toward this option as needed. Conversely, the ever-growing population of the Innocenti is testimony to the willingness to abandon.

Our sources allow little ability to ascribe agency to Florentine bastards. We have encountered them as objects of parental and kindred actions more than anything. Still, as Marilyn Strathern reminds us, "another person may be the cause of action, not as one mind overriding another's, but in terms of the requirement of a relationship in which the presence of one party is necessary to and created by the other, and the necessity is construed as a matter of the difference between them."[5] Even that most quintessential legal *persona* of Renaissance Florence—the paterfamilias and head of household—did not attempt to claim control and sole responsibility for actions. The imperatives of relationships were presented as dictating actions. To return to a central source for our study, statements by heads of household in the catasto reveal again and again a sense of passivity before the demands of the city and economic vagaries, but also before those of kinship and other relationships.[6] Heads of household posed themselves caught in the demands of supporting a family, including illegitimate children at times. Of course, the catasto generically recognized these demands by allowing deductions for related dependents *(bocche)*. Demands on heads of household, in turn, were said to rest on relationships—the need to feed children or others, dower daughters, bury or memorialize parents, leave a sufficient patrimony to one's children. The paterfamilias occupied a position of transgenerational trust, and for

4. Kent, *Household and Lineage,* 127–32, 136–40; Molho, *Marriage Alliance,* 7 and 334; and generally Litchfield, *Emergence of a Bureaucracy.*

5. Strathern, conclusion to *Dealing with Inequality,* 294–95.

6. Conti, *L'imposta diretta a Firenze,* 341–48. Emblematic are statements such as "'non m'è possibile poterli pagare, che . . . non m'è restato nulla o piccola cosa'" or "'non è possibile a me poterli paghare, che come vedete non mi resta nulla.'"

our purposes it is necessary to recognize that illegitimate children muddied the waters.

The requirements of relationships continued to constrain fathers in relation to their bastards in the centuries following the fifteenth. The moralistic activism and control of the marriage process by the church following the Council of Trent has generally been seen as contributing to harsher treatment of bastards—to ending the so-called golden age. Jean-Pierre Bardet has observed a devaluing of the bastard even as matters of familial succession increased in importance versus the sort of collective solidarity that could shelter and accommodate the bastard. Pious fear of sexual sin slid quickly to condemnation of the child in his or her origins and an inability to integrate the bastard socially lest society face the risk of contamination.[7] It would require a separate extensive study of bastardy for the later period to confirm or deny this sense for Florence or anywhere else.

Initially foundling homes like the Innocenti played out a social function of containing demographic pressures. They took in not only "the fruits of relations that did not figure within the norm" but also showed that "this same norm was not so rigid and binding on the ethical level" as to criminalize the abandoning of legitimate children. Trent changed this.

> The same hospitals that had gathered [bastards] in ever growing numbers, progressively lost that social legitimacy that justified their existence and reinforced their functions. They became a lesser evil, the place that had permitted the secret abandonment of the baby and prevented the unnatural and sinful mother from resorting to infanticide. They became infamous places that ever more were felt as institutions in contrast to the new social ethic and in which the same legitimate children whom the fate and poverty of their parents had brought there lost the very presumption of legitimacy.[8]

The foundling homes became places for illegitimates only. Concomitant with this shift was a relieving of paternal responsibilities toward the illegitimate. Authorities ceased to try to learn the identity of fathers, to try

7. Jean-Pierre Bardet, "La société et l'abandon," in *Enfance abandonnée et société,* 8–13.

8. Povolo, "Dal versante dell'illegittimità," 126–27.

to get them to contribute to their offspring's support.[9] "[T]he vision of the illegitimate child of unknown parentage, deprived of any identity, tended to prevail over that of the natural child whose origin was known to all."[10]

The "optional" existence of the bastard illuminated the attributes of the automatic position of the legitimate (who, it must be acknowledged, could, and on rare occasion did, so misdistinguish himself as to merit disinheritance and exclusion from the family). Illegitimacy was a powerful, if highly ambiguous, stigma whose effects could not be thoroughly mitigated even by legitimation—even if this stigma had less to do with sexual sin than with the lack of position and relationships of the bastard.

The frustration of this subject is that those we study did not leave us their thoughts or even their actions. Their silence precludes us coming to any sense of the "self" a bastard may have had—individualistic or not. Those bastards we know best—Alberti, da Vinci—like second-generation immigrants eager to assimilate, did not advertise their origins or dwell on them. But these men are also proof that the bastard could produce, did have some social relationships, and in that sense had a sense of self akin to that of others as a location in a web of relationships.[11]

9. Ibid., 113, 115–16, 120–21; also Povolo's "Aspetti sociali e penali del reato d'infanticidio: Il caso di una contadina padovana nel '700," *Atti dell'Istituto Veneto di Scienze Lettere ed Arti* 138 (1979–80): 415–32; and Kertzer, *Sacrificed for Honor,* 72–101.

10. Cavallo and Cerrutti, "Female Honor," 101.

11. Cf. Carrier, *Gifts and Commodities,* 160–62.

Appendix

Legitimation of Cessino di Salvestro Cessini, 5 February 1411/2

(*Source:* Notarile antecosimiano 9037 [1408–11], fols. 373v–376r)

In dei nomine, amen. Antonius natus et heres quondam Tedicis quondam Jacopi de Albizis de Florentia, dei gratia ac sacri imperii lateranensis palatii comes, dilecto nobis in Christo Cessino nato Silvestri Lodovici Cessini lanificis de Florentia salutem in domino sempiternam.

Licet imperialis maiestatis super omnium temporalium dignitatum speculum constit populos fide Christianitatis inhabites suo salutifero iusto et equo intuitu regat et dirigat universos, attamen quia illa gloriosa persona qui imminet semper et ubique non potest variis et diversis exigentibus negotiorum meritis exibere et tradere se petentem, et plerumque contingit quod ipsa de medio divino subtracta iudicio mundus caret, propter que necessario expedit ut romanus princeps sue potestatis et iurisdictionis honores inter proteres suos et alios nobiles et egregios excelsos Christi fideles privilegiis et rescriptis cesareus partiatur, qui vice sua et imperii fidelibus munera offerant pretiosa, hinc est quod serenissimus princeps et dominus dominus Karolus quartus romanorum imperator semper augustus antistes dictum olim Tedicem patrem dicti Antonii et ipsius Tedici heredes masculos in cesareis privilegiis et rescriptis et largifluis gratiis multipliciter decoravit per suas patentes libras et imperiale privilegium sub isto tenore, videlicet:

In nomine sacre et individue trinitatis feliciter, amen. Karolus quartus divina favente clementia romanorum imperator semper augustus et Boemie rex ad perpetuam rei memoriam, nobilibus Alexio et Tedici natis Jacopi de Albizis de Florentia sacri lateranensis palatii comitibus suis et [374r] imperii sacri fidelibus dilectis gratiam suam et omne bonum sceptrigera cesaree dignitatis sublimitas sicut inferioribus potestatibus offitii et dignitatis elatione prefertur. Et commissus sibi fideles optate gubernet consolationis presidio et tronus cesareus tanto solidatur felicius et uberiori prosperitate profierat quanto in deficientis sue virtutis donaria largiori benignitatis munere fuderit in subiectos sic acoruscante splendore imperialis solii nobilitates alie velud a sole radii prodeuntes ita fidelium status et conditiones illustrent, quod prime lucis integritas minorati luminis detrimenta non patitur, ymo ampliores scintillantis iubaris expectato decore perfunditur dum in circuitu sedet augmentum spectabilium comitum et procerum numerus ad imperii sacri decorem feliciter adaugetur sane de vestre fidei et circumspectionis industria plenam habentes fiduciam, vos et heredes vestros legiptimos masculinis sexus a vobis in perpetuum descendentes sacri lateranensis palatii comites creamus facimus et prout melius possumus ordinamus decernentes et hoc imperiali statuentes edicto. Quod omnibus iuribus privilegiis gratiis et libertatibus uti et gaudere possitis quibus ceteri comites lateranenses palatii de iure vel consuetudine quomodolibet potuissent, dantes et concedentes vobis et heredibus vestris supradictis autoritatem et plenariam potestatem tabelliones seu notarios publicos faciendi, et eos cum penna et calamario, ut moris est, de tabellionatus offitio investendi dum tamen ad praticam et executionem eiusdem offitii habiles eos inveneritis super quo vestram et successorum vestrorum conscientias oneramus. Nec non instituendi iudices ordinarios iuxta sacrarum legum legitima instituta et a tabellionibus et iudicibus ordinariis tempore creationis et institutionis eorum iuxta iuramenta recipiendi, ut tabellio iuret in hec verba: Ego N. promicto et iuro quod fidelis ero serenissimo et invictissimo principi et domino domino Karolo quarto divina favente clementia romanorum imperatori semper augusto et Boemie regi illustri domino meo glorioso et omnibus successoribus suis romanorum imperatoribus et regibus legictime intrantibus. Neque unquam ero in consilio ubi periculum eorum tractetur bonum et salutem eorum promanebo dampna eorum pro mea possibilitate avertam fideliter et instrumenta seu contractus quoscunque non scribam in papiro seu carta veteri aut ab rasa sed in membrana munda et nova testamenta codicillos et quascunque ultimas voluntates, nec non dicta testium conscribam fideliter et ea occulte servabo nullique pandam donec debeant aut mandato iudicis seu alia exigente iustitia publicari causas miserabilium personarum nec non pontes hospitalia emendationes viarum publicarum omni tempore promovebo [374v] et offitium meum exercebo fideliter non actendendo munera odium vel amorem, sic me deus adiuvet et gratia dei evangelia. Iuramentum vero iudicis ordinarii erit in hec verba: Ego N. iuro et promicto quod fidelis ero serenissimo ac invictissimo principi ac domino domino Karolo quarto divina favente clementia romanorum imperatori semper augusto et Boemie regi illustri domino meo glorioso et omnibus successoribus eius romanorum imperatoribus sive regibus legictime intrantibus, neque unquam ero in consilio ubi periculum eius tractetur bonum et salutem eorum promovebo dampna eorum pro mea possibilitate advertam fideliter et offitium meum exercebo fideliter non actendendo munera hodium vel amorem, sic me deus adiuvet and sacra dei evangelia. Decernentes et hoc imperiali statuentes edicto quod tabelliones seu iudices ordinarii per vos creati facti et instituti modo quo premictur, postquam iuramenta predicta presenterint offitia sua valeant, ubique locorum absque impedimento quolibet exercere et operationes eorum vim habeant omnimodam. Et vigorem preterea auctoritate imperiali predicta damus concedimus et largimur vobis et predictis successoribus vestris quod legiptimare possitis bastardos, manseres, nothos, spurios, et quoslibet alios ex illicito et inconcesso coitu procreatos in vita seu in morte parentum ipsosque et eorum quemlibet ad legiptima iura reducere et omnem ab eis tollere maculam geniture, ut offitiis quibuscunque preesee valeant et ad actus singulos publicos et privatos admicti ad instar aliorum qui sunt de legitimo matrimonio derivati. Natis illustrium principum comitum et baronum dumtaxat exceptis et quod virtute legiptimationis huiusmodi in testamento et ab intestato ad equales succedant cum legiptimis portiones, non obstantibus aliquibus legibus imperialibus sive constitutionibus quibuscunque. Quibus omnibus si et in quantum presenti nostri largitioni adversari censentur per omnia derogamus etiam si de hiis iure vel consuetudine deberit in presentibus fieri mentio spetialis. Nulli ergo animo hominum liceat hanc nostre creationis factionis, ordinationis, decreti, statuti, concessionis, largitionis, et derogationis paginam infringere seu ei quovis ausu temerario contrarie. Siquis autem contrarium actentare presupserit indignationem nostram gravissimam et penam centum marcarum auri purissimi totiens quotiens contra factum fuerit, se moverit inremissibiliter in cursurum quarum medietatem imperiali nostro erario sive fisco residuam vero partem iniuriam passorum usibus decernimus applicari. Signum serenissimi principis et domini Karoli quarti romanorum imperatoris invictissimi et gloriosissimi Boemie regis. Testes huius rei sunt venerabiles Johannes archepiscopus Pragensis apostolice sedis legatus, Johannes Clemucensis, Albertus Lathomistensis, Henricus Voarimensis, et Johannes Nissuensis ecclesiarum episcopi, illustres Lodovicus et Henricus Brigensis, Conradus Olissincenis, Heinricus [375r] senior Saganensis, Pazemislaus Teschinensis, Heinricus Falbengergensis, Ralbeo Opdicun, Johannes et Voenceslaus Opanie, Bunzilaus Lignicensis duces spectabiles, Johannes comes de Hardechre et nobilis Patrus de Voartemberg, imperialis curie nostre magister Timo de Coldicz, Benessius de Voartenberg dictus de Voessel, Jaroslaus de Stermberg, Andreas de Daka, Johannes de Burkeristem, et aliquis plures nostri et imperii sacri principes nobilis et fideles presentium, sub imperialis nostre maiestatis sigillo testimonio litterarum datum Prage anno millesimo trecentesimo septuagesimo sexto, indictione quarta, decima nona Decembris regnorum nostrorum anno trigesimo primo, imperii vero vigesimo secundo.

Cum igitur, coram nobis Antonio comiti predicto per dictum Silvestrum genitorem tuum fuerit et sit coram nobis supplicatum quod ipse Silvester intendit, cupit, et desiderat te Cessinum filium ipsius Silvestri non de legiptimo matrimonio natum sed progenitum, natum, et creatum ex ipso Silvestro, tempore quo solutus erat et nullam legitimam uxorem habebat, et ex quadam muliere nomine Lucia soluta et matrimonio non ligata, serva tamen dicti Silvestri, restituere vere et antique ingenuitati et iuri legiptimo, ut sub potestate eius etiam consistas et in omnibus et per omnia et quo ad omnia legiptimare et legiptimum constituere nil a legiptimis filiis differendo et te ipsum Cessinum licet de non legiptimo geniture sue, sis naturalis sive spureus natus, incestuosus sive adulterinus, sive ex quacunque coitu natus legiptimare et legiptimum constituere et ad omnia iura habilitare omnem tue geniture maculam abolendo cum omnibus clausibus opportunis ex auctoritate nobis concessa, non obstante alicuius macula geniture benigniter dignaremur. Nos vero ipsius Silvestri patris tui supplicationibus et petitionibus annuentes et benigniter inclinati cum illis se reddere debeat imperialis celsitudo propria et benigna, qui virtutibus prefulgent et moribus et quos fama decorat et nobilitat, te Cessinum in conspectu nostro personaliter existente et genuflexum coram nobis humiliter ac constitutum, dicto Silvestro genitore tuo presente et devote petente et volente, et de ipsius Silvestri consensu et voluntate expressa, auctoritate imperiali prefata quocunque modo natus sis sive ex soluto et soluta, sive ex ligato et ligata, sive ligato et soluta, sive soluto et ligata, sive notus sive incestuosus, sive adulterinus, sive ex quocunque dampnato coitu natus, restituimus vere et antique ingenuitati et iuri legiptimo et sub potestate dicti Silvestri genitoris tui consistas et in omnibus et per omnia legiptimamus et legiptimum facimus et constituimus nil a legiptimis filiis differendo seu differentiam facientes et omnem geniture tue predicte notam maculam, [375v] defectum, seu impedimentum astergentes et penitus abolentes, et auctoritate eadem te ad omnia iura legiptima in integrum restituimus et habilitamus, ipsaque tibi concedimus volumus, decernimus, et mandamus quod tu prout et tanquam legiptimus et de legiptimo matrimonio natus in omnibus bonis paternis et maternis et aliorum adscendentium et descendentium colateralium sive transversalium, cognatorum et agnatorum, propriis et feudalibus et cuiuscunque generis acquisitis vel acquirendis ex testamento vel ab intestato succedere possis. Ita tamen quod per hanc legiptimationem non preiudicet in totum aliis liberis et descendentibus pereuntum tuorum, si supersunt vel supererunt, sed equali portione succedas prout per alias iura succederis si defectus natalium non obstaret, et quemadmodum si esses de legiptimo matrimonio procreatus, agnatisque et cognatis parentum tuarum in quovis gradu constitutus agnatus et cognatus efficiaris et sis, et reciproce sint ipsi tibi et etiam ad omnes actus publicos et civiles, offitia et honores, si se casus ingesserit, admictaris et admicti valeas et tuam possis in omnibus persequi actionem, macula quacunque cuiuslibet prolis inlegiptime non obstante, et auctoritate imperiali predicta volumus et mandamus in omnibus et per omnia et quo ad omnia te esse et perinde haberi ac si tu ipse Cessinus essis filius legitimus et naturalis dicti Silvestri et de legiptimo matrimonio etiam ab initio procreatus, non obstantibus quibuscunque legibus, iuribus, vel constitutionibus que huic legiptimat, et hiis que premissa sunt quomodolibet obstant vel obstare possent, et illis potissime que legiptimari spurios, naturales, natos incestuosos, manzeres, seu adulterinos nisi ex certa scientia autoritate imperiali prefata spetialiter derogamus et pro expressis hic haberi volumus et mandamus.

In cuius legiptimationis et habilitationis predicte signum te prefatum Cessinum tenore presentium et anulo aureo nostro legiptime et actualiter investimus. Rogantes nec non et monentes omnis et singulus cuiuscunque status et conditionis existant et eisdem sub penis imperialibus in privilegio de quo supra fit mentio contentis comminantes et nichilominus strictissime, et iungentes quatenus te Cessinum pro legiptimo et ut legiptimum de cetero recipiant et admictant et habeant atque tractent cum effectu et hanc paginam legiptimationis non infringant, vel ausu temerario quomodolibet contradicunt alioquin imperiali indignatione et centum marcarum auri purissimi penam incurrant, quarum medietatem imperiali errario supradicto sive fisco, residuam vero parte nobis nostrisque successoribus decernimus applicari. Ad cuius exactionem quantum in nobis erit possibile procedemus decernentes ex nunc irritum et inane si secus a quaquam contra predicta vel aliquid predictorum quicquam fuerit actentante. In quorum testimonio predictas litteras fieri fecimus et in publicam formam redigi et registrari per ser Franciscum Pieri Giacomini notarium florentinum. Data et acta fuerunt omnia [376r] predicta in populo sancti Martini de Florentia in apoteca dicti Antonii comitis predicti, anno domini incarnationis millesimo quadringentesimo undecimo, indictione quinta, tempore sanctissimo in Christo patris et domini domino Johanni divina clementia pape xxiii, die quinto mensis februarii. Et presentibus testibus ad predicta omnia vocatis, habitis, et rogatis, Johanni filio olim dicti Lodovici Lippi Cessini et fratre carnali suprascripti Silvestri, et Michaele Johannis lanifice populi sancti Simonis de Florentia, et Francisco domini Johannis de Zatis populi sancti Pauli de Florentia, et Agnolo Laurentii de Machiavellis populi sancte Felicitatis de Florentia, et civibus honorabilibus florentinis et aliis pluribus.

Item postea dictis anno et indictione et die et loco et coram dictis suprascriptis testibus ad infrascripta vocatis, habitis, et rogatis. De imperiali plenitudine potestatis in egregios viros Alexium et Tedicem natos Jacopi de Albizis de Florentia et eorum descendentes comites lateranenses palatii idcirco creandum tabellionem et iudicem ordinarium iurisdictio emanavit ut eiusdem iurisdictio gratiam imperii refunderet in subiectos. Eapropter ex indulto eis super hoc at imperiali culmine privilegio spetiali, ut in eodem evidentius contingenti, vir nobilis Antonius olim dicti Tedicis comes suprascriptus suprascriptum Cessinum Silvestri publicum et autoritate notarium et tabellionem ac etiam iudicem ordinarium creavit et fecit ipsumque Cessinum flexis genibus devote recipientem de arte et officio tabellionatus et iudicis ordinarii cum anulo ac etiam penna et calamario lege investivit etc. Qui Cessinus etc. promisit etc. iuravit etc. ut supra in forma privilegii etc. omnia facere etc. ad que tenor etc. Qui Antonius decrevit eum notarium etc. et quod acta per eum valeant etc. sub pena in suprascripto restitutionis ad positam etc. Rogantes et mandantes mihi notario publico de predictis confici instrumentum etc.

Bibliography

Manuscript Sources

Archivio di Stato, Florence (ASF)
- Acquisti e Doni
- Arti:
  - Arte degli Albergatori
  - Arte di Calimala
  - Arte di Cambio
  - Arte dei Fornai
  - Arte della Lana
  - Arte dei Medici e Speziali
  - Arte dei Vinattieri
- Carte strozziane
- Catasto
- Diplomatico
- Manoscritti
- Notarile antecosimiano (old designation, pre-1988, alphanumeric; new designation numeric)
- Podestà
- Provvisioni—registri
- Signori e Collegi, Deliberazioni in forze d'ordinaria autorità
- Statuti del comune di Firenze

Biblioteca Apostolica Vaticana
- Ottob. Lat.
- Vat. Lat.

Biblioteca Nazionale Centrale, Florence (BNF)
- Landau Finaly
- Magliabechiano
- Principale

Primary Sources

Alberti, Leon Battista. *De iciarchia.* In *Opere volgari,* edited by Cecil Grayson, 2:187–286. Turin: Einaudi, 1966.

———. *I libri della famiglia*. Edited by Ruggiero Romano and Alberto Tenenti. Turin: Einaudi, 1969.

Barbaro, Francesco. *De re uxoria*. Edited by A. Gnesotto. *Atti e memorie della R. Accademia di scienze, lettere ed arte di Padova*, n.s. 32 (1915): 6–105.

Bartolo da Sassoferrato. *In primam digesti novi partem commentaria*. Venice, 1580.

———. *In primam ff. veteris commentaria*. Venice, 1585.

———. *In primam infortiati partem commentaria*. Lyons, 1544.

———. *In primam infortiati partem commentaria*. Venice, 1581.

———. *In secundam codicis partem commentaria*. Venice, 1580.

———. *In secundam digesti novi partem commentaria*. Lyons, 1544.

———. *In secundam infortiati partem commentaria*. Venice, 1581.

———. *Opera omnia*. 10 vols. Venice, 1615.

———. *Opera omnia*. 10 vols. Venice, 1602.

Barzi, Benedetto. *Tractatus de filiis non legitime natis*. In *Tractatus universi iuris*, vol. 8, part 2, fols. 24ra–29vb. Venice, 1584.

Boccaccio, Giovanni. *The Corbaccio*. Translated by Dennis J. McAuliffe. Urbana: University of Illinois Press, 1975.

———. *Decamerone*. Edited by Vittore Branca. Turin: Einaudi, 1980.

Bottrigari, Jacopo. *Lectura super codice*. Reprint ed., Bologna, 1973.

Brucker, Gene, ed. *The Society of Renaissance Florence: A Documentary Study*. New York: Harper and Row, 1971.

———, ed. *Two Memoirs of Renaissance Florence*. Translated by Julia Martines. New York: Harper and Row, 1967.

Carnesecchi, Carlo. "Un fiorentino del secolo xv e le sue ricordanze domestiche." *Archivio storico italiano*, 5th ser., 4 (1889): 147–73.

Castellani, Francesco di Matteo. *Ricordanze*. Vol. 1: *Ricordanze A (1436–1459)*, vol. 2: *Quaternuccio e Giornale B (1459–1485)*. Edited by Giovanni Ciappelli. Florence: Olschki, 1992, 1995.

Cino da Pistoia. *In codicem et aliquot titulos primi pandectorum*. 2 vols. Frankfurt am Main, 1585. Reprint ed., Turin: Bottega d'Erasmo, 1964.

Corpus iuris canonici. Edited by Emil Friedberg. 2 vols. Leipzig: Tauchnitz, 1879.

Cotrugli, Benedetto. *Della mercatura et del mercante perfetto*. Venice, 1573.

da Butrio, Antonio. *In librum quartum decretalium commentaria*. Venice, 1578.

da Certaldo, Paolo. *Libro di buoni costumi*. Edited by A. Schiaffini. In *Mercanti scrittori: Ricordi nella Firenze tra Medioevo e Rinascimento*, edited by Vittore Branca, 1–99. Milan: Rusconi, 1986.

da Imola, Giovanni. *In primam digesti novi*. Bologna, 1580.

da Maino, Giasone. *In secundam codicis partem commentaria*. 1573.

d'Ancarano, Pietro. *Super quinto decretalium commentaria*. Bologna, 1581.

———. *Super tertio decretalium commentaria*. Bologna, 1581.

Decio, Filippo. *Consilia*. 2 vols. Venice, 1575.

———. *In primam et secundam codicis partem commentaria*. Venice, 1568.

Dino del Mugello. *Tractatus de successionibus*. In *Tractatus universi iuris*, vol. 8, part 1, fols. 318ra–319vb. Venice, 1584.

Diplovataccio, Tommaso. *Liber de claris iuris consultis, pars posterior.* Edited by Fritz Schulz and Hermann Kantorowicz. *Studia gratiana* 10 (1968).

Documenti inediti o poco noti per la storia della Misericordia di Firenze (1240–1525). Florence: Misericordia, 1940.

Durantis, Guglielmus. *Speculum iudiciale.* 1479.

———. *Speculum iudiciale.* Lyons, 1556.

Gherardi da Prato, Giovanni. *Il paradiso degli Alberti.* Edited by Enrico Malato. In *I Novellieri italiani,* edited by Antonio Lanza, vol. 10. Rome: Salerno Editrice, 1975.

Glossa ordinaria. 5 vols. Lyons, 1612.

Guicciardini, Francesco. *Ricordi, diari, memorie.* Edited by Mario Spinelli. Rome: Editori Riuniti, 1981.

Guido dell'Antella. "Ricordi." Edited by F. L. Polidori. *Archivio storico italiano,* 1st ser., 4 (1843): 3–24.

Hellman, Robert, and Richard O'Gorman, eds. *Fabliaux.* New York: Thomas Y. Crowell, 1965.

Hostiensis. *Summa aurea.* Venice, 1605.

Innocent IV. *Commentaria in v libros decretalium.* Frankfurt am Main, 1570. Reprint ed., Frankfurt am Main: Minerva, 1968.

Jacopo di Benvenuto. "Giardino di consolazione." In *Prosatori minori del Trecento: Scrittori di religione del Trecento volgarizzamenti,* edited by Giuseppe de Luca, 3:489–97. Milan: Riccardo Ricciardi, 1954. Reprint ed., Turin: Einaudi, 1977.

Karmin, Otto, ed. *La legge del catasto fiorentino del 1427.* Florence: Seeber, 1906.

Il libro di ricordanze dei Corsini. Edited by Armando Petrucci. Rome: Istituto Storico Italiano per il Medio Evo, 1965.

Lodovico a Sardi. *Tractatus de naturalibus liberis.* In *Tractatus universi iuris,* vol. 8, part 2, fols. 29vb–45va. Venice, 1584.

Macinghi negli Strozzi, Alessandra. *Lettere di una gentildonna fiorentina del secolo xv ai figliuoli esuli.* Edited by Cesare Guasti. Florence: Sansoni, 1877.

Martines, Lauro, ed. and trans. *An Italian Renaissance Sextet.* New York: Marsilio, 1994.

Morandini, Francesca, ed. "Statuti e ordinamenti dell' Ufficio dei pupilli et adulti nel periodo della Repubblica fiorentina (1388–1534)." *Archivio storico italiano* 113 (1955): 522–51.

Morelli, Giovanni. *Ricordi.* Edited by Vittore Branca. Florence: LeMonnier, 1956.

Niccolini di Camugliano, Ginevra. *The Chronicles of a Florentine Family, 1200–1470.* London: Jonathan Cape, 1933.

Ordinamenta iustitiae communis et populi Florentiae, anni mcclxxxxiii. Edited by Francesco Bonaini. Florence: Archivio storico italiano, 1891.

Palmieri, Matteo. *Della vita civile.* Edited by Felice Battaglia. Bologna: Zanichelli, 1944.

Paolo di Castro. *Consilia.* 2 vols. N.p., 1522.

———. *Consilia.* 3 vols. Frankfurt am Main, 1582.

———. *In secundam codicis partem commentaria.* Lyons, 1553.
———. *In secundam digesti novi partem commentaria.* Lyons, 1553.
Pistarini, Geo, ed. *Testi per lo studio del Medioevo in Liguria.* Genoa, n.d.
Roselli, Antonio. *Tractatus legitimationum.* In *Tractatus universi iuris,* vol. 8, part 2, fols. 75ra–90va. Venice, 1584.
Sacchetti, Franco. *Il trecentonovelle.* Edited by Antonio Lanza. Florence: Sansoni, 1984.
Scala, Bartrolomeo della. "Dialogus de legibus et iudiciis." Edited by L. Borglia. *Bibliofilia* 42 (1940): 252–82.
Sercambi, Giovanni. *Novelle.* 2 vols. Edited by Giovanni Sinicropi. Bari: Laterza, 1972.
Sozzini, Bartolomeo. *Consilia.* 5 vols. Venice, 1579.
Statuta antiquissima Saone (1345). 2 vols. Edited by Laura Balletto. Genoa: Collana Storica di Fonti e Studi, 1971.
Statuta populi et communis Florentiae, anno salutis mccccxv. 3 vols. Freiburg [Florence], 1778–83.
Statuti di Perugia dell'anno mcccxlii. Edited by Giustiniano degli Azzi. Rome: E. Loescher, 1913.
Gli statuti veneziani di Jacopo Tiepolo del 1242 e le loro glosse. Edited by Roberto Cessi. Venice: Carlo Ferrari, 1938.
Lo statuto del Bergamo del 1331. Edited by Claudia Storti Storchi. Milan: Giuffrè, 1986.
Statuto di Arezzo (1327). Edited by Giulia Marri Camerani. Florence: Deputazione per la Storia Patria per la Toscana, 1946.
Storia degli stabilimenti di beneficenza e d'istruzione elementare gratuita della città di Firenze. Edited by Luigi Passerini. Florence: Le Monnier, 1853.
Sozzini, Mariano. *Nova et utilissima commentaria super secunda parte libri quinti decretalium.* Venice, 1593.
Ubaldi, Angelo degli. *Consilia.* Frankfurt am Main, 1575.
———. *In primam digesti veteris commentaria.* 1580.
———. *Opus ac lectura autenticorum.* Venice, 1485.
Ubaldi, Baldo degli. *In decretalium volumen commentaria.* Venice, 1595. Reprint ed., Turin: Bottega d'Erasmo, 1971.
———. *In primos libros codicis commentaria.* Lyons, 1546.
———. *Opera omnia.* 10 vols. Venice, 1577.
Vasari, Giorgio. *Lives of the Most Eminent Painters, Sculptors, and Architects.* 2 vols. Translated by Jonathan Foster. London: George Bell and Sons, 1878.
Velluti, Donato. *Cronica domestica di Messer Donato Velluti.* Edited by Isidoro del Lungo and Guglielmo Volpi. Florence: Sansoni, 1914.

Secondary Sources

Airaldi, Gabriella. ". . . bastardos, spurios, manzeres, naturales, incestuosos . . ." In *Studi e documenti su Genova e l'Oltremare,* 319–55. Genoa: Università di Genova, Istituto di Paleografia e Storia Medievale, 1974.
Albini, Giuliana. "I bambini nella società lombarda del Quattrocento: Una realtà

ignorata o protetta?" In *La Famiglia e la vita quotidiana in Europa dal '400 al '600: Fonti e problemi,* 23–50. Atti del convegno internazionale, Milano, 1–4 December 1983. Rome: Ministero per i Beni Culturali e Ambientali, 1986.

Ariès, Philippe. "The Indissoluble Marriage." In *Western Sexuality: Practice and Precept in Past and Present Times,* edited by Philippe Ariès and André Béjin, 140–57. Translated by Anthony Forster. Oxford: Blackwell, 1985.

Ariès, Philippe, and Georges Duby, eds. *A History of Private Life.* Vol. 3: *Passions of the Renaissance.* Edited by Roger Chartier. Cambridge: Harvard University Press, 1989.

Ascheri, Mario. " 'Consilium sapientis,' perizia medica e 'res iudicata': Diritto dei 'dottori' e istituzioni comunali." In *Proceedings of the Fifth International Congress of Medieval Canon Law,* edited by Stephan Kuttner, 533–79. Vatican City: Biblioteca Apostolica Vaticana, 1980.

———. "Le fonti e la flessibilità del diritto comune: Il paradosso del *consilium sapientis.*" In *Legal Consulting in the Civil Law Tradition,* edited by Mario Ascheri, Ingrid Baumgärtner, and Julius Kirshner, 11–53. Berkeley: Robbins Collection, 1999.

———. *Tribunali, giuristi e istituzioni dal Medioevo all'età moderna.* Bologna: Il Mulino, 1989.

Ascheri, Mario, Ingrid Baumgärtner, and Julius Kirshner, eds. *Legal Consulting in the Civil Law Tradition.* Berkeley: Robbins Collection, 1999.

Astarita, Tommaso. *Village Justice: Community, Family, and Popular Culture in Early Modern Italy.* Baltimore: Johns Hopkins University Press, 1999.

Autrand, Françoise. "Naissance illégitime et service de l'État: Les enfants naturels dans le milieu de robe parisien xive–xve siècle." *Revue historique* 267 (1982): 289–303.

Aznar Gil, Federico R. "Die Illegitimen auf der Iberischen Halbinsel im Spätmittelalter." In *Illegitimität im Spätmittelalter,* edited by Ludwig Schmugge, 171–206. Munich: R. Oldenbourg, 1994.

Baker, J. H. *Introduction to English Legal History.* London: Butterworths, 1971.

Balletto, Laura. "Stranieri e forestieri a Genova: Schiavi e manomessi (secolo xv)." In *Forestieri e stranieri nelle città basso-medievali,* 263–83. Florence: Salimbene, 1988.

Barbagli, Marzio. *Sotto lo stesso tetto: Mutamenti della famiglia in Italia dal xv al xx secolo.* Bologna: Il Mulino, 1984.

Bardet, Jean-Pierre. "La société et l'abandon." In *Enfance et abandonnée et société en Europe xive–xxe siècle,* 3–26. Collection de l'École Française de Rome 140. Rome: École Française de Rome, 1991.

Baudin, Maurice. *Les bâtards au théâtre en France de la Renaissance à la fin du xviiie siècle.* Baltimore: Johns Hopkins University Press, 1932.

Baumgärtner, Ingrid. "Consilia: Quellen zur Familie in Krise und Kontinuität." In *Die Familie als sozialer und historischer Verband: Untersuchungen zum Spätmittelalter und zur frühen Neuzeit,* edited by Peter-Johannes Schuler, 43–67. Sigmaringen: Jan Thorbecke, 1987.

———. "Rechtsnorm und Rechtsanwendung in der venezianischen Terraferma des 15. Jahrhunderts: Die Consilia von Bartolomeo Cipolla." In *Consilia im späten Mittelalter: Zum historischen Aussagewert einer Quellengattung,* edited by Ingrid Baumgärtner, 79–111. Sigmaringen: Jan Thorbecke, 1995.

———. "Stadtgeschichte und Consilia im italienischen Spätmittelalter: Eine Quellengattung und ihre Möglichkeiten." *Zeitschrift für Historische Forschung* 90 (1990): 129–54.

———, ed. *Consilia im späten Mittelalter: Zum historischen Aussagewert einer Quellengattung.* Sigmaringen: Jan Thorbecke, 1995.

Bec, Christian. *Les marchands écrivains: Affaires et humanisme à Florence, 1375–1434.* Paris: Mouton, 1967.

Bell, Rudolph M. *Fate and Honor, Family and Village: Demographic and Cultural Change in Rural Italy since 1800.* Chicago: University of Chicago Press, 1979.

Bellomo, Manlio. *The Common Legal Past of Europe, 1000–1800.* Translated by Lydia G. Cochrane. Washington: Catholic University of America Press, 1995.

———. "Erede e eredità (diritto intermedio)." In *Enciclopedia del diritto,* 15:184–95. Milan: Giuffrè, 1966.

———. *Problemi di diritto familiare nell'età dei comuni: Beni paterni e "pars filii."* Milan: Giuffrè, 1968.

———. *Ricerche sui rapporti patrimoniali tra coniugi: Contributo alla storia della famiglia medievale.* Milan: Giuffrè, 1961.

———. *Saggio sull'università nell'età del diritto comune.* Catania: Giannotta, 1979.

———. *Società e istituzioni in Italia dal medioevo agli inizi dell'età moderna.* 3d ed. Catania: Giannotta, 1982.

Belloni, Annalisa. *Professori giuristi a Padova nel secolo xv: Profili bio-bibliografici e cattedre.* Frankfurt am Main: Klostermann, 1986.

Berengo, Marino. *Nobili e mercanti nella Lucca del Cinquecento.* Turin: Einaudi, 1965.

Berlinguer, Luigi. "Considerazioni su storiografia e diritto." *Studi storici* 15 (1974): 3–56.

Besta, Enrico. *Le successioni nella storia del diritto italiano.* Milan: Giuffrè, 1936.

Bestor, Jane Fair. "Bastardy and Legitimacy in the Formation of a Regional State in Italy: The Estense Succession." *Comparative Studies in Society and History* 38 (1996): 549–85.

Black, J. "Constitutional Ambitions, Legal Realities." In *Florentine Tuscany: Structures and Practices of Power,* edited by William Connell and Andrea Zorzi, 48–64. Cambridge: Cambridge University Press, 2000.

Black-Michaud, Jacob. *Cohesive Force: Feud in the Mediterranean and the Middle East.* New York: St. Martin's Press, 1975.

Blum, Carol. "Of Women and the Land: Legitimizing Husbandry." In *Early Modern Conceptions of Property,* edited by John Brewer and Susan Staves, 161–69. London: Routledge, 1995.

Boehm, Christopher. *Blood Revenge: The Enactment and Management of*

Conflict in Montenegro and Other Tribal Societies. Philadelphia: University of Pennsylvania Press, 1987.

Bornstein, Daniel E. *The Bianchi of 1399: Popular Devotion in Late Medieval Italy.* Ithaca, N.Y.: Cornell University Press, 1993.

———. "The Wedding Feast of Roberto Malatesta and Isabetta da Montefeltro: Ceremony and Power." *Renaissance and Reformation,* n.s. 12 (1988): 101–17.

Boswell, John. *Christianity, Social Tolerance, and Homosexuality: Gay People in Western Europe from the Christian Era to the Fourteenth Century.* Chicago: University of Chicago Press, 1980.

———. *The Kindness of Strangers: The Abandonment of Children in Western Europe from Late Antiquity to the Renaissance.* New York: Pantheon, 1988.

Bourdieu, Pierre. "The Force of Law: Toward a Sociology of the Juridical Field." *Hastings Law Journal* 38 (1987): 814–53.

———. "Rites as Acts of Institution." In *Honor and Grace in Anthropology,* edited by J. G. Peristiany and Julian Pitt-Rivers, 79–89. Cambridge: Cambridge University Press, 1992.

Branca, Vittore. *Boccaccio: The Man and His Works.* Translated and edited by Dennis J. McAuliffe. New York: New York University Press, 1976.

Braunstein, Philippe. "The Emergence of the Individual: Toward Intimacy, the Fourteenth and Fifteenth Centuries." In *A History of Private Life,* edited by Philippe Ariès and Georges Duby. Vol. 2: *Revelations of the Medieval World,* edited by Georges Duby, 535–630. Translated by Arthur Goldhammer. Cambridge: Harvard University Press, 1988.

Brinton, Crane. *French Revolutionary Laws on Illegitimacy.* Cambridge: Harvard University Press, 1936.

Brucker, Gene. "A Civic Debate on Florentine Higher Education (1460)." *Renaissance Quarterly* 34 (1981): 517–33.

———. "Florence and Its University, 1348–1434." In *Action and Conviction in Early Modern Europe: Essays in Memory of E. H. Harbison,* edited by Theodore K. Rabb and Jerrold E. Siegel, 220–36. Princeton: Princeton University Press, 1969.

———. *Florentine Politics and Society, 1343–1378.* Princeton: Princeton University Press, 1962.

———. *Giovanni and Lusanna: Love and Marriage in Renaissance Florence.* Berkeley and Los Angeles: University of California Press, 1986.

Brugi, Biagio. "Sentenze di giudici antichi o opinioni comuni di dottori." In *Per la storia della giurisprudenza e delle università italiane: Nuovi saggi,* 81–96. Turin: UTET, 1921.

Brundage, James. *Law, Sex, and Christian Society in Medieval Europe.* Chicago: University of Chicago Press, 1987.

———. "The Medieval Advocate's Profession." *Law and History Review* 6 (1988): 439–64.

Bulst, Neithard. "Illegitime Kinder—viele oder wenige? Quantitative Aspekte der Illegitimität im spätmittelalterlichen Europa." In *Illegitimität im Spätmittelalter,* edited by Ludwig Schmugge, 21–39. Munich: R. Oldenbourg, 1994.

Burckhardt, Jacob. *The Civilization of the Renaissance in Italy.* Translated by S. G. C. Middlemore. Revised ed. by Irene Gordon. New York: Penguin, 1960.

Burke, Peter. "Representations of the Self from Petrarch to Descartes." In *Rewriting the Self: Histories from the Renaissance to the Present,* edited by Roy Porter, 17–28. London: Routledge, 1997.

Cain, Maureen, and Kalman Kulcsar. "Thinking Disputes: An Essay on the Origins of the Dispute Industry." *Law and Society Review* 16 (1981–82): 375–402.

Calleri, Santi. *L'arte dei giudici e notai di Firenze nell'età comunale e nel suo statuto del 1344.* Milan: Giuffrè, 1969.

Cammarosano, Paolo. "Les structures familiales dans les villes de l'Italie communale, xiie–xive siècles." In *Famille et parenté dans l'Occident médiéval,* edited by Georges Duby and Jacques Le Goff, 181–94. Rome: Ecole Française de Rome, 1977.

Campbell, J. K. *Honour, Family, and Patronage.* Oxford: Clarendon Press, 1964.

Canning, Joseph P. "A Fourteenth-Century Contribution to the Theory of Citizenship: Political Man and the Problem of Created Citizenship in the Thought of Baldus de Ubaldis." In *Authority and Power: Studies on Medieval Law and Government Presented to Walter Ullmann on His Seventieth Birthday,* edited by Brian Tierney and Peter Linehan, 197–212. Cambridge: Cambridge University Press, 1980.

———. *The Political Thought of Baldus de Ubaldis.* Cambridge: Cambridge University Press, 1987.

Cappellini, Paolo. "'Status' accipitur tripliciter: Postilla breve per un'anamnesi di 'capacità giuridica' e 'sistema del diritto romano attuale.'" *Annali dell'Università di Ferrara, scienze giuridiche,* n.s. 1 (1987): 29–97.

Caravale, M. "Fedecommesso (storia)." *Enciclopedia del diritto,* 17:109–14. Milan: Giuffrè, 1968.

Carbasse, Jean-Marie. "Currant nudi: Le répression de l'adultère dans le Midi médiéval (xiie–xve siècles)." In *Droit, histoire et sexualité,* edited by Jacques Poumarède and Jean-Pierre Royer, 83–104. Toulouse: Publications de l'Espace Juridique, 1987.

Carlier, Myriam. "Paternity in Late Medieval Flanders." In *Secretum scriptorum: Liber alumnorum Walter Prevenier,* edited by Wim Blockmans, Marc Boone, and Thérèse de Hemptinne, 235–58. Leuven: Garant, 1999.

Caroci, G. "Notizie e curiosità storiche fiorentine." *Arte e storia,* 3d ser., 18 (1899): 131–35.

Carrier, James G. *Gifts and Commodities: Exchange and Western Capitalism since 1700.* London: Routledge, 1995.

Carrithers, Michael, Steven Collins, and Steven Lukes, eds. *The Category of the Person: Anthropology, Philosophy, History.* Cambridge: Cambridge University Press, 1985.

Casey, James. *The History of the Family.* Oxford: Blackwell, 1989.

Cavallar, Osvaldo. *Francesco Guicciardini giurista: I Ricordi degli onorari.* Milan: Giuffrè, 1991.

———. "Lo 'stare fermo a bottega' del Guicciardini: giuristi consulenti, procuratori e notai nel Rinascimento." In *Consilia im späten Mittelalter: Zum historischen Aussagewert einer Quellengattung,* edited by Ingrid Baumgärtner, 113–44. Sigmaringen: Jan Thorbecke, 1995.

Cavallar, Osvaldo, Susanne Degenring, and Julius Kirshner, eds. *A Grammar of Signs: Bartolo da Sassoferrato's "Tract on Insignia and Coats of Arms."* Berkeley: Robbins Collection, 1995.

Cavallo, Sandra, and Simona Cerruti. "Female Honor and the Social Control of Reproduction in Piedmont between 1600 and 1800." In *Sex and Gender in Historical Perspective,* edited by Edward Muir and Guido Ruggiero, 73–109. Translated by Margaret A. Gallucci with Mary M. Gallucci and Carole C. Gallucci. Baltimore: Johns Hopkins University Press, 1990.

Cavanna, Adriano. "Il ruolo del giurista nell'età del diritto comune." *Studia et documenta historiae et iuris* 44 (1978): 95–138.

Chambers, D. S. *A Renaissance Cardinal and His Worldly Goods: The Will and Inventory of Francesco Gonzaga (1444–1483).* London: Warburg Institute, University of London, 1992.

Chevailler, Laurent. "Observations sur le droit de bâtardise dans la France coutumière du xiie au xve siècles." *Revue historique de droit français et étranger,* 4th ser., 35 (1957): 376–411.

Chiodi, Giovanni. *L'Interpretazione del testamento nel pensiero dei glossatori.* Milan: Giuffrè, 1997.

Chittolini, Giorgio, and Dietmar Willoweit, eds. *Statuti città territori in Italia e Germania tra Medioevo ed età moderna.* Annali dell'Istituto Storico Italo-Germanico, Quaderno 30. Bologna: Il Mulino, 1991.

Chojnacki, Stanley. "Marriage Legislation and Patrician Society in Fifteenth-Century Venice." In *Law, Custom, and the Social Fabric in Medieval Europe: Essays in Honor of Bryce Lyon,* edited by Bernard S. Bachrach and David Nicholas, 163–84. Kalamazoo: Medieval Institute, 1990.

Clanchy, M. T. *From Memory to Written Record: England 1066–1307.* 2d ed. Oxford: Blackwell, 1993.

Clarke, Paula C. *The Soderini and the Medici: Power and Patronage in Fifteenth-Century Florence.* Oxford: Oxford University Press, 1991.

Cohn, Samuel K., Jr. *The Cult of Remembrance and the Black Death: Six Renaissance Cities in Central Italy.* Baltimore: Johns Hopkins University Press, 1992.

———. *Death and Property in Siena, 1200–1800: Strategies for the Afterlife.* Baltimore: Johns Hopkins University Press, 1988.

———. "Ultime volontà: Famiglia, donne e peste nera nell'Italia centrale." *Studi storici* 32 (1991): 859–75.

———. *Women in the Streets: Essays on Sex and Power in Renaissance Italy.* Baltimore: Johns Hopkins University Press, 1996.

Colli, Vincenzo. "*Consilia* dei giuristi medievali e produzione libraria." In *Legal Consulting in the Civil Law Tradition,* edited by Mario Ascheri, Ingrid Baumgärtner, and Julius Kirshner, 173–225. Berkeley: Robbins Collection, 1999.

Collier, Jane F. *From Duty to Desire: Remaking Families in a Spanish Village.* Princeton: Princeton University Press, 1997.

Collier, Jane F., Bill Maurer, and Liliana Suárez-Navaz. "Sanctioned Identities: Legal Constructions of Modern Personhood." *Identities* 2 (1995): 1–27.

Collins, Steven. "Categories, Concepts, or Predicaments? Remarks on Mauss's Use of Philosophical Terminology." In *The Category of the Person: Anthropology, Philosophy, History,* ed. Michael Carrithers, Steven Collins, and Steven Lukes, 46–82. Cambridge: Cambridge University Press, 1985.

Collison-Morley, Lacy. *The Early Medici.* New York: E. P. Dutton, 1936.

Comaroff, John L., and Simon Roberts. *Rules and Processes: The Cultural Logic of Dispute in an African Context.* Chicago: University of Chicago Press, 1981.

Conti, Elio. *L'imposta diretta a Firenze nel Quattrocento (1427–1494).* Rome: Istituto Storico Italiano per il Medio Evo, 1984.

Cooper, J. P. "Patterns of Inheritance and Settlement by Great Landowners from the Fifteenth to the Eighteenth Centuries." In *Family and Inheritance: Rural Society in Western Europe, 1200–1800,* edited by Jack Goody, Joan Thirsk, and E. P. Thompson, 192–327. Cambridge: Cambridge University Press, 1976.

Corsini, Carlo A. " 'Era piovuto dal cielo e la terra l'aveva raccolto': Il destino del trovatello." In *Enfance abandonnée et société en Europe xive–xxe siècle,* 81–119. Collection de l'École Française de Rome. Rome: École Française de Rome, 1991.

Crescenzi, Victor. *"Esse de Maiori Consilio": Legittimità civile e legittimazione politica nella repubblica di Venezia (secc. xiii–xvi).* Rome: Istituto Storico Italiano per il Medio Evo, 1996.

Darnton, Robert. "The Symbolic Element in History." *Journal of Modern History* 58 (1986): 218–34.

Davidsohn, Robert. *Storia di Firenze.* Vol. 4: *I primordi della civiltà fiorentina,* part 3: *Il mondo della chiesa, spiritualità e arte, vita pubblica e privata.* Translated from the German by Eugenio Dupré-Theseider. Florence: Sansoni, 1973.

Davies, Jonathan. *Florence and Its University during the Early Renaissance.* Leiden: E. J. Brill, 1998.

Davis, Natalie Zemon. "Boundaries of the Self in Sixteenth Century France." In *Reconstructing Individualism: Autonomy, Individuality, and the Self in Western Thought,* edited by Thomas Heller, Morton Sosma, and David E. Wellbery, 53–63. Stanford: Stanford University Press, 1985.

———. *The Gift in Sixteenth-Century France.* Madison: University of Wisconsin Press, 2000.

———. "Ghosts, Kin, and Progeny: Some Features of Family Life in Early Modern France." *Daedalus* 106, n. 2 (1977): 87–114.

———. *The Return of Martin Guerre.* Cambridge: Harvard University Press, 1983.

de Grazia, Sebastian. *Machiavelli in Hell.* Princeton: Princeton University Press, 1989.

Demonet, M., J. Dupaquier, and H. LeBras. "A Repertory of Stable Populations." In *Population Patterns in the Past,* edited by Ronald Demos Lee, 297–309. New York: Academic Press, 1977.

Dorini, Umberto. *Il diritto penale e la delinquenza in Firenze nel sec. xiv.* Lucca: Domenico Corsi, 1923.

du Boulay, Juliet. "Lies, Mockery, and Family Integrity." In *Mediterranean Family Structures,* edited by J. G. Peristiany, 389–406. Cambridge: Cambridge University Press, 1976.

———. *Portrait of a Greek Mountain Village.* Oxford: Oxford University Press, 1974.

Dubuis, Pierre. "Enfants refusés dans les Alpes occidentales (xive–xve siècles)." In *Enfance abandonnée et société en Europe xive–xxe siècle,* 573–90. Collection de l'École Française de Rome. Rome: École Française de Rome, 1991.

Duby, Georges. *The Knight, the Lady, and the Priest: The Making of Modern Marriage in Medieval France.* Translated by Barbara Bray. New York: Pantheon, 1983.

Enriques, Anna Maria. "La vendetta nella vita e nella legislazione fiorentina." *Archivio storico italiano* 91 (1933): 85–146, 181–223.

Epstein, Steven A. *Genoa and the Genoese, 958–1528.* Chapel Hill: University of North Carolina Press, 1996.

———. *Speaking of Slavery: Color, Ethnicity, and Human Bondage in Italy.* Ithaca, N.Y.: Cornell University Press, 2001.

———. *Wage Labor and Guilds in Medieval Europe.* Chapel Hill: University of North Carolina Press, 1991.

Esmein, Adhémar. *Le mariage en droit canonique.* 2 vols. Paris, 1891. Reprint ed., New York: Burt Franklin, 1968.

Ettlinger, Helen S. "Visibilis et Invisibilis: The Mistress in Italian Renaissance Court Society." *Renaissance Quarterly* 47 (1994): 270–92.

Fabbri, Lorenzo. *Alleanza matrimoniale e patriziato nella Firenze del '400: Studio sulla famiglia Strozzi.* Quaderni di "Rinascimento" 12. Florence: Olschki, 1991.

Fajans, Jane. "The Person in Social Context: The Social Character of Baining 'Psychology.'" In *Person, Self, and Experience: Exploring Pacific Ethnopsychologies,* edited by Geoffrey M. White and John Kirkpatrick, 367–97. Berkeley and Los Angeles: University of California Press, 1985.

Farr, James R. *Authority and Sexuality in Early Modern Burgundy (1550–1730).* Oxford: Oxford University Press, 1995.

Felstiner, William L. F., Richard Abel, and Austin Sarat. "The Emergence and Transformation of Disputes: Naming, Blaming, Claiming . . ." *Law and Society Review* 15 (1980–81): 631–54.

Fine, Agnes. "A Consideration of the Trousseau: A Feminine Culture?" In *Writing Women's History,* edited by Michelle Perot, 118–45. Translated by Felicia Pheasant. Oxford: Blackwell, 1992.

Fink, Janet. "Natural Mothers, Putative Fathers, and Innocent Children: The Definition and Regulation of Parental Relationships outside Marriage, in England, 1945–1959." *Journal of Family History* 25 (2000): 178–95.

Flandrin, Jean Louis. *Families in Former Times.* Translated by Richard Southern. Cambridge: Cambridge University Press, 1979.

Fox, Robin. *Reproduction and Succession: Studies in Anthropology, Law, and Society.* New Brunswick, N.J.: Transaction, 1993.

Fransen, Gérard. "La valeur de la jurisprudence en droit canonique." *Ius canonicum* 15 (1975): 97–112.

Freud, Sigmund. *Leonardo da Vinci: A Study in Psychosexuality.* Translated by A. A. Brill. New York: Random House, 1955.

Frigo, Daniela. *Il padre di famiglia: Governo della casa e governo civile nella tradizione dell' "economica" fra Cinque e Seicento.* Rome: Bulzoni, 1985.

Gavitt, Philip. *Charity and Children in Renaissance Florence: The Ospedale degli Innocenti, 1410–1536.* Ann Arbor: University of Michigan Press, 1990.

Geertz, Clifford. *Local Knowledge: Further Essays in Interpretive Anthropology.* New York: Basic Books, 1983.

Génestal, Raoul. *Histoire de la légitimation des enfants naturels en droit canonique.* Paris: Ernest Leroux, 1905.

Godelier, Maurice. *The Enigma of the Gift.* Translated by Nora Scott. Chicago: University of Chicago Press, 1999.

Goldthwaite, Richard. *Private Wealth in Renaissance Florence.* Princeton: Princeton University Press, 1968.

———. *Wealth and the Demand for Art in Italy, 1300–1600.* Baltimore: Johns Hopkins University Press, 1993.

Goode, William J. *The Family.* 2d ed. Englewood Cliffs, N.J.: Prentice-Hall, 1982.

Goodich, Michael. "*Ancilla Dei:* The Servant as Saint in the Late Middle Ages." In *Women of the Medieval World,* edited by Julius Kirshner and Suzanne F. Wempel, 119–36. Oxford: Blackwell, 1985.

Goodrich, Peter. *Oedipus Lex: Psychoanalysis, History, Law.* Berkeley and Los Angeles: University of California Press, 1995.

———. *Reading the Law: A Critical Introduction to Legal Method and Techniques.* Oxford: Oxford University Press, 1986.

Goody, Jack. *The Development of Family and Marriage in Europe.* Cambridge: Cambridge University Press, 1983.

———. *Production and Reproduction: A Comparative Study of the Domestic Domain.* Cambridge: Cambridge University Press, 1976.

Grassi, G. Nicolosi. "Analisi di manoscritti vaticani per uno studio dei 'Consilia' di Giovanni e Gaspare Calderini." *Rivista di storia del diritto italiano* 50 (1977): 127–49.

Greenblatt, Stephen. "Fiction and Friction." In *Reconstructing Individualism: Autonomy, Individuality, and the Self in Western Thought,* edited by Thomas Heller, Morton Sosma, and David E. Wellbery, 30–52. Stanford: Stanford University Press, 1985.

Greenhouse, Carol. "Looking at Culture, Looking for Rules." *Man,* n.s. 17 (1982): 58–73.

Gregory, Heather J. "Chi erano gli Strozzi nel Quattrocento." In *Palazzo Strozzi: Metà Millennio, 1489–1989,* 15–29. Atti del Convegno di Studi, Florence, 3–6 July 1989. Rome: Istituto della Enciclopedia Italiana, 1991.

Grossi, Paolo. *Il dominio e le cose: Percezioni medievali e moderne dei diritti reali.* Milan: Giuffrè, 1992.

———. *"Locatio ad longum tempus": Locazione e rapporti reali di godimento nella problematica del diritto comune.* Naples: Morano, 1963.

———. *L'ordine giuridico medievale.* Bari: Laterza, 1995.

———. "La proprietà e le proprietà nell'officina dello storico." In *La proprietà e le proprietà,* edited by Ennio Cortese, 205–72. Milan: Giuffrè, 1988.

———. *Le situazioni reali nell'esperienza giuridica medievale.* Padua: CEDAM, 1968.

———, ed. *Storia sociale e dimensione giuridica: Strumenti d'indagine e ipotesi di lavoro.* Atti del Incontro di Studio, Firenze, 26–27 April 1985. Milan: Giuffrè, 1986.

Guarducci, Piero, and Valeria Ottanelli. *I servitori domestici della casa borghese toscana nel basso Medioevo.* Florence: Salimbeni, 1982.

Guarini, Elena Fasano. "Gli statuti delle città soggette a Firenze tra '400 e '500: riforme locali e interventi centrali." In *Statuti città territori in Italia e Germania tra Medioevo et età moderna,* ed. Giorgio Chittolini and Dietmar Willoweit, 69–124. Annali dell'Istituto Storico Italo-Germanico, Quaderno 30. Bologna: Il Mulino, 1991.

Gurevich, Aaron. *The Origins of European Individualism.* Translated by Katharine Judelson. Oxford: Blackwell, 1995.

Hanawalt, Barbara. *The Ties That Bound: Peasant Families in Medieval England.* Oxford: Oxford University Press, 1986.

Harsgor, Mikhail. "L'essor des bâtards nobles au xve siècle." *Revue historique* 253 (1975): 319–54.

Hartley, Shirley Foster. *Illegitimacy.* Berkeley and Los Angeles: University of California Press, 1975.

Hatfield, Rab. "Cosimo de' Medici and the Chapel of His Palace." In *Cosimo "il Vecchio" de' Medici, 1383–1464,* edited by Francis Ames-Lewis, 221–44. Oxford: Oxford University Press, 1992.

Heers, Jacques. *Esclaves et domestiques au Moyen Age dans le monde méditerranéen.* Paris: Fayard, 1981.

———. *Family Clans in the Middle Ages: A Study of the Political and Social Structures in Urban Areas.* Translated by Barry Herbert. Amsterdam: North-Holland, 1977.

Helmholz, R. H. "Bastardy Litigation in Medieval England." *American Journal of Legal History* 13 (1969): 360–83.

———. *Roman Canon Law in Reformation England.* Cambridge: Cambridge University Press, 1990.

———. "Support Orders, Church Courts, and the Rule of *Filius Nullius:* A Reassessment of the Canon Law." *Virginia Law Review* 63 (1977): 431–48.

Henderson, John. *Piety and Charity in Late Medieval Florence.* Oxford: Oxford University Press, 1994.

Herlihy, David. "Family and Property in Renaissance Florence." In *The Medieval City,* edited by Harry A. Miskimin, David Herlihy, and A. L. Udovitch, 131–57. New Haven: Yale University Press, 1977.

———. "Medieval Children." In *Essays on Medieval Civilization: The Walter Prescott Webb Lectures,* edited by Bede Karl Lackner and Kenneth Roy Philip, 109–41. Austin: University of Texas Press, 1978.

———. "The Rulers of Florence, 1282–1530." In *City-States in Classical Antiquity and Medieval Italy: Athens and Rome, Florence and Venice,* edited by Anthony Molho, Kurt Raaflaub, and Julia Emlen, 197–221. Stuttgart: Franz Steiner, 1991.

———. "Vieillir à Florence au Quattrocento." *Annales* 24 (1969): 1338–52.

Herlihy, David, and Christiane Klapisch-Zuber. *Les toscans et leurs familles.* Paris: Fondation Nationale des Sciences Politiques, 1978.

———. *Tuscans and Their Families.* New Haven: Yale University Press, 1985.

Herrmann, H. *Die Stellung der unehelichen Kinder nach kanonischem Recht.* Amsterdam: Grüner, 1971.

Herzfeld, Michael. *Anthropology through the Looking Glass: Critical Ethnography in the Margins of Europe.* Cambridge: Cambridge University Press, 1987.

———. *The Poetics of Manhood: Contest and Identity in a Cretan Mountain Village.* Princeton: Princeton University Press, 1985.

Hesse, Christian. "Vorgezeichnete Karriere? Die Bemühungen von Eltern, ihre unehelichen Söhne mit Pfründen zu versorgen, dorgelegt an Beispielen aus den Diozesen Basel und Konstanz." In *Illegitimität im Spätmittelalter,* edited by Ludwig Schmugge, 275–92. Munich: R. Oldenbourg, 1994.

Hoffman-Nowotny, Hans-Joachim. "Soziologische Marginalien zur Marginalisierung durch 'illegitime' Geburt." In *Illegitimität im Spätmittelalter,* edited by Ludwig Schmugge, 11–20. Munich: R. Oldenbourg, 1994.

Hufton, Olwen H. *The Poor of Eighteenth-Century France, 1750–1789.* Oxford: Oxford University Press, 1974.

Hughes, Diane Owen. "From Brideprice to Dowry in Mediterranean Europe." *Journal of Family History* 3 (1978): 262–96.

Hunecke, Volker. "Intensità e fluttuazioni degli abbandoni dal xv al xix secolo." In *Enfance abandonnée et société en Europe xive–xxe siècle,* 27–72. Collection de l'École Française de Rome. Rome: École Française de Rome, 1991.

Hurtubise, Pierre, O.M.I. *Une famille-témoin: Les Salviati.* Vatican City: Biblioteca Apostolica Vaticana, 1985.

Jacobs, A. C. "Illegitimacy." *Encyclopedia of the Social Sciences,* 7:582–83. 1932.

James, T. E. "The Illegitimate and Deprived Child: Legitimation and Adoption." In *A Century of Family Law, 1857–1957,* edited by R. H. Graveson and F. R. Crane, 39–55. London: Sweet and Maxwell, 1957.

Kent, Dale V. *Cosimo de' Medici and the Florentine Renaissance: The Patron's Oeuvre.* New Haven: Yale University Press, 2000.

Kent, Dale V., and F. W. Kent. *Neighbours and Neighbourhood in Renaissance Florence: The District of the Red Lion in the Fifteenth Century.* Locust Valley: J. J. Augustin, 1982.

Kent, F. W. "La famiglia patrizia fiorentina nel Quattrocento: Nuovi orientamenti nella storiografia recente." In *Palazzo Strozzi: Metà Millennio,*

1489–1989, 70–91. Atti del Convegno di Studi, Florence, 3–6 July 1989. Rome: Istituto della Enciclopedia Italiana, 1991.

———. *Household and Lineage in Renaissance Florence: The Family Life of the Capponi, Ginori, and Rucellai.* Princeton: Princeton University Press, 1977.

———. "Palaces, Politics, and Society in Fifteenth-Century Florence." *I Tatti Studies* 2 (1987): 41–70.

Kertzer, David I. *Sacrificed for Honor: Italian Infant Abandonment and the Politics of Reproductive Control.* Boston: Beacon, 1993.

Kirshner, Julius. "*Ars Imitatur Naturam:* A Consilium of Baldus on Naturalization in Florence." *Viator* 5 (1974): 289–331.

———. "Baldus de Ubaldis on Disinheritance: Contexts, Controversies, *Consilia.*" *Ius Commune: Zeitschrift für Europäische Rechtsgeschichte* 27 (2000): 119–214.

———. "Between Nature and Culture: A Consilium of Baldus of Perugia on Venetian Citizenship as Second Nature." *Journal of Medieval and Renaissance Studies* 9 (1979): 179–208.

———. "*Civitas Sibi Faciat Civem:* Bartolus of Sassoferrato's Doctrine on the Making of a Citizen." *Speculum* 48 (1973): 694–713.

———. "*Consilia* as Authority in Late Medieval Italy: The Case of Florence." In *Legal Consulting in the Civil Law Tradition,* edited by Mario Ascheri, Ingrid Baumgärtner, and Julius Kirshner, 107–40. Berkeley: Robbins Collection, 1999.

———. "Messer Francesco di Bici degli Albergotti d'Arezzo, Citizen of Florence (1350–1376)." *Bulletin of Medieval Canon Law,* n.s. 2 (1972): 84–90.

———. "Mulier alibi nupta." In *Consilia im späten Mittelalter: Zum historischen Aussagewert einer Quellengattung,* edited by Ingrid Baumgärtner, 147–75. Sigmaringen: Jan Thorbecke, 1995.

———. "Paolo di Castro on *Cives Ex Privilegio:* A Controversy over the Legal Qualifications for Public Office in Early Fifteenth-Century Florence." In *Renaissance Studies in Honor of Hans Baron,* edited by Anthony Molho and John A. Tedeschi, 227–64. Dekalb: Northern Illinois University Press, 1971.

———. *Pursuing Honor while Avoiding Sin: The Monte delle doti of Florence.* Milan: Giuffrè, 1978.

———. "Some Problems in the Interpretation of Legal Texts *re* the Italian City-States." *Archiv für Begriffsgeschichte* 19 (1975): 16–27.

Kirshner, Julius, and Anthony Molho. "The Dowry Fund and the Marriage Market in Early Quattrocento Florence." *Journal of Modern History* 50 (1978): 403–38.

Klapisch-Zuber, Christiane. "Déclin démographique et structure du menage." In *Famille et parenté dans l'Occident médiéval,* edited by Georges Duby and Jacques Le Goff, 255–68. Rome: Ecole Française de Rome, 1977.

———. *La famiglia e le donne del Rinascimento a Firenze.* Bari: Laterza, 1988.

———. "Les généalogies florentines du xive et xve siècle." In *Le modèle familiale européen: Normes, deviances, contrôle du pouvoir,* 101–31. Rome: Ecole Française de Rome, 1986.

———. "Kinship and Politics in Fourteenth-Century Florence." In *The Family in*

Italy from Antiquity to the Present, edited by David I. Kertzer and Richard P. Saller, 208–28. New Haven: Yale University Press, 1991.

———. "Le nom 'refait': La transmission des prenoms à Florence (xive–xvie siècles)." *L'Homme* 20, no. 4 (1980): 77–104.

———. "Parents du sang, parents du lait: La mise en nourrice à Florence (1300–1500)." *Annales de démographie historique* 20 (1983): 33–64.

———. "Ruptures de parenté et changements d'identité chez les magnats florentins du xive siècle." *Annales* 43 (1988): 1205–40.

———. *Women, Family, and Ritual in Renaissance Italy.* Translated by Lydia G. Cochrane. Chicago: University of Chicago Press, 1985.

Kogler, Ferdinand. *Die legitimatio per rescriptum von Justinian bis zum Tode Karls IV.* Weimar: Bohlaus, 1904.

Kohl, Benjamin G., and Allison Andrews Smith, eds. *Major Problems in the Italian Renaissance.* Lexington, Mass.: D. C. Heath, 1995.

Koschaker, Paul. *Europa und das römische Recht.* 4th ed. Munich: C. H. Beck, 1966.

Krautheimer, Richard. *Lorenzo Ghiberti.* Princeton: Princeton University Press, 1956. Reprint ed., 1982.

Kuehn, Thomas. "Adoption à Florence à la fin du Moyen Age." *Médiévales* 35 (1998): 69–81.

———. "Antropologia giuridica dello stato." In *Origini dello stato: Processi di formazione statale in Italia fra Medioevo ed età moderna,* edited by Giorgio Chittolini, Anthony Molho, and Pierangelo Schiera, 367–80. Bologna: Il Mulino, 1994.

———. "'As If Conceived within a Legitimate Marriage': A Dispute concerning Legitimation in Quattrocento Florence." *American Journal of Legal History* 29 (1985): 275–300.

———. "*Consilia* as Juristic Literature in Private Law." In *Legal Consulting in the Civil Law Tradition,* edited by Mario Ascheri, Ingrid Baumgärtner, and Julius Kirshner, 229–53. Berkeley: Robbins Collection, 1999.

———. "Il diritto e l'uso del diritto nelle famiglie fiorentine nel Rinascimento." In *Palazzo Strozzi: Metà Millennio, 1489–1989,* 108–25. Atti del Convegno di Studi, Florence, 3–6 July 1989. Rome: Istituto della Enciclopedia Italiana, 1991.

———. *Emancipation in Late Medieval Florence.* New Brunswick, N.J.: Rutgers University Press, 1982.

———. "Honor and Conflict in a Fifteenth-Century Florentine Family." *Ricerche storiche* 10 (1980): 287–310.

———. "Inheritance and Identity in Early Renaissance Florence: The Estate of Paliano di Falco." In *Society and Individual in Renaissance Florence,* edited by William J. Connell. Berkeley and Los Angeles: University of California Press, forthcoming.

———. "Law, Death, and Heirs in the Renaissance: Some Meanings of the Repudiation of Inheritance." *Renaissance Quarterly* 45 (1991): 484–516.

———. *Law, Family, and Women: Toward a Legal Anthropology of Renaissance Italy.* Chicago: University of Chicago Press, 1991.

———. "A Medieval Conflict of Laws: Illegitimacy and Legitimation in *Ius Commune* and *Ius Proprium*." *Law and History Review* 15 (1997): 243–73.

———. "*Memoria* and Family in Law." In *Art, Memory, and Family in Renaissance Florence,* edited by Giovanni Ciappelli and Patricia Lee Rubin, 262–74. Cambridge: Cambridge University Press, 2000.

———. "'Nemo mortalis cognitus vivit in evo': Moral and Legal Conflicts in a Florentine Inheritance Case of 1442." In *The Moral World of the Law,* edited by Peter Coss, 113–33. Cambridge: Cambridge University Press, 2000.

———. "Person and Gender in the Laws." In *Gender and Society in Renaissance Italy,* edited by Judith A. Brown and Robert C. Davis, 87–106. New York: Longman, 1998.

———. "Reading between the Patrilines: Leon Battista Alberti's *Della Famiglia* in Light of His Illegitimacy." *I Tatti Studies: Essays in the Renaissance* 1 (1985): 161–87.

———. "Reading Microhistory: The Example of Giovanni and Lusanna." *Journal of Modern History* 61 (1989): 512–34.

———. "Social Processes and Legal Processes in the Renaissance: A Florentine Inheritance Case from 1452." *Quaderni fiorentini per la storia del pensiero giuridico moderno* 23 (1994): 365–96.

———. "Vicissitudini di un patrimonio fiorentino del xv secolo." *Quaderni storici* 88 (April 1995): 43–61.

La Roncière, Charles M. de. "Portraits: Tuscan Notables on the Eve of the Renaissance." In *A History of Private Life,* edited by Philippe Ariès and Georges Duby. Vol. 2: *Revelations of the Medieval World,* edited by Georges Duby, 157–309. Translated by Arthur Goldhammer. Cambridge: Harvard University Press, 1988.

Ladurie, Emmanuel LeRoy. "The Court Surrounds the King: Louis XIV, the Palatine Princess, and Saint-Simon." In *Honor and Grace in Anthropology,* edited by J. G. Peristiany and Julian Pitt-Rivers, 51–78. Cambridge: Cambridge University Press, 1992.

———. *Montaillou: The Promised Land of Error.* Translated by Barbara Bray. New York: George Braziller, 1978.

LaFontaine, J. S. "Person and Individual: Some Anthropological Reflections." In *The Category of the Person: Anthropology, Philosophy, History,* ed. Michael Carrithers, Steven Collins, and Steven Lukes, 123–40. Cambridge: Cambridge University Press, 1985.

Landau, Peter. "Das Weihehindernis der Illegitimität in der Geschichte des kanonischen Rechts." In *Illegitimität im Spätmittelalter,* edited by Ludwig Schmugge, 41–53. Munich: R. Oldenbourg, 1994.

Lansing, Carol. *The Florentine Magnates: Lineage and Faction in a Medieval Commune.* Princeton: Princeton University Press, 1991.

———. "Gender and Civic Authority: Sexual Control in a Medieval Italian Town." *Journal of Social History* 31 (1997–98): 33–59.

Laslett, Peter. *Family Life and Illicit Love in Earlier Generations: Essays in Historical Sociology.* Cambridge: Cambridge University Press, 1977.

Laslett, Peter, Karla Oosterveen, and Richard M. Smith, eds. *Bastardy and Its*

Comparative History: Studies in the History of Illegitimacy and Marital Nonconformity in Britain, France, Germany, Sweden, North America, Jamaica, and Japan. Cambridge: Harvard University Press, 1980.

Lefebvre-Teillard, Anne. "Beati possidentes." In *À cheval entre histoire et droit: Hommage à Jean-François Poudret,* edited by Eva Maier, Antoine Rochat, and Denis Tappy, 247–59. Lausanne: Bibliothèque Historique Vaudoise, 1999.

———. *Introduction historique au droit des personnes et de la famille.* Paris: Presses Universitaires Françaises, 1996.

———. "*Ius sanguinis:* L'émergence d'un principe (Eléments d'histoire de la nationalité française)." *Revue critique de droit international privé* 82 (1993): 223–50.

———. "'Pater is est quem nuptiae demonstrant': Jalons pour une histoire de la présomption de paternité." *Revue historique de droit française et étranger* 69 (1991): 331–40.

———. "'Tanta est vis matrimonii': L'écho français d'une vieille controverse." In *Hommage à Romuald Szramkiewcz,* 95–108. Paris: Litec, 1998.

Leicht, Pier Silverio. *Storia del diritto italiano, Il diritto privato.* 3 vols. Milan: Giuffrè, 1943–48. Reprint ed., Milan: Giuffrè, 1960.

Leineweber, Anke. *Die rechtliche Beziehung des nichtehelichen Kindes zu seinem Erzeuger in der Geschichte des Privatrechts.* Königstein: Peter Hanstein, 1978.

Lemosse, Maxime. "L'enfant sans famille en droit romain." In *Recueils de la société Jean Bodin pour l'histoire comparative des institutions.* Vol. 35: *L'enfant,* part 1: *Antiquité-Afrique-Asie,* 257–70. 1975.

Lesnick, Daniel R. "Insults and Threats in Medieval Todi." *Journal of Medieval History* 17 (1991): 71–89.

Lewin, Linda. "Natural and Spurious Children in Brazilian Inheritance Law from Colony to Empire: A Methodological Essay." *The Americas* 18 (1991–92): 351–96.

Litchfield, R. Burr. *Emergence of a Bureaucracy: The Florentine Patricians, 1530–1790.* Princeton: Princeton University Press, 1986.

Lombardi, Luigi. *Saggio sul diritto giurisprudenziale.* Milan: Giuffrè, 1967.

Lopez, Robert S. "Hard Times and Investment in Culture." In *The Renaissance: Six Essays,* 29–54. New York: Metropolitan Museum of Art, 1953. Reprint ed., New York: Harper and Row, 1962.

Maffei, Domenico. *La donazione di Costantino nei giuristi medievali.* Milan: Giuffrè, 1964.

Malinowski, Bronislaw. "Kinship." *Encyclopedia Britannica,* 13:403. 1929.

Mallett, Michael. *The Florentine Galleys in the Fifteenth Century.* Oxford: Oxford University Press, 1967.

Marek, George R. *The Bed and the Throne: The Life of Isabella d'Este.* New York: Harper and Row, 1984.

Mariottini, Jean-Marc. "'Il corredo e la legittima.'" In *Femmes et patrimoine dans les sociétés rurales de l'Europe méditerranéenne,* ed. G. Ravis-Giordani, 163–68. Paris: Centre Nationale de la Recherche Scientifique, 1987.

Martin, John. "Inventing Sincerity, Refashioning Prudence: The Discovery of the

Individual in Renaissance Europe." *American Historical Review* 102 (1997): 1309–42.

Martinelli, Bruno. "Matrimoine et patrimoine: Sur les fonctions successorales des femmes dans quelques exemples provençaux." In *Femmes et patrimoine dans les sociétés rurales de l'Europe méditerranéenne,* ed. G. Ravis-Giordani, 75–87. Paris: Centre Nationale de la Recherche Scientifique, 1987.

Martines, Lauro. *Lawyers and Statecraft in Renaissance Florence.* Princeton: Princeton University Press, 1968.

———. *Power and Imagination: City-States in Renaissance Italy.* New York: Knopf, 1979.

Martone, Luciano. *Arbiter-Arbitrator: Forme di giustizia privata nell'età del diritto comune.* Naples: Jovene, 1984.

Mayali, Laurent. "Le droit des autres dans la France médiévale: Système de différenciation et mode d'harmonisation." In *Identité et droit de l'autre,* edited by Laurent Mayali, 183–200. Berkeley: Robbins Collection, 1994.

———. *Droit savant et coutumes: L'exclusion des filles dotées, xiième-xvème siècles.* Ius Commune, Sonderhefte: Studien zur Europäischen Rechtsgeschichte 33. Frankfurt am Main: Klostermann, 1987.

———. "Note on the Legitimization by Subsequent Marriage from Alexander III to Innocent III." In *The Two Laws: Studies in Medieval Legal History Dedicated to Stephan Kuttner,* edited by Laurent Mayali and Stephanie A. J. Tibbetts, 55–75. Washington, D.C.: Catholic University of America Press, 1990.

Mazzi, Maria Serena. "Il mondo della prostituzione nella Firenze tarda medievale." In *Forestieri e stranieri nelle città basso-medievali,* 127–47. Florence: Salimbene, 1988.

———. *Prostitute e lenoni nella Firenze del Quattrocento.* Milan: Il Saggiatore, 1991.

McDevitt, Gilbert Joseph. *Legitimacy and Legitimation: An Historical Synopsis and Commentary.* Washington, D.C.: Catholic University of America Press, 1941.

McKnight, Joseph. "Legitimation and Adoption on the Anglo-Hispanic Frontier of the United States." *Tijdschrift voor Rechtsgeschiedenis* 53 (1985): 135–50.

McLaughlin, Mary Martin. "Survivors and Surrogates: Children and Parents from the Ninth to the Thirteenth Centuries." In *The History of Childhood,* edited by Lloyd deMause, 101–82. New York: Harper and Row, 1974.

Medick, Hans, and David Warren Sabean. "Interest and Emotion in Family and Kinship Studies: A Critique of Social History and Anthropology." In *Interest and Emotion: Essays on the Study of Family and Kinship,* edited by Hans Medick and David Warren Sabean, 9–27. Cambridge: Cambridge University Press, 1984.

Migliorino, Francesco. *Fama e infamia: Problemi della società medievale nel pensiero giuridico nei secoli xii e xiii.* Catania: Giannotta, 1985.

Miller, William Ian. *Humiliation: And Other Essays on Honor, Social Discomfort, and Violence.* Ithaca, N.Y.: Cornell University Press, 1993.

Mitterauer, Michael, and Reinhold Sieder. *The European Family: Patriarchy to*

Partnership from the Middle Ages to the Present. Translated by Karla Oosterveen and Manfred Horzinger. Chicago: University of Chicago Press, 1982.

Molho, Anthony. "Deception and Marriage Strategy in Renaissance Florence: The Case of Women's Ages." *Renaissance Quarterly* 41 (1988): 193–217.

———. *Marriage Alliance in Late Medieval Florence.* Cambridge: Harvard University Press, 1994.

———. "*Tanquam vere mortua:* Le professioni religiose femminili nella Firenze del tardo Medioevo." *Società e storia* 43 (1989): 1–44.

Molho, Anthony, Roberto Barducci, Gabriella Battista, and Francesco Donnini. "Genealogia e parentado: Memorie del potere nella Firenze tardo-medievale, il caso di Giovanni Rucellai." *Quaderni storici* 86 (August 1994): 365–403.

Montorzi, Mario. *Fides in rem publicam: Ambiguità e tecniche del diritto comune.* Naples: Jovene, 1984.

Moore, Sally Falk. *Law as Process: An Anthropological Approach.* London: Routledge, 1978.

Muir, Edward. *Mad Blood Stirring: Vendetta and Factions in Friuli during the Renaissance.* Baltimore: Johns Hopkins University Press, 1993.

Niccolai, Franco. *La formazione del diritto successorio negli statuti comunali del territorio lombardo-tosco.* Milan: Giuffrè, 1940.

Nicholas, David. "Childhood in Medieval Europe." In *Children in Historical and Comparative Perspective: An International Handbook and Research Guide,* edited by Joseph M. Hawes and N. Ray Hiner, 31–52. New York: Greenwood Press, 1991.

———. *The Domestic Life of a Medieval City: Women, Children, and the Family in Fourteenth-Century Ghent.* Lincoln: University of Nebraska Press, 1985.

Onory, Sergio Mochi. "*Personam habere:* Studio sulle origini e sulla struttura della 'persona' nell'età del Rinascimento." In *Studi di storia e diritto in onore di Enrico Besta,* 3:417–39. Milan: Giuffrè, 1939.

Origo, Iris. "The Domestic Enemy: The Eastern Slaves in Tuscany in the Fourteenth and Fifteenth Centuries." *Speculum* 30 (1955): 321–66.

———. *The Merchant of Prato: Francesco di Marco Datini.* Rev. ed. Harmondsworth: Penguin, 1963.

Ottokar, Nicola. *Il comune di Firenze alla fine del Dugento.* Reprint ed., Turin: Einaudi, 1962.

Pagliano, Graziella. "Il motivo dell'infante abbandonato in letteratura: Considerazioni su alcuni testi italiani." In *Enfance abandonnée et société en Europe xive–xxe siècle,* 879–95. Collection de l'École Française de Rome. Rome: École Française de Rome, 1991.

Pandimiglio, Leonida. "Giovanni di Pagolo Morelli e la ragion di famiglia." In *Studi sul medioevo cristiano offerti a Raffaello Morghen,* 553–608. Rome: Istituto Storico Italiano per il Medio Evo, 1974.

———. "Giovanni di Pagolo Morelli e la continuità familiare." *Studi medievali,* 3rd ser., 22 (1981): 129–81.

Park, Katherine. *Doctors and Medicine in Early Renaissance Florence.* Princeton: Princeton University Press, 1985.

Pecorella, Corrado. "Filiazione (storia)." *Enciclopedia del diritto,* 17:449–56. Milan: Giuffrè, 1968.

Pennington, Kenneth. "Pope Innocent III's Views on Church and State: A Gloss to *Per Venerabilem.*" In *Law, Church, and Society: Essays in Honor of Stephan Kuttner,* edited by Kenneth Pennington and Robert Somerville, 49–67. Philadelphia: University of Pennsylvania Press, 1977.

Peristiany, J. G., ed. *Honour and Shame: The Values of Mediterranean Society.* Chicago: University of Chicago Press, 1966.

Pertile, Antonio. *Storia del diritto italiano dalla caduta dell'impero romano alla codificazione.* 2d ed. 6 vols. Turin: Unione Tipografico, 1894.

Petrucci, Armando. *Writers and Readers in Medieval Italy: Studies in the History of Written Culture.* Edited and translated by Charles M. Radding. New Haven: Yale University Press, 1995.

Philips, Mark. *The "Memoir" of Marco Parenti: A Life in Medici Florence.* Princeton: Princeton University Press, 1987.

Pia di Bella, Maria. "Name, Blood, and Miracles: The Claims of Renown in Traditional Sicily." In *Honor and Grace in Anthropology,* edited by J. G. Peristiany and Julian Pitt-Rivers, 151–65. Cambridge: Cambridge University Press, 1992.

Piergiovanni, Vito. "Diritto e giustizia mercantile a Genova nel xv secolo: I consilia di Bartolomeo Bosco." In *Consilia im späten Mittelalter: Zum historischen Aussagewert einer Quellengattung,* edited by Ingrid Baumgärtner, 65–78. Sigmaringen: Jan Thorbecke, 1995.

Pinto, Giuliano. "Il personale, le balie e i salariati dell'Ospedale di San Gallo di Firenze negli anni 1395–1406: Note per la storia del salariato nelle città medievali." *Ricerche storiche* 2 (1974): 113–68.

Pistarini, Geo. "Tra libere e schiave a Genova nel Quattrocento." *Annuario de estudios medievales* 1 (1964): 353–74.

Pitkin, Donald S. *The House That Giacomo Built: History of an Italian Family, 1898–1978.* Cambridge: Cambridge University Press, 1985.

Pitt-Rivers, Julian. *The Fate of Shechem: Essays in the Anthropology of the Mediterranean.* Cambridge: Cambridge University Press, 1977.

———. "La veuve andalouse." In *Femmes et patrimoine dans les sociétés rurales de l'Europe méditerranéenne,* ed. G. Ravis-Giordani, 261–68. Paris: Centre Nationale de la Recherche Scientifique, 1987.

Pitzorno, Benvenuto. *La legittimazione nella storia delle istituzioni familiari del medioevo.* Sassari: Satta, 1904.

Pomata, Gianna. "Legami di sangue, legami di seme: Consanguinità e agnazione nel diritto romano." *Quaderni storici* 86 (August 1994): 299–334.

Povolo, Claudio. "Aspetti sociali e penali del reato d'infanticidio: Il caso di una contadina padovana nel '700." *Atti dell'Istituto Veneto di Scienze lettere ed Arti* 138 (1979–80): 415–32.

———. "Dal versante dell'illegitimità: Per una ricerca sulla storia della famiglia: Infanticidio ed esposizione d'infanti nel Veneto nell'età moderna." In *Crimine, giustizia e società veneta in età moderna,* edited by Luigi Berlinguer and Floriana Colao, 89–163. Milan: Giuffrè, 1989.

Quaglioni, Diego. "The Legal Definition of Citizenship in the Late Middle Ages." In *City-States in Classical Antiquity and Medieval Italy: Athens and Rome, Florence and Venice,* edited by Anthony Molho, Kurt Raaflaub, Julia Emlen, 155–67. Stuttgart: Franz Steiner, 1991.

Quaife, G. R. *Wanton Wenches and Wayward Wives: Peasants and Illicit Sex in Early Seventeenth Century England.* New Brunswick, N.J.: Rutgers University Press, 1979.

Raggio, Osvaldo. "La politica nella parentela: Conflitti locali e commissari in Liguria orientale (secoli xvi–xvii)." *Quaderni storici* 63 (December 1986): 721–57.

Ravenscroft, Judith. "The Third Book of Alberti's *Della Famiglia* and Its Two *Rifacimenti.*" *Italian Studies* 29 (1974): 45–53.

Ravis-Giordani, G., ed. *Femmes et patrimoine dans les sociétés rurales de l'Europe méditerranéenne.* Paris: Centre Nationale de la Recherche Scientifique, 1987.

Regnault, H. *La condition juridique du bâtard au Moyen Age.* Pont-Audemer: Lescuyer Frères, 1922.

Rheubottom, David B. "Genealogical Skewing and Political Support: Patrician Politics in Fifteenth-Century Ragusa (Dubrovnik)." *Continuity and Change* 9 (1994): 369–90.

Roberts, Simon. "The Study of Dispute: Anthropological Perspectives." In *Disputes and Settlements: Law and Human Relations in the West,* edited by John Bossy, 1–24. Cambridge: Cambridge University Press, 1983.

Rocke, Michael. "Il controllo dell'omosessualità a Firenze nel xv secolo: Gli Ufficiali di Notte." *Quaderni storici* 66 (December 1987): 701–23.

———. *Forbidden Friendships: Homosexuality and Male Culture in Renaissance Florence.* New York: Oxford University Press, 1996.

Romano, Andrea. *Famiglia, successioni e patrimonio familiare nell'Italia medievale e moderna.* Turin: Giappichelli, 1994.

———. "La giurisprudenza consulente e Paolo di Castro." *Rivista di storia del diritto italiano* 61 (1988): 141–70.

Romano, Dennis. *Housecraft and Statecraft: Domestic Service in Renaissance Venice, 1400–1600.* Baltimore: Johns Hopkins University Press, 1996.

Rossi, Giovanni. *"Duplex est ususfructus": Ricerche sulla natura dell'usufrutto nel diritto comune.* 2 vols. Milan: Giuffrè, 1996.

Rossi, Guido. *Consilium sapientis iudiciale: Studi e ricerche per la storia del processo romano-canonico.* Milan: Giuffrè, 1958.

Rossiaud, Jacques. *La prostituzione nel Medioevo.* Bari: Laterza, 1986.

Ruggiero, Guido. *The Boundaries of Eros: Sex Crime and Sexuality in the Renaissance.* Oxford: Oxford University Press, 1985.

Saalman, Howard. *The Bigallo: The Oratory and Residence of the Compagnia del Bigallo e della Misericordia in Florence.* New York: New York University Press, 1969.

Sablonier, Roger. "The Aragonese Royal Family around 1300." In *Interest and Emotion: Essays on the Study of Family and Kinship,* edited by Hans Medick

and David Warren Sabean, 210–39. Cambridge: Cambridge University Press, 1984.
Salisbury, Joyce E. *The Beast Within: Animals in the Middle Ages.* London: Routledge, 1994.
Saller, Richard P. "Patria Potestas and the Stereotype of the Roman Family." *Continuity and Change* 1 (1986): 7–22.
Salvemini, Gaetano. *Magnati e popolani in Firenze dal 1280 al 1295.* Florence: Sansoni, 1899. Reprint ed., Milan: Feltrinelli, 1966.
Sandri, Lucia. "Modalità dell'abbandono dei fanciulli in area urbana: Gli esposti dell'Ospedale di San Gallo di Firenze nella prima metà del xv secolo." In *Enfance abandonnée et société en Europe xive–xxe siècle,* 993–1015. Collection de l'École Française de Rome. Rome: École Française de Rome, 1991.
———. *L'Ospedale di S. Maria della Scala di San Gimignano nel Quattrocento: Contributo alla storia dell'infanzia abbandonata.* Biblioteca della "Miscellanea Storica della Valdelsa," vol. 4. Florence: Società Storica della Valdelsa, 1982.
Sbriccoli, Mario. *L'interpretazione dello statuto: Contributo allo studio della funzione dei giuristi nell'età comunale.* Milan: Giuffrè, 1969.
Schimmelpfennig, Bernhard. "*Ex Fornicatione Nati:* Studies on the Position of Priests' Sons from the Twelfth to the Fourteenth Century." *Studies in Medieval and Renaissance History* 2 (1979): 1–50.
Schmugge, Ludwig. *Kirche, Kinder, Karrieren: Päpstliche Dispense von der unehelichen Geburt in Spätmittelalter.* Zurich: Artemis und Winkler, 1995.
———, ed. *Illegitimität im Spätmittelalter.* Munich: R. Oldenbourg, 1994.
Schneider, Jane. "Of Vigilance and Virgins: Honor, Shame, and Access to Resources in Mediterranean Societies." *Ethnology* 10 (1971): 1–24.
Schreiner, Klaus. "'Defectus natalium': Geburt aus einem unrechtmäßigen Schoß als Problem klösterlicher Gemeinschaftsbildung." In *Illegitimität im Spätmittelalter,* edited by Ludwig Schmugge, 85–114. Munich: R. Oldenbourg, 1994.
Schulz, Knut. "Die Norm der Ehelichkeit im Zunft- und Bürgerrecht spätmittelalterlicher Städte." In *Illegitimität im Spätmittelalter,* edited by Ludwig Schmugge, 67–83. Munich: R. Oldenbourg, 1994.
Schweder, Richard A. *Thinking through Cultures: Expeditions in Cultural Psychology.* Cambridge: Harvard University Press, 1991.
Segoloni, Danilo, ed. *Il diritto comune e la tradizione giuridica europea.* Perugia: Libreria Universitaria, 1980.
Sella, Pietro. *Il procedimento civile nella legislazione statutaria italiana.* Milan: Hoepli, 1927.
Sergène, André. "Le précédent judiciaire au moyen âge." *Revue historique de droit français et étranger* 39 (1961): 223–54, 359–70.
Shahar, Shulamith. *The Fourth Estate: A History of Women in the Middle Ages.* Translated by Chaya Galai. London: Methuen, 1983.
Sheedy, Anna. *Bartolus on Social Conditions in the Fourteenth Century.* New York: Columbia University Press, 1942.
Sigle, Wendy, David I. Kertzer, and Michael J. White. "Abandoned Children and

Their Transition to Adulthood in Nineteenth-Century Italy." *Journal of Family History* 25 (2000): 326–40.

Silverman, Sydel. "The Life Crisis as a Clue to Social Function: The Case of Italy." In *Toward an Anthropology of Women,* edited by Rayna R. Reiter, 309–21. New York: Monthly Review Press, 1975.

Simon, Kate. *A Renaissance Tapestry: The Gonzaga of Mantua.* New York: Harper and Row, 1988.

Simons, Patricia. "Alert and Erect: Masculinity in Some Italian Renaissance Portraits of Fathers and Sons." In *Gender Rhetorics: Postures of Dominance and Submission in History,* edited by Richard C. Trexler, 163–86. Binghamton, N.Y.: Medieval and Renaissance Texts and Studies, 1994.

Snyder, Francis G. "Anthropology, Dispute Processes, and Law: A Critical Introduction." *British Journal of Law and Society* 8 (1981–82): 141–80.

Stein, Peter. "Civil Law Reports and the Case of San Marino." In *The Character and Influence of the Roman Civil Law: Historical Essays,* 115–30. London: Hambledon Press, 1988.

———. "Safety in Numbers: Sharing of Responsibility for Judicial Decisions in Early Modern Europe." In *The Character and Influence of the Roman Civil Law: Historical Essays,* 101–13. London: Hambledon Press, 1988.

Stewart, Frank Henderson. *Honor.* Chicago: University of Chicago Press, 1994.

Stone, Patricia. "Illegitimacy." *New York Review of Books,* 26 April 1984, 21.

Strathern, Marilyn. *After Nature: English Kinship in the Late Twentieth Century.* Cambridge University Press, 1992.

———. *The Gender of the Gift: Problems with Women and Problems with Society in Melanesia.* Berkeley and Los Angeles: University of California Press, 1988.

———. "Self-Interest and the Social Good: Some Implications of Hagen Gender Imagery." In *Sexual Meanings: The Cultural Construction of Gender and Sexuality,* edited by Sherry B. Ortner and Harriet Whitehead, 166–91. Cambridge: Cambridge University Press, 1981.

———, ed. *Dealing with Inequality: Analyzing Gender Relations in Melanesia and Beyond.* Cambridge: Cambridge University Press, 1987.

Strocchia, Sharon. *Death and Ritual in Renaissance Florence.* Baltimore: Johns Hopkins University Press, 1992.

Stuard, Susan Mosher. "Urban Domestic Slavery in Medieval Ragusa." *Journal of Medieval History* 9 (1983): 155–71.

Swain, Elizabeth. "Faith in the Family: The Practice of Religion by the Gonzaga." *Journal of Family History* 8 (1983): 177–89.

Takahashi, Tomoko. "I bambini abbandonati presso lo spedale di Santa Maria di San Gallo di Firenze nel tardo medioevo (1395–1463)." *Annuario dell'Istituto Giapponese di Cultura* 24 (1990–91): 59–79.

———. "I bambini e i genitori-espositori dello spedale di Santa Maria degli Innocenti di Firenze nel xv secolo." *Annuario dell'Istituto Giapponese di Cultura* 25 (1991–92): 35–75.

Tamassia, Nino. *La famiglia italiana nei secoli decimoquinto e decimosesto.* Milan: Sandron, 1910.

Tamba, Giorgio, ed. *La società dei notai di Bologna*. Rome: Istituto Poligrafico, 1988.

Teichman, Jenny. *Illegitimacy: An Examination of Bastardy*. Ithaca, N.Y.: Cornell University Press, 1982.

Tenenti, Alberto. "Famille bourgeoise et idéologie au Bas Moyen Age." In *Famille et parenté dans l'Occident médiéval,* edited by Georges Duby and Jacques Le Goff, 431–40. Rome: Ecole Française de Rome, 1977.

Thomas, Yan. "'Auctoritas legum non potest veritatem naturalem tollere': Rechtsfiktion und Natur bei den Kommentatoren des Mittelalters." In *Recht zwischen Natur und Geschichte,* edited by François Kervégan and Heinz Mohnhaupt, 1–32. Frankfurt am Main: Klostermann, 1997.

———. "The Division of the Sexes in Roman Law." In *A History of Women in the West,* edited by Georges Duby and Michelle Perot. Vol. 1: *From Ancient Goddesses to Christian Saints,* edited by Pauline Schmitt Pantel, 83–137. Translated by Arthur Goldhammer. Cambridge: Harvard University Press, 1992.

Tierney, Brian. *The Idea of Natural Rights: Studies on Natural Rights, Natural Law, and Church Law, 1150–1625*. Atlanta: Scholars Press, 1997.

Torelli, Pietro. *Lezioni di storia del diritto italiano: Diritto privato*. Milan: Giuffrè, 1947.

Trexler, Richard. "The Foundlings of Florence, 1395–1455." *History of Childhood Quarterly* 1 (1973–74): 259–84.

———. "Infanticide in Florence: New Sources and First Results." *History of Childhood Quarterly* 1 (1973–74): 98–116.

———. *Synodal Law in Florence and Fiesole, 1306–1518*. Vatican City: Biblioteca Apostolica Vaticana, 1971.

Twinam, Ann. *Public Lives, Private Secrets: Gender, Honor, Sexuality, and Illegitimacy in Colonial Spanish America*. Stanford: Stanford University Press, 1999.

Vallerani, Massimo. "I processi accusatori a Bologna fra Due e Trecento." *Società e storia* 78 (1997): 741–88.

van de Walle, Etienne. "Illegitimacy in France during the Seventeenth Century." In *Bastardy and Its Comparative History: Studies in the History of Illegitimacy and Marital Nonconformity in Britain, France, Germany, Sweden, North America, Jamaica, and Japan,* ed. Peter Laslett, Karla Oosterveen, and Richard M. Smith, 264–77. Cambridge: Harvard University Press, 1980.

Vernier, Bernard. "Putting Kin and Kinship to Good Use: The Circulation of Goods, Labour, and Name on Karpathos (Greece)." In *Interest and Emotion: Essays on the Study of Family and Kinship,* edited by Hans Medick and David Warren Sabean, 28–76. Cambridge: Cambridge University Press, 1984.

Vidari, Gian Savino Pene. *Ricerche sul diritto agli alimenti.* Vol. 1: *L'obbligo 'ex lege' dei familiari nel periodo della Glossa e del commento*. Turin: Giappichelli, 1970.

Villata, Gigliola di Renzo. "Persone e famiglia nel diritto medioevale e moderno." *Digesto,* 4th ed. vol. 13 (Civile): 457–527.

Vismara, Giulio. "Adozione (diritto intermedio)." *Enciclopedia del diritto,* 1:581–84. Milan: Giuffrè, 1958.

Weber, Max. *Economy and Society.* 2 vols. Edited by Guenther Roth and Claus Wittich. Berkeley and Los Angeles: University of California Press, 1968.

Weiner, Annette B. *Inalienable Possessions: The Paradox of Keeping-While-Giving.* Berkeley and Los Angeles: University of California Press, 1992.

Weissman, Ronald F. E. "Reconstructing Renaissance Sociology: The 'Chicago School' and the Study of Renaissance Society." In *Persons in Groups: Social Behavior as Identity Formation in Medieval and Renaissance Europe,* 39–45. Binghamton, N.Y.: Medieval and Renaissance Texts and Studies, 1985.

———. *Ritual Brotherhoods in Renaissance Florence.* New York: Academic Press, 1982.

Weitnauer, Albert. *Die Legitimation des ausserehelichen Kindes im römischen Recht und in der Germanenrechten des Mittelalters.* Basel: Helbing und Lichtenhahn, 1940.

White, Geoffrey M., and John Kirkpatrick, eds. *Person, Self, and Experience: Exploring Pacific Ethnopsychologies.* Berkeley and Los Angeles: University of California Press, 1985.

Whitehead, Ann. "Women and Men; Kinship and Property: Some General Issues." In *Women and Property—Women as Property,* edited by Renee Hirschon, 176–92. London: Croom Helm, 1984.

Willoweit, Dietmar. "Dominium und Proprietas: Zur Entwicklung des Eigentumsbegriffs in der mittelalterlichen und neuzeitlichen Rechtswissenschaft." *Historisches Jahrbuch der Goerres Gesellschaft zur Pflege der Wissenschaft im Katholischen Deutschland* 94 (1974): 131–56.

———. "Von der natürlichen Kindschaft zur Illegitimität: Die nichtehelichen Kinder in den mittelalterlichen Rechtsordnungen." In *Illegitimität im Spätmittelalter,* edited by Ludwig Schmugge, 55–66. Munich: R. Oldenbourg, 1994.

Winterer, Hermann. *Die rechtliche Stellung der Bastarden in Italien von 800 bis 1500.* Munich: Arbeo, 1978.

Wolff, H. J. "The Background of the Post-classical Legislation on Illegitimacy." *Seminar* 3 (1945): 21–45.

Wrightson, Keith. "The Nadir of English Illegitimacy in the Seventeenth Century." In *Bastardy and Its Comparative History: Studies in the History of Illegitimacy and Marital Nonconformity in Britain, France, Germany, Sweden, North America, Jamaica, and Japan,* ed. Peter Laslett, Karla Oosterveen, and Richard M. Smith, 176–91. Cambridge: Harvard University Press, 1980.

Zatti, Paolo. *Persona giuridica e soggettività: Per una definizione del concetto di "persona" nel rapporto con la titolarità delle situazioni soggettive.* Padua: CEDAM, 1975.

Zorzi, Andrea. "I fiorentini e gli uffici pubblici nel primo Quattrocento: Concorrenza, abusi, illegalità." *Quaderni storici* 66 (December 1987): 725–51.

———. *L'Amministrazione della giustizia penale nella repubblica fiorentina: Aspetti e problemi.* Florence: Olschki, 1988.

Index